Not as a Lamb

He was oppressed, and he was afflicted, yet he
opened not his mouth: he is brought as a lamb
to the slaughter, and as a sheep before her
shearer is dumb, so he openeth not his mouth.

Isaiah LIII 7—8

Not as a Lamb

The Jews against Hitler

by

Lucien Steinberg

Translated by Marion Hunter

SAXON HOUSE

SAXON HOUSE, D.C. Heath Ltd,
1 Westmead, Farnborough, Hants, England.

© 1970 Librairie Arthème Fayard
First published in French as
La Révolte des Justes
© Translation 1974 D.C. Heath Ltd

ISBN: 0 347 00003 7

LIBRARY OF CONGRESS
CATALOG CARD NUMBER 73-10623

PHOTOSET BY ST PAUL'S PRESS LTD, MALTA

Printed in Great Britain by
ROBERT MACLEHOSE AND CO LTD
The University Press, Glasgow

CONTENTS

Part 6
The Ghetto Uprisings

Part One

The Jews Against Hitler

CHAPTER 1

THE JEWISH RESISTANCE

'RESISTANCE' was the word used during the Second World War to describe the manifestations and attitudes of the inhabitants of occupied countries, and the action they took in their attempts to drive out the invader.

Later, the sense of the term was enlarged to include the campaign waged by anti-Fascist Italians and anti-Nazi Germans, both at home and abroad, in their efforts to rid themselves of their hated regimes.

The same definitions apply to the Jewish campaign against Hitler. For in every country that suffered Nazi and Fascist occupation Jews were found taking part in the struggle against the enemy, from without, when it was a question of occupied countries, from within as far as Italy and Germany were concerned. This aspect of the anti-Nazi Jewish campaign took many different forms and reached considerable proportions.

Some time in the spring of 1941, as Adolf Hitler was putting the finishing touches to his preparations for the invasion of Russia, he calmly announced his decision to annihilate every Jew in Europe. Here he was simply affirming what he had already proclaimed before the *Reichstag* on 30 January 1939:

> *If the international Jewish financiers, inside and outside Europe, should again succeed in plunging the nations into a world war, the result will not be the bolshevisation of the world and victory for Israel, but the annihilation of the Jewish race throughout Europe.*

The fact that it was not the international Jewish financiers, but the *Führer* of the Third Reich who plunged the world into armed conflict in no way discouraged him from issuing a decree for the 'suppression of the Jewish race in Europe'.

Perhaps a clarification of what is intended by the term 'Jew' is necessary at this point.

A characteristic of the Jew is that he eludes any cut and dried scientific definition, whatever specialist branch of learning is invoked. Historians, ethnologists, geneticists, fail to provide a definitive and wholly convincing answer, but these are *bona fide* scholars who hesitate to commit themselves unless they are absolutely sure of their facts, and theologians and politicians follow a different line of reasoning, and can and do provide an answer.

3

As far as the Jewish theologian is concerned, any person born of a Jewish mother is Jewish, which takes us back to principles of law established long before Roman Law, and though this approach may appear somewhat outmoded to the Western intellectual, it is, in fact, the ruling concept of traditionalist Judaism and helps to maintain a balanced home policy by constituting the law in the State of Israel.

The politician, by the very nature and circumstances of his profession, has an entirely different approach to the problem. Let us isolate two extreme points of view given by politicians of widely contrasting backgrounds.

When Hermann Goering was faced with the dilemma of seeing his close associates accused of having Jewish ancestry, he took a firm stand: *'Wer Jude ist, bestimme ich!'* ('I am the one to decide who is Jewish!').

David Ben Gurion, on the other hand, declared: 'Whoever considers himself to be Jewish is Jewish.'

The second statement clearly appeals most to Western reasoning — despite the fact that Ben Gurion was defeated on this very issue. The general opinion today, among Jews and Gentiles alike, is that a Jew is a Jew whether he likes it or not.

The Nazis adopted Goering's criterion, but whereas Goering had uttered these words in order to 'exonerate' a high-ranking military official accused of 'Judaism', the German authorities, and particularly the SS and the Gestapo, interpreted the conception in a much more restrictive sense.

In Nazi Europe, there were two types of Jews: those who were Jews because they considered themselves to be so, and those who were Jews only because the Nazis made them so.

In this book we refer to the Jews in Ben Gurion's use of the term — which will not deter us, should the occasion arise, from mentioning the actions of individuals who were Jews only by the 'grace' of Hitler — but a clear differentiation will be made in every case.

The European Jews were not a united body, and within no single European country were there 'the Jews' but 'Jews' of all shades and kinds. Relations between Jewish communities on an international level had practically ceased with the German Occupation, and in those countries, particularly in Eastern Europe where ghettos had been set up, there was no longer any communication even between the different ghettos; but then the European Jews had never made any effort to unite themselves in a single organisation and seemed to find it impossible to do so. To mention only one important example, various initiatives, including the one that led to the creation of a Jewish World Congress, got no further than the Russian frontier, and in other countries, only a small number of Jews ever banded together, and these only for very limited purposes.

But if the European Jews did not form a unity from the Jewish point of view, the Nazis held quite a different opinion, and the official report of the Wannsee

Congress, 20 January 1942, made it clear that Europe had to be purged of its Jews from East to West — priority being given to the Reich itself; so that in all the European countries under the Hitler regime one saw the same scenes of deportation being repeated over and over again. Heinrich Himmler, *Reichsführer SS* and Chief of the German Police, had supreme control over the extermination of the Jews throughout Europe. Service IV B 4 of the *Reichssicherheitshauptamt* had jurisdiction over the whole of occupied Europe, with the exception of the Soviet-occupied territories, for everything connected with the deportation of the Jews. In occupied Russia, there were other command circuits, but with a few exceptions, there had never been any 'deportation of Jews' from there: they were assassinated on the spot.

So it was that throughout Europe the Jews were condemned to death. For every Jew in occupied Europe, passively obeying the orders of the authorities could have no other effect — except by a miracle — than death; which was perfectly 'normal' since orders were that the Jews must be killed. We prefer to speak of 'killing' and of 'killers' and of 'assassinations', for the word 'genocide' tends to make us forget that we are concerned here with the massacre of human beings. The only way a Jew in France, Belgium, Poland, White Russia, the Netherlands, Germany, Austria, Czechoslovakia or any other German-occupied or German-dominated country could hope to survive and to permit his family to survive, was by disobeying the orders of the German occupying forces.

This disobedience could take many different forms; armed resistance was only one of them — the most inspiring perhaps. It began with refusing to be registered as a Jew, refusing to wear the yellow star, refusing to go to the assembly points, refusing to live in the ghettos. Some Jews infringed German orders by procuring false identity papers and ration books. They tried to go into hiding and above all to ensure that their wives and children were out of harm's way, and here they were often obliged to depend upon the non-Jewish population. In most cases, and particularly in Western Europe, national resistance movements considered it one of their main duties to come to the aid of Jews on the run, and especially of old people, women and children. A great number of men and women of good will, who were not otherwise involved in the Resistance, participated in it through their efforts on behalf of the persecuted Jews.

Hitler's war against the Jews was in a way 'a war within a war'; and, from the Jewish point of view, every time one of these 'small' actions succeeded, the Nazis suffered a setback; and since it was a question of killing all the Jews, each Jew who escaped represented a defeat for the Third Reich. It is also true to say that the anti-Jewish measures in Western Europe led to a fresh surge of anti-German resistance, and a rather paradoxical aspect to the problem is that every time a Jew provided himself with false papers and went into hiding, either to take part in resistance activities or simply to avoid being deported, he accomplished an anti-German act, an act of resistance, while, in contrast to what happened to non-Jewish Resistance fighters, such an act of resistance, far from increasing the dangers that threatened the Jews, considerably diminished them.

There are no exhaustive statistics available of the losses suffered by the Resistance movements in the various occupied countries, but it is possible to establish that throughout the different groups these varied at a rough estimate from 25 to 75 per cent of the complement, some groups being completely annihilated.

On the other hand, the losses of civilians who did not directly participate in the Resistance, losses caused by famine, bombardments, repression by the Occupants, or other causes, were proportionally much less. In the Balkans, the USSR, and Poland, a high percentage of civilians perished; but these losses were mainly confined to the regions where guerrilla warfare was particularly intense.

For the Jews it was the reverse. When they punctiliously obeyed Nazi laws and regulations, or those of their local accomplices, they suffered enormous losses. The more closely they conformed to the law, the less were their chances of surviving.

Where they disobeyed the law by changing identity, leaving their homes or their ghettos, or going into hiding, the percentage of losses visibly diminished, sometimes showing a spectacular drop.

In Kiev, capital of the Ukraine, only one Jew survived out of the 33,000 or so resident in the city when the Germans entered, while in the Jewish Resistance in the swamps of White Russia, where whole families had sought refuge under the armed protection, such as it was, of the Jewish Resistance fighters, at least half of the fugitives survived.

It is easy, now that it is all over, to define the paradoxical aspect of the Jewish condition under Nazi occupation.

The Jews were living in the heart of non-Jewish populations and had more or less adopted their way of life, and psychologically speaking it was less difficult for them to infringe a law, knowing that all they risked was a fine, than to disobey the Germans who as they were fully aware had all the strength and power on their side and would not hesitate to make full use of it.

Added to these psychological stumbling blocks were objective factors. All over Eastern Europe the Jews, taken as a body, were recognised as such and were therefore pin-pointed and easily located, while in Central Europe this was less frequently the case, and in Western Europe still less so. The registration of the Jews, carried out on Nazi orders in all occupied countries and followed by the introduction of yellow stars or arm-bands, aimed primarily at taking a census of the Jews and isolating them from the rest of the population, and even before local ghettos had been set up, the distinctive symbols were more than sufficient to permit the eventual arrest and deportation of the Jews, which made it more difficult for the Jews to take an active part in the Resistance; for by discarding their emblems they ran the risk of drawing the attention of their neighbours who could be kindly disposed or not. In Eastern Europe and particularly in Poland, goodwill was the rare exception.

Even in the ghettos, Jewish collectivities *par excellence*, the Resistance came up against enormous obstacles. The ceaseless surveillance of the Gestapo and the local police was by no means the only problem. Sheer terror of the Nazis drove most of the ghetto population to oppose any action liable to cause reprisals. In an extreme case at Vilna, the leader of the ghetto Resistance organisation was literally forced by the other inhabitants to give himself up to the Gestapo; and even when the Jewish communities were less timorous, the Resistance fighters very often remained isolated so that when the final hour came only a few were in a position to fight.

This sort of reaction is in no way confined to European Judaism, and in all the occupied countries only a minority took part in the Resistance, though this minority increased proportionally as the enemy's position grew weaker and his final defeat became inevitable, the number of Resistance fighters reaching a peak at the time of the battles of the Liberation, to say nothing of 'the Resistance fighters of the thirteenth hour'. Counter-Resistance groups, often very strong ones, sprang up everywhere, accusing the Resistance of trouble-making, while in many countries local authorities enjoying the support of a large proportion of the population openly condemned the campaign against the German occupying forces and opposed it by all the material and moral means at their disposal.

Of all the ethnic groups of Hitler's Europe, only the Jews were forced to break the law if they were to survive physically; and they were no better prepared psychologically than anyone else. When they joined forces it was because of external pressure: that of Hitler's law; it was not a spontaneous reaction based on immutable tradition; for, up to then, the Jews of different countries were only linked by very slender bonds, and had no common reaction until they were attacked as Jews, and little enough even then. Hitler's attacking them *en bloc* was not sufficient to unite them, so that there were at least as many Jewish groups as there were occupied countries even though they were attacked on the scale of a whole continent.

The national Resistance movements of every occupied country could rely to a considerable extent on a free centre or nucleus: the section of the French Resistance movement inside France could count on the section outside as well as on English, and eventually American support; and this was true, in varying degrees, of the groups in other occupied countries, including the Soviet Partisans, who received direct aid from Moscow. There was already sufficient air transport to parachute British arms even into Czechoslovakia and Poland.

The Jews had no such outside support. There was no Jewish state; but only a Jewish community of 500,000 living in Palestine under British colonial rule, and variously sized Jewish communities scattered throughout the free countries, the largest and most important of these being in the United States.

Even today, and perhaps even more today than a quarter of a century ago, there is speculation in Jewish circles as to whether or not the Jewish communities of the free countries did all that they ought or even could have done, to help European Judaism in its hour of need, but we consider it simply was not possible for these Jews to bring positive aid to their persecuted brothers.

In spite of all these disadvantages, the Jews faced up to Hitler. They fought back, but they were defeated in a number of ways and for a number of reasons.

It would serve no useful purpose to justify the Jewish resistance; nor do we claim that all the Jews or even the majority of them took part in it. There is no more excuse for exaggeration than for false modesty, and we will not draw a veil over the mistakes, the inadequacies and the false appraisals of the few. Nor will we, simply because it concerns Jews, broaden the meaning of 'resistance' to include those perfectly commendable, admirable, praiseworthy phenomena which have no real place within the concept of the resistance: for example, to organise soup kitchens; to keep the synagogues open even during the most dangerous times; to set up strictly Jewish children's homes and orphanages so that even during the worst period the children might have the sort of education that would encourage them to become worthy Jews; and many of those who devoted themselves to ensuring the success of these enterprises were arrested by the Gestapo or by its local representatives, deported, or gassed; as indeed were the starving who came to eat at the soup kitchens; the faithful who came to pray in the synagogues; the children and their teachers in the homes and orphanages.

Consequently, one cannot help feeling a prickling of doubt. Had there not been this devotion to duty, these starving people, albeit still starving, these faithful, obliged to find moral strength within themselves, would probably still have been alive today; above all, one cannot help wondering if the insistence on Jewish education at all costs for the children justified the risks when other, no less devoted, Jews found a way of retaining the confidence and co-operation of the non-Jewish populations, to the extent of entrusting the children to them and thus saving their lives. Was it so very important that a few 'souls' were lost in the process; in other words, that some children had their lives saved while being lost to Judaism? As a practising Jew I suggest that on the very rare occasions when this happened, the 'fault' lay in the loving influence of the adoptive parents on the children they took into their homes.

In the same way, it is not feasible to put the Resistance — in the strictest sense of the term — in the same category as certain Jewish defence actions inherited from centuries of persecution for however successful these may have been in their time their effects would have been disastrous for the Jews between 1939 and 1945.

On the basis of the fundamental concept of the eternity of Israel, it was accepted that the waves of persecution inflicted by the Gentiles were in their very nature temporary phenomena, comparable, say, to thunderstorms, which take time to pass over; and the best way to encourage this storm to pass over, was to obey the regulations of the persecutors, and every effort should be made to establish relations with the 'good' anti-Semite, that is to say one who could be persuaded by one means or another, usually by monetary inducement, to put an end to anti-Jewish measures, or at least to limit or delay their import.

Finally, and most important, the German must be persuaded that such persecution went against his own interests, for the presence of the Jews, so long as they were comparatively speaking free, was an asset to the persecutor and to the country he occupied.

During the war both the Jewish Councils set up by the Germans and the freely constituted Jewish organisations could be found applying these methods in an attempt to save the various Jewish communities, and they also established networks of charitable and philanthropic institutions to help the distressed.

Where these defence mechanisms were used to combat Nazi persecution, they behaved like antibodies secreted by the human body, coming into play not only in the case of physical illness and injury but also in the event of an organ from another body being grafted on to it.

The Nazis attempted quite simply to kill all the Jews, and all the measures enacted were directed towards this end; and to obey, to conform to the regulations enabled them to achieve their ends more easily.

Though the Nazis massacred members of a given community, they never seriously interfered with their religious and philanthropic activities, or with any other aspect of community life; on the contrary, if the Jews were not already living in a community the Nazis established one for them. They had created the *Zwangs-gemeinde*, and where individual Jews insisted on remaining outside an existing community they forced them to become part of it if only by submitting them to community jurisdiction. The ideal name for these obligatory communities was, of course, the ghetto, with its Jewish Council; and Jews who considered themselves as such, assimilated Jews, and even Christians who had been born Jews or who had one Jewish parent were all shut away in these ghettos; so that one can hardly compare the Resistance to the setting in motion of those ancient defence mechanisms which led to death rather than life. On the other hand, it was a blessing that the Resistance, and more precisely the Jewish Resistance, opposed the obligatory communities, the blind application of ancient systems and obedience to the occupying forces.

CHAPTER 2

THE GREAT REVERSAL

EVER since the anti-Jewish reign of terror became a reality, there has been speculation as to whether or not the Jewish leaders can be blamed for having executed Nazi orders[1], and at times, the behaviour of the Jewish leaders has been likened to that of collaborators, a few noted writers even asserting that the Jewish leaders of the *Judenräte* were as much responsible as the Nazis themselves for the death of millions of Jews, if not more so.

At the other end of the scale, there are writers — again of some standing — who maintain that these same leaders, or a very large proportion of them, were actually among the bravest members of the Resistance.

The principal authority of the anti-Jewish campaign, the one acting 'at an executive level' as its leaders loved to say, in other words the one that could arrest, deport and deal out the death penalty, was the Gestapo.[2]

Basically, the *Geheime Staatspolizei* (Secret State Police) was composed of two main branches:

The Security Police (*Sicherheitspolizei*, abbreviation *Sipo*) of the German State. Besides this secret police force there were the municipal police force, the regimented constabulary (*Ordnungspolizei*) and the crime squad (*Kriminalpolizei* or *Kripo*). All these police forces later came under the jurisdiction of Himmler.

The Intelligence Service of the Nazi party (*Sicherheitsdienst*, abbreviation SD). This had been set up before the Nazis seized power and, as its name indicates, was used essentially for the Nazi Party's own needs.

At the outbreak of the war, Heinrich Himmler, *Reichsführer SS* and Chief of the German Police, regrouped all the services of the crime squad and of the SD, in a single superorganisation, the Reich Central Security Office (*Reichssicherheitshauptamt*, abbreviation RSHA), comprising a series of bureaux (*Aemter*) similar to district headquarters. The *Aemter* I and II, common to the State Police and the SD was in charge of personnel and domestic administration. *Amt III* was the branch of the SD which acted inside Germany. *Amt IV* was the Gestapo proper which officially existed to unmask and fight 'the ideological enemy'. *Amt V* was the crime squad; *Amt VI*, another SD branch, was responsible for foreign espionage; finally there was an *Amt VII*, charged with investigating rather obscure scientific problems, but on occasion also engaged in foreign espionage.

At the head of the RSHA was Himmler's brilliant Second-in-Command,

Reinhard Heydrich. Born in 1904, he began his career in the Naval Intelligence Service under Admiral Canaris. Later, master and pupil found themselves alternating as collaborators and rivals, without this affecting their friendship. Canaris was appointed head of military espionage (*Abwehr*); Heydrich became head of the SD which he had helped to found in 1931; and when he later became head of *Sipo* as well, he continued to display a taste for espionage. Following the reform of the German police in 1936, the 'Jews' department was handed over *en bloc* to the Gestapo, where the sigla of this branch II — 112 were changed first to IV A 4, then to IV B 4. The head of IV A 4 was Adolf Eichmann, also a former SD man, who like Heydrich, had no previous connections with the official police.

Which of the two had the idea of reducing costs to a minimum by enlisting the aid of the Jews in their anti-Jewish policy? According to available documents it was Eichmann. Most of the details of these events are recorded, including the fact that the strategy was applied for the first time, and with resounding success, in Vienna, just after the *Anschluss* in the spring of 1938.

Adolf Eichmann's flash of inspiration consisted in enlisting the active co-operation of the Jewish leaders, not by provoking their aggressive instincts, but by appealing to their finer feelings and their devotion to the cause of their fellow Jews.

His first concern in Vienna was to speed up Jewish emigration, and to this end he must co-ordinate all the formalities of German administration: no easy task. Next, he must have the co-operation of the Jewish leaders. The few people at his disposal were capable of causing a reign of terror but not of conducting the whole operation. A central office of Jewish Emigration (*Zentralstelle für judische Auswanderung*) was set up in Vienna, and between March and November 1938 was directly responsible for driving at least 50,000 Jews out of Austria, that is to say one in every four, compared to the 19,000 Jews who left Germany during the same period.

While it is true that Eichmann began by threatening the leaders of the Jewish community of Vienna with the worst brutalities if the emigration did not come up to his expectations, menaces alone would certainly not have been enough, and he gave them to understand that their support was vital to the Jews, rich and poor alike, if they were to leave the country and escape Nazi persecution. He was right in supposing that the Jewish leaders would respond to this argument hoping that in so doing they would save a large number of their compatriots and fellow Jews.

In 1939, an administrative act was passed replacing the general organisation of Judaism in Germany by the Jewish Union of Germany (*Reichsvereinigung der Juden in Deutschland*), not a religious or secular organisation this time but one in which all the Jews were assigned positions; and when the deportations began the *Reichsvereinigung* was charged with the proceedings, first collecting extremely detailed inventories of the possessions of the deportees, later to be confiscated by the SS. Printed forms issued to the Jews of the various districts were returned when completed to the Gestapo. Later, when the date of deportation had been fixed, individual summonses were dispatched to the Jews concerned, notifying them to present themselves at a given time at an assembly point, often a railway station.

In the event of a Jew choosing not to accept the invitation, the *Reichsvereinigung* could and did send henchmen to the home of the recalcitrant with orders to bring him by force. These Jewish aiders and abettors knew that their freedom, precarious as it was, depended on the successful performance of their task, and that if they themselves were to escape deportation, they must round up the Jews in hiding; yet a great many Jews bore absolutely no resentment towards these particularly unnatural auxiliaries.

It was the duty of the leaders themselves to ensure that the trains carrying the Jews to their various destinations, and more often than not to their death, were not too crowded or overheated, and that the deportees had adequate food supplies for the journey, and milk for their children.

To those who asked their advice on whether or not to disobey the summons and try to go into hiding, leaders replied that clandestinity was hopeless and jeopardized not only their own lives, but those of their families and the whole community; which advice was not reprehensible in itself, and was given in good faith by these good and compassionate men, anxious to aid their fellow Jews. All the same, their actions played into Nazi hands, making the deportation plan run more smoothly, and thanks to their intervention, the Gestapo was saved the trouble of engaging outside help. The Jews left quietly, without causing scandal, and the Gestapo was not even obliged to publish the anti-Jewish regulations in the Press: the *Reichsvereinigung* was responsible for that. Later, when the great Rabbi Leo Baeck, living in the Theresienstadt ghetto, learned that the deported Jews were being dispatched to Auschwitz and the gas chambers, he kept the news from the other Jews in the ghetto, and here it might be said that if they had known what fate awaited them, many of them might have escaped; but the eminent Rabbi, whose nobility of character no one questions, reasoned that since his fellow Jews were doomed in any case, it was better to spare them mental anguish, by keeping them in ignorance of their fate until the very last moment.

Such then was the situation in Germany, the first country to possess, in the *Reichsvereinigung*, a *Judenrat*. With few exceptions, the same conditions prevailed in Austria and in the 'Protectorate' of Bohemia-Moravia. In this region of Czechoslovakia, enemy of the Germans *par excellence*, where a large part of the population was sympathetic towards the Jews, around 70,000 Jews were deported by the system of individual summons, less than a thousand choosing to avoid deportation by going into hiding.

Sometimes it happened that the non-intervention of the *Reichsvereinigung* placed the Nazis in an embarrassing position as on the occasion in Berlin in March 1943, when Jewish male partners of mixed marriages were arrested and their wives assembled outside the headquarters of the Gestapo clamouring for their release. Being Aryans these women were in no way answerable to the *Reichsvereinigung*, and the Gestapo was obliged to let them state their case, finally choosing to satisfy their demands rather than forcibly disperse a demonstration of women in the heart of the capital.

There is no indication in the Nazi texts at our disposal of the deep-seated reasons for the setting up of the *Reichsvereinigung*, but we do know the reasons given for establishing the Jewish Councils (*Judenräte*) in Poland; and can confirm that when organisations of this nature were eventually introduced in Western Europe, in France, Belgium, and the Netherlands, and in Eastern Europe, in Hungary and occupied Soviet countries, the ultimate aim was the same.

On 21 December 1939, as the German campaign against Poland was drawing to a close, Heydrich summoned the heads of departments and special task forces to Berlin, a total of 15 persons attending, among them Adolf Eichmann in his capacity as Head of the Office for Jewish Emigration. The conference took place during luncheon, when a broad policy was drafted for the benefit of the leaders of the Special Action Groups (*Einsatzgruppen*) concerning the Jewish problem in occupied territory.

This directive mentioned a 'final solution', the precise nature of which was not disclosed, and went on to dictate immediate top-secret measures, the first of which, a step towards achieving the 'final solution', consisted in bringing all the Jews who lived in the country into the towns, the number of Jews in each community not to exceed 500. A whole chapter of the directive was then devoted to the setting up of 'Jewish Councils':

1. A Jewish 'Council of Elders' must be set up in each Jewish community; it will be composed as far as possible of any prominent persons who are still in residence, and of Rabbis. It will include not more than 24 male Jews (depending on the size of the Jewish community) and will be held *fully responsible* (in the literal sense of the term) for seeing that regulations already in force, and future regulations are strictly carried out.
2. The Councils will be warned that failure to obey these orders will entail the most severe penalties.

Expert spy as he was, Reinhard Heydrich had applied a two-pronged technique in his anti-Jewish campaign, which was to become a model in the secret service: reversal of agents, on the one hand; deception of the adversary on the other; in the anti-Jewish campaign, the two techniques were often combined; and as the enemy was not fighting on equal terms, success was assured every time.

It was by playing on their noblest sentiments that the Gestapo succeeded in obtaining the Jewish leaders' co-operation, and once they became part of the system these leaders were powerless to do anything but contribute to the destruction of their fellow Jews, for in order to save a minority, they were obliged to abandon the rest: but there were occasions when the leaders of the Jewish Councils rebelled.

Adam Czerniakov, president of the Warsaw *Judenrat*, chose to commit suicide when the Gestapo asked him to select Jews for deportation to Treblinka. Ovsej Itzikson, president of the Baranovichi *Judenrat* in Western Bielorussia, faced with the same exigency, told the Germans that he would rather be shot, as he was, and his family along with him; and there were similar instances, at Bialystok for example, where the *Judenrat* co-operated with the underground movement; and others where the *Judenrat* acting on its own behalf, called the Jewish population to insurrection.

There were occasions when the Jewish Resistance, interpreting the functional aim of the *Judenrat* in its own way, adapted it to serve its own purposes by reversing the roles and turning it against the Germans, this sort of tactical manoeuvre being most evident in Belgium and France where it was usually carried out without the knowledge of the Jewish Councils; but unfortunately for the Jews, their leaders were not of the same calibre as the enemy. Though morally superior, and by far, they were desperately inferior otherwise, with a few rare exceptions, so that even when they finally grasped the Nazis' true intentions, they were seldom able to avert them, for nothing had prepared them for this kind of responsibility.

Two courses of action lay open to the Jewish Resistance fighters: they could try to destroy the machine, or they could devise a way of turning it to their own advantage. Later we shall see the two methods in operation and be better able to appreciate the results of this unequal struggle between professional murderers skilled in deceit, and amateurs, and the wonder is that the amateurs occasionally succeeded in defeating the professionals.

How did the 'Jewish front' appear to the Nazis after 1939?

First of all there were the Jews who had found themselves under German domination at the outbreak of the war: those of the Third Reich, which is to say of Germany and Austria, of the 'Protectorate' of Bohemia-Moravia, and of the puppet state of Czechoslovakia.

Later, two-thirds of Polish Judaism were to fall into the hands of the Nazis, the rest of that great mass remaining temporarily out of reach behind the Soviet-German frontier.

In June 1941, the Soviet territories acquired in 1939—1940 fell into German hands, their dominion now extending over much of the European section of the

USSR, in which area was the largest concentration of Russian Jews, Moscow and Leningrad apart.

The Germans took very few Jewish prisoners in occupying Denmark and Norway, for there were only about 10,000 in the two countries put together, but it was quite a different matter in Western Europe, where there were more than 500,000 Jews living between the Pyrenees and the North Sea; approximately 120,000 in the Netherlands; 90,000 in Belgium; around 350,000 in France: a considerable number though decidedly inferior to that of Eastern Europe. In Poland the number of Jews was reckoned at more than three million, and in Western Soviet territories, comprising the Baltic countries, at more than a million and a half.

Then there was South-Eastern Europe and the Balkans, where about 150,000 Jews resided, more or less equally distributed between Yugoslavia and Greece: the only German enemy countries in that part of the globe. There were close on 800,000 in the territory belonging to Hungary in 1941; around 400,000 in Romania; nearly 50,000 in Bulgaria: these three countries being allies of the Third Reich. Finally, there were just over 35,000 Jews in Fascist Italy.

While Germany lost no time in launching her campaign against the Jews in directly occupied countries, she made her allies responsible for those in their own territories; and the way in which these discharged their duties was inconsistent to say the least, so that apart from instances where the Germans ended up by intervening directly, an enormous number of Jews managed to escape, and even when the Germans did intervene, the Jews often had time to take action, if they did not always grasp their opportunities. The tragedy of the Hungarian Jews is evidence enough.

We have already observed that the Jews of different allied or occupied countries of the Reich, as well as those of the Reich itself, were totally isolated from each other, and that there was no co-ordinate action across the frontiers. Any Resistance offered was confined within the frontiers of the various countries, if not within the boundaries of the provinces or even of the ghettos themselves.

NOTES

1. Readers who wish to know more about the subject will find a short bibliography at the end of this volume.

2. *L'Histoire de la Gestapo* by Jacques Delarue, published by Fayard, contains an extremely comprehensive description of the structures of this organisation, and we sketch the broad outlines here simply to show the mechanisms of the anti-Jewish campaign.

Part Two

In the Heart of the Nazi Empire

CHAPTER 3

THE JEWISH RESISTANCE FIGHTERS OF THE THIRD REICH

FIVE hundred thousand Jews were living in Germany at the time of the birth of Nazism, and it was here that the process called Jewish assimilation was most advanced. It was also in Germany, and in the German countries of the former Austro-Hungarian dual monarchy, that 'modern' anti-Semitism, based on racial rather than religious prejudice, saw the light of day.

Today, Hitler and anti-Semitic bestialities mean much the same to us; and the main reason why Nazism is rejected by most people, and why even those whose political leanings dangerously approach Fascism and anti-Semitism violently deny all association with it, is the horror that the revelations of Bergen-Belsen, Buchenwald, Auschwitz and Treblinka inspire in a world that we persist in calling civilised. Even an anti-Semite rejects the idea of mass murder, either by pretending that it never happened or by attempting to conceal his beliefs under the cloak of less compromising notions; anti-Zionism is one of these and currently very widespread, although anti-Zionists are not necessarily anti-Semites.

In 1933, the situation was reversed inside as well as outside Germany and there is no doubt that vast sections of society rejected anti-Semitic atrocities. Even in the National Socialist Party itself, there was very little support for the proposed 'final solution'; but at the same time the idea that the rights of the Jews ought to be restricted, that they were 'not like other Germans', met with general approval, and anti-Semitism certainly did not cause Hitler to lose favour; in fact it increased his prestige if to a lesser degree than it would have done a few years earlier.

Nevertheless the Judæo-German symbiosis was so ancient and so deep-rooted that Nazi anti-Jewish measures inside Germany, measures intended to isolate the Jews and set them apart, did not receive unanimous support, and at the outset, Nazi internal courts often had to institute proceedings against Party members who continued to patronise Jewish shops, while in 1941, when the yellow star was introduced in Germany, the Gestapo was ordered to arrest Germans 'guilty of public manifestations of sympathy' towards the wearers of the symbol. The fact that 20,000 German Jews managed to go into hiding and half of these survived proves that quite a large number of Germans took the risk of coming to their aid.

By comparison, when the Red Army liberated Kiev, in the autumn of 1943, no more than a handful of Jews crawled out of hiding. According to some accounts there was only one survivor.

From the birth of the German Gestapo, its aim was the annihilation of the opponents of Nazism, and suddenly most of those dissenters who did not succeed in reaching safety abroad found themselves in concentration camps specially created for them. It follows that the far from negligible anti-Nazi Resistance could only have been brought about by two categories of men and groups: the militants of parties and movements opposed to Nazism who had managed to escape arrest, and the individuals and groups who, having put their trust in Nazism, and given it more or less their full support, then broke away — this for a variety of reasons, but most of all because it finally dawned on them that Hitler's regime was leading the country to total ruin.

In the first category were men and movements that could be classified as leftist including a small number of Christians, more Protestants than Catholics[1], and also quite a large number of Jews.

The second category was quite different: gradually built up over the years it consisted of some Conservatives, a number of more or less extremist Nationalists, and a handful of Liberals; it had also managed to win over several army officers. Its most spectacular action was the attempted assassination of Adolf Hitler on 20 July 1944, which was also its most bloody defeat.

By force of circumstances, this category contained only a very small number of Jews, and indeed, practically all German Nationalist movements associated themselves with anti-Semitism. For example Karl Goerdeler, one of the ringleaders of the plot of 20 July 1944, who was to take over the Reich if all went well, never tried to conceal his anti-Semitism, and even the proposals in the proclamation to be given the day after his seizure of power contained characteristic anti-Semitic elements; yet a number of Jews and half-Jews living in hiding, who may or may not have been involved in the plot itself, were dragged into the consequences of its failure. To cite only one example, General Lindemann, fleeing from the Gestapo, could only find refuge with the half-Jew Erich Gloden. When the General was arrested, and subsequently condemned to death and executed, his host paid for his sense of hospitality with his life. Goerdeler himself, after his ill-fated attempt to escape from the Gestapo, sometimes hid with Jews who were themselves in hiding, and Baron von Hammerstein relates in his memoirs that he was greatly helped by a number of half-Jewish friends.

A brief digression at this point will explain the term 'half-Jew': a Nazi refinement for which we disclaim all responsibility, since a person is Jewish or he is not. Hitlerian Germany adopted its own definition of Jew; using the term not in accordance with racial criteria, but simply where the persons concerned, or his forebears, belonged to the Jewish religious community.

In practice, Nazi law considered a person to be Jewish if both his parents were Jews, and this even if the person concerned had abandoned his faith. It also defined half-Jews, quarter-Jews and three-quarter Jews, there being numerous provisions governing the status of the different members of the sub-divisions, though Hitler himself took the view that there were simply Jews and non-Jews; and it fell to a jurist in the Home Office of the Reich, Dr. Bernhard Loesener, a dedicated Nazi — at least at the outset — to perceive that in excluding the half-Jews, or the fractional Jews, from the German racial community there was a risk of depriving German blood of the non-Jewish part of the persons concerned.

That this argument appeared specious, even in Loesener's eyes, did not prevent his putting forward a second argument, political this time, and much more convincing: that the racial measures might have a harmful effect on purely German families having partially Jewish parents.

The number of *bona fide* Jews rose by at least half a million in 1935, when these laws came into force, no one then foreseeing that they would be singled out for special treatment; while at the same time the number of 'fractionary' Jews having any amount of non-Jewish relations rose to a much greater extent.

It must be pointed out that even though the *Mischlinge* (crossbreeds), as they were so elegantly called in the Third Reich, did not suffer the same fate as the Jews, they were forcibly made to understand that they were unworthy of trust, and that, classified among the adversaries of the regime, they acted accordingly[2].

The principal resistance group, formed almost entirely of half-Jews, operated not in Germany itself but in Vienna where in 1942 and 1943, the *Wehrmacht*, which had other things in mind, had quite simply dismissed a number of soldiers from its ranks when a study of their forebears revealed too strong a dose of Jewish blood. In Vienna the number discharged was relatively high.

As military men they had been no better or worse than the others; some had been decorated with the Iron Cross, others had fought at Stalingrad and elsewhere, but all of them had the same defect. On their discharge they set up a Communist-inspired, military-type resistance group, which showed evidence of a resurgence of nationalist fervour, but this network, as many others like it, was broken up.

The same fate befell the section directed by Franz Kaufmann, Helene Jacobs and Ernst Hallermann, a group operating in Berlin from 1942—1943 and chiefly concerned with supplying false identity and ration cards to the Jews living in clandestinity. Kaufmann, a senior state official, had been thrown out of office in 1935, stigmatised as a Jew, but as he had long since been converted to Protestantism he benefited from a compromise: dismissed from office, he retained his right to a pension, so that he was not particularly put out. Hallermann was a 'crossbreed of the first degree', whereas Helene Jacobs was 'a hundred per cent Aryan'. Kaufmann was not even tried, but was put to death in the Gestapo prison at Berlin. Hallermann, Helene Jacobs and nine others were tried on 11 January 1944, when the court ruled that the accused had acted out of altruism, and passed only relatively light sentences upon them ranging from one to eight years' imprisonment — a rare event indeed. The report of the trial goes on to state that three of the nine others were 'crossbreeds of the first degree' and six were 'Aryans'; one of these 'Aryans' having another defect: married to a Jewess, he had failed to abandon her despite the fact that they were childless.

However, most of the Jewish members of the German Resistance belonged to left-wing political groups, in particular to the various Socialist splinter groups, the Social Democratic Party of the epoch being very much divided, and to the Communist Party, and on 11 January 1935, the Gestapo conducted large-scale investigations throughout Germany in an attempt to discover the extent of Jewish participation in 'subversive' movements, particularly Marxist and Communist groups; and in Gestapo jargon, 'Marxist' meant Social Democratic or, more generally, Socialist, as opposed to its notion of 'Communist'. The final report, giving the total results of the survey, recorded 193 cases in the whole of the country, though the true figure was more like 118, for the Nuremberg Police, one of the principal Gestapo bureaux, had included in its report those Jews who had been engaged in left-wing activities, in whatever capacity, even prior to 1933.

The geographical repartition of these cases broadly corresponded to the size of the Jewish communities in the respective regions, and apart from the Nuremberg example already mentioned, where it was stated categorically that there were practically no subversive activities after 1933, for the simple reason that the Jews who had managed to escape were recaptured immediately or had found refuge abroad, about fifteen cases of participation in 'subversive' movements were reported in the region of Baden; the same number in the Gestapo circumscription of Frankfurt-on-the-Main; 15 in Silesia; 11 in Berlin; the remainder divided up in 'small lots'. A drop in Jewish leftist activities was noted in Saxony and the Rhineland.

The Jews were further broken down according to their political leanings, more than half being listed as members of the Communist Party and related organisations (Communist youth organisations, *Secours rouge*, revolutionary trade unions); just over a third were Socialists, more or less equally divided between the orthodox Social Democratic Party and the Socialist Workers' Party; and there were a few dissident Communists, a handful of anarchists and some 'miscellaneous'.

One of the most striking cases was that of twenty-five-year-old Heinz Brandt, arrested on 4 December 1934 for distributing illegal Communist tracts. He became one of the Communist leaders of post-War East Germany, then switched to the West, then went back and had himself arrested, or kidnapped, in East Berlin. After several years of detention in the German Democratic Republic, he was eventually 'expelled' to West Berlin where he died a few years ago.

In Constance, there was a left-wing Zionist among the Communists: twenty-one-year-old Adolf Purwin. At Mannheim, Erhard Alterthum, a forty-three-year-old pharmacist, was imprisoned for being a militant of the *Reichsbanner*, a war veterans' organisation affiliated to the Social Democratic Party. He was also a member of the Jewish war veterans' organisation[3].

The signature of the future camp commander of Drancy, Brunner, appears at the bottom of a report from Munich, dated 29 January 1935, in which the question of James Todtman, and others, is raised. Also a militant in the Jewish war veterans' organisation, he was accused of preparing to commit 'an act of high treason', in his attempt to reconstitute the dissolved Social Democratic Party; but he was able to turn his British origin to advantage — though it was distant and had not prevented his fighting in the Kaiser's army. This put an end to the proceedings and he escaped with a deportation order.

The Bremen Gestapo report contains a quite astonishing statement. No Jews being discovered among the arrested Communists and Social Democrats, it was pointed out that 'there are very few Jews in Bremen itself'. Various Gestapos, including that of Frankfurt-on-the-Main, reported the arrest of Emil Carlebach, then twenty years old, who was to become one of the first Communist deputies of Hesse when the war ended.

An entry in the records of the Nuremburg police, under the signature of Dr. Martin, future Commander-in-Chief of the SS and Nuremburg Police, describes the first of the Dachau camp assassinations; that of the economist Rudolf Benario, who was imprisoned on 6 April 1933 and was shot a week later while attempting to escape.

We know of no other 'comprehensive survey' detailing the role played by the Jews in the anti-Nazi left-wing Resistance movements, only a number of individual cases, such as the Felix Jonas affair in which ten or so Berlin militant Social Democrats, working under cover of a popular Berlin choral society called *Arion*, were arrested between May and June 1937, accused of 'intending secretly to reestablish the Social Democratic organisation *Reichsbanner*'. Jonas and two of his accomplices were Jews.

A year later, in Frankfurt-on-Oder, another group was broken up: commanded by the former Social Democratic municipal councillor Oskar Hertz, (apparently Jewish), it consisted of workers and artisans drawn from the Kirchhain district, and was chiefly responsible for relaying the news from Radio Strasbourg.

Another militant Socialist tried and condemned for his political actions was Gunther Salomon (Salter in clandestinity). Arrested in Berlin on 16 May 1939, he was sentenced to six years' penal servitude for having been connected with a distribution centre run by Social Democrats who had sought refuge in Copenhagen. He had circulated their propaganda material in Germany, and had tried unsuccess-

B

fully to establish a printing press and distribution centre for this literature in Berlin itself.

The musicologist Rudolf Israelski was among the vast number of Jewish militant Communists convicted under Nazi law, a number of other Jewish militants being mentioned in the report of his trial. He was accused of having directed underground Communist activities for more than two years in the Schöneberg district of Berlin and was sentenced to twelve years' criminal detention in 1937. Moreover, the Goethe University of Frankfurt was persuaded to withdraw his doctorate of philosophy.

Israelski was imprisoned in the Brandenberg Penitentiary, and later moved to the Hameln. His tubercular condition deteriorated so rapidly that, in November 1942, the prison board was driven to ask authorisation for his transfer to the Israeli hospital in Berlin, the request being directed to Service IV B 4 of the Gestapo, at that time in charge of all Jewish affairs. It made its objections known, on 9 December 1942, in a letter addressed to the Public Prosecuter of the Reich, care of the People's Court, in which it referred to the Minister of Justice of the Reich's circular of 16 April 1942, reference 4300 IIIa 4586-42. Otto Hunsche insisted that Israelski should not be sent to the Jewish hospital, but set at liberty and placed at the disposal of the Berlin Gestapo, so that he could be 'evacuated', in other words, sent to Auschwitz; but Hunsche's communiqué was defeated by events, and on 4 December 1942, the Public Prosecutor received a note from the board of governors of the Hameln Penitentiary, informing him that the Jewish writer Rudolf Israelski had died in the hospital of that prison on the first of December 1942.

By force of circumstances fewer Jews participated in the Resistance against National Socialism. There were far fewer of them, about 300,000 at the outbreak of war, and the most dynamic members either had emigrated or were already under lock and key, while the underground political organisations had been systematically broken up.

However, two large Jewish groups continued to militate, one up to 1942, the other up to the end of 1944, and their action deserves closer study.

NOTES

1. The anti-Nazi Christians were only a small minority at the beginning and their numbers never increased to any great extent. The ecclesiastical hierarchies did sometimes successfully oppose the regime in specific directions, but never openly. It was they, for example, who brought about the arrest of those responsible for murdering the sick under the guise of euthanasia in the summer of 1941.

2. That said, we have no intention whatsoever of 'annexing' these brave men and women to Judaism. The fact that a common enemy classed them in a category that he intended to be ignominious does not enter into account.

3. This war veterans' association was one of the few German organisations to envisage the possibility of offering armed resistance to the Nazis if they attempted to seize power by force; but, even in 1932, this splendid lead met with no response. The Social Democrats, who held power in Prussia, representing more than half of Germany, considered the Communists to be their most serious threat and directed all their efforts against them.

CHAPTER 4

THE HERBERT BAUM CAMPAIGN

O NE of the most extraordinary Resistance groups was founded by Herbert and Marianne Baum at the end of summer 1937, extraordinary in that it was set up right in the heart of the capital of the Nazi Reich, and was composed mainly of members of those sections of the community most zealously pursued and persecuted by the Nazis: the Jews, the Communists and the Communist Jews.

Very few investigators of any persuasion have been concerned with the fortunes of this group, astonishing though they were, the reason perhaps being that here in particular we have that ever-recurring problem of how to define a Jew and how to define a Communist, there being, for example, Communists and Communist-sympathisers who pursued their activities practically independently of the Party and were rarely even in touch with it; while there were Jews who tended to disclaim true Jewish values but proved by example that armed resistance was possible even in Germany. A handful of German Resistance fighters even established friendly relations with Belgian and French workers sent to Germany by the STO.

Most of the Jewish Resistance fighters were young, but the Baum group was exceptionally so. In 1933, the year of the advent of Nazism, only four of the future members of this group of about thirty, Herbert Baum and his future wife Marianne, Richard Holzer and his future wife Charlotte Paech, were over nineteen years old.

Herbert Baum had wanted to be an engineer, but when the Jews were denied entry to the universities and university colleges, he had to change his plans and became an electrician. Born in 1912, he had founded a German-Jewish movement in 1928 and in 1932 had gone over to the Communist Youth movement. Other young Jews, future members of the Baum group and also affected by the dissolution of the German-Jewish movement in 1932, set up a group called *Werkleute*, while the remainder joined the Socialist Youth movement.

When Hitler seized power Baum was directed by the Communist Party to reestablish contact with his old comrades and at the beginning of 1934, he and a number of Communists and Communist-sympathisers, joined the German-Jewish Youth movement, the *Ring-Bund Judischer Jugend*, which was to remain legal up to 1938, while other friends of Baum joined the Zionist movement *Hachomer Hatzair*.[1]

The members of the Baum group were from modest backgrounds, sometimes extremely modest, Baum's father being a clerk, while among the parents of his comrades were pedlars, travelling salesmen, a dressmaker, a secondhand dealer, several petty artisans, a town council employee given job-priority as a war invalid, etc. The highest on the social scale was a dentist.

A dozen young Jews belonged to a nucleus attached to the Communist group of south-west Berlin militating in an area covering the districts of the Centre (*Mitte*), Kreuzberg and Neukölln, today separated by the Berlin Wall. In 1936, in the words of Margot Pikarski, 'following a succession of arrests and sentences in the south-west sub-district ... a number of Jews and their friends formed a Resistance nucleus. As Herbert Baum was the only one in touch with the administration of the south-west sub-district, and as he alone directed the splinter group, the safety of the conspiracy was assured. If the worst came to the worst, the young Jews could not be accused of Communist activities since they were all members of a legal Jewish organisation.'

In the same way, the Nazi plan to exclude the Jews from German society encouraged the formation of illegal anti-Nazi organisations such as the German Communist Party, and here circumstantial logic outmanoeuvred Party doctrine.

The situation of the Jews in Germany underwent a dramatic change at the end of 1938, when on the night of 9—10 November the embassy attaché Ernest von Rath was assassinated in Paris by the young Jew, Herszel Grynszpan. Using this as a pretext, the Nazi Party launched a pogrom throughout Germany. Synagogues went up in flames; Jewish shops were wrecked or burnt to the ground; homes were looted; and more than 20,000 Jews were imprisoned, filling the prisons and the concentration camps of Sachsenhausen, Dachau and Buchenwald to overflowing.

A series of measures sanctioned the exclusion of the Jews from the German economy. The Jewish community was fined one billion marks, and all bank accounts, stocks and shares were blocked. Jews were forbidden to dispose of their properties, or even to sell their possessions, and commissioners were put in charge of shops. Ghettos of the sort imposed in Eastern Europe were never set up in Germany, but Jews were now denied access to certain main streets, to parks, cinemas, theatres and sleeping cars. At the end of 1938, a secret order was issued which authorised the expulsion of the Jews from premises owned by Aryans and obliged Jewish landlords and tenants to give accommodation to the evicted Jews, so that from 1939 to 1942 all the principal German towns had a number of *Judenhäuser* (Jewish houses). When, in 1941—1942, it was decided to go a step further and deport the Jews, most of the work had already been done.

One of the immediate effects of this series of measures — and the one the Germans most sought — was to force the Jews to emigrate or flee. Internees and

their families were informed that they would be set at liberty if they could produce
entry visas to any country whatsoever, and from this point on Adolf Eichmann was
able to introduce in Berlin, on a scale embracing the whole of Germany, the technique he had perfected in March 1938 in Vienna, where he had gathered all the
services concerned with Jewish emigration under one roof — from the police and
the inland revenue, down to the travel agencies, all being directly responsible to
him — and with the worst jobs reserved for the Jews. The Berlin department took
the same name: *Zentralstelle für judische Auswanderung* (Central Office for Jewish
Emigration), and its potentials can be judged by the report of Reinhard Heydrich,
chief of the Sipo-SD, at the high-level conference held on 12 November 1938, when
the Viennese measures were halted. This meeting was presided over by Goering,
and several ministers, including Goebbels and Funk, attended. On this occasion
Heydrich declared:

> *Thanks to our Jewish emigration centre in Vienna we have been
> able to encourage 50,000 Jews to leave Austria. During the same
> period only 19,000 Jews left Germany itself (*Altreich). *This has been
> achieved with the co-operation of the Ministry of Economy and of
> philanthropic foreign organisations. . . . We asked wealthy Jews
> wishing to emigrate to deposit a fixed sum of money in the hands
> of the Jewish community. With this money and currency payments
> from abroad, we were able to get rid of a number of Jewish paupers.
> The problem was not so much getting rid of the wealthy Jews, as
> disposing of the rabble.*

During the months that followed, tens upon tens of thousands of Jews left
German territory. It may well be asked under what circumstances. The Jewish
tragedy of this epoch: the wretchedness of people whom no one wanted and in the
face of whom so many doors were swiftly closed, constitutes a sad chapter beyond
the scope of this book. Hundreds of thousands of Jews from Germany, and from
countries threatened by Germany, wanted to leave but had nowhere to go; for no
country could, or would receive such a large number of them.[2]

By this time Herbert Baum had acquired such authority among the young Berlin
Jews that those who wished to emigrate, even when they were not true Communists
but merely Communist-sympathisers, came to ask him for the moral authorisation
to do so. No one was refused, though Baum himself remained where he was, and
with his wife did everything he could to keep up the spirits of those who, willingly
or not, had remained in Germany. A literary, artistic and musical circle was set up
in the Baum home, consisting mainly of young Communists like Hildegard Jadamowitz, but including such Zionists as Hildegard Loewy, who retained her convictions right to the end. Arrested and tried in 1942, she blazoned before the

court her solidarity with her comrades and with the Soviet Union, principal enemy of the Third Reich, the fact that she had lost an arm doing nothing to diminish her courage.

The links between the Baum group and the Party were, at that time, extremely tenuous. The German Communist Centre in Czechoslovakia, which had managed to keep going, though the Czechoslovakian government was very sensitive to the protestations of the German Embassy in Prague, rapidly disappeared between the annexation of the Sudetenland in October 1938 and the occupation of the rest of Czechoslovakia on 15 March 1939.

Herbert Baum and other members of his group, Hildegard Jadamowitz and Richard Holzer in particular, were in personal contact with other Berlin militants and Communist groups, but these were very much reduced in number and strength. The most important, in effectiveness rather than size, was that of Harro Schulze-Boysen and d'Arvid Harnack, known under the name of *Rote Kapelle* (Red Orchestra) given it by the Gestapo, but there was no liaison between this and the Baum group, and though a meeting between the last survivor of the Baum group and the women members of the Schulze-Boysen-Harnack group did take place in 1943 this was in the women's prison of Berlin Moabit.

The most important contact was the one Herbert Baum made with his old classmate Werner Steinbrink, who, although half-Jew, had managed to obtain the status 'Aryan' and was a chemist employed by the *Kaiser Wilhelm* institute like his Party comrade, Joachim Franke.

Another Communist group with which Baum was in touch was the *Europäische Union*, so called because of its multiple relations with French and Belgian workers.

As well as musical evenings, the Baums organised outings to the forests and to the numerous lakes around Berlin, but after 1941 Jews were denied access to such places; and the dissolution of the legal Jewish organisations caused a number of Baum's old comrades and friends to draw closer to him for like all true leaders he had tremendous personal magnetism. The general situation weighed heavily upon the young men to whom emigration was excluded, either as undesirable or impossible, and who simply had to make the best of the situation and be prepared to stay and fight on the spot.

Here Herbert Baum had his own solution, which he proposed to his friends and comrades: the Communist solution; and in the years that followed, he was to expound the principles of Communism to them all, reading and encouraging others to read the main ideological Communist texts, of which Lenin's *The State and Revolution* seems to have been one of the most popular, perhaps because the conclusions to be drawn from it were relatively straightforward and easily assimilated by young minds: the principal enemy of the Jews, in Germany and outside it, was Nazi Fascism; the most bitter and powerful enemy of Nazi Fascism, against which it directed its most single-minded opposition, was Communism, having as its instigator the Soviet Union. It followed logically that the only lasting solution for the German-Jewish problem in Germany would be reached through Communism and the Soviet Union.

This is a considerably simplified version of the explanations given by Herbert Baum and, at a later stage, by his comrades Martin Kochmann and Hilde Jadamowitz: we must bear in mind that we are dealing with German Jews who were particularly fond of theoretical discussion, and as Communist texts were prohibited in Nazi Germany, and what literature had escaped the auto-da-fé could only be circulated with the greatest difficulty and under the threat of very severe penalties — and there were cases where these were surreptitiously recopied by hand or photostated — these young people were more and more obliged to fall back on their own reasoning powers.

Two young women members of the group, neither of them Jewish, who shared the same struggles, joys and sorrows and the same fate as Herbert Baum and his comrades, were Irene Walther, who kept the young Resistance fighters supplied with various material necessities, particularly paper, and Suzanne Wesse (née Vasseur), of French extraction, who had married a half-Jew, from whom she was separated. How her left-wing sympathies had drawn her to a Jewish rather than to a German group we do not know, for none of her close friends survived, though Charlotte Holzer remembers that she was the girl friend of one of the group, and that the Vasseur family lived in the north of France, and was very wealthy. In fact, for a long time it was Suzanne Wesse's financial assistance that allowed the group to survive.[3]

Situated on the fringe of other illegal Communist groups in Berlin, the Baum group militated as best it could within its limits, and in the autumn of 1940 it organised a semi-public demonstration, aimed at two objectives.

The group had just learnt of the death at Buchenwald of Rudi Arndt, a very special militant Communist Jew who had been interned in concentration camps since 1933, having served previous prison sentences for his Communist activities.

This veteran internee, who had arrived at Buchenwald the day the camp opened, had set his mind on procuring better conditions for the Jewish prisoners, of whom there was a particularly large number as a result of the *Kristallnacht* (Night of the Broken Glass) of November 1938. Many of these had been freed and allowed to emigrate; but when war was declared, others, more numerous still, had taken their place.

These Jewish internees were abandoned to the double despotism of the SS guards and the 'Jerries', common-law internees who, in the circumstances, had become the aristocracy of the camp, and Rudi Arndt intervened, as far as he could, to spare them at least some of the worst forms of victimisation and suffering inflicted on them: perhaps not very much, but for the internees of Buchenwald, the mere fact of receiving the camp soup more regularly, of being less often cheated of their rations, meant a great deal, and Rudi Arndt won the respect of his gaolers, who called him, with a derision that could not quite conceal a certain grudging admiration 'the King of the Jews'.

Herbert Baum and his comrades felt impelled to pay homage to his memory, at the same time taking advantage of the occasion to boost the morale of the militants of the group, and to this end, one day in the autumn of 1940, some fifty members of the group gathered together in the Jewish cemetery of Berlin-Weissensee, the cemetery where they all now lie.

For someone who has never had to organise a secret public gathering it is almost impossible to grasp the strain and stress, not to mention the danger involved in gathering fifty people together, in Berlin itself and at this time; these were not ordinary people, but Jews who were suspects, and treated as such.

The ceremony went off without incident, an inspiring occasion that rekindled the fervour of everybody present.

The cohesion of the group was further strengthened by the fact that most of them, including Herbert Baum, worked in the same factory, *Elmo* (*Elektromotoren*), part of the Siemens group, situated on the outskirts of Berlin. They did not enjoy the same working conditions as their German companions, for they had no right to holidays, paid or unpaid, nor could they claim Social Security benefits, or any of the voluntary benefits provided by the firm, while their wages were far inferior to those of the Germans and even fell below the minimum living wage, seldom rising above 80 to 90 marks a month. Jews in the group who worked elsewhere were seldom better off, and one of their number, employed as a baker's assistant at 70 marks a week, was considered the 'Mr. Moneybags' of the group.

Herbert Baum was swiftly voted representative of the Jewish labourers who worked in homogeneous groups, and as far as possible were segregated from the rest, particularly the German workers, not being allowed to appeal to the factory manager or even to the German foremen. Only the Jewish representative could do that, and his possibilities were severely limited, as Herbert Baum soon realised.

A much better relationship existed between the Jews and the French and Belgian workers who were considerably handicapped by their ignorance of the German tongue, and here again Suzanne Wesse played an important role: although she did not work at Siemens, she managed to make contact with these workers through her Jewish comrades and these contacts deepened into friendship, the STO workers appreciating the spontaneous display of solidarity offered by this German-speaking group of aliens who were so much more unfortunate than themselves. The Resistance group *Europäische Union*, directed among others by Robert Havemann, also proved to be very useful in forming liaisons, and once the relationship was firmly established, the Jewish Resistance was able to procure a number of false French and Belgian papers, though the transactions were difficult and expensive, an identity card costing about 150 marks, or two to three months' pay.

These were petty considerations compared with the two Nazi measures issued in the second half of 1941 when suddenly the situation of the Jews became desperate, and they were face to face with the last two stages of the 'final solution': the compulsory wearing of the yellow star and the beginning of the deportations to the east.

The gas chambers of Auschwitz were not yet in use but from the autumn of 1941 German Jews were deported to Riga, Minsk, Lodz and Lublin, and shot by the thousands. No details were published but everyone was well aware that Jews deported to the east ran the greatest risks.

From the beginning of 1941, the underground activities of the group consisted in the preparation and distribution of propaganda leaflets. One, aimed at doctors, disclosed that there were many more wounded on the Russian front than the authorities admitted, that they were badly cared for, that the medical equipment was inadequate, etc. Other documents — one ran to 19 typed pages — were distributed most frequently via the army postal service. How effective these documents were remains an open question. We know that the Gestapo and the military police seized a large number of them, both at the front and in the towns. A German citizen finding one in his letter box, could not tell if it was an authentic illegal document or a provocation from the Gestapo, and he generally conformed to official orders which required that he deliver the document to the head of the *bloc* (block of houses) of the National Socialist Party.

If it was a genuinely illegal document the Gestapo found it quite easy to trace the diffusion area and close in on the centre of distribution, whether or not the document was sent by post.

We refer here only to the documents produced at the trial of one section of the Baum group which are nothing more nor less than Communist texts, the other material distributed by the Baum group consisting of propaganda posters denouncing the Nazi regime and prophesying its inevitable defeat in the face of the Anglo-American-Soviet coalition, which were stuck on the walls of the Reich capital.

Herbert Baum and certain members of his group found this propagandist activity far too tame, and looked for the opportunity to deal a vital blow, though in achieving this they were to lose their lives. They had a deep-rooted moral urge to show that they, as Jews, were at least as courageous as the others; though this meant that they must take greater risks than non-Jews; that they must in effect, do more than others in order to be considered their equals.

We already know something of Herbert Baum's background, though hardly anything of his wife Marianne, and police and legal dossiers provide us with rather prejudiced character sketches of the other conspirators.

A Nazi law, perpetrated it seems by Dr. Hans Globke, who was to end his career in the German bureaucracy as Secretary of State to Federal Chancellor Konrad Adenauer, made it compulsory for male German Jews to adopt, besides their own Christian name, the Christian name of Israel, while female Jews had to adopt the name of Sara; so that to the authorities of the Third Reich, Herbert Baum was Herbert-Israel Baum; Heinz Birnbaum, Heinz-Israel Birnbaum; and so on.

Heinz Birnbaum, a turner by trade, was born in Berlin on 22 September 1920, became friendly with Herbert Baum in the Zionist Youth movement and shared lodgings with him between 1938 and 1940, in which year Heinz began a course on Communist politics; and it was he who, at the end of 1941, was entrusted with the 19-page document we have mentioned, which bore the title *Organise the mass revolutionary struggle against Fascism and the Imperialist war*. The donor was another Jew whom we only know as Hopp.

In the spring of 1942, Birnbaum, Marianne Baum and Sala Kochmann, under Herbert Baum's direction, prepared a treatise on the German food situation, in direct response to an article written by Doctor Goebbels, Minister of Propaganda of the Reich, which had appeared in his weekly paper *Das Reich*. The completed text was dictated to Irene Walther, who typed the stencil for duplication. Birnbaum managed to get hold of a false 'French worker's' identity card and participated with Baum and Steinbrink in the 'expropriation' operation of Lietzenburger Strasse. The supplementary 'crime' of not wearing the yellow star was also committed.

Charlotte Holzer was born in December 1909, and was now thirty-two years old, this 'great age' earning her the nickname of 'grandmother' in the group. She had wanted to be a doctor, but her family's limited means prevented this and she trained as a nurse, taking up employment in the Berlin Jewish Hospital in 1931. Charlotte was the divorced wife of Gustav Paech and had custody of their seven-year-old daughter. In her younger days she had belonged to a German-Jewish youth movement militating for a united Germany; and Baum and she had met some years before, and again in 1940 when he spent a period in the hospital where she was a nurse and persuaded her to attend the courses of political instruction he was conducting at his home.

Her friend and future husband, Richard Holzer, who was linked to various

Communist groups, also attended the meetings though he did not share all Herbert Baum's ideas, and particularly distrusted his activist tendencies.

At the beginning of May 1942, Dr. Goebbels' propaganda services organised a gigantic exhibition, *The Soviet Paradise*, in the Lustgarten in the centre of Berlin.

The Red Orchestra group, led by Schulze-Boysen, replied by preparing an enormous number of placards and posters denouncing Dr. Goebbels' scheme and plastering the walls around the exhibition under cover of blackout, which operation was carried through without incident. Schulze-Boysen and his friends were arrested shortly afterwards, but for entirely different reasons.[4]

Herbert Baum and his comrades had joined the others in pasting up the posters, and now wanted to go a step further and set fire to the exhibition buildings.

This would be no easy task. They must first procure the necessary materials, and learn the basic principles of fire-raising. Werner Steinbrink and Franke volunteered for these two missions. The material had to be hidden in such a way as to avoid unnecessary risk to human lives, and above all, the strictest security measures must be taken, a precaution more necessary in Berlin than anywhere else in Europe. Nowhere did the Resistance fighters run greater risks; for their actions went not only against the State and established order but against popular feeling. A militant who found himself in difficulties in Paris, Brussels, or even in Warsaw could at least count upon the passive complicity of his fellow citizens — but not in Berlin where the normal reaction of an honest citizen was to denounce all suspicious-looking activities to the police or to the leader of the National Socialist *bloc*.

Some members of the group considered the action too risky, not only for the participants but for the Berlin Jews as a whole. A much larger number could hardly wait to participate in the attack, but most of these were turned down, either because there were not sufficient explosives or because their too characteristic physiognomy would have given them away.

The explosives were delivered to Herbert Baum on Friday, 15 May 1942, when he decided that seven members would take part in the operation: he and his wife Marianne, Hans Joachim, Gerd Meyer, Sala Kochmann, Suzanne Wesse and Irene Walter, three men and four women. On the Sunday evening, 17 May, the seven made their way to the spot, but finding there were too many people around, put off the action until next day. On Monday evening they placed their miniature incendiary bombs at different points in the exhibition, the idea being that several conflagrations should burst out simultaneously.

Was the Gestapo warned of the attack?[5] At all events, firemen extinguished the fires and the German Press did not breathe a word about the affair, which would hardly have gone unnoticed had a fire got out of control at the Lustgarten in the heart of Berlin.

Within a few days of the event, the seven participants and most of the other members of the group were seized by the Gestapo. Steinbrink and Franke were also arrested.

On 11 June 1942, the Gestapo informed the public prosecutor that Herbert Baum had committed suicide. Those who had been directly involved in the outrage, Franke, Steinbrink and eight others, were tried on 16 July 1942. All were executed on 18 August.

Doubts persist as to how exactly Herbert Baum died. Some prison comrades think that he succumbed to the tortures inflicted upon him by the Gestapo; others believe that he did in fact commit suicide. It is known that after being tortured he was taken to the entrance of the Siemens factories one morning when the Jews were clocking in for work. It was hoped that he would give the game away when he caught sight of former accomplices, or that the latter would betray themselves by recognising him. The ruse failed.

What is known for certain is that members of the group were tortured in the course of preliminary investigations. The dossier of the trial of the second batch of prisoners has been found intact, and in it appear the names of a dozen members who had not personally taken part in the outrage: Heinz Rotholz, Heinz Birnbaum, Hella and Alice Hirsch, Edith Fraenkel, Hanni Meyer, Marianne Joachim, Lothar Salinger, Helmuth Neumann, Hildegard Loewy, Siegbert Rotholz and his wife Lotte.

The same dossier contains a letter from the Gestapo dated 5 December 1942 addressed to the Public Prosecutor of the Reich, care of the People's Court. It reports that both Heinz Rotholz and Heinz Birnbaum were twice subjected to 'forced interrogation in the form of beating with a stick' and this with the consent of the Chief of the principal bureau of the Berlin Gestapo, the *SS-Obersturmbann-führer und Oberregierungsrat* Bovensiepen. The document does not mention how many blows of the stick were administered to these two unfortunates nor the results obtained by such methods of interrogation.

Incidentally, even though no account of the attack on the anti-Bolshevik exhibition appeared in the German Press controlled by Dr. Goebbels, the incident none the less provoked a violent reaction from him. In his capacity — not as Minister of propaganda of the Reich — but as *Gauleiter*[6] of Berlin, Goebbels ordered the immediate execution of five hundred Berlin Jews, and these were shot at the SS barracks of Lichterfelde-West, and at Sachsenhausen. All Jews who had 'legal' residence in Berlin were deported soon afterwards and all were gone by the end of

1943. It can therefore be assumed that the five hundred victims would have perished whether there had been an outrage or not.

The members of the Rotholz group were tried on 10 December and with the exception of Lotte Rotholz, Alice Hirsch and Edith Fraenkel, were condemned to death, and executed on 4 March 1943. Strange to relate, their execution was publicly announced by a 'red poster'[7] which limited itself to listing the names of the victims and mentioning the fact that they had been condemned to death for participating in an 'attempt to commit an act of high treason'.

Though there was no indication that this was a Jewish undertaking, it was self-evident, since 'Israel' and 'Sara' were affixed to the Christian names of the accused.

The defence of the accused was entrusted to lawyers designated by the court, for Jewish lawyers had no longer the right to plead, and the accused were not authorised to choose their own defence counsel. It is only fair to point out that the lawyers in question, members of the National Socialist Party, did all that they could in an effort to save their clients — to the extent of incurring the displeasure of both prosecutor and court. They managed to obtain prison sentences for three of them: eight years for Lotte Rotholz, five years for Edith Fraenkel, three years for Alice Hirsch. True, these sentences had only a symbolic value, as the three young women were deported to Auschwitz and did not return.

One of the condemned, Hildegard Loewy, tried to escape from prison but was recaptured as she attempted to scale the boundary wall.

The official reports of the execution, a series of photostated documents with the requisite blanks for the names, are contained in the same dossier:

The Public Prosecutor of the Berlin-Plötzensee of the Reich, 4 March 1943, the People's Court (place of execution).

IO J 207/42

Execution of the sentence of death
upon
HEINZ ISRAËL ROTHOLZ

Present:

Director of the execution. . . . .   *Judge*: Dr. Beselin

Official of the Court. . . . .   *The clerk*: Karpe

At 18.40 the condemned, his hands tied behind his back, was led out by two prison officials. The executioner Röttger, of Berlin, and his three assistants, were in attendance.

Also present was the prison official, inspector of administration Rohde. After having confirmed the identity of the condemned, the director of the execution ordered the executioner to proceed. The condemned man appeared calm and untroubled and allowed himself to be positioned on the block without resistance. Thereupon the executioner effected decapitation with an axe, upon which he announced that the sentence had been carried out. The duration of execution from the moment that the accused was led out, to the announcement of the execution was 18 seconds.

Signed: Dr. Beselin   *Signed*: Karpe

All the reports on Nazi trials include a detailed statement of the costs and taxes incurred by the condemned. Their next-of-kin were accountable for all legal costs including that of the execution where that applied. Any sum of money found on the person of the accused at the moment of his arrest was confiscated and if this was not sufficient to cover all costs, the administration referred to the relatives.

In the case of Marianne Joachim, however, the official report dated 30 July 1943 declared that a debt of 144.90 marks, owed to the Reich by the condemned had been annulled and the amount carried over to the debit of the Reich. This was not a matter of a favour, as the report makes abundantly clear:

> *The estate has been liquidated. No other successor is known. The next-of-kin, (father and mother) have been deported to the east. There is no prospect of any ultimate recovery of the funds.*

The third trial took place on 29 July 1943 and concluded with the passing of death sentences on three other members of the group, Martin Kochmann, Felix Heymann and Herbert Budzislawski.

The case of Charlotte Paech (Holzer), who was tried at the same time, was treated separately because the accused had to make a preliminary appearance before another court to answer for the offence of illegal possession of false ration books.

During the trial it was pointed out that Martin Kochmann was called 'widower' because his wife Sala Kochmann had been condemned to death and executed with the first batch. She had tried to commit suicide by jumping out of a window, but had only succeeded in breaking both legs. She appeared before the court in a wheelchair and was still in a wheelchair when she was taken to the scaffold.

On 16 July 1943, it was the turn of Gustav Paech, former 'Aryan' husband of

Charlotte Paech. He was accused of having been in touch with his first wife after the outrage — she having gone to entrust him with their child — and of not having denounced her to the authorities. He was only sentenced to two years' imprisonment but when this period expired he was shut up in a concentration camp. He survived up to the Liberation, but died a few days later in the camp hospital.

Other people were tried and sentenced for coming to the aid of one or other of the Baum group. Only twenty-eight names are inscribed on the monument commemorating the sacrifice of Herbert Baum and his companions. There should be many, many more.

Charlotte Paech, whose trial had been disjointed, was tried separately and duly sentenced to death, but her execution was postponed due to an exigency of German bureaucracy: having been committed to prison for illegal possession of ration books, she was obliged to serve this sentence first, and as according to regulations this term could not be served in Berlin, where she was on detention awaiting trial, she was transferred to Leipzig.

There other complications arose: the local gaols had all been declared 'purged' of their Jewish prisoners, and the truck transporting Charlotte had to go from prison to prison in search of one willing to take a Jewish detainee for a brief period, even if it meant forfeiting their claim to the coveted title of *Judenrein*. The ninth of these establishments agreed to open its doors, and swiftly closed them again on Charlotte Paech.

Shortly before her sentence expired, the prisoner realised that she had scarlet fever. A doctor came the following day and diagnosed the case by peering through the grille. Still outside the door, he announced: 'Scarlet fever. Quarantine.'

Forty days later the doctor returned and flinging open the door declared: 'Recovery. End of quarantine.'

During that period Charlotte Paech had received no medicine of any sort. Her cell had no lighting, natural or artificial and she was not allowed out once into the light of day.

On her recovery, which can only be described as miraculous, Charlotte was taken back to Berlin, to the prison of Moabit. There she had the opportunity of 'meeting' Erika von Brockdorff and other members of the Red Orchestra group detained there. They did not actually see each other but were able to communicate by knocking on the walls or singing at the pitch of their voices. The wardresses of the prison, former Social Democratic militants, turned a deaf ear.

Twice a week, a number of women were taken from their cells. As a general rule, Monday was for interrogations or for giving evidence in court; Thursday was for executions.

From time to time, over the next few months, Charlotte Paech was summoned to appear before the various Berlin courts, the same courts where decent Aryan Germans were tried when found guilty of harbouring Jewish belongings. Sometimes these possessions had been entrusted to them by deported Jews who hoped to be able to collect them again on their return. In other cases, the accused had procured the belongings in rather more dubious circumstances. The attitude of the Gestapo was always the same: all Jewish belongings, whether the owners had been deported or not, were legally theirs, and they reacted energetically when mere individuals, although good Aryans or even good Nazis, dared to question their monopoly.

The evidence Charlotte Paech gave at these trials was minimal. Not knowing either the accused or the goods concerned, she limited herself to saying that she knew nothing whatsoever about them.

It is interesting to note in passing that the evidence of Jews greatly embarrassed the Nazi jurists. Stripped of their German nationality, they had no longer the right to be sworn in. The courts therefore found themselves confronted with witnesses who could freely sidestep the truth, without risk of punishment: an insoluble problem, as one can see. Again, how could a sentenced person be deprived of civic rights which he no longer had?

These stumbling blocks were not removed until 13 October 1942, when Thierack, Minister of Justice of the Reich, let it be known that he would hand all Jews, gypsies, Poles and Russians over to the *Reichsführer SS* and Chief of the German Police since 'Justice could only contribute in a very small way to the extirpation of these peoples' and 'there was no sense at all in keeping such persons for years and years in the prisons and penitentiaries of the Reich'. This ruling received the force of law on 1 July 1943: the 13th decree of application of the 'law on the citizenship of the Reich' stipulated that 'offences committed by the Jews are punishable by the police'. It was by virtue of this decree that Lotte Rotholz, Edith Fraenkel and Alice Hirsch were deported to Auschwitz.

One Thursday morning, an execution day, Charlotte Paech was taken from her cell. For weeks she had been quietly preparing herself for this moment and was morally ready to face death. Her only worry was that she might be handicapped at the last moment by some physical debility. The long months in prison had weakened her eyesight and even wearing strong spectacles she could barely see. In the prison truck she was astonished to find she had a travelling companion — a man without fetters, wearing a yellow armband. From him, she learned that the truck was not going in the direction of Plötzensee. For the time being, at least, she was not going to her death. But when it transpired that she was being transferred from the 'official' prison to the Gestapo camp where this man was imprisoned, she had a moment of despair, fearing that instead of being allowed to die a dignified death she was about to face an ignoble one.

The camp was situated on the outskirts of Berlin and contained half-Jews, awaiting 'clarification of civil status'; Jews seized while living illegally in Berlin; others who had managed to escape from Theresienstadt, or even from Auschwitz.

Once again Charlotte Paech was lucky. After weeks of terrible suspense she was summoned to the *Kommandantur*. It had been discovered from her dossier that she was a qualified nurse, and now, as it happened, the camp *Kommandant* was in the throes of a severe attack of nephritic colic.

Charlotte Paech cared for him as well as she could, refusing to let her real feelings get the better of her, and gradually, the *Kommandant's* condition improved, so that one day he behaved, as it were, like a human being and asked his nurse if he could do something for her.

'I want to know what is in store for me,' said Charlotte Paech. 'That depends on the position of the dossiers in the central bureau. If your dossier is at the bottom of the pile you must wait; if it is on the top of the pile you will soon be moving on.'

Several days later, the *Kommandant* summoned her to his office and told her that her dossier was on top of the pile.

Knowing that her last die had been cast, Charlotte Paech decided to try to escape, but in such a way as to bring no repercussions on her imprisoned comrades. In the course of an air raid that had ripped apart the barbed wire entanglements, the prisoner slipped away. As she could not distinguish a human figure at 50 centimetres, she walked calmly on without once turning round to see if she was being followed.

She knew only one address and that at the other end of Berlin. Here an unknown Protestant, a member of the Confessional Church, took her in and hid her for some time, then sent her off to another charitable soul, and as her situation was still dangerous she was supplied with false papers alleging her to be a French worker. She still had a smattering of French from her school-days, and finished up in an industrial centre on the outskirts of Stettin, where her fellow workers were very careful not to ask questions.

When the Soviet Army arrived Charlotte Paech came out of hiding and got in touch with other militant Communists. Her main concern was to trace the whereabouts of her mother-in-law, who had taken charge of her daughter, now aged eleven years. She found the child; alive but only just. The grandmother had treated her abominably, holding the child responsible for her son's imprisonment; in her eyes, she was the daughter not so much of her son as of a Jewish Communist.

Though Charlotte was reunited with her daughter, both of them were seriously ill. One day she was called to an infirmary: Gustav Paech had sent for her, and she was just in time to see him before he died.

All alone in Berlin, sick, exhausted, at the limit of her endurance, Charlotte found a home for Jewish children established near Hamburg that would be willing to accept her daughter, and there, at least, the child would have enough to eat and would be decently cared for. It was an incredible piece of good fortune in the devastated Germany of 1945.

Shortly afterwards, a piece of stupefying news reached her from Budapest: Richard Holzer was still alive! He had escaped death under even more adventurous circumstances than her own. Armed with a Hungarian passport, he had escaped from Germany to Budapest where, as a Jew, he was mobilised for hard labour in the so-called *Keret* units. These tattered columns of Jews rigged out in old army uniforms were attached to the Hungarian army units and had to work at the front line under military discipline. Barely a quarter of the Jewish conscripts survived because they escaped being captured by the Red Army, those who suffered this misfortune being considered by the Russians — to begin with at any rate — as soldiers of the Hungarian Fascist Army.

In Eastern Galicia where he was stationed, Richard Holzer established contact with some Polish priests who showed him a number of hideouts, in churches and sacristies, where a score or two of Polish Jews were concealed, and Holzer organised food supplies for them as best he could.

During a Soviet offensive, he and his unit of conscripts managed to cross the frontier, only to be captured in the Soviet lines. It took Holzer weeks of effort to persuade the Russians that he was not a Hungarian military Fascist but an anti-Fascist German soldier, and here the intervention of some Jewish Red Army officers proved very useful.

Back in Germany he joined a unit of the 'Committee of Free Germany' helping to publish a newspaper and propaganda material aimed at German prisoners-of-war, urging them to desert.

Richard Holzer knew the German psychological make-up well and was often stupefied and dismayed at the propagandist content of this literature. The average German was heartily sick of the exaggerated claims that had been fed him for years and could not stomach any more. But orders were orders.

About this time Holzer first heard about the gas chambers, and his reaction was that of the average German: it was just propaganda. He advised his colleagues not to circulate information of this kind.

Reunited in Berlin, Richard and Charlotte Holzer decided to take an active part in the building up of the German Democratic Republic, but first they had a mission to accomplish: to trace the remains of Herbert Baum and his comrades and give them a decent burial. They succeeded in the end in identifying them, and now came the problem of where to bury them.

In the big cemetery of Friedrichsfelde, east of Berlin, there is a cordoned-off area where fallen German revolutionary militants, Communist leaders and private soldiers lie buried, and it was suggested that Herbert Baum and his comrades should be laid here. Charlotte and Richard Holzer did not agree, and as sole survivors of the group, demanded that the Jewish heroes of the Resistance should be buried in the Jewish cemetery of Berlin-Weissensee. They won their case, and a star was placed above the grave inscribed with the names of the entire Herbert Baum group, Jewish or not.

In every town of the German Democratic Republic one comes across streets named after heroes of the Resistance. Herbert Baum Street in East Berlin leads to the cemetery of Weissensee, where he and his comrades rest.

NOTES

1. A young historian of the German Democratic Republic, Margot Pikarski, who has studied the political activities of the Baum group, considers that these young people joined the Zionist movement not through conviction but on the instructions of Herbert Baum. (Margot Pikarski, *Sie bleiben unvergessen*, East Berlin, 1968.)

2. At this period, France was the country that showed most humanity and understanding. Practically all German Jews who tried to enter France in the autumn of 1938, with or without papers, were more or less free to do so, and tens of thousands grasped the opportunity.

3. We have tried without success to trace the Vasseur family. Perhaps some reader can help.

4. These men played a very important role in the Soviet spy network in Germany and procured some vitally important information; and one wonders how militants already burdened with such heavy responsibilities could risk sticking up posters. More experienced militant Communists would never have undertaken such activities but would have respected the principle of job allocation and non-interpenetration of action. Schulze-Boysen was not just a cog in the machine, but a young man who militated because he was convinced that Nazism was evil and Communism was good. Although his espionage activites were very useful to the Soviet Military Command, they did not bring him personal and moral fulfilment; while to go out and stick up bills himself, denounce Nazi crimes in person, in short set his own life at risk, probably gave him a much greater sense of achievement.

5. A Gestapo report gives this impression.

6. Cf. *Wollt ihr den totalen Krieg? Die geheimen Goebbels-Konferenzen 1939—1943*, DTV, Munich, 1968, pp. 314—318.

7. Tens of thousands of so-called 'official' death sentences — that is, those following a court trial — were passed in Germany during the war, apart from the far greater number of executions that took place in the concentration camps. But it was very unusual for death sentences to be publicly announced through the medium of the red posters.

CHAPTER 5

THE UNION FOR PEACE AND LIBERTY

*A*RBEITSGEMEINSCHAFT *für Friede und Freiheit* — 'Union for Peace and Liberty' is in the name of a little-known but extremely active Resistance group. The high-sounding title tends to overstate the scope of the group — although not necessarily its aims. A young Jewish electrician from Berlin, pursued by the Gestapo, arrested, escaped, arrested again, deported, escaped once more, succeeded in founding this group, and directed its operations in Berlin and in many other towns of north, north-east and southern Germany from 1943 to 1945. The group would have achieved much had it been able to count upon wider support.

The electrician Werner Scharff was born in Poznan, which was then German, in 1912 and was therefore the same age as Herbert Baum. There is no evidence that the two youths ever met or had occasion to work together, when they would have complemented each other perfectly.

Scharff had great personal charm which enabled him to win over not only those whose co-operation he sought, but even Gestapo officers: a truly remarkable achievement considering the hatred and contempt these people had for the Jews.

Scharff began operations at the end of 1941, as the deportations of the Berlin Jews got underway, the first being to the Lodz ghetto, on 16 October. As a trained electrician, he was ordered to install the lighting in the assembly centre of the Berlin Jews, the synagogue of the *Levetzowstrasse*. He often managed to slip a little food or tobacco or other small items to the deportees before they set off, and, since his trade gave him unlimited access, he managed to suppress filing cards and even complete filing systems by putting the cards of the people to be deported in the 'deported' file.

He also tried to enlist the support of Germans in finding hiding places for the clandestine Jews or helping them to change their identity. Scharff himself did not go into hiding until 10 June 1943, when the time came for the last Jewish workers of the *Reichsvereinigung* to be deported.

He remained at liberty only until 14 July, when he was recognised in the street by a Gestapo police officer accompanied by two Jews who in such cases had to serve as auxiliaries. Scharff was armed, but because of the Jews he allowed himself to be arrested without resistance. It is not for us to say whether or not this manifestation of Jewish solidarity was justified.

Scharff was removed to the *bunker* of the Jewish prison where Charlotte Holzer was to pass several months, while he himself was deported with his comrade-in-arms Friedel Fancia Grün on 4 August, with the privilege of being sent not to Auschwitz, but Theresienstadt.

This ghetto-camp was the responsibility of the RSHA and not of the concentration camps' administration board. The Theresienstadt prisoners were not exterminated; at the worst they died of hunger or sickness as many did. It was a sort of model camp which delegates from the Red Cross were allowed to inspect when necessary, and in the main it was specially deserving German, Austrian or Czech Jews who were sent there: decorated war veterans, employees of the *Reichsvereinigung*, or Jews well known abroad, who had powerful sponsors intervening on their behalf. The several hundred Danish Jews the Danish Resistance movement had not succeeded in transferring to Sweden were imprisoned in Theresienstadt, since the Danish authorities never ceased making representations on their behalf.

But when Theresienstadt became overcrowded the surplus was sent to Auschwitz, where the formerly 'privileged' were treated exactly like their fellow Jews, 60 to 100 per cent of them being packed off to the gas chambers, the rate depending on the convoy. The fact that Theresienstadt was still considered a veritable paradise in comparison with other camps did not prevent Scharff and his comrades from escaping on 7 September 1943, barely a month after their arrest.

The small 18th-century fortress town of Theresienstadt was encircled by walls and bastions like a Vauban fortress, the whole of which had been emptied of its German and Czech inhabitants and transformed into a ghetto. There were two citadels, the smaller of which, a sort of prison-within-a-prison, was reserved for Jews and political prisoners.

Escape was slightly less difficult for a German Jew, not inconvenienced by the language, for Theresienstadt was situated on the border of the German territory of the Sudetenland.

Scharff and Fancia returned to Berlin where they lost no time in obtaining false papers, Scharff assuming the identity of 'Hans Wieczorek', travelling salesman. His appearance was in his favour; he was one of those rare blue-eyed, flaxen-haired Semites, anything but Jewish.

Scharff's main contact, a clerk called Hans Winkler, lived in Luckenwalde, a small town some thirty-five miles east of Berlin, and the two men created a 'Union for Peace and Liberty', Winkler taking command and adopting the title of *Reichsführer* (national leader). He also created a clandestine savings bank, *Höher Einsatz* (higher stake), with the object of collecting funds for the Jews in hiding.

We have no record of the pair's exact movements, but we do know that they prepared and distributed a series of propaganda leaflets relaying news bulletins

taken from the BBC; and that with the help of contacts in the area and in particular that of the agronomic inspector Alfred Stein; the butcher, Henry Landes;
and the carpenter Walter Klatt[1]; they managed to hide a number of Jews, beginning
with those drawn from Scharff's close circle.

In Berlin itself, another supporting group was established — a predominantly
female one. Its members kept the Luckenwalde group supplied with hiding-places
and funds and also distributed propaganda leaflets. All of them were German,
and older than the militant Jews: Pelagia Kozlowski was thirty-eight, Johanna
Schallschmidt forty-two, Ida Röscher forty-eight and Frieda Wiegal fifty-three.

The Werner-Scharff group included a brother of Fancia Grün, Gerhard, with his
wife Ilse, the Samuel couple and Eric Sojka, a Franco-Jewish prisoner-of-war and
interpreter at *Stalag IIIA* which was right there in Luckenwalde. It is not known how
he came to be associated with the movement.

The group had other antennae in Eisenach, Thuringia, Hamburg and probably
in Munich.

Scharff knew how to turn the circumstances to his advantage. It had become more
and more apparent — even for those who tried to close their eyes to it — that the war
was lost, and Scharff often talked to Nazis who seemed lukewarm towards the
regime or had been made lukewarm by the way the war was going. Both Winkler
and he saw to it that all those who volunteered to help the union in any way were
given anti-Nazi attestations, and it was a sign of the times that the market value
of these attestations was about the same as that of the 'foreign workers' identity
papers which the members of the Herbert Baum group had bought two years before.

Scharff, like Baum, longed to strike a lethal blow with some bearing on the Jews
which would have far-reaching effects on their general situation, and it was decided to launch a surprise attack on the Schulstrasse Jewish prison and free the
prisoners. This attack was to coincide with the Allied Berlin offensive which would
decide the war.

The plan was a tremendously ambitious one and had the disadvantage of requiring a large number of participants if it was to succeed, and in fact no one did
escape — an informer saw to that; and on 12 October 1944, the whole group, including Gertrude Scharff and Fancia Grün, was arrested, Werner and Winkler being
taken two days after, and within two months the entire Luckenwalde group was
wiped out.

Werner Scharff was immediately recognised by the Gestapo as an escapee from
Theresienstadt, particularly as his passage had been marked by massive distri-
butions of leaflets. It was imperative to get him to talk.

Werner Scharff refused to utter a word; certainly not because the Gestapo dealt
gently with him. After keeping him for three long weeks in a dark cell with his hands
and feet bound, they submitted him to all sorts of tortures including being dangled

by his feet, and having his thumbs crushed in an ingenious screw device. But Scharff did not wish to talk and nothing could make him, and after several weeks they stopped torturing him: others had spoken for him.

On 16 March 1945, six weeks before the fall of Berlin, Scharff was shot at Sachsenhausen. Gerhard Grün seems to have been shot at the same time. Fancia Grün suffered the same fate. Gertrude Scharff and Ilse Grün managed to survive until the Liberation: when the German women members of the group, imprisoned in the Fehrbellin camp and the prison of Bayreuth were almost all saved.

NOTES

1. Hildegard Bromberg was another 'Jewish terrorist' who was arrested and escaped. She was more fortunate than Scharff and managed to survive until the Liberation, but she committed suicide in Berlin soon after. Why she did so remains a mystery.

CHAPTER 6

MUTINY OF THE SACHSENHAUSEN JEWS

A BOUT twenty-five miles north of Berlin, near the little town of Orianienburg, lay Sachsenhausen, one of the thirteen principal concentration camps of the Third Reich. Here, in addition to the usual watch-towers, camp henchmen, areas set aside for atrocities, executions and suchlike, were a few extra refinements: the measuring apparatus, for instance, under which condemned men, for whom no other provision had been made, were forced to pass, and in so doing received a bullet in the back of their necks. There were also a small gas chamber, several crematoria, dungeons, etc.

Sachsenhausen was unusual in another respect: it was next door to the SS Central Office of Administration and Economy (WVHA), which was responsible for the administration of all concentration camps. The barracks of the Waffen-SS, where the recruits learned the routine and the camp guards received their professional training, were also in Oranienburg-Sachsenhausen.

The relations established between prisoners and guards in this camp were of a rather special kind, for the simple reason that by the end of their training the debutant guards had come to know their charges very well. Later, when they were sent to other camps and happened to come across prisoners they had known in the early stages of their career, they sometimes treated them in a less barbarous, even humane manner. Had this attitude been the rule rather than the exception, the mortality rate would have shown a marked fall, especially in the latter years of the war. But it did sometimes happen at Auschwitz, Dachau, and Buchenwald, for instance, that guards who had trained at Sachsenhausen arranged for prisoners they recognised to have the less arduous tasks.

There were large Jewish contingents at all the camps, including Sachsenhausen. The particular concentration camp a prisoner was sent to depended upon where he was picked up; Sachsenhausen, for example, received the prisoners of the Berlin suburbs, though later large numbers of non-German prisoners hailing from every part of Europe from Smolensk to Bordeaux were sent there and very often died there. There were also Soviet prisoners.

In every camp Jewish internees were placed in separate huts: at Sachsenhausen in blocks 37, 38 and 39, which can still be seen today, for they have been preserved, and indeed restored. This area is one of the most starkly depressing parts of the Sachsenhausen Memorial.

The first Jews to arrive were political prisoners, mostly Communists, sent there either without trial, or after serving prison sentences. Similarly, a large number of militants who had been given relatively light sentences, of two, three or five years' imprisonment, turned up again at Sachsenhausen, Buchenwald, Dachau, etc.

Political prisoners 'freed' from the penitentiaries around Berlin were also handed over to Sachsenhausen.

When the Jews imprisoned in Sachsenhausen began to reach large figures the 'political Jews' took charge of them. There were two main 'deliveries': one following the *Kristallnacht* in November 1938, most of whom were liberated a few months later; and another in September 1939 just after war was declared, when about a thousand Berlin Polish Jews were dispatched to Sachsenhausen. Many of these were young.

Following the *Kristallnacht*, the Jews were particularly badly treated in the camp, but their general situation improved slightly from the autumn of 1939, when their quarters ceased to be totally isolated from the rest of the camp, consolidating relations between the prisoners and making combined action possible. Hans Hüttner, one of the future protagonists of the Jewish revolt in the camp, recalls that around this period prisoners allocated to hospital duties managed to smuggle themselves into the Jewish quarters and organised what he calls 'flying ambulances'. Other prisoners, working in the central kitchen or the clothes shop, smuggled food and clothing to the Jews: little enough, no doubt, but sometimes sufficient to save a man's life. Some SS guards who knew what was going on did nothing to stop it and as time went on these interdependent actions became fairly generally tolerated.

The arrival in 1939–1940 of new waves of prisoners, particularly Czech and Polish Resistance fighters, drew some of the attention of the SS from the Jews for a time, but the situation changed for the worse in 1941, and deteriorated even more when the Russo-German war broke out.

There is no trace of the document in which Hitler prescribed the systematic extermination of the Jews, and though it may one day come to light, in all likelihood the order was not given in writing.

It frequently happened that the *Führer* expressed his wishes verbally and these were noted by whichever of his collaborators happened to be near him at the time, when the order would be signed by Hitler. Few original documents have been found, only copies charging different administrative grades to execute his orders. All the same, such an order must have been given in the course of spring 1941, probably at the time Hitler was issuing his directives preparatory to the invasion of the Soviet Union; and orders have been found recommending that Soviet political representatives and Soviet Jews in general should be executed; the latter being qualified in the interests of the case as 'principal bearers of Bolshevist ideas'.

That autumn saw the first of the Jewish deportations from Germany, Austria and the 'Protectorate' of Bohemia-Moravia; 'purging' the concentration camps of Jews only came in 1942, when during the summer and autumn Jews in concentration camps in Germany itself were moved eastwards to the camps of Lublin-Maidanek and Auschwitz. (Strictly speaking Auschwitz was situated in the eastern part of Upper Silesia which had been part of the Reich since 1939.) Nevertheless it was at Auschwitz that the most advanced type of gas chamber was installed: yet another example of Nazi inconsistency.

In May 1942, tragedy struck at Sachsenhausen. A reprisal action following the attack on the exhibition *Soviet Paradise* ended in the imprisonment and execution of 250 Berlin Jews, and soon after, 97 Jews were shot in retaliation for the attempted assassination of the Supreme Head of the Gestapo, Reinhard Heydrich, on 28 May 1942.

Reaction was particularly violent among the younger prisoners, who felt they must act; they could not tolerate the idea of allowing themselves to be murdered without offering some sort of resistance and were particularly sensitive to the jibes of non-Jewish fellow prisoners who accused them of passivity. The only reason there was not a desperate uprising of the young Jews just then was that the illegal Communist administration of the Jewish quarters intervened, convinced that desperate action could only lead to the assassination of the Jewish prisoners and endanger the lives of non-Jewish fellow prisoners at Sachsenhausen and elsewhere. It was doubtful too whether such a sacrifice would achieve anything.

The situation was more or less back to normal up to 21 October 1942 when at evening roll call the SS announced that Jews were not to report for work the following morning.

If no one had any idea what lay behind this decision, no one had any illusions, and when immediately following the announcement, the illegal leaders of blocks 37, 38 and 39, including those in charge of the huts of the various blocks, were arrested and shut up in the *bunker* (the camp prison) the Jews knew they must expect the worst.

From then on rumours in the *Industriehof*, the yard where the various camp workshops were situated, flew thick and fast.

The clandestine Jewish group formed in the weeks preceding the event decided to take action straight away. It was not a very large group, thirty to forty men perhaps, most of them young, with a hard core of young Communists like Hans Hüttner, called Nathan Hirschtritt at this time, Horst Jonas, Walter Blass, Gottfried Ballin, Arnold Edberg, Adam Koenig, Leo Swirski, Jakob Goldmann, Leo Hauser, Oskar Heim, Arnold Hirschhorn, 'old Brenner' and others. They were not all Communists, nor did all the Communist Jews belong to the group, but they were all bound by the common decision not to allow themselves to be murdered without offering some sort of resistance, which decision they made known to the clandestine political leaders of the camp.

The clandestine leadership showed strong reservations about the plan. As Horst Jonas, one of the members of the group, now mayor of the town of Neu-Branden-burg in the German Democratic Republic, wrote:

> Only a small number gave an enthusiastic response to our Jewish friends' decision. Many challenged it. Some objected because they feared that the whole camp would suffer from the reprisals that were bound to follow. Others considered that there was little danger of that. (They did not want to add strength to the rumours that were already circulating.) All the same, very few indeed gave their full support to the prisoners of block 39.

At 8 a.m. on 22 October 1942, the *Blockführer SS* burst into the huts flailing their truncheons and drove the Jews towards the *Appelplatz* where they joined the sick Jews, who had been chased just as brutally from the infirmary. The *Appel-platz* was 'reserved for the Jews'. They were made to line up three yards apart and underwent a rigorous search, in the course of which everything they had on them was removed. The rain poured steadily down as the proceedings dragged on and on.

Suddenly there was a brisk change of programme. The prisoners were gathered together in groups of fifty and marched towards the disinfestation hut where normally prisoners supervised the undressing, the shower and the subsequent dressing. This time only the SS was present and in a trice the few precious objects which had not been taken away in the morning, toothbrushes, hunks of bread, were whipped away. The prisoners were stripped of their clothes and marched off naked to the dressing room where they received a new 'wardrobe': denim shirt and trousers and a pair of sabots.

It took no one very long to grasp that they were about to receive a bullet in the back of their necks in the *Industriehof*.

Some were seized with despair; others resigned themselves to their fate; but the young people still managed to hold their meeting; not that all the members were present, for the roll call and the shower had considerably diminished their numbers, but if there were only eighteen of them left, eighteen would take action, and zero hour was fixed at ten minutes after the evening roll call.

At 6 p.m. the bell sounded and the 12,000 prisoners gathered together on the *Appelplatz*, duly lined up according to rooms, huts, blocks; but the Jewish prisoners were not among them. They remained shut up in their three blocks.

Suddenly pandemonium broke loose. Prisoners were shouting: 'Shoot, you cowardly dogs! Go on, shoot!'

The figures of prisoners came into view on the right-hand side of the *Kommandantur*. They advanced rapidly and SS guards who tried to stop them were roughly pushed aside. More and still more guards arrived, but the prisoners continued to advance in spite of the punches and the truncheon blows.

That group of eighteen had smashed the windows of block 39 and had succeeded in advancing right up to the *Lagerführer*, but there they were overcome. But the miracle had happened: eighteen men had broken the iron discipline of the camp, and had not been shot dead on the spot, even though they had committed the unpardonable crime of striking the SS: and not just anyone, but the Second in Command of Sachsenhausen himself! The 12,000 prisoners looking on could hardly believe their eyes. The SS guards were equally stunned. The impossible had happened! And there was the *Lagerführer* in person approaching the eighteen, who by this time were completely surrounded by guards brandishing revolvers and machine guns.

The order was given for the guards to withdraw. Addressing himself to the prisoners, the *Lagerführer* barked out: 'Stand up!'

For a long breathless moment no one budged. Then briskly one of the prisoners repeated the order: 'Stand up!' and with deliberate slowness, the eighteen got to their feet.

A guard indicated one of the prisoners with the muzzle of his machine gun: 'That's the leader!'

The *Lagerführer* motioned him to step forward and demanded: 'What is this all about?'

The reply rang out clipped and clear:

'We don't want a bullet in the back of our necks!'

'Absurd! You are about to be transferred. And you will kindly convey this information to your companions still in the huts.'

'I will only tell my comrades what I consider to be the truth.'

The incredible dialogue continued. The eighteen had calmed down. Whatever fate had in store for them they had won a great victory, and the SS guards became more and more ill at ease.

The Camp *Kommandant*, senior in rank to the *Lagerführer* arrived on the scene and the exchange continued.

Finally the Jewish spokesman declared: 'If it is truly a matter of our being transferred elsewhere, then I must say that I have never seen prisoners in transit from this camp so disgustingly treated!'

The *Kommandant* turned to the embarrassed SS guards for an explanation, giving the impression that the measures had been taken without his authority; and withdrew, leaving the eighteen under SS guard.

Finally, his orders arrived. The eighteen were allowed to return to their huts. Everything that had been taken from the prisoners was restored to them and the meals of which they had been deprived were duly distributed.

By rebelling, the eighteen had gained a tremendous moral victory over the SS. Further than that they could not go. Had there been eighteen hundred of them instead of eighteen, they still would not have been able to stop the transfer to Auschwitz. Not even the insurrection of the entire camp could have prevented that.

The handful of Sachsenhausen prisoners continued to benefit from their action at Auschwitz. Instead of being sent to the gas chambers with the other prisoners they were allotted the easiest tasks. Only three or four of the eighteen perished, including 'Old Brenner' when he attempted to escape. We know of no Jewish group imprisoned at Auschwitz that could claim such a high percentage of survival.

The fact that there were former Sachsenhausen acquaintances among the SS guards certainly played in the prisoners' favour. But were these guards really more humane?

Here is Horst Jonas's opinion:

> After the war, I was informed that one of these guards had cited me as a witness when he had to appear before a tribunal. He alleged that he had saved my life. My reply to the Soviet officer in charge of the proceedings was as follows: 'Yes, this man did save my life, but at the same time he was responsible for the loss of hundreds if not thousands of others.'

So the only riot recorded in the 12-year history of the Nazi concentration camps in Germany itself was victorious to the very end.[1]

NOTES

1. Other Jewish acts of Resistance behind the barbed wire of the German concentration camps may since have been forgotten. The revolts that took place in the extermination camps situated outside the frontiers of the Reich will be dealt with later. Emil Carlebach (see page 23) should be mentioned for his activities, first at Dachau, then at Buchenwald. He was in charge of a Jewish hut and saved many of his fellow captives. He was moreover a very active member of the international camp organisations, particularly at Buchenwald.

Part Three

Inside Fascist Italy

CHAPTER 7

AMBIGUITIES IN ·MUSSOLINI'S POLICIES

T HERE were about 35,000 Jews in Italy prior to the war, of which 7,500 or so were deported to Auschwitz and Mauthausen. About 600 returned.

These crude statistics show that the destiny of the Italian Jews was still on the whole less harsh than that of their fellows in neighbouring countries. Much of the credit for this goes to the Italian people and to the Italian Jews themselves. Two factors, two hierarchies had a bearing on their attitude: the National Fascist Party and the Catholic Church. There is also much to say about relations between Benito Mussolini and the Jews, unstable to say the least — on both sides.

As a young revolutionary Socialist anarchist in Switzerland, Mussolini had had an affair with Angelica Balabanova, a militant Menshevik, formerly bound to Lenin and Trotsky. The fact that the young woman was Jewish had no connection what-soever with her exemplary revolutionary activity.

Later the Fascist *Duce* had an affair with another Jewess, one that had far-reaching repercussions, for the lady became his enthusiastic biographer. Even when the liaison had come to an end and Margherita had withdrawn to the Argentine, she remained faithful to Mussolini and to Fascism. As a result, those Jews, and there were many of them, who had the habit of judging by appearances, a type as frequently found among the non-Jews as among the Jews, came to the conclusion that Fascism was and always would be on their side, a fatal mistake for many of them.

There have always been Jews in Italy: those living in the ghetto of Rome today can trace their origins to an epoch long before the birth of Christ; and on 13 May 1929, Mussolini felt it incumbent upon him to declare to Parliament in Rome;

> *The Jews have lived in Rome since the epoch of the Magi. Perhaps it was they who supplied the apparel for the kidnapped Sabines. There were 50,000 of them at the time of Augustine, and they asked permis-sion to weep on the tomb of Julius Caesar.*[1]

We disclaim all responsibility for the historical accuracy of these remarks, but they could well be true. In fact, the Italian Jews were very largely assimilated into the non-Jewish community; they had the same general attitudes and held the same political views, and many Italian Jews, like the non-Jewish Italians, started off by joining the Fascist movement and the National Fascist Party even when they did not always wholeheartedly agree with their ideology.

Mussolini's attitude towards the Jews was inconsistent to say the least. In June 1919, he violently denounced them as the instigators of Bolshevism; a year later he wrote the very opposite. He cited a number of Jewish Communist leaders in Russia and Hungary; then went on to state that after the crushing of Bela Kun's Hungarian Soviet Republic, the Hungarian Jews were the victims of anti-Semite pogroms. In his own words:

> Contrary to general opinion, Bolshevism is not a Jewish phenomenon. But there is no doubt that it will lead to the total ruin of the Jews in Eastern Europe. Every European Jew is aware of this impending danger and knows that the fall of Bolshevism in Russia will be followed by a pogrom of unheard-of proportions.[2]

At a later date Mussolini was to make a clear differentiation between the Fascist, pro-Fascist, opportunistic and out-and-out anti-Fascist Jews, and did not hesitate to exert pressure on the first two categories to force them to react in their turn on the others. 'We hope,' he said, 'that the Italian Jews will be intelligent enough not to stir up anti-Semitism in the one country where it has never existed.'

At one point, and for highly political motives principally concerned with ousting Great Britain from the Eastern Mediterranean, Mussolini even went to the extent of flirting with the Zionist movement. Zionist leaders such as Chaim Weizmann, Nahum Sokolov and Nahum Goldmann were all received by him at one stage or another.[3]

One of the splinter groups of the Zionist movement at that time, the Zionist-Revisionists, led by Vladimir Jabotinski, went even further. Jabotinski received official backing to establish a college in Italy for the purpose of training cadets for the navy of the future Jewish State, and this school was able to function right up to 1937. Jabotinski was convinced — and managed to convince others — that it would be better for the Palestine Jews, for the Zionist movement, and for Jews all over the world if Fascist Italy became the mandatory power in Palestine instead of Great Britain.

What caused Mussolini to constantly change his attitudes? The historian of the Italian Jews under Fascism, Renzo de Felice (who, incidentally, was not Jewish) can offer no definite facts, but states,

> In our opinion there is more than one reason: the first, that he probably managed to get hold of additional information; the second that he was given advice (possibly by some of the large number of influen-

tial Jews in his entourage). The latter provided valuable financial assistance to Fascism and to its paper Il Popolo d'Italia.

Renzo de Felice also mentions that about 750 Jews who had belonged to the Fascist Party before the March on Rome were still alive at that period. The total membership in 1938 was 10,370 adults. Non-members totalled 23,000.

At the outset, there were as few anti-Fascist Italian Jews as there were anti-Fascist non-Jewish Italians; and there were very few anti-Fascist emigrants, a small number of them Jews. Similarly a number of Jews among the university professors refused to swear allegiance to the *Duce* and were consequently deprived of their posts. Some of the emigrants such as Claudio Trèves had been friends of Mussolini during his Socialist period prior to 1915. Others were younger, like the brothers Carlo and Nello Rosselli.

The last two had already served prison terms for their anti-Fascist activities in Italy. In 1929, Carlo was placed under house arrest in the Lipari Islands, but managed to escape to Tunisia by boat. Later the two brothers helped to create the anti-Fascist movement *Giustizia e Libertà* and played an active part in its operation, particularly in France. This movement contained a large number of militant anti-Fascists, who, despite their leftist and even extreme leftist leanings, still kept apart from the Italian Communist Party. In 1937, Mussolini decided to rid himself of the threat that the Rosselli brothers represented to his regime and had them disposed of at Bagnoles-de-l'Orne by French assassins.

There were also a number of Jews in the top ranks of the Italian Communist Party, such as Umberto Terracini, Mario Montagnaga and Emilio Sereni. All of these passed long years in prison for their anti-Fascist activities and were only released on the fall of Mussolini in July 1943. They later played an important part in the Italian Resistance against the German Occupation and its Fascist allies.

Other Jewish emigrants who took an active part in the Toulouse Resistance movement were Silvio Tretin and Gustavo Camerini. The latter, under his *nom de guerre* of Clarence was made a *Compagnon de la Liberation* by General de Gaulle.

Nevertheless most of the Italian Jews stayed on in Italy and most of them eventually became anti-Fascists. Take the group of young Zionists who frequented the Allasons' home in Turin in 1931. Neither they nor Barbara (the life and soul of the group) were Jewish, but all were anti-Fascists. There was a hard core of them around Léone Ginzburg, consisting of the young painter and writer Carlo Levi

(*Christ Stopped At Eboli*), Professor Giuseppe Levi, Sion Segre and a few others. This nucleus was allied to the *Giustizia e Libertà* group in Paris.

Besides the Ginzburg group, there was a young Zionist group known as *Oneg Shabat*, and some Jews, such as Sion Segre, belonged to both groups. Among the regular visitors to the Allasons' home was the noted philosopher Benedetto Croce and the young Zionist Enzo Sereni, who had been domiciled in Palestine since 1922 — unusual for an Italian Jew — and made a point of visiting the Allasons on his occasional trips home.

Enzo Sereni, younger brother of the Communist Emilio Sereni, enlisted in the British Army during the war and volunteered to be parachuted behind the enemy lines, beginning his training in 1943 when he was over forty years old. In May 1944 he and an Italian officer were dropped over Northern Italy and were to have landed in the region of Ferrara, but owing to a navigational error Enzo Sereni found himself inside a German fortified zone. He was sent first to a *Stalag* as a British officer prisoner-of-war, but this special treatment did not last long and on 8 October 1944 he was moved to Dachau, reclassified as both an Italian political prisoner (red triangle) and Jew (yellow triangle). He was shot on 18 November 1944 along with several Italian political detainees.

In him was lost both a gifted philosopher and a man of action: it had taken Hitler's war to convince this fighting pacifist that armed aggression was necessary.

The younger *Oneg Shabat* group was formed after an extremely successful sojourn at a holiday camp at Courmayeur in 1931. The organisers of the camp and the holiday-makers have since taken widely divergent paths. Anna Foa was a Socialist and remained one; her brother Vittorio became a Socialist deputy after 1945; Corrado Corinaldi settled in Israel, while his sister Lia, having relinquished an important position in the Communist Party is now a full-time professor of philosophy.

Emmanuele Artom, also a professor of philosophy, was another member of the group as was his young brother Ennio, who died in 1940. Carlo Levi was already well known as a painter at this time — his literary talent being still untapped. Leo Levi was even then more of a mystic than a politician and in this respect has changed very little. He now lives in Israel.

On 11 March 1934, Sion Segre and Mario Levi, two members of *Giustizia e Libertà*, were intercepted by the Fascist political police at the Italo-Swiss frontier post of Ponte Tresa. Mario Levi flung himself into the Lake of Lugano and managed to swim back to Switzerland. The police ransacked the car and discovered the *Giustizia e Libertà* clandestine newspapers and leaflets all ready for distribution. They seized Segre's diary which was chock-full of addresses as one would expect. There was also a list of people who were to be present at a coming *Oneg Shabat* meeting. The outcome was 39 arrests in the course of the following couple of days, and of this number only 17 were kept in prison for any length of time.

In the meantime a section of the Press kicked up a great fuss about the fact that of the 14 men arrested 11 were Jews. The newspaper *Tevere* (the same one that was to 'spit on France' in 1938) laid great emphasis on the fact that a group of the imprisoned Jews were Zionists, pointing out that anti-Fascism had always depended for the most part on Jewish support, and that from Trèves to Modigliani, from Roselli to Margari the leaders of anti-Fascist subversive activity had always belonged and still belonged to the 'Chosen Race'.

The two prisoners convicted at the trial in the autumn of 1934 escaped with comparatively light sentences (Ginzburg got four years; Segre three, of which two were deferred[4]).

The relative clemency of the sentences was due to Mussolini's personal intervention. According to Renzo de Felice, the aim of the trial was not to unleash an anti-Semite campaign in Italy, but rather to put the Italian Jews on their guard against the dangers of anti-Fascism.

In fact, Fascist Italy was at this time conducting an extraordinarily ambivalent policy. In the spring of 1933, Mussolini, Minister of Foreign Affairs, had asked all his diplomats posted abroad to send him reports on Hitler's anti-Jewish policy, and these reports varied considerably in tenor and spirit.

The Italian embassies and consulates in Germany expressed horror and disgust at Hitler's anti-Semite manifestations such as the boycotting of Jewish enterprises, and were especially critical of the scathing diatribes of the Nazi Press. The Italian diplomatic mission in France pointed out with evident displeasure that the Jewish emigrants from Germany were anti-Fascist, and placed the French who protested against Hitler and his regime in the same category. The French politicians who denounced Hitler's excesses were severely taken to task in these reports, as were church dignitaries, and in 1933, at least, a large number of these denounced Hitler's anti-Semitism.

The Italian consul stationed at Casablanca reported with undisguised pleasure that any attempts of the Moroccan Jews to organise protest demonstrations had the immediate effect of releasing anti-Jewish repercussions on the part of the Arabs.

Italy's attitude to the German anti-Jewish measures was just as ambiguous, some newspapers rejecting them with horror; others welcoming them. The Italian authorities allowed several thousand German Jews to seek refuge in Italy, but only on the understanding that the matter was not to be publicised, and a rabbinic school from Germany took up quarters in Fiume. At the same period Mussolini was cautioning the leaders of the international Zionist movement to be prudent and trying to dissuade them from organising, or attempting to organise, an anti-German movement.

The Jews played a very active part in anti-Fascist nuclei operating outside Turin — particularly in Trieste, where there had been a small Jewish community since the time of the Austro-Hungarian monarchy. The situation of Eugenio Colorni (although born in Milan) gives us an idea of how matters stood there.

Born in 1909, he had been tempted to join *Giustizia e Libertà* in his university days. Soon after his appointment as professor of philosophy at the Trieste College of Education, he began to have sympathies for the Socialist Party and went to see the leader in Paris, and on his return he set about trying to get the clandestine groups back on their feet.

On 7 September he was captured, and after five months' imprisonment, he was placed under house arrest, first on the island of Ventotene, then on Melfi.

He managed to escape in the spring of 1943 and within a few months had resumed his activities in the Socialist Party, playing a leading role in the negotiations between the Party and Marshal Badoglio immediately after Mussolini's overthrow; but like many others he was taken by surprise on 8 September 1943 by the announcement of armistice and especially by the virulence of the German reaction — which ended in the military occupation of Italian territory.

Finding himself shut up in Rome, Colorni courageously pursued his activities. He rescued a defunct clandestine military centre belonging to his party and successfully directed it almost until the capital was liberated early in June 1944. We say 'almost' for on 26 May he was recognised and attacked by a Fascist patrol. He died two days later.

At the beginning of his activities in Trieste, Colorni had had occasion to collaborate with a Jewish pediatrician a few years older than himself, Bruno Pincherle, himself a former militant of *Giustizia e Libertà* who had been won over to Socialism. Pincherle was well known for his anti-Fascist activities and had been arrested for the first time along with Carlo Rosselli. He settled in Paris and succeeded in smuggling his writings into Italy. Although he avoided arrest in September 1938, he was kept under close observation, and a year later he was violently beaten up in the street for having refused to doff his cap at the passage of a Fascist flag.

When Italy entered the war on 10 June 1940, he was of course arrested 'as a preventitive measure' and he and his brother were interned in the concentration camp of Urbisaglia.

He must have found a large number of Jews there: some arrested as anti-Fascist; some as enemy aliens; some simply because they were non-Italian Jews, refugees from Germany and from the whole of Central and Eastern Europe. He was released after a year and resumed his anti-Fascist activities by organising small nuclei of Resistance, embryos of the future detachments of Venezia Giulia, even succeeding in establishing liaisons with the Slovene partisans of Istria and Slovenia who proved extremely valuable after the capitulation of Italy.

At that time it was no easy matter to establish this type of contact. The conspirators disliked the job and unless they took the most careful precautions they ran the risk of falling into police hands. In the end the Yugoslavian and Italian fighters were more or less obliged to reach some sort of understanding — after all they were fighting the same battle — but it was not without considerable misgivings and hesitation on both sides. Pincherle was used to it: as far back as the thirties he and Colorni had weighed up the difficulties of establishing contact with clandestine Communist groups in the region. In 1943 they often met up with the same men they had tried to co-operate with a score or so years before.

It is interesting to note that Pincherle was not only a political militant in the thick of the fight, but a brilliant doctor and a noted Stendhalian.

The introduction of anti-Jewish measures in Italy in 1938 was a severe blow for the Italian Jews in general and an even worse one for the dedicated Fascists, although particularly deserving Fascists were protected by provisos. Most Italians, including the members of the Fascist Party, disapproved of the measures,[5] and this made the lot of the Jews much better than it might otherwise have been.

Besides, Mussolini's characteristic ambivalence was just as much in evidence in this affair. He had not changed his mind about the Jews, but in 1938 he thought it wise, in view of the political situation, to launch anti-Jewish legislation.

This does not change the political judgment brought upon the *Duce* and upon his actions in general, and the fact that his ambivalent attitude probably saved tens of thousands of Jews from being massacred by the Nazis in no way justifies the part the Fascists played in the slaughter of thousands of others; nevertheless, however conclusive the evidence against Fascism, it is rather less so against Mussolini and some of the Fascist leaders.

NOTES

1. Renzo de Felice, *Storia degli ebrei italiani sotto il fascismo*, Turin, Einaudi, 1962, p. 114.
2. Renzo de Felice, *op. cit.*, pp. 81—82
3. On the other hand, during one of his visits, Weizmann did not hesitate to intervene in favour of an imprisoned Jew, who was as far removed from Zionism as could be. Emilio Sereni, future deputy and prime minister was imprisoned for being a militant Communist. The only reason Chaim Weizmann intervened in his favour was that a brother of the prisoner, Enzo Sereni, was one of the leaders of the Zionist movement in Palestine.
4. Nevertheless the trial had dramatic consequences for Italian Judaism. In a large number of towns the leaders of Jewish communities had to report to the Prefects and renew their oaths of allegiance to Italy, to Fascism, and to the person

of the *Duce*. In Turin itself, epicentre of the upheavals, a group of important Fascist Jews completely dissociated themselves from community life and created their own newspaper *La Nostra Bandiera* whose rampant Fascism was enough to shock even non-Jewish Fascists.

5. Three members of the Fascist Grand Council, Marshals Balbo and Emilio de Bono, and the Minister Federzoni, openly opposed the measures when they were brought before the Grand Council.

CHAPTER 8

THE DOWNFALL OF THE *DUCE*

W HEN Italy entered the war, the Jewish refugees of Central Europe were sent *en masse* to concentration and internment camps. Their lot was a far from enviable one, but there was no comparison between the regime of these camps and those that the Vichy government planned to put in their place.

The Italians led an extremely rich spiritual, cultural and religious life inside their camps and Italo-Jewish organisations were more or less free to help the prisoners, but complete chaos reigned on the administrative side. The food was deplorable and got even worse as Italy's situation deteriorated. However, one by one, the camps were closed down and most of the prisoners were set free, though one of the largest camps of all, Ferramonti Tarsia in Calabria, was still operating when the British Army reached it after the Salerno-Naples battle in the autumn of 1943.

Naturally, the Italian anti-Fascists, who opposed official anti-Semitism, were on very good terms with the Jews, who were to be found in varying numbers in all the Italian Resistance groups, though always as individuals taking part on their own account, for there were no established Jewish groups or organisations.

On 25 July 1943, Mussolini was ejected by the Grand Fascist Council and subsequently arrested by royal command, on the instigation of his successor and the new Prime Minister, Badoglio. A certain Italo-Jewish politician played a prominent role in the plots and conspiracies that led up to this event: the lawyer, historian and journalist Eucardio Momigliano, former deputy, and an enemy of Fascism since its birth. On behalf of his party the 'Democracy of Labour', subsequently integrated with the Social Democratic Party, he endeavoured to persuade some of the military leaders, among them Badoglio, to overthrow the *Duce* and Fascism. The moment was particularly ripe in March 1943, for the big strikes that had flared up in Northern Italy at that time had dealt a terrible blow to the regime and strongly contributed to the country's collapse in July.

However, Badoglio and the other generals refused to follow Momigliano, considering themselves bound by oath to King Victor Emmanuel III, who was still not ready to separate himself from Mussolini, particularly while the strike crisis continued in the north.

The Italo-German capitulation in Tunisia took place two months later, at the beginning of May 1943, just after the simultaneous fall of Tunis and Bizerta, the

Italian islands of Lampedusa and Pantelleria capitulating a few weeks later. It was not even necessary to effect a landing: the air raids were more than sufficient.

The next blow struck at Italy was a telling one for the Mussolini regime and one from which it never recovered: the landing of the Anglo-American Allied forces in Sicily on 10 July 1943.

In desperation, seeing that defeat was inevitable, Mussolini took himself on 19 July 1943 to Feltre in the Veneto. There he had another meeting with Hitler, hoping to persuade him to make peace in the Mediterranean, or at least to send powerful reinforcements in Italy. He did not manage to get a word in edgeways.

At Feltre, the *Duce* learned that Allied planes had bombed Rome for the first time. (It is interesting to note that whereas the Bishop of Rome, Pope Pius XII, protested loudly against the bombardment of the Eternal City, he did not feel the same exigency when the issue was the gassing of Jews.)

On the return of the *Duce*, the crisis exploded in the heart of the Fascist hierarchy and on 25 July 1943 King Victor Emmanuel informed Mussolini that he had been dismissed from office and that Marshal Badoglio would form a new government in his place. The first official declaration had no doubt the object of letting the Italian people, and especially the German allies, know that the war would continue. Political prisoners were gradually released, but by no means all of them. The Communist leader Emilio Sereni, for instance, who had been arrested by the Vichy police a short time before and handed over to the Italian Occupation authorities, was transferred to Italy and sentenced — long after 25 July — to eighteen years' hard labour[1].

He had travelled a long way since that distant day in Toulouse in October 1941, when he and his Party comrade and future mayor of Bologna, Dozza, had added their signatures to the agreement between *Giustizia e Libertà* and the Socialist Party: the former represented by the Jew Silvio Trentin and Fausto Nitti, the latter by Pietro Nenni and Giuseppe Saragat.

The 'forty-five day' period from the fall of Mussolini to the official proclamation of the capitulation of Italy and its occupation by the German Army on 8 September 1943, was a very strange one indeed. Badoglio wished to make peace, for he was in a very delicate situation and trembled to think what the Nazis would do. Knowing exactly what they were about, the Germans sent large contingents of troops into Italy. The size and equipment of these divisions far exceeded Mussolini's wildest dreams.

At the same time, the Allies were trying to reach a peace agreement with the Italian government in their own fashion. Subjecting the Italian towns to heavier and heavier bombardments, more and more often, during the 'forty-five days', to convince Badoglio and King Victor Emmanuel that such shilly-shallying did not pay.

Nevertheless, political life took up where it had left off, although not openly. Eugenio Colorni, who had been one of the principal editors of the clandestine Socialist newspaper *Avanti!* resumed his post. Another Jewish intellectual from Trieste — Eugenio Curiel, professor of mathematics and physics and a brilliant philosopher — was then writing for the still clandestine Communist newspaper *Unità.*

Emmanuele Artom, Professor in the Jewish school in Turin, militated in the ranks of the Action Party — a political emanation of *Giustizia e Libertà.* A note in his private diary dated 13 August 1943, refers to an article that had appeared the day before in the *Gazzetta del Popolo*, in which Tullio Giordana demanded the restitution of the Jews' civil rights:

> We have seen that the conception of liberty embraces both religious and cultural life. . . . By means of so-called radical laws Fascism has placed the Jews in a situation of inferiority compared to other citizens, thus violating one of the fundamental concepts of liberty, no less important than the acquisition of the rights of man: legal equality for all.

Artom commented,

> We must stand up to Badoglio, force his hand and show him that the voice of the Italian people has not been silenced; there is still a chance of getting him to do something.

Another young Jewish intellectual, Vito Volterra, went even further: he interrupted his university studies in neutral Switzerland to return to his family in Italy. After all, Fascism had fallen, the country was free and peace was on the way, so what was the point of continuing to live in Switzerland?

On 16 October 1943, barely a month after the capture of Rome, the Germans organised a large scale round-up in the Jewish quarter and deported 1,007 Jews. This episode has been the subject of many investigations and of a very powerful dramatic work: *The Deputy* (*The Representative*) by Rolf Hochhuth. The fact remains — despite attempts to explain it away — that over a thousand Jews were rounded up in the Eternal City and not once did Pope Pius XII openly protest. Was his silence on this and on other occasions where the lives of the Jews were in jeopardy due to the fact that the Pope considered it useless to intervene? Or did he consider it dangerous not only for the Jews, but for Catholics, the Church and the

Vatican to interfere at that time? Whatever the reason, these are the facts. A few years ago, the Holy See began publication of Vatican archives that have a bearing on this period of the war; but at the time of writing documents relative to this episode have not been made public. As a non-Christian, I prefer to reserve judgement until they are. In the meantime, Pius XII must be given the benefit of the doubt[2].

NOTES

1. Emilio Sereni was only freed in 1944 following a surprise attack by the Resistance. He ended the war in Milan as a member of the Committee of National Liberation of Northern Italy. In a communiqué dated 26 April 1945 in which the Committee of National Liberation of Lombardy announced that it was assuming full governmental powers, Emilio Sereni's signature headed the list.

2. It is only fair to point out that in Rome and throughout Italy, all the churches, convents, religious schools, parish presbyteries and institutions, directly or indirectly dependent on the Roman Catholic Church — and goodness knows they were numerous enough in Italy — sheltered and hid the hunted Jews. Italian Jews talk feelingly of men like Torquato Fraccon, a Christian Democratic militant, shot by the Germans for having concealed Jews; and women like Ida Batistella, a modest peasant woman who hid a Jewish family in her home for more than a year and later refused to accept even the smallest financial compensation for her hospitality when the family was able to offer it.

CHAPTER 9

THE ITALIAN PARTISANS

IT is impossible for us to do justice here to the Italian Partisan movement, an immense movement in the extent of its territory and in the strength of its numbers. It was also a great movement in the many bitter battles fought and won with heavy losses on both sides. The Italian Resistance combatants were of a different calibre altogether from the Italian Fascist Army that attacked France in June 1940, and the Italian troops who were defeated in Albania, Greece, Libya, Ethiopia, Egypt, Tunisia, even in Russia, though they were often the same men, the same soldiers. The only difference was that from the day the Germans invaded their country they knew what they were fighting for. From now on they were face to face with the real enemy.

The several phases of the Italian armed Resistance progressed at their own pace in the different regions, in some carried through to a successful conclusion; in others coming to an abrupt halt because of the reduced strength of the Partisans, or because Liberation intervened.

In Southern Italy, close to the Allied front, there were spontaneous uprisings, of which the best known is the Four Days of Naples (27—30 September 1943). After Kesselring's vain attempt to foil the Allied landing at Salerno, one of his German units, trying to withdraw through Naples, came up against a veritable tidal wave of the population who attacked the *tedesco traditore* (the traitorous Germans) and ended by overwhelming them.

Rome never reached the extent of armed uprisings owing to strong opposition from Royalist elements on the one hand, the Vatican on the other. However, in Latium, on the outskirts of the capital, and particularly in the region of *Castelli Romani*, an important guerrilla movement rapidly developed, fed by military Resistance fighters and abandoned arms. The political leadership was chiefly in the hands of the Communists and the militants of *Giustizia e Libertà*. There was a number of Jews among them, from Rome and elsewhere, notably Pino Levi Cavaglione. Similar nuclei sprang up all over the country. Beginning in the towns and large villages of the plains and spreading to the mountains they were often reinforced by Allied prisoners-of-war, liberated when armistice was declared and on the run from the Germans.

The Resistance suffered considerably in the course of winter 1943—44. The slowness of the Allied advance, coming immediately after the defeat suffered at

Cassino, lowered their morale, while paradoxically this same delay increased their political strength and importance: the very difficulties impeding the Allies' progress north led them to depend more and more upon the co-operation of the Partisans. Liaisons were established, parachutings were effected, military envoys were sent.

Spring and summer saw a considerable intensification of Partisan operations both in towns and in the mountains, with numerous uprisings behind enemy lines only just preceding the Allied advance. The Germans were driven from Rome, then from the whole of Central Italy.

At the same time, further north, obviously expecting the Allied advance to continue right up to the Alps, the Partisans rose up *en masse* and took over entire regions. It was at this time that numerous 'Partisan Republics' were born in the zones liberated by the Resistance. They were found in Val d'Ossola, Piedmont, the Veneto and in Emilia. In all these 'Republics' the Partisans had the upper hand, declaring themselves members of the Committee of National Liberation of Northern Italy centred in Milan; this, like all the other committees with localised or provincial headquarters, was composed of delegates from the five anti-Fascist political parties: Communists, Socialists, 'Actionists', Liberals, and Christian Democrats. The party representation was equal although the Communists were numerically stronger among the Partisans — particularly in the plains.

In the mountains, the various nuclei and detachments grew rapidly in strength, transforming themselves into brigades and even divisions.

At the top of the scale reigned the Committee of National Liberation of Northern Italy (CLNAI), headed by the Communists Luigi Longo and Emilio Sereni, the 'Actionists' Ferrucio Parri and Leo Valiani (the latter not only Jewish, but also a distant relative of Dr. Theodor Herzl, founder of Zionism), and representatives of the Christian Democratic, Liberal and Socialist parties. A number of anti-Fascist political groups also acknowledged the Committee as their authority. On the military side, a Voluntary Freedom Corps (CVL) was set up to control the *ensemble* of Partisan movements and units. It was commanded by General Cadorna, who had been sent north by the Italian government in Rome. The latter had become resolutely anti-Fascist since the fall of Badoglio.

When the Allied offensive was forced to pause for breath, the Partisans found themselves in a difficult position. In Bologna, for instance, where they had managed to seize several districts of the town and its suburbs, the operation threatened to turn against them when the Allied front came to a halt at some distance from the town. In fact they had several fierce battles to fight before they were able to beat a retreat and lose themselves in the population. They succeeded but at the cost of several lives.

In the autumn, the Germans and their Fascist allies, having made sure that the front line was stabilised, launched the usual offensives and a series of round-ups inside the Free Zones, managing to retake most of them. The Partisans suffered another major setback on 15 November 1944, when Field-Marshal Viscount Alexander, Commander-in-Chief of the Allied forces in the Mediterranean, issued a series of dispositions stating quite simply that the Allied winter offensive had been halted and that consequently the Partisans, while remaining on the alert, should rest and prepare themselves for the spring campaign.

This amounted in fact to a demobilization order, and the Partisans were faced with a very difficult situation. Unlike the soldiers of the regular army, they could not simply supply themselves with leave passes and return home, for more likely than not their enemies would be there waiting for them.

The Committee of National Liberation and the Voluntary Freedom Corps of Northern Italy, although stunned by this bolt from the blue, reacted vigorously. Under the pretext of following the instructions of Field-Marshal Alexander, they did their utmost to keep the Partisan units together. A certain number gave up the fight, especially when Mussolini's government, delighted with this stroke of good luck, hastened to proclaim general amnesty for all those who returned home; but, generally speaking, the ranks of the Partisans held firm, and in the spring of 1945 rapidly reorganised themselves. On 29 March, the Voluntary Freedom Corps finally asserted its leadership over the Partisan formations, and all these emanations of different political and party movements became regular forces of the Italian Army.

On 10 April, the Communist Party published the 'insurrectional directive no. 16'. Despite this, the Resistance forces, and especially in the Communist ranks, continued to suffer heavy losses. Both Eugenio Curiel, editor of *Unità* and founder of the Youth Front, and Sergio Kasman, commander of Milan Square, were shot in Milan by a Fascist commando. Curiel was Jewish, Kasman probably of Jewish origin.

The national insurrection began on 14 April, nine days after the Allied offensive. On 17 April the German front was penetrated. The Partisans already held Carrara, Imola and part of Bologna. In fact, throughout the offensive, the Allies had simply to walk in and take possession of the towns, for the Partisan rebels had already done all the fighting. They forced the German General Meinhold, commander of the town and sector of Genoa, to surrender, and took Milan, Turin, Venice, Parma, Piacenza, La Spezia, and many other large towns.

Negotiations for the separate peace, led on the German side by the SS General Karl Wolff, concluded on 30 April with the surrender of the German forces in Italy. But it was the Italian Partisans who liberated most of the inhabited centres of North Italy, and they who seized the *Duce* and the ministers of his phantom republic rather than let them fall into Allied hands.

Jewish Resistance fighters played a part wherever the Partisan war was waged. Feruccio Valobra, leader of the Committee of National Liberation of San Bernardo in Carmagnola, was shot at the age of forty-six years. Franco Cesena, a Partisan liaison agent, fell at the age of thirteen years. There may well have been as many as 2,000 Jews among the armed Italian Partisans.

To appreciate the relative size of this number, it is sufficient to say that there were only around 35,000 Jews in German-occupied Italy. Of these 7,500 had been deported by the Gestapo, and 1,500 to 2,000 others interned in concentration camps by the Fascist authorities.

In Italy, as elsewhere, women shared in the struggle. Rita Rosani, a teacher in the Jewish school in Trieste, was only twenty-four when she was killed on active service. She is the only woman to have received posthumously an Italian military gold medal. This was inscribed with the following citation:

> *Politically persecuted, she joined an armed detachment and shared in the rough life of the other fighters. She was a comrade, a sister, an inspiring person with indomitable courage and burning faith, shirking neither danger nor death nor suffering in the accomplishment of the difficult and dangerous missions that were entrusted to her. When her formation was encircled by far superior Nazi-Fascist forces, she took arms and covered the retreat of her companions. She fought up to the moment when she fell, gloriously sacrificing her young and heroic life for her country's cause.*
> Monte Commune (Verona), 17 September 1944

Reserve captain Mario Jacchia was forty-seven years old in 1943. Racial discriminatory laws had banned him from the regular army and he had joined the Partisans on 8 September 1943 in Bologna, his native city. He rapidly rose to become Partisan Military Inspector of Emilia and Commander of the Partisans of northern Emilia.

From the military point of view Emilia was very important to the Germans, for the province was immediately behind the so-called Gothic line, which the Germans had extended across the northern part of Central Italy following the Apennines from the Adriatic to the Tyrrhenian Sea.

One evening in the summer of 1944, Jacchia was presiding at a meeting when a German patrol took him by surprise. He could have escaped as he ordered all his subordinates to do, but he was determined to destroy all incriminating documents first — and what document was not! He was captured and given the usual treatment, particularly refined in his case for his captors were well aware that they were holding an important person; but at the end of several days they realised that they were wasting their time: Mario Jacchia was not going to talk. They shot him without any other form of trial, on 20 August 1944.

Emmanuele Artom died on 7 April 1944. He was political commissary for his unit and had been captured during a round-up in west Piedmont, not far from Perero, in the Val Pellice. The SS identified him and subjected him to particularly odious tortures, even by their standards. Artom refused to talk. When his torturers finally decided to kill him, they discovered he was already dead. So they fired their bullets into his corpse.

Giorgio Latis did not survive either. Intellectual influences had estranged him from Judaism but the anti-Jewish persecutions brought him swiftly back to the fold.

There is a long list of Jewish Resistance fighters who died in captivity, victims of ill-treatment. Léone Ginzburg for instance, sentenced as we have seen, as early as 1934, for his anti-Fascist activities, and arrested again in 1944 while engaged in the same activities. He died in the prison in Rome that bears the idyllic name of *Regina Cœli*.

A great many Jewish fighters held high-ranking posts in the Resistance. Curiel was founder and national leader of the Youth Front; the engineer Ettore Pacifici became a general in the underground movement under the *nom de guerre* of 'Cæsar' and led the Mingo division. Attacked by the SS division in the autumn of 1944, during the Partisans' bad season, he was lucky enough to escape from the enemy, having stood his ground right up to the last moment. After the war his Partisan grade was recognised and he became a colonel in the Engineering Corps.

Another Jewish Partisan who climbed rapidly in rank was Silvio Ortona, who began as a simple Partisan in the Biella region of Piedmont, became deputy leader, then leader of the *Fratelli Bandiera* detachment. He was then appointed Second in Command of the 5th *Garibaldi* division, and finally Chief of Staff of the *Garibaldi*[1] divisions of the Biella zone and of the 1st Piedmont zone.

Raffaele Jona, a thirty-eight year old engineer, had been forbidden as a Jew to continue to run the small metallurgical business in Turin which had been his occupation since he qualified. Jona was related to the great Olivetti family, also of Jewish origin, and actively anti-Fascist. He had always been anti-Fascist himself and was now free to take positive action.

He moved back to his native town of Ivrea and following the German invasion, 15 September 1943, he set up a Resistance group at Maletto, near by. His plan was to recover abandoned arms — and there were plenty of these around — and to provide shelter for the Allied prisoners-of-war, who had been liberated after the September armistice and were now being pursued by the Germans. This activity had excellent results and paved the way to an accord with the American authorities.

In December, Jona moved to Lanzo Torinese, where he fought for four long months, seizing stocks of weapons and attacking small garrisons in the valley of Viù and Lanzo. Here he came up against an enemy offensive.

These were the typical actions of a locally-based Partisan leader, but the situation changed entirely in the spring of 1944. Jona had established contacts — if rather laboriously — with the FFI of Lanzo Torinese which operated on the French side of the Alps, and was sent to the Val d'Aosta to fight against the Nazis and their Fascist accomplices. There he was able to collaborate with the FFI, and by September 1944 with the FFL. He also established solid relations with the Italian and American authorities in Switzerland, especially in Lugano and Berne. The Italian Partisans had only one thing in mind at this time: that when the moment came to drive out the Germans, they and not the French forces must be the ones to do it. And as the Val d'Aosta was a French-speaking region and had suffered a great deal from having Italianization thrust upon it by the Fascist regime, Jona's task was far from easy. (Not only had the names of localities and people been Italianized but even the inscriptions on tombstones.) Jona was helped by another Italian Jew, Giulio Colombo, who made his appearance in the region under the *nom de guerre* of Jules Cross. Both made a great success of their mission and were able to use American influence to such good advantage that the Val d'Aosta became Italian in 1945, and has remained so ever since.

As if all his military, political and diplomatic responsibilities were not enough, Jona took a very active part in bringing relief to the Italian Jews living in rather uneasy hiding in the Alps. He got in touch with the Jewish charity organisations operating in Switzerland and received large sums of money which he distributed with the help of a wide network composed of a number of Jews, among them Edi Consolo, Cesare Arton, Giorgina Segri and Lia Corinaldi. These relief funds were destined for hundreds, even thousands of people, not necessarily all Jewish, for Jona had succeeded in recruiting a large number of non-Jews, either directly or through the intermediacy of Segri. One of these Gino Giuganino, manufacturer and retailer of church candles, had business connections with clergymen of all grades of the hierarchy, and as 'Distributor no. 551', as Jona refers to him in one of his reports, was in charge of more than a hundred persons hidden in convents, parish presbyteries, etc. Jona himself, having become a member of the Committee of National Liberation of Piedmont did not hesitate, when occasion demanded, to distribute the funds personally.

Philatelists — especially Italian ones — will probably be surprised to learn that the author of the principal Italian stamp catalogue, Giulio Bolaffi was responsible for setting up a Partisan division: the 4th Alpine Division, Duccio Galimberti 'Stellina'.

Under the pseudonymn of Giulio Bossi, he took to the underground (or rather to the mountains) on 9 September 1943, the day after armistice was declared, and organised armed Action Party groups in the valleys of Lenzo and Susa. Attacked by the Germans in January and March 1944 in the Viù Valley, his men managed to stand firm and even to gather reinforcements. The division *Stellina* was founded in May 1944 and commenced operations a month later by organising attacks on the trunk road Susa-Monte Cenis. A neo-Fascist formation sent to dislodge it was smartly routed. Twenty-five days later, on 26 August, the Germans enlisted the help of an independent force composed of two SS companies on special mission (*zur besonderer Verwendung* — ZBV). They had underestimated the Partisans and 160 of their number were captured. This action in the Grange Sevine has remained a celebrated event in the annals of *Stellina.*

After the battles of Liberation, the division took the Monte Cenis pass by force and captured the lower valley and the town of Susa. Aldo Laghi (his last *nom de guerre*) was able to become Giulio Bolaffi again; and the general gave place to the publisher.

Another Jewish Partisan, the journalist and lawyer Bruno Segre, attached to the 1st Alpine division of *Giustizia e Libertà* in the province of Cuneo, helped to look after the Jewish refugees flowing in from Italian-occupied territory in France when it was taken over by the Germans.

At the opposite end of German-occupied Italy, in the mountainous province of Le Marche that skirts the Adriatic, another Jewish militant showed what he was capable of. In the early stages, however, Vito Volterra, twenty-two year old anti-Fascist engineer could not boast a very keenly developed sense of political foresight. It was he who, after the fall of Mussolini, left Switzerland and the protection it offered against anti-Semitic measures to return to Ancona.

Vito had close links with *Giustizia e Libertà* and the Action Party, so after the armistice he took to the mountains. There the young engineer found a large number of Italian military men, mostly members of fragmented units, who were wandering about more or less aimlessly trying to avoid being taken by the Germans. Many wanted nothing more than to return home. Others, shocked by the disintegration of the regular army, wanted to continue fighting. There was certainly no shortage of weapons.

Vito Volterra joined up with Lieutenant Mostardo, a man of about his own age. The engineer had had hardly any military training, but he was a *dottore*, an educated man, and the soldiers, drawn for the most part from modest town and country backgrounds, adopted him as their leader, while Mostardo became the military expert. That was how the independent Monte San Martino group originated in the province of Macerata.

The group switched to action, attacking the road and the railway line that ran along the Adriatic. Other operations followed, some successful, some not. One of them stands out particularly: the attack on the Jewish concentration camp at Servigliano, in the province of Ascoli Piceno. Several hundred Jews owe their lives to the Partisans' attack led by Vito Volterra.

We leave the details of the operation to Haim Vito Volterra, who became an Israeli some fifteen years ago and is now employed by the Israeli government as an architect in Nazareth:

> When Italy entered the war, a British prisoner-of-war camp was set up at Servigliano. Then armistice was declared (8 September 1943) and the English and American prisoners were set free. But a few days later the Nazis occupied the region, took over the lines of communication and the camp of Servigliano was put back into use again. This time the prisoners were the many Jews captured in the region — most of them Jewish refugees who had already been in other camps, but who had been liberated when armistice was declared. They included a number of Italian Jews who had been captured by the Nazi-Fascists as they were trying to slip south to the part of Italy already liberated by the Allies.
>
> During this period, groups of Partisans had formed up in the villages and hamlets on both sides of the Tenna Valley, in the mountains and in the hills . . . . These detachments consisted of non-Jewish Italians, Italian and non-Italian Jews, and former Allied prisoners of war who had joined the ranks of the Partisans. An Italian Jew, officer and lawyer, Höllander-Ogliani was in charge of the Committee of Liberation in the province of Macerata, bounding Ascoli Piceno. . . .
>
> About six miles as the crow flies from the camp of Servigliano, in the ancient walled city of Monte San Martino (or Monsammartino) on the northern side of the Tenna Valley, there was a strong autonomous Partisan detachment set up and commanded by myself. It was later integrated with the 86th Adriatic Sector, a famous territorial unit of the Italian Resistance. This unit had established close radio contact with the Allied Command in South Italy.

From their vantage points on Monte San Martino, the Partisans could observe the movements of the enemy in the valley below. It was early May 1944, and the Allies had begun their offensive on the River Sangro. It was then that the local detachment learned through its informers that the local Nazi command was preparing to evacuate the camp at Servigliano and dispatch the Jewish internees to the extermination camps in Central Europe. The camp was guarded by Italian carabinieri. . . .

As soon as the time of the first deportation was known, the commander of the sector was informed and he, in his turn, radioed Allied Command in the south of Italy.

The latter took immediate action and on the evening preceding the day of deportation a number of Allied planes dive-bombed the boundary walls of the camp causing a breach.

A Partisan formation went immediately to the spot to clear away the debris and enlarge the gap. Evacuation of the Jewish internees began immediately. The Partisans knew that certain of the carabinieri would co-operate loyally but feared that others might take a hostile stand either by directly opposing the operation or by calling for reinforcements. So a second Partisan formation cut the telegraphic and telephone cables and besieged the camp guards.

The liberation of the internees was rapidly effected. Soon only a handful remained inside the camp. They were the ones who did not believe there was a risk of deportation and who feared the hardships of life outside the camp. The freed prisoners were looked after by the Committees of Liberation of the provinces of Ascoli and Macerata.

We may add that the internees who refused to have faith in the liberators were indeed deported.

The Servigliano operation was unique of its kind and for two reasons: it was the only occasion — in Western Europe at least — where Jewish and non-Jewish Partisans directly attacked a Jewish concentration camp — and we have just seen that they did so victoriously; it was also the one and only time that Allied military forces, in this case the Royal Air Force, intervened directly in support of a campaign to save Jews threatened with deportation.

Servigliano, alas, was an isolated case. Most of the credit must be given to Vito Volterra for his initiative and organising ability. He continued his military activity right up to the liberation a month and a half later, he and his detachment helping in the final combats by seizing the bridgehead of Villa Molino and holding it until the arrival of the British Eighth Army.

Soon after liberation was proclaimed on 21 June 1944 at Monte San Marino, Volterra and Mostardo declared themselves, by decree, territorial commissioners of the Free Territory of San Martino. The Allied authorities recognised the *fait accompli* and Volterra became mayor of the small town, and so remained until the end of the war, when he returned to Ancona and launched himself into an active business life.

What did the non-Jewish combatants think of the role played by their Jewish companions-in-arms in the Italian Resistance movement?

On the death of Emmanuele Artom, his former companions gave his name to a Partisan brigade which formed part of the 16th Division of *Giustizia e Libertà* (Como-Lecco zone). Another, Matteotti, brigade was named after the Jewish Partisan Davide Pugliese.

The 9th Garibaldian brigade of Turin bore the name of Eugenio Colorni. At Bologna there was the 66th Garibaldian brigade Jacchia. There were at least two Eugenio Curiel brigades; one at Turin, the other at Cremona; there was a 'Polacco band' in Latium, and as many as seven formations (battalions and brigades) bearing the name of Rosselli.

NOTES

1. The units that adopted the name of *Garibaldi* had Communist leanings while those that were called *Matteotti* were predominantly Socialist. The Action Party Resistance fighters were found mostly in the units of *Giustizia e Libertà*. But there were no fixed rules.

Part Four
The Jews in the French Resistance

CHAPTER 10

THE JEWS IN FRANCE

I N 1939 there were several hundred thousand Jews in France. An exact estimation has not been established, those who have tried to make the calculation ending up with widely differing totals. The Nazis and their French supporters hoped to discover that France was overflowing with Jews, and recognising the danger, the latter retaliated by returning an assessment far below the true figure of the resident Jewish population.

The French Jews were largely traditionalists who deplored the secular character of the French Republic and particularly their habit of dispensing with religious categorisation in official documents; but it was precisely this absence of religious endorsement that permitted a good number of Jews to escape anti-Jewish measures altogether. It was not until after the Vichy Government took over that Jews were registered in both Free and Occupied Zones.

We reckon that there were from 300,000 to 350,000 Jews living in France at the outbreak of World War II.

The social composition of the Jews in France was extremely diverse. Small and large groups, all of different origin, were scattered about the country, sometimes united, at other times doing their utmost to avoid each other.

There were, for example, French Jews whose families had lived in France for decades, if not for centuries. Some of these were strongly attached to their religious foundation and Jewish traditions; others had no religious ties, but considered themselves Jews, by atavism rather, and in the face of anti-Semite attacks, these would have considered it dishonourable to have denied their origins.

Another group of Jews originated in North Africa and the Mediterranean basin. The two categories of this group claiming to have had exactly the same education from the primary school onwards, there was little apparent difference between the Colmar-born Jew and the Smyrna-born Jew.

Then came the Jews calling themselves immigrants who had been arriving from Eastern Europe in successive waves since the beginning of the century, if not before. A large number of Jewish artisans settled in Paris in the years following the Commune to fill up the gaps caused by the Versailles repression. Most of them had led a very meagre existence in their country of origin on account of the anti-

Semitism flourishing there. Others — and particularly the Russian Jews — had emigrated following the upheaval caused by the October Revolution of 1917. The remainder had been driven out by political persecution and consisted mainly of Communists or Communist sympathisers. All of them had begun to integrate into French life, and as usual this integration was much more advanced at the children's level. Many had naturalised themselves — whether they were the subject of political dossiers or not — at a time when it was not always very easy to do so, especially for the poorer people.

The language was an enormous obstacle, and one which the children surmounted more quickly than their elders, who continued to speak their Jewish tongue, their beloved Yiddish, just as the Russian and Romanian Jews clung to their native tongues.

An important characteristic of this immigrant group was its tendency to organise itself. They had all arrived in France with the same tradition of committees, commissions and associations of every kind, so that Jews of the same country, the same province, even of the same town, were already grouped together. Just as there were Auvergnat *amicales* in Paris, there were *amicales* of the natives of Bessarabia, Galicia, even of the Polish town of Ostrow-Mazowiecka. Even today there are dozens of these *amicales* still in existence. Their aim at the beginning was mutual aid, which even went to the extent of including the acquisition of vaults in the cemeteries for society members and their families. Later, *amicales* and societies tended to federate, particularly in the Federation of Jewish Societies in France. The Federation and its composites were all purely immigrant organisations.

Relations between the Jewish autochthons (comprising Jews born outside the French mainland but of French culture) and the immigrant Jews were often difficult. Attempts to achieve mutual understanding were rare and for the most part unsuccessful, the two groups mistrusting one another. The autochthons had not much sympathy for those who spoke no French at all, or who spoke it badly. As for the immigrants, they often wondered if the Jewish French were still Jews, and even had the temerity to put the question to them, which did nothing to improve relations. For example, it was exceptional for an immigrant practising Jew to frequent the large synagogue in the rue de la Victoire in Paris. They preferred to go to their own synagogues. Not all were believers.

The Zionist movement, born at the turn of the century, had never really gained a foothold in France, even though a number of the founder fathers were French.

It took no time at all for the Communist Party to realise the potentiality of members and sympathisers among the Jews as a whole, for Communist ideas were just as widespread among the autochthonous Jews as among the non-Jewish French. However, the majority of the immigrant Jews supported Communism, and a large number of Jewish immigrant *amicales* had Communist learnings. Through the intermediacy of an organisation entitled MOI (*Main-d'oeuvre immigrée*) the Communist Party had succeeded in associating itself with a large number of immigrants (and not only Jewish ones) by creating linguistic groups. Established before the war, these were to play an important part in the Resistance.

From 1933 onwards, tens of thousands of Jewish refugees from Germany, Austria, and to a lesser degree Czechoslovakia, joined these two large Jewish strata. Some settled in France but most of them were simply in transit. Although these refugees, or neo-immigrants, were much better prepared for rapid assimilation, their cultural formation being much closer to that of the French than that of the East European Jews, they still had not had time to make this a reality.

The French authorities took a very contradictory attitude with regard to the refugees. Every government in power from 1933 to 1939 authorised the central European Jews to seek refuge in France, but this authorisation was more often than not one *de fait* rather than of right, and the government closed its eyes rather than authorised. And whether because of the French strikes — and there were plenty of those between 1933 and 1939 — or so as not to displease the xenophobe *milieux* overmuch, foreigners allowed to seek refuge in France were not always given work permits, and it was absolutely essential for them to find work, not only in order to earn their keep, but also to obtain a permit, for on this depended the granting of a certificate of registration. It was a vicious circle.

At the beginning, the refugees could live off what they had been able to bring with them (in most cases not very much). Then they became the responsibility of Franco-Jewish international philanthropic organisations including the American *Joint*, and were at last able to bring political relations into play in order to obtain the much desired permits. Once these legal or paralegal resources were exhausted, they had no option but to seek work without a permit.

The French Jews, therefore, did not constitute a community in any sense of the word. On the religious side only a tiny fraction of autochthonous Jews were attached to the Consistory of French and Algerian Israelis, while there were hardly any immigrant members. On the legal side the situation was no better. The Federation of Jewish (Immigrant) Societies certainly did not represent the majority of the Jews; and morally speaking, they were no more closely united. This being so, there was no question of there being a 'Resistance of the French Jews', though they certainly participated in the Resistance, the extent of this participation depending upon which group the Jews belonged to; the form it took depended upon particular circumstances.

The autochthonous Jews naturally followed the same road as the non-Jewish French, integrating themselves in all the various networks of the Resistance, often even helping to establish them. According to their personal and political affinities as well as their individual circumstances, they were found in traditionalist groups such as *Alliance* or *l'Organisation civile et militaire* (OCM); in groups which could be regarded as non-Communist left wing (*Combat, Franc-Tireur, Libération*, etc.) and in those directed or actuated by the Communist Party. In Free France they were found in every rank ranging from commissary to General de Gaulle to private soldier in the Free French Forces.

'There was no Jewish Resistance movement in France,' declared André Manuel, former adjutant to Colonel Passy in the BCRA in London, on 13 November 1968, going on to declare that a large number of Jewish men and women had fought in the Resistance but had done so for motives that had no bearing on the fact that they were Jews. 'There was no Jewish Resistance in France,' reiterated Jerome Stroveis of the *Interallié* networks, F2 and others, one of the first to organise the setting up of transmitting stations on a large scale in Occupied France.

Jean Rosenthal, *Compagnon de la Libération*, states that his reasons for participating in the Resistance had nothing to do with the fact that he was a Jew, but in 1967 he was running purely Jewish, even pro-Jewish, philanthropic organisations.

Daniel Mayer, who helped to set up the French Socialist Resistance movement kept in touch with the Franco-Jewish organisations during the war solely for the purpose of earning his living and procuring official cover. Who could suspect an employee of a Jewish organisation of being a high-ranking Resistance fighter?

All the men mentioned are Jewish, and the list could go on indefinitely and include the most illustrious members of the Resistance movement. There was Jean-Pierre Lévy, for instance, organiser and leader of *Franc-Tireur* who shared the same point of view; or again Marc Bloch, who in his book *l'Étrange Defaite*, another clandestine publication, denied that his Jewishness had been the spur to his action.

Pierre Mendès France, Jean-Pierre Bloch, Jules Moch, René Meyer and many others became linked with Free France because they were patriotic French politicians. Admiral Louis Kahn, Pierre Dreyfus-Schmidt, Jacques Mayer and many others did so because they were French officers. The founders and militants of all the Resistance networks, Jewish or non-Jewish, were first and foremost French patriots. René Cassin, *Compagnon de la Libération*, winner of the Nobel Peace Prize in 1968, was always a devoted Jew, but it was his allegiance to France, not his Judaism, that made him the first civilian to leave France and rejoin General de Gaulle in London in June 1940.

Suzanne Dijian and Francis Cohen, both Jews, and François de Lescure were responsible for reorganising the Union of Communist Students in Paris early in the autumn of 1940. The former were dedicated militant Communists and played a leading part in the preparations for 'the march to the Étoile', 11 November 1940. They knew that as Jews they ran much greater risks than the others, but the fact that they were Jews had no bearing on how they behaved; any more than it had a bearing, for example, on the behaviour of Lazare Rachline, recently disappeared. Better known under his *nom de guerre* of Lucien Rachet he was a devoted Gaullist and a loyal Jew.

Other militant Communists, such as Georges Politzer and Jacques Salomon, both shot — as was Yvon Dijian, Suzanne's brother — were looked upon as Jews, but only by the Germans. Indeed, official German documents[1] recording their execution make it quite clear that as far as Politzer and Salomon (and Louis Salomon Weiler) were concerned they were dealing with 'Jews and Communists'.

Although more Jews were found in the 'leftist' movements, they were also associated with movements which, in peacetime, would have been situated 'on the right'. Philippe Koenigswerther, who perished in the ranks of the *Alliance* network, was no less Jewish than the Jews we have mentioned.

Emigrant Jews, too, were found in all the networks, but, there again, mostly in the left-wing groups.

Jewish formations of the MOI participated, as Jews, in operations actuated by the French Communist Party. On the other hand Jews who specifically claimed to be acting for their race ended up by grouping together under a 'parent structure', the Jewish Combat Organisation, which co-operated closely with all the French Resistance networks — and also with the Jewish MOI. For obvious reasons, the collaboration of German or German-speaking Jews (and especially the women) was particularly sought after by all the Resistance groups, whatever their leanings.

Finally there was a special category consisting of the French or foreign Jews (particularly British ones) who militated in the British services in France, mostly in the SOE (Special Operations Executive). Two of them, Jacques Weill ('Robin') and Roger Landes, have written books on the subject in the series *The Secret War* edited by Constantin Melnik. One group, set up by Haim Victor Gerson ('Captain Vic') was nicknamed the 'Palestine Express' because of its homogeneous Jewish composition. This group smuggled people into Great Britain, especially those in desperate situations: distressed pilots shot down over France, Resistance fighters, politicians .

Many an SOE agent was captured by the enemy and put to death: Denise Bloch, Violette Szabo, Sonia Olschanecki, André Bloch, Alec Rabinovitch (Peter Churchill's companion), Markus Bloom, Maurice Pertchuk, to mention only a few. Others such as Bernard Aptaker, Gaston Cohen, Roger Boiteux, managed to survive despite the countless dangers they had to face.

All French Jews suffered persecution at the hands of the Vichy Government and the Nazis — simply for being Jews. Though this is not the story of Jewish suffering, a swift survey of anti-Jewish measures will perhaps help the reader to assess the situation.

In August 1940, the Occupation authorities, headed at the time by Field Marshal Walter Heinrich Hermann Alfred von Brauchitsch, set about preparing anti-Jewish measures, and at that period Jewish shops in the Champs-Elysées had their windows smashed by hooligans acting on their behalf.

The first anti-Jewish decree, dated 27 September 1940, ordered the Jews to present themselves for registration, and in Paris 149,734 Jews, 7,737 individual Jewish firms and 3,456 Jewish companies did so.

The real meaning of the measure escaped them. In the capital and elsewhere in occupied Europe, the vast majority — all those who had even the remotest connection with Judaism — presented themselves for registration. An astounding case was that of Henri Bergson, old and sick at the time, who had become to all intents and purposes a Catholic long before the occupation but, acting out of a feeling of solidarity with the harried Jews, renounced his conversion to Catholicism and had himself registered as a Jew.

The only ones not included in the census were some militant Communists already living in clandestinity or preparing to do so. The latter simply did not present themselves at their local police station where the registrations took place.

The German decree was followed immediately by a Vichy one: the Jewish Statute, promulgated on 4 October 1940. Then on 18 October 1940 and 26 April 1941, other German decrees struck at the Jews on an economic level.

On 15 May 1941, several thousand Jews were arrested in the Paris region and imprisoned in the Pithiviers and Beaune-la-Rolande camps, situated in the Loiret. Thousands of foreign Jews had been in captivity in the so-called Free Zone of Vichy since the armistice and the number went on increasing right up to the day the Germans began emptying the camps and dispatching their occupants to Auschwitz.

Two other German economic decrees, on 28 May and 28 September 1941, were again aimed at the Jews. And there was yet another — an 'unpaginated' one drawn up by Colonel Hans Speidel[2] around the same time. This ordered the confiscation of all radio sets belonging to Jews.

On 20 August, several thousand foreign Jews living in Paris, mostly in the XIe *arrondissement*, were arrested and sent to a camp specially created for them at Drancy, in the north-eastern suburbs of the capital.

These arrests, as the May ones, represented a personal triumph for the *SS-Hauptsturmführer*, Theodor Dannecker, who was in charge of the Paris antenna of the Eichmann service (officially Section IV B of the RSHA). In January 1941,

Dannecker used the German Embassy in Paris to help him put pressure on Vichy with a view to the setting up of a central Jewish bureau. According to Dannecker, this bureau, which would have jurisdiction over all Jews, would be especially useful in the evacuation of 100,000 to 120,000 Jews from the Occupied Zone. The planned deportation of the Jews was entitled *Endlösung* (final solution) — a locution which was to become very familiar indeed.

On 27 March 1941, the *SS-Brigadeführer*, Dr. Werner Best, sent a note to the commanders of the German military regions[3] requesting them to give assistance to French Prefects who might wish to set up concentration camps for the Jews. On 2 April 1941, he sent them an even more explicit note advising them not to send undesirable Jews in their areas to the Free Zone. According to Best, the expelled Jews would be even more harmful away from German surveillance. Moreover, and still according to Dr. Best, this type of measure contributed nothing to the *Endlösung* of the Jewish question.

In mid-December 1941, disaster struck. Out of about a hundred hostages shot, 53 were Jews while a thousand Jewish intellectuals, mostly French, were imprisoned at Compiègne. A billion-franc fine was imposed on the Jewish community, also a *Judenrat* entitled *Union Générale des Israélites de France* (UGIF), whose first task was to collect the fine.

The sixth anti-Jewish decree, of 7 February 1942, imposed personal restrictions on the Jews: they had no longer the right to change residence as they wished, and were subjected to a curfew from 8 p.m. to 6 a.m; and on 24 March 1942 the seventh anti-Jewish decree was promulgated and extended the definition of the term 'Jewish' to embrace other categories of the population. Two German anti-Jewish decrees were yet to come: one imposed the wearing of the yellow star (29 May 1942): the other forbade Jews access to public places and specified the one hour in the day when they were allowed to go shopping (15 July 1942).

On 16 July 1942, 12,884 foreign Jews were arrested in the Paris region and were imprisoned in the Vél' d'Hiv', which had been transformed into a reception centre, then sent to Auschwitz, via Beaune-la-Rolande, Pithiviers or Drancy. Five Jewish transports had already left France, carrying 5,137 Jews to Auschwitz.

Before the Occupation ended, about 83,000 Jews were to be deported from France as racial deportees (in the Gestapo jargon: *Transportjuden*).

What is more, from 15 August 1942, the Vichy authorities, who up to this moment had abstained from arresting Jews in the Free Zone, began to do so, handing their prisoners over to the Germans. It was not until 1943, when the defeat of Germany was becoming more and more probable, the Allies occupying Morocco, Algeria, Tunisia and the battle of Stalingrad over, that the French police ceased to be put at the disposal of the occupying forces for Jewish round-ups. Anyway,

D

Dannecker's successor, Brunner, preferred to arrest the Jews systematically in his own way.

The Jews, prompted by very varied motives, were active in a great number and variety of Resistance groups, and were always able to count upon the wholehearted co-operation of the Resistance in general, as well as the sympathy of the population. These facts complicate the task of a historian who endeavours to grasp the problem as a whole.

It could be imagined that under the Occupation the Resistance spirit was shared by all French people, and that the majority participated in the Resistance from beginning to end, but the facts prove otherwise.

In 1940 there were very few Resistance fighters, and though their numbers grew in 1941 and 1942, they were depleted again in 1943 following the disbanding of the Resistance groups in an operation led by the Gestapo and the SD on the one hand, and the military counter-espionage (*Abwehr*) on the other.

The Vichy Government under Marshal Pétain was truly representative of French public opinion, at least in 1940, but rapidly lost support, though Marshal Pétain himself continued to hold the sympathies of a considerable number of French people right up to the end of the Occupation, and even after the war. Those closest to the Marshal, and the members of General de Gaulle's entourage, insisted that the two positions were directly opposed and therefore irreconcilable; but very large sectors of public opinion persisted in believing that the two men had in some way shared out the roles and that consequently one could be a Gaullist and still revere Pétain.

Aware of how matters stood, the Germans and their French collaborators tried to present the Resistance movements as instruments, created, manipulated, and directed by the Jews for their own gain, in the interests of Bolshevism and even with a speculative eye cast in the direction of the City and Wall Street.

We wonder if this convinced anyone, but it would be very remiss to fall into the same bad habits as those whose ideas are diametrically opposed to our own; so to avoid all equivocation, let us say that even if a large number of Jews took part in the French Resistance, the French Resistance was a French phenomenon. It would be absurd to categorise the different members of the Resistance movement; in other words to create a ghetto within it.

Suffice it to say that in a very large number of cases, Jewish Resistance fighters were fully aware that their being Jewish added an extra dimension to their military engagement. There were famous Resistance fighters who, without for a moment repudiating their Jewishness, considered that it had nothing to do with their participation in the Resistance. There are even those who have made it known clearly and unequivocally that they did not wish to see their names appearing in any publication concerned with the part the Jews played in the Resistance.

NOTES

1. In this case, a note from Dr. Werner Best, co-founder of the Gestapo, who quarrelled with Heydrich and had himself transferred to the Germany military administration in France. He headed the section 'Administration' at head-quarters.

2. After the war, Hans Speidel, promoted to the rank of General, pursued a brilliant career in NATO.

3. *Gross-Paris*, Dijon, Saint-Germain (Nord-Ouest), Bordeaux, Angers.

CHAPTER 11

THE COMMUNIST JEWS

FOLLOWING the armistice of June 1940 and the German Occupation, some members of the French Communist Party thought they might be able to obtain supplementary benefits by resorting to legal action. Such an idea had never even crossed the minds of the Communist Jews or the Jewish immigrants, and for once it was their non-Jewish comrades who suffered, not they.

The official history of the *Parti communiste français dans la Résistance*[1] describes the various approaches made to the German authorities in Paris with a view to obtaining permission for the legal republication of *l'Humanité* and adds,

> *The mere terms of the German conditions brought home the grave error of this action — upon which opinion among the Party leaders had been so much divided in the first place.*

Now the majority of the immigrant members and sympathisers of the Communist Party had already had personal experience of anti-Semitism. More often than not, the very reason for their immigration to France had been the intolerable situation created for them in their countries of origin.

For some militant French Communists, the German soldier that he passed in the street could appear — at least in the beginning — to be simply a misguided brother. A generous illusion which was probably the result of their internationalist education. To the Jewish militants the same German soldier was a Nazi like all the others who had oppressed them in Germany, Czechoslovakia, Poland — above all in Poland, for most of the pro-Communist immigrant Jews came from there and, to a lesser extent, from Bessarabia.

After the Spanish Civil War in the thirties, the militant Jewish Communists had received reinforcements which, although they were not numerous, were of the highest calibre. These were Jewish volunteers, mostly Palestinians, from the International Brigades, who, through either choice or necessity, had settled in France after the fall of the Spanish Republic.

Some of these became officers in the Resistance movement: Marcel Langer and Zeev Gottesmann (Captain Philippe), for instance, in Toulouse; and Jonas Geduldig, of the Manouchian-Boczov group, in Paris.

The immigrant Jews — and especially the Communists among them — were by and large of modest origin. Most of them held the lower-paid jobs in the various branches of the textile industry; the remainder were only slightly better off. The small knitwear factories where they worked were not very prosperous enterprises and even the owner himself was of very modest standing. The general economic situation of the thirties was far from rosy, and the Jewish proletariat, a very large one at that time, was a proletariat in the fullest sense of the word.

The majority of the immigrant Communist Jews had been engaged in underground activity in their country of origin. Indeed, the Communist Party was clandestine in most East European countries and repressive measures in Poland, Romania and Hungary were very harsh, especially when the Communists happened to be Jews as well.

It is well known that one of the main concerns of the Communist Party is propaganda, and it is not surprising that the immigrant Communist Jews were very active in this sphere.

They were obliged to act on three levels:

First of all they had to communicate with people who did not know French at all or at the most knew it very badly, which meant they had to publish newspapers in the Yiddish language, and a great many of these were circulated.

They then turned their attention to the French-speaking autochthonous Jews, and particularly to the French-speaking immigrants. The latter had only a smattering of Yiddish and were not always capable of reading it, but they had learned to speak passable French. The most important members of this category were the young Jews who, despite being fluent French speakers, lived in the same *milieu* as their parents. The second series of newspapers, therefore, was published in French.

Finally, there was a third series, also written in French, whose purpose was to stir up the sympathies of the general public, or at least make it aware of the plight of the Jewish people.

The first two series of newspapers were in circulation from the beginning of the Occupation, the Yiddish newspapers leading the way and having the widest circulation. The carefully compiled newspapers destined for the general public were distributed over a wide area just after the large-scale round-ups.

The complexity of the Jewish situation in France led the Jewish Communists to militate on different levels in the various frameworks, within the differentiated structures. Later they succeeded in creating *ad hoc* organisations to deal with situations of special importance in order to encourage Communists and non-

Communists who shared a particular problem to tackle it together. These organisations developed, remained static, or disappeared altogether.

To integrate the French-speaking militant Jews, immigrants or not, did not pose any special problems, their natural place being at the side of their French comrades. For the others, it was a different story: they had to be fitted into proper organisations.

In this respect, the Jewish immigrants found themselves in an analogous, if not identical, situation to that of the non-Jewish Communist immigrants — Polish, Italian, Spanish, Hungarian, Romanian, etc. These immigrants, many of whom were political refugees, could not — if only for material reasons — militate in the regular organisations of the Communist Party. It was for their benefit that the structure of the *Main-d'oeuvre immigrée* was created. Within this parent organisation were to be found various groups: Yiddish, Polish, Hungarian, Romanian, Italian, Spanish, etc., logically divided up according to their language.

These homogeneous immigrant nuclei within the Communist Party had an upper structure, a sort of governing body affiliated to the local sections; and this structure, the Jewish, Italian or Spanish organisation, as the case might be, was directly responsible to the Central Committee of the Communist Party.[2]

At the head of the Jewish group of the MOI in 1939, we find men like Kowalski, Bruno (Lerman) and Hervé (Kaminsky).

Joseph Boczov, chemical engineer by profession, was thirty-nine years old when he was shot along with his comrades on Mount Valérien on 21 February 1944. Born in Transylvania, of Hungarian parents, Boczov became Romanian in 1918. He was doubly discriminated against, being both Hungarian and Jewish, but after a hard struggle managed to qualify as a chemical engineer.

In 1936, he set out for Spain on foot and arriving six months later, enlisted in the International Brigade and fought until the defeat of the Spanish Republic. He was imprisoned first in Argelès, then in Gurs, and was there when the occupation of France began. In the meantime, he and the other Romanian internees had been deprived of their nationality. Eventually they were dispatched by train to Germany as stateless persons. Boczov managed to force the lock of the carriage and jumped — having first persuaded all his comrades to do the same.

On reaching Paris, he took command of the 1st detachment of immigrant *Francs-Tireurs* and Partisans (FTP). This was called the Hungaro-Romanian detachment because, like Boczov, most of the members were Transylvanian Jews.

They launched a series of attacks, particularly against railways, and at a later date Boczov was placed at the head of the 4th detachment, which was responsible for railway sabotage on a larger scale.

He was arrested on 27 November 1943 at the same time as most of the members of the 'FTP-immigrants' and in the same way. At his trial he was accused of 20 derailments — he had in fact been responsible for quite a few more — and was condemned to death and shot along with his comrades.

His photograph and those of his comrades appeared on the Nazi propaganda poster that Louis Aragon immortalised in his poem *L'Affiche Rouge* (The Red Poster). Running along the top of this poster was the inscription LIBERATORS?; in the centre appeared the photographs of ten FTP members, seven of them Jews; below these the photographs of several outrages, and finally at the bottom another inscription: LIBERATION BY THE CRIME SQUAD!

The photograph of Boczov bore the caption: *Hungarian Jew — Leading Derailer* —20 outrages.

The French Communist Party, clandestine since the autumn of 1939, remained so during the German Occupation, while the immigrant Communist Jews found themselves in a rather different situation after September 1939. Their Yiddish newspaper, *Presse nouvelle*, not only refused to condemn the 'imperialist character' of the war against Germany, but called on the Jewish immigrants to enlist in the French Army, as many of them did.

A welfare organisation was then set up, ostensibly charged with caring for the families of the volunteers, often in straitened circumstances. That was how *Solidarité* originated, and it very soon took over responsibility for those militants who, for one reason or another, had been obliged to take to the underground.

Immediately after armistice was declared, the leaders of the MOI Jewish section held a meeting in occupied Paris. They decided to maintain and develop the structures and activities of *Solidarité*. The trio in charge settled in the city.

The immigrant Communist Jews (like Communist immigrants in general) adapted themselves far more easily to underground activities — or illegal action — than did their French comrades, perhaps because the MOI, especially in the thirties, was for the most part a politically motivated immigration.

On 15 July 1940, the Communist Jews succeeded in launching a clandestine Yiddish newspaper[3] in Paris. Other clandestine newspapers were to appear all the way through the Occupation. The editors, printers, distributors and readers of this press naturally suffered very heavy losses, but that did not stop publication. The press began in 1940 and 1941 by denouncing Nazi and Vichy anti-Jewish measures. Shortly afterwards, Yiddish newspapers were seen to take a very close interest in the development of the situation in the Balkans. The German advance into Romania and Bulgaria, followed by their offensive against Yugoslavia and Greece, received top priority in the news bulletins.

As the war approached the frontiers of the USSR, there was an outcry in the Jewish Communist Press denouncing the 'imperialist' threat to the birthplace of Socialism. All the same, one could not help feeling that the editors were impatient to see the USSR join the war against Nazi Germany.

The need to prepare false papers in quantity made itself felt in May 1941, when the concentration camps of Beaune-la-Rolande and Pithiviers were established. These were in operation for just over a year. In June-July 1942, their occupants were dispatched to Auschwitz.

Neither the Communist nor the non-Communist Jews had any idea of the real purpose of these camps, and while several prisoners escaped — among them young Maurice Fefferman, who was to distinguish himself later in an armed action against the Germans in Paris — the bulk of the prisoners made no attempt to get away, no one having given them any encouragement to do so.

The Communists organised a very lively cultural and spiritual life inside the camps, and it was they — atheists *par excellence* — who were responsible for the building of a hut to serve as a synagogue.

Nothing in the clandestine press of the Jewish Communists suggests that they had the slightest idea at the time of what lay in store for the internees, and later, when the Jewish Communists did receive precise information about Auschwitz, it was a long, long time before they published it. First of all they had to convince themselves that the information was correct — and this took time. That done, they had to bring the news to the notice of the Jewish people in such a way as to incite them to take action against the occupying forces and not in a fashion to discourage them or cause them to draw back. The information was gradually released in the course of successive editions, and from a propagandist point of view, this campaign was a success.

The third branch of the MOI activities, working under the initials TA (German Labour) depended upon the collaboration of the large number of German-speaking Jews who knew the Germans as well as they knew their language. There were primarily three national groups detailed for this type of action, under the tri-national leadership of Arthur London, Czech; Otto Niebergall, German; and Oskar Grossman, Austrian. London and Grossman were Jews.

Following the example of the Czechs, a large number of Austrians had themselves sent to their country of origin as 'voluntary workers' under assumed names. The Gestapo got wind of them, and their leader, Oskar Grossman, fell at Lyons; his deputy, Franz Marek, and Tilly Spiegel his fiancée were more fortunate. This Austrian group, which was among those that suffered the heaviest losses, contained a large number of Jews.

Arthur London was captured by the Gestapo in 1942 and deported to Mauthausen a year later where he became one of the leaders of the international Resistance movement in the camp. In 1945 he was liberated, and four years later returned to Czechoslovakia to become a deputy minister. In 1951 he was imprisoned and got caught up in the Prague trials. He is now living in France.[4]

The head of the Department of General Information and Strategies of the Préfecture de Police in Paris mentions the arrest in April and May 1941 of a number of editors and distributors of the Yiddish Communist paper *Unser Wort* (Our Word), also the seizure of a typewriter with Yiddish characters used in its preparation.

The fourth branch of MOI action — armed action — made its appearance in the summer of 1941 after the German invasion of Russia.

The Communists knew from the start that vigilance was imperative, but did not recognise immediately what practical forms this should take, and as late as spring 1941, the collectors of funds gave the Jews receipts in the form of 'solidarity stamps' which, when there were police raids, rose to the status of valuable documentary evidence.

NOTES

1. *Éditions sociales*, Paris 1967.
2. Interview on 28 October 1968 with M. Jacques Duclos, confirmed in writing on 8 November 1968.
3. *La Presse antiraciste sous l'occupation hitlérienne*, Paris, 1950, UJRE (p. 15, survey by A. Rayski).
4. See his memoirs *L'Aveu*, published by Gallimard.

CHAPTER 12

THE JEWS IN THE COMMUNIST COMBAT GROUPS

I N June 1941, the Communist Party in France and elsewhere in Europe found itself facing an entirely new situation, due to Russia's entry into the war.

The Party had offered stout resistance to the Germans up to then and had been responsible for instigating the National Front about a month before the German attack on the USSR, but after 22 June, the French CP was able to increase its hearing in the country considerably and this led to much more effective anti-German operations, on a far wider scale.

Some of the most successful combat groups in the Paris region were the *Bataillons de la Jeunesse*, these combat organisations, created by the young Communists, containing a large number of young Jews, already largely assimilated.

Albert Ouzalias, leader and historian of the *Bataillons de la Jeunesse*[1], refers to some of the very early Resistance demonstrations of this organisation which took the form of writing inscriptions on walls and circulating propaganda leaflets, particularly in the XI[e], XII[e], and XVIII[e] *arrondissements* of Paris, and in some suburban districts. We note that one group in the XI[e] *arrondissement* was mainly composed of Jews: Liliane Levy, Jean Caplevic, Fernand Zalkinov, Acher Semhaya, with his sister Sarah, and the brothers Chevit, this particular *arrondissement* having a large Jewish population, which was to be sadly depleted.

In July 1940 twenty-year-old Jacques Grinbaum from the XVIIIe *arrondissement* wrote on the walls of Sacré-Coeur: '*Down with the Occupant! Long live France! Long Live the USSR!*'

Another Jewish militant, Henry Segal, managed to retain a file of the FSGT, the parent organisation of the workers' sports clubs, which included that of the immigrant Communist Jews who supplied the Resistance with a large number of combatants.

Ouzalias had been a prisoner-of-war in the *Stalag* of Wels, near Linz, but had escaped on 26 July 1941, and Danielle Casanova and André Leroy appointed him leader of the *Bataillons de la Jeunesse* when his first duty was to report that three young Jewish Communists, Samuel Tyszelman, Elie Wallach, and Charles Wolmark had just recovered 55 lbs of explosives from the Seine-et-Oise.

None of these three lived to see the Liberation. At that period, Communist youth organisations thought it was still possible to organise demonstrations in the streets of Paris and launched several between mid-July and 13 August 1941, on which day the demonstrators were confronted by German troops. Tyszelman and Henri Gautherot, both in their early twenties, were captured and were sentenced to death two days later by a military tribunal. They were shot on 19 August.

According to the German Poster:

> The Jew Tyszelman and a man by the name of Gautherot were condemned to death on 15 August 1941 for enemy activity. They took part in a Communist demonstration against the German Occupation Forces.

A young Jewish friend Georges Ghertman, survived, as did another of Tyszelman's friends, Pierre Georges, better known under his *nom de guerre*: Colonel Fabien.

When Fabien launched the 'Paris war' on 23 August 1941, by shooting down a German officer at the métro station Barbès-Rochechouart, he declared: 'I have avenged Titi!'

Young Communist Jews in the process of assimilation were not particularly attracted to Jewish Resistance action because it was chiefly directed by their 'elders', of whom Leon Pakin, just over thirty years old, was one. Born at Pabianice, near Lodz in Poland, and a militant Communist in his country of origin, where he had served a seven-year prison sentence for his activities, Pakin did not appear in France until after the defeat of the Spanish Republic. He had fought with the Jewish company Botwin and spent more than two years in the internment camps of the Midi before his comrades arranged his escape. Back in Paris, he resumed his militant activities and helped to set up the Jewish detachment of the MOI, soon to become famous as the 2nd FTP Paris detachment.

Some opportunistic German businessmen took advantage of the Occupation to move to Paris, among them a number of manufacturers who had the bright idea of using cheap labour, particularly qualified Jewish artisans, and used Jewish decoys to bring them in. Recruits were asked to bring their own sewing machines and other tools with them, and the pay was minimal; but the security that was guaranteed — to them and their families — was priceless. This false security was symbolised by a special *Ausweis* (identity card).

There was a whole series of these workshops in Faubourg Saint Denis and

Saint Antoine, as well as in the adjoining streets, where large quantities of leather clothes, sheepskin jackets, textiles, and other goods were made available to the *Wehrmacht*, while the enterprising Germans quietly amassed fortunes.

The Jewish Communists rightly considered that this activity was demoralising to the Jewish masses — not to mention the material aid it brought to the *Wehrmacht* — and decided to fight it. They began by distributing leaflets and by urging the Jews to stop working for the Germans, and when persuasion was not enough they resorted to more energetic methods.

On 21 July 1942, Ghertman and one of his comrades forced an entry into the workshop of one of the procurers. Armed with a revolver, Ghertman made the occupants of the workshop line up, soundly thrashed the proprietor and, with the help of his comrade, smashed up some of the machines. When they calmly left the building the proprietor raised the alarm, and the two Resistance members were caught near the *métro* Poissonier. They escaped with their lives solely due to Ghertman's presence of mind in convincing the French police, both at the police station and at the Préfecture, and even the examining magistrate, that this was a common-law case. His claim that his intention was to effect a holdup was believed, and even the Gestapo, officially informed of the arrest and knowing that Ghertman was armed, did not intervene.

A similar operation by Leon Pakin and Elie Wallach a few days later had a less happy ending: they were captured and did not escape.

Colonel Fabien's outrage was the first of a long series which was to continue right up to the Liberation of Paris. During the summer and autumn of 1941, the *Bataillons de la Jeunesse* launched a great many attacks in the region of Paris. Maurice Fefferman, the Pithiviers escapee, and his friend Maurice Feld shot several German officers, mostly in the X^e *arrondissement*, sometimes operating singly, sometimes together; Acher Semhaya took part in attacks against the German police stations of the Gare de l'Est; Fernand Zalkinov made a grenade raid on a German garage — all in the X^e *arrondissement*. A combined operation was also launched against the German transmitting stations at Goussainville in the northern suburbs of Paris.

All these young people were seized and shot by the enemy, with the exception of Maurice Fefferman who, wounded in an attack, chose to keep the last bullet for himself.

At the end of the year 1941, we read in a synthesis report of Gestapo action against the various Resistance movements in occupied Europe:

> In Paris two groups have been identified to date, structured in the following way:
> — head of operations;
> — intelligence agent;

- former members of International Brigades;
- Communist youth groups;
- French adults.

Plans were being made to engage another group of eight men, comprising:

- 2 doctors or nurses;
- 2 chemists;
- 2 young Communists;
- 2 couriers.

The two groups had ramifications in all districts and in all the important French towns and contained a strong Jewish element.

To date we have arrested more than 70 persons, including important leaders; and seized large quantities of firearms, hand grenades and rifles, incendiary mixtures, explosives, chemical and toxic products, etc.

The Gestapo, an experienced, competent organisation, was not a very large one and few of its members knew France very well, but they were greatly helped by other experts, at least as competent as themselves, who knew the country intimately: the French police gave the occupying forces their full co-operation, especially when it was a question of repressing the Communists[2].

Semhaya and Zalkinov were shot in March 1942 on the orders of a German military tribunal. Zalkinov's father was to be killed as a hostage on 11 August 1942, at the same time as Bernard Kirschen, one of his son's comrades; and other Communist Jews had been shot as hostages in that year: Salomon Calmanovic on 22 January; Guitlevitch and Klabinski on 3 February; 5 *Ostjuden*, Karpenstein, Lewin, Libermann, Rosenwasser and Glueck, on 20 May.

Two lines of action stand out in the strategy of the Communist Resistance fighters at this time, the first being to undermine the morale of the occupation forces.

The Germans looked upon Paris as the very symbol of life *wie Gott in Frankreich* (like God in France), and whatever may have been said or written on the subject since, relations between the German military and the French civilians were not bad: the Vichy Government's policy of collaboration, echoed by the more or less sincere dispositions of the Germans stationed in Paris, had yielded results, and the stereotyped phrase 'The Germans are correct' was apparently a true reflection of general opinion. Indeed, they had no need whatsoever to pillage at machine-gun point since, thanks to the armistice, they had more French money than they could possibly spend, even on the black market.

The Germans' correctness was on the whole reciprocated by the French, so that everyone was happy. All the Germans wanted was to be left in peace to exploit

France, and anyway, the leaders of the Reich attached little importance to active collaboration,[3] on which only a few members of the Vichy Government pinned their hopes. Germans like Otto Abetz and Helmut Knochen, who staked everything on collaboration and whose star was to pale as the possibility of it dwindled, were exceptions.

The Communists were not unaware that their attacks against the German soldiers led to reprisals; on the contrary — and this is where their second line of action came in — they attached a great deal of importance to the fact that these reprisals infallibly put an end to the peaceful co-existence between the occupying forces and the French and the mutual good behaviour gave place to ever-growing hostility.

In wartime, the life of an individual does not amount to very much, and Colonel Remy claimed that the mathematics of the French Communists took the following progression: 1 shot German = 10 shot hostages = 100 new combatants against Germany: a rather exaggerated estimate perhaps, but the basic argument seems to correspond fairly well to the politico-military strategem of the PCF in 1941–1942, an element of which was closely related to the game of poker where stakes may be increased only within limits. There were two possible outcomes: the population would eventually weary and force the Communists to change tactics, or the Germans would abandon their automatic system of execution. It was the Germans in the end who felt obliged to give up the spectacular executions of the hostages, with all its trimmings of *Bekanntmachungen*, appeals to the good sense of the French, etc., and after 1942 there were no more executions of hostages in France,[4] but this did not mean that German oppression had ceased; on the contrary it was intensified, and henceforth the captured Resistance fighters, even suspects, were deported to Germany by virtue of NN (*Nacht und Nebel*, Night and Fog), unless they were guilty of capital crimes, when they were tried by a German military tribunal. The NN deportees totally disappeared: not only were they forbidden to correspond with their families, but these were not even informed, and strict orders were given that if a request for information regarding an NN detainee was received from any French source whatsoever, the reply was to be that the person referred to was unknown. Later most of the NN detainees were slaughtered in the concentration camps.

This does not mean that the French Communists had won in the terrible game of outbidding; but up to this time the hostage system, over and above the arrests of the members of the combat groups, had sadly depleted the ranks of the Resistance fighters, and particularly the Jewish ranks. Indeed, the stereotyped formula of the German communiqués relating to these reprisals mentions the execution of x Communists and Jews, or of x Judeo-Communists acting for Britain; or again the deportation to the East of x Communists and Jews. In this last category, the mortality rate for the Communist deportees varied from 50 to 80 per cent. For the Jews deported as a reprisal measure it was much higher. In the largest deportation convoy of this category, which left Drancy and Compiègne, there were fifty survivors out of 1,100 deportees.

After the disappearance of this first line of combatants during 'the terrible spring' of 1942, a second line rose up, most of whom were to form the backbone of the 2nd detachment FTP of Paris which went into action immediately after 16 July 1942.

July 16, 1942, is a crucial date in the history of Judaism in France, a gaping wound whose implications extend far beyond the history of the war and of the Resistance, On that day 12,884 Parisian Jews — men, women and about 4,000 children — were arrested at their homes in the city by the Paris police and imprisoned for days in the Paris Vélodrome d'Hiver. They were then sent to the transit camps of Drancy, Beaune-la-Rolande and Pithiviers, and from there to Auschwitz.

The sixteenth of July imposed agonising reappraisals on all the Jews of France, but particularly on the immigrants, for on that day only immigrants were arrested; the turn of the French Jews was to come later.

Up to then the Jewish MOI had believed that the well-tried technique of demonstrations, delegations, etc., could yield results, but shortly before 16 July 1942, the MOI militants had sensed that some sort of change was in the air and began to arrange for some of their number and certain families to go underground and to search for institutions or private dwellings where they could leave their children.

When after 16 July, the dimensions of the action changed, the Jewish MOI tried to persuade the Jews to go underground, to give up wearing the yellow star, to avoid making themselves conspicuous, not to speak Yiddish in public, especially when they had assumed Aryan identities, etc. The party machine was put severely to test.

At the same time, a peripheral organisation created a short time before, the *Mouvement National Contre le racisme* (MNCR), expanded. Probably some enterprising Communists had been responsible for setting up this organisation that grouped together intellectuals like the writers Colette and Roger Martin du Gard with tradesmen and clergy. Its aim was to help the hunted Jews and, most important of all, to rescue the children, but it was not a purely Communist organisation: militants like A. Rayski, V. Kowalski and hundreds of others, not all Communists and only a few of them Jews, played an active part in the rescue of thousands of children.

We may say that the intervention of experienced militant Communists could occasionally place the MNCR and all its humanitarian work in jeopardy. Suzanne

Spaak (Suzette), for instance, was arrested by the Gestapo, not for having helped in the rescue of the Jewish children, but because of the aid she had given to the head of the Soviet network of the *Red Orchestra*, Trepper-Domb, after his escape. Trepper-Domb survived; Suzanne Spaak did not, and at the moment of her arrest the whole MNCR network with which she was involved was in danger of disintegrating. Rayski deserved much of the credit for holding it together.

Some of the leading militants who were transferred to the 2nd detachment after 16 July 1942 were to perish after the trial called the '23' or the 'Affiche Rouge' in 1945: Marcel Rayman (nineteen years old in 1942), Léon Goldberg (eighteen years old), Maurice Fingercwaig (nineteen years old), Wolf Wajsbrot (seventeen years old): four out of the twelve Jews of the group.

The 2nd all-Jewish detachment was in operation for a year almost to the day. Created by Pakin, Sevek Kirschenbaum and Arco, it launched its first action at the end of May 1942 with the destruction of machines and raw materials in a Jewish workshop belonging to the *Wehrmacht*, in the X^e *arrondissement*, and its last on 27 May 1943, a grenade attack on a passing German platoon in rue de Courcelles, and between the two dates the communiqués of the detachment reported fifty different operations: attacks on passing German units, assaults on sentries, tossing of bombs into hotels, attacks on restaurants and garages occupied by the Germans; and some of these operations were particularly daring, like the offensive on the German DCA batteries in the neighbourhood of the Eiffel Tower on 3 February 1943.

Meanwhile, though the Gestapo had succeeded in identifying a large number of the combatants and arrested several at the beginning of the year 1943, the detachment continued its operations right up to the end of May, giving the Germans the opportunity to more or less break up the group.

Rayman and most of his Jewish companions of the trial of the 23 were captured in November 1943, and more than a hundred militant Communists fell around this time, many of them Jewish. Rayman was arrested on 17 November, during a *rendezvous* with Golda Bancic, and on the same day the Armenian poet Missak Manouchian was captured, during a *rendezvous* with Colonel Gilles (Epstein) Commander-in-Chief of the FTP in the Île-de-France.

On the fall of the 2nd detachment, the leaders of the Jewish MOI were forced to leave Paris, and the few survivors were evacuated to Pas-de-Calais where most of them, being Polish, were able to lose themselves among the mass of Polish miners in the region.

Gordon (Tygier), who had come up to Paris from the South Zone to save what could be saved, managed to identify a former member of the detachment who had served as an auxiliary to the Germans in the breaking up of the group. The

Gestapo had arrested him and made a deal with him: he would either betray his comrades or be deported to Auschwitz with his family.[5]

Rayski transferred to the South Zone.

Other MOI units in Paris had Jewish combatants, particularly the 1st and 4th detachments: Joseph Boczov the derailment expert; Marcel Rayman, who worked with Czechs, Italians and Spaniards; and others too numerous to mention. One of the most spectacular successes was the assassination of the German *Gauleiter* Julius Ritter, special representative in France of the *Commissariat général allemand pour la Main d'oeuvre* and nicknamed the Slave Driver in Chief. He was shot along with his chauffeur near Trocadero on 28 September 1943 by the Spaniard Celestion Alfonso, accompanied by Marcel Rayman, a Polish Jew, and Spartaco Fontano, an Italian anti-Fascist.

Besides the 150 to 200 Jewish Partisans in the Parisian FTP detachment, there was quite a large number of young women who were charged with extremely dangerous missions. Though they were seldom asked to do any shooting they had the equally perilous task of taking arms and ammunition to the combatants, and recovering the weapons after the operation, for only under exceptional circumstances were the FTP fighters allowed to retain their arms. Golda Bancic (Olga) was one of these women and the only one sentenced in the trial of the 23. She was not shot right away but was sent to Germany, no doubt as a result of her activities in the TA.

The Jewish MOI in Paris, led by Joseph Clisci and Golda Bancic, planned the attack against a German bus at Clichy, on 6 June 1943 when the Germans suffered heavy losses. Clisci was wounded and took refuge in a basement, 2 rue de l'Abreuvoir. He still found the strength to throw a grenade, which fell among his besiegers. Eight bullets were left in his pistol, of which seven found their mark. The eighth he kept for himself.

Other types of organisation had to be set up in the South Zone, as there were no longer sufficient Yiddish-speaking men willing to fight in the MOI type of formation, and the advent of the *Union des Juifs pour la Résistance et l'Entraide (UJRE)* helped to solve this situation. At the same time the number of French newspapers was on the increase: the second generation had taken over. The FTP Jewish detachment set up in Lyons chose the name of *Carmagnole* — a striking testimony to how the young Jews identified themselves with the France of 1789 — and later a second name, that of the Jewish combatant *Simon Fryd*, who was killed at this period, was added.

Other UJRE detachments sprang up: in Grenoble, Toulouse, Limoges, on the

Côte d'Azur (the *Maurice Korsec* detachment, called after an eighteen-year-old boy killed in Marseilles after tossing grenades into a German cinema). The *Marcel Rayman* company in the north consisted of the survivors of the battle of Paris and local reinforcements.

Groups of 'patriotic militia', mainly Jewish, had been constituted earlier on in the spring of 1944. A detachment of this militia liberated several hundred Jews imprisoned in the Nexon camp of Upper Vienne. Others took part in the Lyon battle of liberation. The Villeurbanne militia suffered particularly heavy losses, having had at one point to face the enemy alone, while other Jewish militia took a very active part in the liberation of Marseilles and played an even more decisive role in the liberation of Paris.

What balance is it possible to strike?

On the debit side, counting the combatants proper and the whole of the sub-structure: from the 'technical machine' to the fund collectors — from the fund collectors to the contacts men, boys and girls, not to mention the men and women who hid the combatants and their weapons — the total would be several thousand.

Some of these, like Joseph Clisci, had fought when no fight seemed possible. Raphaël Fiegelson, arrested at Toulouse, lost no time in forming an AFTP group at the camp of Drancy. He kept up the struggle at Auschwitz and finally joined the ranks of the Red Army, where he was responsible for destroying large enemy forces. Ritter has already been mentioned. Others, such as Marc Carrel, local delegate of the *Commissariat général aux Questions Juives*, captured arms and munitions; but even more noteworthy was the immigrants' achievement in their own domain, in persuading their fellow Jews to take measures to avoid deportation, and they deserve great credit for making the struggle against deportation more of a French affair than a Jewish one. It was a Jewish Communist lawyer, M. Charles Lederman, who informed Mgr. Saliège, Archbishop of Pau, of the special dangers threatening the Jewish population. Mgr. Saliège responded with courage, denouncing the deportation of the Jews from the pulpit, and circulating a Pastoral Letter on the subject in his diocese, so that his word reached the ears of tens of thousands of Catholics, who lost no time in coming to the aid of the Jews.

But before convincing 'our French brothers', to quote the title of an appeal launched in the wake of the round-ups of 16 July, the Jews themselves had to be made to understand that deportees went to their death.

Several thousand Communist Jews were actively engaged in combat, if the infrastructure and logistics are included, and it is they who deserve much of the credit for the rescue of several thousand children, and for having convinced a large number of adult Jews that their lives were in serious danger: over and above all ideological and political considerations, the credit for these two actions goes unquestionably to the Jewish branch of the MOI.

NOTES

1. *Les Bataillons de la Jeunesse*, Editions Sociales, Paris, 1967.

2. Later, in 1943 and especially in 1944, there were cases where the French police were more co-operative with the Resistance, although, it seems only rarely with the Communists; but in 1942, at least in Paris, this was not the case.

3. On 16 July 1941 at a meeting in his general headquarters, Adolf Hitler made no bones about his views on the matter. Three weeks after the beginning of the German offensive against the USSR, he became furiously angry at an impertinent allusion of a Vichy newspaper, according to which the war against the Soviet Union would be a European war and would therefore be conducted throughout Europe. This Vichy newspaper was obviously insinuating that the Germans would not be the sole beneficiaries of the war, but that other European states would profit from it. The *Führer* went on to say that it was simply a matter of 'cutting the enormous cake into equal slices'. Nazi-French collaboration, it is evident, was not what he had in mind.

4. Except during the combats of the Liberation which began immediately after the Allies disembarked in Normandy. At that time, however, it was a matter of decisions taken at a local level. The massacres of Tulle and Oradour, as well as other more obscure massacres, belong to this category. Cf. Delarue, *op. cit.* pp. 277—491.

5. How did the Resistance fighters fall into enemy hands? Rayski, who had the opportunity during and after the war to study police techniques employed by the Germans and that of their French auxiliaries at very close quarters, notes that both showed proof of enormous patience during the tracking down process. Once they suspected someone, they had him patiently followed to try to trace where the centre of activities lay. The shadowing was extremely skilful and very difficult to spot, let alone outmanoeuvre. There were cases where Partisans were followed while they were in operation, and if their shadowers had received no orders to arrest them, they were simply watched; but sooner or later the combatants would fall into the hands of the enemy.

One of the survivors, Abraham Lissner, was instructed to disperse the detachment (see his book *Un Partisan Juif Raconte* . . . , Paris 1969), where he asserts that one informer was an MOI leader who talked after his arrest on 20 October 1943, after which it was pointless to let the others carry on; and from 15 November onwards they were rounded up one after another.

CHAPTER 13

JEWISH ORGANISATIONS IN FRANCE

IN 1939, the organisation of Judaism in France was distinguished by its dual character, and in this respect has hardly changed since. On the one hand, there was a whole series of central and local social, cultural, political and religious organisations, while, on the other, the vast majority of French Jews had nothing whatsoever to do with any of these organisations; either because they did not feel so inclined, or because the splinter groups themselves were more concerned with the racial quality — rather than the quantity — of their members.

Not one of the Franco-Jewish organisations was psychologically or materially prepared to transform itself overnight into a Resistance movement. This was perfectly understandable, for they had been created for a special purpose and were planned accordingly but later, in face of Jewish persecution and the ever-increasing number of deportations, they had to take action and members of the various organisations, men and women, whatever their position, courageously entered the fight, taking up positions where they would be most useful and serving through success and failure. But in doing so, they had to leave the ranks of their official organisation and step outside the bounds of the law.

When they did this resolutely, they were generally successful; when they tried to compromise, by pretending to keep within the law, while at the same time acting illegally, the results were generally disastrous.

The activity of the Jewish chaplains in the prison camps quite often assumed the character of Resistance action — indeed many Rabbis belonged to the movement. Rabbi R. S. Kappel, stationed at Toulouse and free to come and go in the numerous camps of the region, was able to recruit a large number of militants, who later joined the ranks of *l'Organisation juive de Combat*[1]. The Chaplain General, Chief Rabbi Hirschel, was also linked with the Resistance.

The Rabbis were first-class Resistance combatants, and at least a score of them died in deportation, but just as large-scale participation in the Resistance by Catholic and Protestant clergy did not necessarily mean that the respective churches, as such, had formed part of the Resistance, the engagement of Rabbis was only binding upon them as individuals.

Far be it from us to blame men of faith and religious spirit, men of God, for not having been the contemporary counterparts of the warrior monks of the Middle Ages, although this was exactly the impression a few of them, notably Rabbi Feuerwerker, made on their interlocutors. But those who did bear testimony to the existence of God, even under the most terrible circumstances, were an inspiration to all of us.

The activities of the *Fédération des Sociétés juives de France*, one of the most important immigrant organisations, were of quite a different character. This Federation, in the Northern Zone, functioned under the name of '*Comité de la rue Amelot*', at the headquarters of a charitable organisation called *la Colonie scolaire*, where besides his official duties, its director, David Rappaport took an active part in the Resistance mainly by supplying large quantities of false papers. The organisation also possessed an official dispensary which was used by clandestine Jews, and even by the sick or wounded members of the FTP. The identity papers of a Jew born at Minsk-Mazowiecki in Poland might establish him as a Catholic born in Valence-d'Agen (Gers) or Carvin (Pas-de-Calais); but one might well ask what protection they offered when he spoke Yiddish from the moment lunch was served to him in the Jewish canteen.

Many a Jew escaped deportation with the false papers of la rue Amelot and was saved from starvation by the canteens, but Rappaport did not survive. He was arrested and deported. On his arrival at Auschwitz the other internees, who knew him well, rallied round, but their efforts were in vain and he disappeared shortly after. Rappaport was in his sixties, and as the SS guards were wont to declare, Auschwitz was not a sanatorium.

The Federation was to suffer one bitter setback after another. Although it had tried to conceal the activites of its various centres under cover of the initials UGIF, the Gestapo eventually effected round-ups at Lyons, Limoges and elsewhere, and prisoners were dispatched to Auschwitz, via Drancy. None remained long at large.

At the beginning of 1943, in despair of their cause, the leaders of the Federation passed the word for exodus to the Italian Occupied Zone, east of the Rhône, where the Jews lived in relatively idyllic conditions. More than once, the Italian occupation authorities intervened *manu militari* in order to prevent the French police, even the Prefects, from releasing the Jews arrested on orders of the Vichy government.

The Italian armistice on 8 September 1943 put an end to the idyll, and tens of thousands of Jews found themselves trapped in Alpes Maritimes and in the upper Alpine valleys. Some of them escaped into Italy; others were captured on both sides of the frontier[2].

The Nice catastrophe sounded the knell of militants of the Jewish organizations, and it took all their courage, intelligence, faith and skill to avert disaster. Although thousands of Jews were rounded up in and around Nice, the vast majority, more than three-quarters, slipped through the meshes, and this was due neither to a miracle, nor to any lack of vigilance on the part of the Gestapo. Indeed, one of the most active of Eichmann's assistants, Brunner, who at that time commanded the camp of Drancy, went down in person to Nice with a whole *Kommando* and saw to it that the region was thoroughly combed. But the militant Jews belonging to the Federation and to the other organisations, among them the future historian Leon Poliakov, Maurice Loebenberg-Cachoud, Claude Gutmann, Weintraub-Wister and Joseph (André) Bass, managed to open countless doors where the Jews were able to go to ground. Jews were hidden in the buildings of the archbishopric, with the Jesuits, and with Catholic and Unionist Scouts; they found refuge with the *Compagnons de France,* a Pétainist group if ever there was one; they were sheltered for months in houses known for their brief rather specialised hospitality. Whatever political divergences there may have been between Communist and other Jews these were shelved in Nice during the crisis. The ubiquitous A. Rayski directed the operations of the Communist Jews.

But Gutmann and Weintraub were arrested by the Gestapo, for there had been indiscretions. The word treason was pronounced and certain names were cited, verbally and in writing; but fairness and prudence forbid us to enter into further details.

On the debit side of the UGIF balance there are far too many arrests and deportations. Apart from the round-ups of the Lyons and Limoges offices, several orphanages set up by the UGIF for children whose parents had been deported were emptied of their occupants by the Gestapo. The UGIF leaders were called to task for not having evacuated the orphanages in time, but one wonders why they were ever created when the children might have been placed with private families in the country as thousands of others were.

Torn between their legal character on the one hand, and the necessity for clandestinity on the other, the Franco-Jewish organisations searched for conciliatory solutions rather than honourable compromise, but were not to achieve positive results until they abandoned this policy.

Many well-intentioned leaders and members of these organisations sacrificed their lives in the course of their duty. In a war as inexorable as that of 1939—1945 this was not, alas, always enough.

A social organisation created to respond to the needs of peacetime is not capable of facing up to a state of war, and especially not to aggression such as the Nazis showed towards the Jews. Men can adapt themselves to the circumstances; organic structures cannot.

This argument is reminiscent of the very lively controversy over Hannah Arendt that shook Jewish opinion a few years ago. Hannah Arendt, a Jewish philosopher of German origin resident in the United States, who had followed the Eichmann trial in Jerusalem 1961—1962, published, in the United States in 1963, then in other countries, including France, a book entitled *Eichmann In Jerusalem: A Report On the Banality of Evil*[3], in which she denounced the role — in her opinion harmful — that the Jewish Councils and leaders in general played during the Occupation. What she blamed them for, fundamentally, was not so much having failed to offer resistance to the Germans, of which they were quite incapable, as having refused to let themselves be passively overcome; for having consented to preserve some at the cost of the lives of others, the Jewish leaders tended, quite naturally in her opinion, to save those nearest to them personally, socially or ideologically, and so unwittingly condemned others to death. Her conclusions, after a virulent attack on the Jewish leaders, can be summed up in a single sentence.

If the Jewish people had really been disorganised and leaderless, chaos would have reigned, and much misery too, but the number of victims would not have been from four and a half to six millions.

This argument provoked a general outcry among the Jewish historians of the catastrophe, but could not be refuted. All they could do was to cite individual cases showing that not all Jewish leaders corresponded to the sombre picture Hannah Arendt drew of them; occasionally expanding the example to the scale of a particular Jewish Council; and at least it was proved that the majority of Jewish leaders had not been spared by the Nazis.

Perhaps we answered Hannah Arendt at the beginning of this book. The circumstances were terrible and men were not always equal to them; and though anarchy seems to have a strange fascination for Madame Arendt, the truth is that it is contrary to man's nature. While it is impossible to write history with 'ifs' we do not wish to give the impression of trying to side-step and would only repeat that it is impossible for men to live in a state of anarchy. The Jewish Councils had been created by the Germans for the sole purpose of destroying the Jews and in the same way the Nazis turned Jewish institutions to their advantage by diverting them from their object and turning them once more against the Jews; so that passive surrender in itself would not have been a solution; the only answer would have been to turn the Nazi army against the Nazis.

The Jewish organisations, particularly the immigrant ones, belonging to the *Fédération des Sociétés juives de France*, distrusted the Communists, and while the feeling was reciprocated, the latter made several attempts, during the war, and especially after 1941, to improve relations politically and in other directions; and men like Henri Bulawko, militant member of the young *Hachomer Hatzair* Zionist movement in Paris-Ville contributed considerably in dissipating the prejudices on both sides, as did Jacques Rabinovitch, lawyer and officer in the pre-revolutionary Russian Army, who succeeded in enlisting the support of a number of emigrant White Russians some of whom changed colour, if not to red, at least to pink.

In the provinces, Federation militants like Leon Glaeser, killed by the Militia, and Communist Jews like A. Rayski also co-operated and a number of Jewish Defence Committees, sprang up in Paris and in the south-east. These were purely political organisations: there was no question of pooling armed forces.

The Jewish Communists, whose very structures were designed for combat, exercised a sort of fascination even on decent middle-class citizens as far removed from Communism as it was possible to be, though some were apprehensive of being swallowed up by the Communists. These fears proved to be exaggerated.

Zionists, Communists and other Jews eventually set up a *Comité représentatif des Israélites de France* (CRIF)[4], still in existence and similar committees were set up at youth organization level; notably one Jewish youth movement consisting mainly of Communists and Bundists.

NOTES

1. The Jewish chaplains were allowed to operate in the camps of the South Zone, and continued to do so long after its occupation by the Germans.

2. The Communist Jews had been much more clear-sighted: taking a more orthodox political attitude, they had estimated that no good could come out of a situation that depended essentially on the good will of the Occupation authorities, especially as they happened to be Fascists. In fact, most of the members of the Italian military administration in Occupied France had never been, or were no longer, Fascists, and if they were unable to help the Jews who had put themselves in their hands, it must be remembered that they could not do anything for themselves either. The 4th Italian Army and most of the large Italian units were carried off in the landslide of September 1943.

3. New York, 1963.

4. Leon Meiss, at that time interim President of the Israeli Consistory; Joseph Fischer-Ariel and A. Rayski helped to found the CRIF.

CHAPTER 14

THE JEWISH COMBAT ORGANISATIONS

THE Jewish *Organisation juive de Combat* (OJC), set up around 1942, became active just after the Toulouse armistice.

In July 1942, Toulouse was still swarming with refugees: French, Belgian, Luxemburgers, and Dutch civilians; Polish and Czechs; Germans, Jewish and non-Jewish British together with newly demobilised soldiers from all the active armed forces, for it had still not dawned on the people that they had been defeated, and the Resistance was still far off. It was then that the *Organisation juive de Combat* was born, with the coming together of two men, a visionary and a man of action experienced in underground activity.

The visionary was David Knout, a Russian-speaking, Russian-born poet and a dedicated Zionist, although not affiliated to any Zionist party, who had just been demobilised and was wondering what he could do for his fellow Jews. He had closely followed the progress of Nazism, first in Germany, then in Central and Eastern Europe; and had painfully lived through the Battle of France and seen his fellow Jews hunted and pursued. Knout's Russian wife, Regina, a granddaughter of the composer Scriabine and related to the USSR Minister of Foreign Affairs, Molotov, was at least as fanatical a Zionist as her husband. At her own desire she had been converted to Judaism on her marriage: an astonishing concession, for to get a Rabbi to ratify such a conversion is a feat indeed.

Knout knew that running away would not improve the fate of the Jews, which already hung in the balance. In his opinion they had to confront the enemy in an organised Jewish fashion, and immediately after the collapse, he outlined his plan to form a Jewish army under Jewish command which would fight under a Jewish flag to defend Jewish interests.

Needless to say, when he disclosed his idea to leading members of Jewish society living in Toulouse — and there were a great number of them forced into exile by the defeat — he was given a cool reception. The more indulgent took him for a visionary and thought this hardly surprising considering that he was a poet, but all the same, they asked him to moderate his views. The others suspected him of being a professional agitator.

Knout eventually came into contact with Abraham Polonski, a young Palestinian engineer who happened to be passing through France and had come to Europe to help in preparations for the Zionist Congress, due to take place in Switzerland at the end of August 1939.

Unlike Knout, Polonski was a disciplined Zionist militant and a staunch supporter of the workers' (Socialist) Party, *Mapai* which, outside Palestine, was known by the name of *Poalei Sion*. Polonski had served in the *Haganah* — a little-known Jewish defence organisation in Palestine. This clandestine organisation, alternately tolerated and persecuted by the British authorities, while Palestine was still under English mandate, had been forced to learn the techniques of clandestine action, which it had done very successfully; its intelligence service was also efficient.

Polonski had therefore been well trained and Knout's idea appealed to him instantly, though he saw it in a slightly different perspective. As an organised Zionist, and a member of the *Ychouv* (Jewish community of Palestine), he could not conceive of any organised Jewish action that was not directly linked to the efforts of this community — the future Jewish State. He went even further: it was, in his eyes, the only guarantee of the continued existence of the Jewish people — whom the Nazis, among others, threatened to exterminate. The only really worthwhile service that the Jews living outside Palestine could offer, was to help build up this Jewish State as quickly as possible.

To the Jews living in Toulouse in July 1940, Polonski's idea seemed no less fantastic than that of Knout. But Polonski did not content himself with thinking: he acted. At that time, the main efforts of the Palestinian population were directed towards creating a Jewish army force in the ranks of British armies. This idea only began to be realised later, in the autumn of 1944, with the creation of the Jewish Brigade. Before that the British colonial authorities had opposed it, despite being strongly advised by Winston Churchill not to do so. The colonial authorities and many high-ranking military men, including General Wavell, Commander-in-Chief of the British Forces in the Eastern Mediterranean, considered that the constitution of this army would lead to Arab uprisings in the Near East. Winston Churchill's protests fell on deaf ears, and there was nothing further he could do. The real — and perhaps more justifiable — reason for this opposition was that the British colonial authorities feared that a Jewish army force might question the position of Great Britain in the Near East when the war was over, and were convinced that this army would be a feather in the Jews' cap after peace was declared. They had in any case only a limited respect for the fighting capacities of the Jews; but in spite of all this, the Zionist leaders did not cease to clamour for the setting up of this armed force, and Polonski, in France, supported the effort. To understand his position, we must compare it, on a more modest scale, to that of General de Gaulle, whose Free French Forces engaged in all the operations — in Africa, in Asia; with the Royal Air Force as well as the Soviet Russian — in order to hasten the liberation of France. Polonski had no objection to the Jews fighting in France against the Germans but, above all, he wanted them to assist in the creation of the Israeli Jewish State. Polonski was, and is, a cool-headed realist with his feet well planted on the ground and knew perfectly well that the Zionist idea was not very widespread in France and that even the organised Zionists were hardly in a position to fight the Germans, especially in July 1940. It was therefore necessary to act shrewdly and cautiously.

Experienced as he was in clandestine activity, he decided upon a two-pronged operation: to create a special organisation, which was to remain as secret as possible; and to do so in such a way that all the Jewish organisations should be represented. Its members must support the actions of their parent organisation without giving themselves away; and Polonski's concern for efficiency was such that he did not hesitate to manipulate others: be they men, groups, or organisations. As he never tried to boost his personal image — always preferring to act behind the scenes — he generally succeeded.

The network that resulted from the meeting between Knout and Polonski took the significant name of *l'Armée juive* (AJ). Tough as this group was, there sprang up an even tougher one within it: *'Main forte'* (MF), responsible for secretly supervising the operations of the Jewish Army. MF had quite an important role to play in the early stages of the AJ, though later its responsibility diminished.

Like other Resistance movements AJ had its own terminology: it was organised not in 'groups' but in 'fortresses'. Its initial membership of a score or two were men of stature and character, well equipped to handle their heavy responsibilities. It was their duty to set the ball rolling, and they succeeded.

Rabbi Hosanski and Rabbi R. Kappel, former military chaplain, helped to bring religious comfort to tens of thousands of Jewish internees in camps like Gurs, Vernet, Noé, Récébédou, Barcarès, Agde and Brams in the Midi of France, where theoretically, the non-French Jews were either internees in the camps or sentenced to hard labour; some being quartered in barracks, others placed under house arrest. Most of them resigned themselves to their fate; the remainder found a way to escape. The camp internees were the most unfortunate of all, the very fact that they were internees indicating that they had neither sufficient money nor the right connections. Kappel and Hosanski tried to help these unfortunates, the role they played not being a purely spiritual one; and they did more: able to move freely between the different camps, they picked out the most dynamic, courageous and enterprising prisoners and helped a large number of them to escape and thus to join the AJ and later the OJC; and here the Rabbis were greatly helped by a Polish Jew, Jacob Kotlicki, who disappeared after 1942, swallowed up by some Auschwitz gas-chamber.

Like all Jewish organisations, the AJ had to have a welfare service to help feed and clothe the internees and, from the beginning of summer 1942, to combat deportation, while tens of thousands had to be supplied with false papers and money to enable them to live outside the law; and homes had to be found for the children.

At the same time it was necessary not to lose sight of the main objective, reinforcements for the Jewish State, and to this end a first delegation of young men, old enough to fight, was sent off to Spain in 1943, with instructions to establish a liaison with the international Jewish organisations, with *Joint* in particular, and to collect the necessary funds.

The young militants' mission was to end in utter failure. Far from convincing the representative of *Joint* in Barcelona, they aroused suspicion and distrust; but a second mission, led by J. Jeffroykin (*Dyka*) was sent in 1944 and was more successful. Several hundred young people were enlisted in the Jewish Brigade and others were sent to Algiers, where they joined the Free French Forces.

The aforementioned 'fortress', the operative unit of the AJ comprised fifteen members: four groups of three, a leader for every two groups, and a fortress commander.

The AJ was the only Resistance movement operating in France that thought it necessary to have a ceremonial of initiation and adhesion taken directly from the *Haganah*. The new adherent was blindfolded and led into a darkened room. When his eyes were uncovered he saw facing him a Hebrew Bible, a Jewish flag, blue and white struck with the Star of David, and a revolver; and he was made to take an oath with his hand on the Bible:

> *Standing in front of our flag, I swear fidelity to the Jewish Army and obedience to its leaders.*
> *I swear to fight for the honour and the rights of Judaism, until the enemy is crushed.*
> *Liberty or Death!*

Those present then repeated in chorus: 'Liberty or Death!'

One can recognise the poetical inspiration of David Knout behind all this. The ceremonial and the text of the oath made a deep and lasting impression, especially on the younger members, and a quarter of a century later those who had pronounced it had not forgotten the inspiration it gave them.

N. Gryn (Tony) was a nineteen-year-old student living in Paris, whose university career had been interrupted by the war, and had only recently become French.

On 3 August 1940 he and a friend, out walking in the Saint-Cloud forest, sat down on the terrace of a café. Some German soldiers entered into conversation with them, expressing their not very flattering views on the French Army, on France, and on the character of the inhabitants.

Gryn and his comrade reacted to these remarks with more hastiness than prudence and were arrested by some German soldiers in mufti, whose presence they had not even noticed. They got off with a year in prison.

Their luck did not stop there: they were freed in August 1941, just before the round-ups of the Jews of the XIe *arrondissement* and the German decision to cease releasing political prisoners even when their sentences expired. The two youths realised that they were 'done for' in Paris because their identities were too well known and sought refuge in the Free Zone. Tony ended up in Grenoble, where he came into contact with a group of Jewish Zionists, joined the AJ and was charged with numerous missions ranging from one end to the other of the so-called Free Zone. On more than one occasion his path crossed that of a young woman, the future writer Françoise d'Eaubonne, who mentioned their meetings in her *Mémoires*. Tony finished the war in Paris taking part in the battles of the Liberation.

Another member of the AJ was Joseph Fuchs (Jo), originally from Strasbourg, son of Polish-born parents like Gryn, who had attended a French school and felt as French as his comrades. When the war came and the defeat was followed by the anti-Jewish measures of the Vichy Government, seventeen-year-old Fuchs underwent a traumatic experience that left its mark intellectually. He became a Zionist, joined the AJ, and did all that he could to get out of France and enlist in the Jewish armies in Palestine. He succeeded too late to take part in the World War, and it was not until 1948 that he had the opportunity to fight in a Jewish army, when he was seriously wounded and practically incapacitated in the course of Israel's War of Independence.

A large proportion of the combatants of the AJ chose to go and live in Israel after the Liberation; the rest stayed in France, as, with the exception of Polonski himself, now a prosperous industrialist in Tel-Aviv, did most of the officers of the AJ who remained. Some have since died. The national commissioner of the Jewish scouts, Gamzon, who succeeded Haguenau when he was arrested and shot by the Gestapo, settled in Israel, but disappeared some years ago.

About 2,000 combatants passed through the ranks of the AJ/OJC: quite a considerable figure when all is said and done, and comparable with the total strength of a large, purely French, Resistance network such as *Alliance*.

The AJ had a series of *maquis* in the Noires Mountains and in the Cevennes: Vabre, Bic, Rècques, which were on excellent terms with the local groups of the

Armée sécrète (AS), and eventually integrated in the MUR (*Mouvements unis de la Résistance*).

On one occasion Polonski, better known under the name of 'Monsieur Pol', gave a practical demonstration of the ideology of his movement. When circumstances permitted the OJC *maquis* carried the French *tricoleur*; but there was an exception. One day while they were recovering arms, equipment and agents, dropped by parachute by the British SOE, they came face to face, with not French but British officers. The Jewish *maquis* proudly raised the blue and white flag struck with the Star of David, the flag of the future Jewish State, which the British officers, brothers-in-arms of those occupying Palestine, recognised immediately.

Later, these same *maquisards*, commanded by Colonel Dunoyer of Segonzac, took part in the combats that ended in the liberation of Castres and Mazamet. Forming themselves into the Marc Haguenau company they seized an armoured German train and the captured soldiers on it. Hubert Beuvemery, who witnessed the incident, was struck by the terror of the German prisoners when one of their captors declared '*Ich bin Jude*'. That was the only vengeance exercised by the Jews on their executioners.

Besides the *maquis*, a series of commando units AJ/OJC operated with varying degrees of success, mainly in the large towns. The commando unit of Toulouse, with which 'Monsieur Pol', as a resident, was most directly concerned, was particularly successful in establishing and maintaining friendly relations with the militant Communists. Unlike the other non-Communist Resistance fighters who were forced to co-operate with the Communists, Polonski was not afraid of being manipulated to suit their ends, for he was sure enough of himself to know that it would be he who would make use of them, not vice versa, and future events confirmed this.

The main assignment of Lyons and Grenoble commando units was the children's rescue operation, and several convoys were sent to Switzerland, though some of the women who accompanied them paid for this enterprise with their lives. These units also tried to maintain contact with the world-wide Zionist organisation through the Geneva office of the Jewish Palestine Agency.

A special commando unit in Roux near the Pyrenees was commanded by Jean Roitman (Morel) and after his arrest by his brother Paul. Its task was to ensure safe passage of the convoys sent by the OJC through Spain, and here the Spanish Republican officer Maura was of invaluable help.

The Nice commando unit was particularly active immediately after the Italian capitulation, when the Italian Occupied Zone, where a large number of Jews had sought refuge, was taken over by the Germans. The Nice region was suddenly transformed into an enormous trap by the clique of toadying citizens gravitating round the Gestapo and other auxiliary German services. Joseph Dornand, Commander-in-Chief and founder of the Militia, being Niçois, his movement had more support in Nice than elsewhere.

A particularly odious industry prospered in Nice, that of denunciation, and the first task of the OJC commando unit was to set about cleaning up the region of such undesirables.

The *Alerte* commando unit of l'Île-de-France, commanded by Lucien Rubel, which later participated in the Liberation of Paris, suffered a severe setback when the Nice militants put an alleged agent of the Intelligence Service, supposedly in direct contact with Britain, in touch with it. He was in fact a German agent of *Abwehr*. All the Paris militants and some of the Niçois fell into the trap.

One of these militants, Maurice Loebenberg (Cachoud), took over the forging of documents for the various OJC groups, and for the *Combat* movement. The Gestapo located him, and he was subjected to the most atrocious tortures to make him talk, but died without uttering a word.

Others who were arrested belonged to the small 'Dutch group' of young Zionist militants from the Netherlands, some Dutch and some German, who up to 1941 had been following courses in husbandry with a view to settling in a *kibbutz* in Palestine.

When the deportations began, they adopted a special type of clandestinity: taking advantage of their type of physique, more Aryan than the Aryans, and of their knowledge of German, they procured false papers and offered themselves as long-distance drivers for the Todt Organisation, and in German lorries, under cover of German papers, got several hundred young Jews out of Holland. They had the same idea as Polonski: they had to get to Palestine, which meant that first of all they had to cross the Pyrenees.

Their first meeting with the AJ militants was a rather uneasy one, for the latter were at a loss to understand how men of the Todt Organisation could be disguised Jews, but once contact was established the collaboration proved to be very fruitful.

After the round-up, the prisoners, numbering about fifty, were sent to Germany in what was to be the last train-load of deportees to leave the Drancy camp, following the same route as some 83,000 French Jews — to the death camps; but in the course of an air raid, the train drew to a halt in the open country and about fifteen of the prisoners escaped, while the remainder had the good fortune to be treated as political prisoners, and were sent, not to Auschwitz, but 'only' to Buchenwald; so that a number of them survived.

Other arrests took a heavy toll of the AJ militants. Polonski himself was captured at Toulouse on 7 June 1944, as were Regina Knout and Joseph Frydman, 'Perrin', who was secretary general of the AJ. 'Pol' managed to give his guards the slip in the street. 'Lieutenant Albert' (Cohen) head of the Toulouse commando unit, tried to mount an operation to extricate Perrin, but the Germans got there first and sent him immediately to an 'unknown destination', from which he never returned.

The leader of the Marseilles commando group 'Guy' (Wolf Wechsler), instigator of various sabotage operations, was also arrested, but he was not credited with being a Jew, and was sent to Buchenwald. He did return.

The Liberation found the OJC with about a tenth of its members arrested, deported, or killed: quite a large percentage of losses, but small compared with those suffered by other networks[1].

One episode at the time of the Liberation might give the impression that the AJ had failed to attain its essential goal. At the time of the march past in liberated Toulouse the *maquisards* of the OJC were forbidden to carry the blue and white Jewish flag, just as the Spanish Republican *maquisards* were forbidden to carry theirs. Jean Cassou, at that time commissioner of the Republic of Toulouse, was responsible for this decision. But this apparent failure was soon forgotten after Pol's negotiations at the beginning of 1945 with 'Colonel' Shadmi who had been sent to Europe to see if there was anything left to salvage and found the AJ, the non-Zionist members of the OJC having gone back to civilian life. In the terms of the agreement drawn up, the AJ was appointed the *Haganah* section in France and in North Africa, and as such played a very active role between 1945 and 1948, making it possible for tens of thousands of immigrants to enter Palestine. These immigrants were 'illegal', that is to say their entry was not authorised by the mandatory power. Later, when the time of Israel's war of independence drew near, Pol's men organised military training camps in France, mostly in the suburbs of Marseilles (la Madrague de Montredon, le Grand-Arénas, and the suburbs of Salon-de-Provence, etc.). Thousands of young people received an intensive military training there, so that when the war began most of them were in a position to go straight to the front line the moment they disembarked.

All this was made possible by the French civilian and military authorities who were fully aware of the object in view and gave all the support they could. Bonds that had been forged during the Resistance were obviously as strong as ever.

NOTES

1. At the time of the Liberation, the leaders of the AJ headed by Polonski (also known as Maurice Ferrer), included Zupraner, Lublin (Lucien), Kowarski (Alexandre). Dyka-Jeffroykin led the AJ mission to Spain, while Knout had been forced to withdraw to Switzerland as did another poet, Arnold Mandel.

CHAPTER 15

THE ALGIERS LANDING

S EVERAL hundred Jews, acting as such, played a decisive role in the plots that led to the capture of Algiers and to the neutralisation of its civil and military forces on 8 November 1942. The disembarkation proceeded smoothly and the Allied troops were able to enter the town without firing a single shot. It was one of these rare occasions when expediency and bluff made up for lack of numbers and finally won the day.

On 8 November 1942, about four hundred insurgents, more than half of them Jews, risked their lives in Algiers. They arrested or immobilised the senior Vichy military officials, among them Admiral Darlan, and unlike the operations that preceded the Casablanca and Oran landings did so swiftly enough to avoid risking several thousand lives.

To visualise what would have happened if the plan had failed, let us take a rapid glance at wartime Europe.

The German attack on Stalingrad had been arrested definitively, but the Russian counter-offensive, which was to end with the crushing defeat of the Sixth German Army, was not due to begin until fifteen days later.

With the exception of Yugoslavia and the USSR, there was not a single armed Resistance movement in the whole of occupied Europe, and Resistance movements in other countries had not progressed beyond the sabotage stage, although some groups were collecting political and military information.

It is true that General Montgomery had inflicted a sharp defeat on Rommel's *Afrika-Korps* a fortnight before, on 23 October 1942, but this corps was beaten, not destroyed. Its defeat was due mainly to lack of supplies, a situation that was considerably eased when the Axis forces occupied Tunisia. The operation *was* militarily possible as events were to show.

The physical extermination of the European Jews lasted for over a year, with the deportations of French Jews, which had begun on 27 March 1942, proceeding at a rapid pace. Vichy had already handed over thousands of Jews from the so-called Free Zone to the Germans, while the head of the anti-Jewish section of the Paris Gestapo, Theodor Dannecker, had decided to send the Algerian Jews to Auschwitz as well, transporting them by sea from Algiers to Marseilles. The plan had not yet come into operation, but only for technical reasons: Dannecker finding it very difficult to procure enough trains to dispatch even the French Jews to Auschwitz, and complaining to Eichmann that he had been supplied with passenger coaches instead of cattle-trucks, which made the guards' task much more complicated. He was told that he would have to make the best of things and that the present arrangement was a blessing in disguise in that it avoided alarming the Jews at the moment of their departure.

We stress the Algerian episode because, unlike most armed actions in the Jewish Resistance between 1941 and 1944, this one was victorious; not that it changed the course of the war, but without it the Allies would have had to pay more dearly for victory.

We have particular reason to believe that if the Anglo-Saxons had been driven from North Africa, the Germans would certainly have taken their place, in which case Franco's Spain would have bartered its non-belligerence, since even though it remained neutral, its sympathies were with the Axis. The Allied forces would probably still have succeeded in establishing the Second Front, but much less easily. The British position in the Mediterranean would have continued to be difficult, and the destiny of Malta, uncertain. Rommell could have launched a counter-offensive.

The deportations of the Jews in France would have been speeded up; the military presence of the Allies in North Africa having indirectly caused the process to slow down, for the Vichy police authorites began to give up lending their support; and instead of 83,000 Jewish deportees from France, there would have been 250,000 or more. Besides, some half-million Jews living in Maghreb would have been swallowed up in the 'Final Solution to the Jewish Problem'. The contribution of Maghrebin Judaism, in manpower, to the Israeli War of Independence (as well as to the successive wars which Israel fought for its existence in 1956 and 1967) gives an idea of how much harm the disappearance of this community would have done to the Israeli cause, not to mention the risk Israel ran of finding itself overwhelmed by the *Afrika-Korps*, and not forgetting the presence of almost 50,000 Jews in Libya.

To sum up, the intervention in Algiers — at the right time and at the right place — of these 200 or so Jews, and less than 200 non-Jews, spared the Anglo-Saxons a North African Dunkirk and the Jewish people dangers that threatened about a million of their fellows.

Chief among the Algerian Jews involved were the Aboulker clan. José, one of the youngest members of the clan, organised a Gaullist student movement, and in September 1940 three other enterprising young Jews, Emile Atlan, André Témine and Bouchara set up a Jewish gymnasium under the name of *Géo Gras*. There had been anti-Jewish pogroms in Algeria prior to 1939, even in face of opposition by the French government. How much more were they to be feared under the Vichy Government, which had promulgated a 'Jewish statute', withdrawing from the

Algerian Jews the privileges of the Crémieux decree, and consequently full exercise of the rights of French citizenship, and had appointed to all the top administrative posts officials notorious for their hostility towards the Jews. The three organisations planned to set up small defence groups, in the hope that, by taking action against pogroms, they would discourage potential aggressors.

In 1942 a French Resistance fighter, Captain Pilafort, arrived in Algiers and contacted his friends, the Aboulkers, to ask for their assistance in setting up Resistance groups. Their first thought was the Géo Gras gymnasium.

The Resistance movement had already been established for some time, having been created in the Oranais, on 7 March 1941, when Roger Carcassonne, 'the Jew Carcassonne', as his enemies called him, formed an alliance with Henri d'Astier de la Vigerie, Abbé Cordier and his colleague — in religion as well as in the Resistance — Father Therry, joining in a few days later. The group tried without success, to establish contact with General de Gaulle through the agency of a Polish branch of the Intelligence Service, and not wishing to take financial aid from this Anglo-Polish centre, and unable to obtain it from General de Gaulle, Carcassonne succeeded in overcoming the scruples of his comrades and made himself personally responsible for all expenses.

At the beginning of 1941, Carcassonne and José Aboulker proposed to mount 'some sort of operation' in Algiers, but the plan had to be shelved until the end of the year when Aboulker was introduced by his friend Guy Cohen-Calvet to one of the first Algerian Resistance fighters, André Achiary, commissary of the DST. In October 1941, Bernard Karsenty, a Paris business man and Algerian Jew, returned to Algiers and joined the group.

Later, Guy Calvet was to play a more and more important role in events, for he had kept up valuable liaisons with the MA office, *le Bureau des Menées anti-nationales* which had acted as camouflage for the 2e Bureau since the time of the phoney war, and had undertaken difficult missions abroad mostly to Italy. These contacts were all the more useful when Achiary was moved from Algiers to Sétif, his loyalty to Vichy being open to question in high places.

It was José Aboulker who introduced Bernard Karsenty to Henri d'Astier de la Vigerie and to Abbé Cordier, Pierre Alexander, and Guy Calvet. The newcomer took over the manufacture of false papers. In his turn, d'Astier put Aboulker in touch with Colonel Jousse, who became the military expert of the group and also supplied it with important material resources.

At the same time, it was necessary to act on a political level. The shock of Mers el-Kebir was still fresh in people's minds, so that the only card that could be played was American, and bore the name of Robert Murphy. This professional diplomat, with the grade of ambassadorial adviser, was not only the Algerian consul general, but also the personal representative of President Roosevelt.

We are not going to retrace here all the various stages of the 'Algerian coup', but simply the action of the Algerian Jews, and the role played, on the French side, by the so-called group of five: Tarbé de Saint-Hardouin, Henri d'Astier de la Vigerie, Jean Rigault, Jacques Lemaigre; also Dubreuil and the leader Van Hecke (*Compagnons de France*).

At one point, an American military mission commanded by General Mark Clark visited Cherchell by submarine, and landed under cover of darkness for a clandestine *rendezvous* with the French military conspirators of Algiers. On this memorable occasion the General presented an American Marine fifteen-stroke carbine to the organiser of the meeting, Bernard Karsenty, and this constituted exactly half the stock of automatic arms supplied by the Americans to the Algerian conspirators; the other half being the Sten gun which was Robert Murphy's gift to José Aboulker. Aboulker demanded 800 similar carbines, so that all the volunteers might be armed, and he also asked for explosive and tear-gas grenades, 400 revolvers, 50 walkie-talkies; all of which were promised to him, none of which he ever received, though on several occasions the conspirators risked being discovered when they ventured out on the beaches at night to scan the horizon for the mythical submarine that was to bring them arms.

Finally, it was decided to launch the assault on Algiers. Eight hundred volunteers were to seize and hold the principal nerve centres of the town, awaiting the arrival of the Americans, that is, in theory, for two to three hours, by which time the Americans should have arrived, and the French army would surrender and fraternise with the liberators.

The 800 volunteers had to oppose an armed force of 11,000 men, to which could be added about 2,000 members of SOL, *Service d'ordre légionnaire*, embryo of the Darnand Militia, and several hundred militants of the Doriat PPF.

The rebels had a few trumps up their sleeves and knew exactly how to deal with these forces. Colonel Jousse, Commander of the *Place d'Alger*, was conversant with the plan of action, *du Maintien de l'ordre*, that would be applied in case of emergency, employing civil volunteers, *volontaires de place*, who were issued simply with arm-bands bearing the initials VP, which Colonel Jousse also supplied to Aboulker's men; but there was no sign of the promised American weapons. Nor could he persuade Colonel Anzelme, in charge of all operations in Algiers, to go back on his last-minute refusal to act when the Americans failed to deliver the promised weapons, he having no guarantee that when zero hour came they would not default again.

The formation charged with taking the town consisted of five groups (A,B,C,D, E), each entrusted with a special mission, and these were to be deployed around general headquarters, set up in the home of Professor Henri Aboulker, where Jousse and d'Astier were in close contact with Murphy and other members of his consulate, in a PC (fighting post) to be installed in the Central Police Station under the command of twenty-five year old José Aboulker, who was supported by his adjutants Bernard Karsenty, Guy Calvet and Jean Athias, still a Jewish, as well as a relief flying squad led by Colonel Tubert which included four other combatants, only two of them Jews. On the police side, besides Superintendent Achiary, there was his colleague Bringard, Head of Security, and Inspector Pilier.

Group A, covering 1^e, 11^e, 111^e and V^e *arrondissements*, was commanded by the Jewish doctor, Morali-Daninos, who was to install himself in the police station of 1^e *arrondissement*. His three groups were to neutralise respectively, the headquarters of the Algerian division in the Pelissier barracks, the *Palais d'hiver*, which housed the military headquarters of the Commander-in-Chief in North Africa, and the Admiralty. The last of these groups, A3, was commanded by André Cohen, with his fellow Jews Lanfrani and Habibou.

Group B, commanded by Dr. Raphael Aboulker, with the assistance of M. de Saint-Blancat and two Jewish combatants, Stéphane Aboulker and Oliver Bokanowski which covered the IVe and X^e *arrondissements*, was to install its PC in the police station of X^e *arrondissement*. Its four sub-groups were charged respectively with seizing the headquarters of the 19th Army Corps, the Préfecture, the General Post Office, and Radio Algiers.

B1, commanded by Captain Pilafort, included most of the students of the Géo Gras, in particular Temime, Bouchara, Atlan, Lieutenant Jaïs and Lucien Fredj. B2 (Préfecture) was commanded by Jacques Zermati, assisted by Ladia Oualid and André Lévy, all of whom were to hear themselves called 'dirty Jews' again, while the commander of B3 Post Office, Lieutenant Jean Dreyfus, did not have that pleasure but was treacherously shot.

Group C1, commanded by a Jewish lawyer, M. Maurice Hayoun, was charged with taking the Governor-General's palace; Group D, also led by a Jew, Paul Ruff, was to take over the town's telephone exchange.

Group E, which was to operate on El-Biar and Colonne-Voiro, was the only one not headed by a Jew. Henri d'Astier de la Vigerie, a staunch Catholic monarchist, was in charge of this group which was to carry out missions of capital importance, involving the arrests of Admiral Darlan and Generals Juin and Mendigal. There were fewer Jews in these groups than in the others, but one Jew, Marcel Felus, leader of Group E3, had the task of neutralising the Air Force Signals Centre.

The *coup* did not go according to plan.

At Algiers only 377 of the 800 volunteers presented themselves when the time came though out of the 200 Jews who volunteered only three or four defected, so that the Jews made up more than half the total strength.

Murphy came up with some 50-year-old Lebel guns and a supply of American cigarettes.

The lack of arms was not a decisive issue, for even the full complement of

800 men, equipped with machine guns, could not possibly have defeated any army of 11,000, especially as most of the 800, or as it fell out the 400, were civilians. José Aboulker gives a good general picture of the situation on the eve of the attack.

> *One can understand the reaction of people, who, after having been promised ultra-modern machine guns for a year, are handed a few ancient Lebels and a fistful of cartridges with which they are expected to face an army. Unfortunately it is impossible to explain to everybody that our real strength lies in our illegal uniforms and false mission orders, which enable us to penetrate the oiled wheels of the military machine; that we as volunteers are up against people who do not wish to fight, because for two years they have had their heads stuffed with propaganda extolling virtues of defeat; our strength lies in the fact that the few weary leaders left have decided to abandon their cause, anyway, having pursued it for too long.*

The real action began at about 10.30 p.m. on Saturday 7 November. The operational command had just taken up its position in the home of Professor Aboulker, 26 rue Michelet, when some police officers, led by Police Superintendent Delgrove, called to investigate the causes of the unusual commotion they had noticed there during the day.

Delgrove was received by his colleague Achiary, and a vaudeville scene followed, each of the police superintendents declaring his colleague arrested, and as Achiary had strength to back up his conviction, Delgrove found himself in an embarrassing situation.

As a junior officer of the Reserve Army, José Aboulker, acting on the spur of the moment for Colonel Anzelme, took over the Central Police Station.

At the beginning everything went off as planned, including the arrest of Darlan and Juin at the *Villa des Oliviers*; then things began to go wrong. Robert Murphy — no longer sure that General Giraud would arrive, decided to bring Darlan and Juin into the game and had them freed, hoping that Juin would order the armed forces not to offer resistance when the landing took place.

Juin would do nothing without Darlan's support and Murphy was obliged to negotiate with both of them.

At 3 o'clock in the morning of Sunday, 8 November, the insurgents held Algiers. Ten minutes later, Algiers knew that it was at war when an English destroyer opened fire and tried to force its way into the port: an attempt which was to end in failure.

Senior officials and superior officers, awakened by the bombardment, rushed to their posts and were immediately immobilised, more or less humanely, by the rebels.

The release of a certain number of them had grave consequences. Among them was a colonel, directly subordinate to General Juin, who at least still had his wits about him. Around four o'clock in the morning he received a message from Darlan. The latter had been able to send it under seal after having assured Murphy that the envelope contained a message to Marshal Pétain calling for his support.

In fact, although no one has been able to trace it, this was probably very similar to an earlier message, sent by Darlan under much the same conditions, which Henri d'Astier intercepted, and in which Darlan indirectly gave the order to oppose the landing by force. The second message remains a mystery, but on receipt of it the colonel concerned ordered his mobile guards and other available troops to take over the positions held by the rebels.

Aboulker was now in an extremely delicate situation, wishing to avoid bloodshed, but still without the promised American support.

At 4.50 a.m. Juin was freed by a platoon of mobile guards. Juin's own 'guards', schoolboys from the neighbouring *lycée*, had just time to get away.

Eventually, the Americans arrived, over 2,000 men, commanded by General Ryder, disembarking on the Sidi-Ferruch beach. The General did not consider himself strong enough to occupy Algiers, which was presumably defended, and surrounded the town.

The rebels tried to persuade Ryder to march directly on Algiers assuring him that the town was not defended whereas if he delayed too long he would have to face 11,000 men.

Murphy negotiated with Darlan and Juin while the official military command threatened to regain control of the town.

One sensational event followed another until 7 p.m. The General Post Office was recaptured and Lieutenant Dreyfus got a revolver bullet in his back, his murderer being awarded the *Croix de Guerre* a few days later for this feat of arms. At about 3 p.m., a car approached the barricade set up by Pilafort in front of the Central Police Station and all hell broke loose. Before he collapsed Pilafort managed to pull out his revolver and empty the charge on the fast-retreating vehicle.

At 7. p.m., Murphy persuaded Juin to order a cease fire. The coup had succeeded.

As to the rebels: in the short run, they had managed to attain their strategic objective, but in doing so they suffered a tactical and personal defeat.

The outcome of the agreements reached by the civil and American military authorities with Darlan and Juin was that the latter retained those powers that the Allied armies had not reserved for themselves.

When General Giraud eventually arrived, Darlan very skilfully immobilised him by making him his Commander-in-Chief. The legitimacy of Marshal Pétain and of the Vichy Government was maintained.

Following the assassination of Admiral Darlan on 24 December 1942, it was decided to take action against the principal protagonists of the Algerian coup, and on 30 December a police swoop ended in the arrest of Achiary, Professor Aboulker, his son José, René Moatti and several others. Karsenty, who was arrested at the same time, managed to escape and raise the alarm, as did Colette Aboulker, José's sister, not only warning Murphy but even more important, informing the British journalists present in Algiers of the state of affairs. These journalists were not at all sympathetic towards the Vichy hierarchy which held sway in Algiers, and disapproved of the fact that Roosevelt and Churchill had come to terms with it. The fugitives also warned René Capitant, a leading Algerian Gaullist, who managed to go into hiding just in time.

Murphy, hearing that Giraud had declared at a press conference that the 'arrested terrorists' wanted to shoot him, was not so foolish as to help to liberate them, and in fact, they were not released until after the Anfa Conference, at which Roosevelt and Churchill drew up among other agreements the 'Casablanca Declaration' on the unconditional surrender of the enemy.

The Generals de Gaulle and Giraud were subsequently forced to meet and to shake hands in front of the cameras.

Murphy manifested a tardy regret by inviting José Aboulker and Pierre Alexander to his home shortly after their release, and this was how the leaders of the insurrection were recompensed, although some were decorated later, José Aboulker being made a *Compagnon de la Libération*.

As for the troops, they hastily moved from Algiers to the Tunisian front. The Jews were remobilised, but great care was taken not to infringe the Jewish statute promulgated by the Vichy Government on 27 September 1940, whereby instead of carrying arms, they were sent to break up stones; and it was even thought advisable to have them supervised by commissioned and non-commissioned officers of the Foreign Legion, Germans, of course, who would have infringed the statute of the Legion had they fought against Germany.

Justice triumphed in the end, if only because of the shortage of fighting men; and once General de Gaulle was in full control in Algiers, these discriminations disappeared and the militant Algerian Jews were able to participate in the battles of Tunisia, Italy, Provence, Alsace, the Rhine and the Danube.

Did the Jews motivate the Algerian coup? Yes, indeed. For, unlike many of their fellow Jews in France, Algerian Jews were not at all torn between their Jewish and French loyalties, and from 1940 onwards they not only reacted as French Republicans, indignant at the impositions of Vichy, but also as Jews directly attacked by the regime.

Professor Henri Aboulker was President of the Algerian Zionist Federation from the Liberation up to his death. His daughter Colette is now living in Israel. José Aboulker has always insisted upon his Jewish heritage despite the fact that he is not a Zionist.

Finally, and perhaps most important of all, the action of some 200 Algerian Jews made it possible for almost a million of their fellow Jews to escape the gas chambers. It is for this reason that we consider the 'Algerian coup' to be one of the few Jewish victories of the Second World War.

Part Five

Submission or Resistance
What happened in Belgium and Holland

CHAPTER 16

THE RESISTANCE OF THE BELGIAN JEWS

O N 10 May 1940 the German forces began moving westwards, crossing at dawn the frontiers of The Netherlands, Belgium and Luxembourg, then penetrating into France; German paratroops rained down on Rotterdam, on the bridges of the Meuse at Moerdijk and on the Eben-Emael fort of the stronghold of Liège, and the hour of destiny ringing out across the skies of Western Europe sounded the knell for more than 200,000 Jews living in what was later to be known as Benelux.

Of the sixty million Europeans whose countries were to be invaded by the Germans in the space of a few weeks over half a million were Jews. By the time the Germans surrendered on 8 May 1945 almost half this number had disappeared, swallowed up in the turmoil, spirited away in the smoke of the crematoria, felled by the firing squads side by side with their brothers in arms.

That the other half of the Jews of Western Europe escaped with their lives was due to the Resistance movements of the various countries and — to a very large extent — the resistance of the Jews themselves.

Proof of this is to be found in Holland, the only Western European country in which the Germans succeeded in breaking down Jewish resistance at the outset and setting up a Jewish Council in its place. This, unfortunately, managed to win the trust of the Jewish population, with the result that more than 105,000 of them were deported and put to death; and this despite the fact that the Dutch Resistance movement was of a considerable size, and that almost the whole of the Dutch population rejected Nazism, particularly in its anti-Semitic aspects.

The first effect the invasion of Europe had in Belgium, and later in France, was to trigger off an immense exodus. More than a million Dutch, Luxemburgers and Belgians rapidly took to the roads, and these included at least half of the 240,000 or so Jews living in the three countries. Their example was quickly followed by the inhabitants of northern France, and later of those further south.

The movement of the Dutch population was halted by the speed of the German advance. The Belgian Jews and those of Luxembourg were able to seek shelter in France, though many did not get beyond the Somme.

It is interesting to note, bearing in mind the movement of repatriation after the Rethondes armistice, that on 1 October 1941, in Belgium alone, the Gestapo registered 42,562 Jews over fifteen years of age, that is to say, counting the children, about 52,000, in other words about 60 per cent of those who had been domiciled there before the war. This meant that around 40,000 Jews had found refuge outside Belgium, principally in France. But according to the statistics of the Belgian Ministry of Health, 25,280 Jews were deported from the General Baron Dossin de Saint Georges barracks in Malines, better known as the Dossin barracks, while 5,803 others were deported from Drancy, and 24 from various prisons in France.

In June 1940, circumstances forced a number of Jews from different parts of Belgium to rise up against the Germans.

Albert Wolf from Liège, a printer by trade, had long been known for his anti-Nazi activities, not only in Liège and its surroundings, but also on the other side of the frontier, an hour's car or train journey away. Albert Wolf was a prisoner-of-war. He had the presentiment that the day the *Stalag* got its hands on the dossier which the Aix-la-Chapelle Gestapo had in its possession he was a dead man. He knew that his name appeared on the wanted list that was posted up at all the frontiers of the Reich[1], and decided to escape while he was still in a *Frontstalag* near Liège.

Others in Brussels did likewise. A group of Jewish students from the independent University of Brussels joined forces in June, but could only take sporadic action, since most of the Jews had not re-entered the country: but were either wandering along the French highways or confined to the 'rest camps', more like internment camps, situated in the region of Saint Cyprien, Gurs and Vernet.

In the autumn of 1940, a mutual aid organisation, *Solidarité juive*, already in operation before the war, resumed its activities in Brussels, Antwerp and other large urban centres. Its members were mainly Eastern European Communists, most of them from Poland and Romania, but quite a large number from Bessarabia.

The great majority — more than 90 per cent — of the Jewish population in Belgium on the eve and the aftermath of the German Occupation, were not of Belgian nationality. There were several reasons for this: one was the strong surge of immigration into Belgium in the twenties, which was followed by a second wave after Hitler came to power. These immigrants and refugees were, of course, people of modest means, and many were extremely poor. In 1938, for example, when war appeared imminent, the number of non-Belgian Jews to enrol as volunteers, to be mobilised if the need arose, reached 8,321. Of these only nine owned a car. Moreover, Belgian naturalisation laws were much stricter than elsewhere, much more so than in France, for instance.

Nevertheless, the situation of the Jews in Belgium during the summer and autumn of 1940 seemed relatively normal. The inhabitants drifted back; business started up again. Apart from a slight uneasiness in the air due to the presence of the Germans, all seemed well[2].

The various Jewish charity organizations, the Zionist organisations, and the cultural organisations, carried on their activities as best they could, in spite of the absence of a large part of their members and many of their leaders.

The publication on 28 October of a 'Statute concerning anti-Jewish measures' took many people by surprise. This enactment, and those that succeeded it, followed the usual lines. It began by defining the Jews, forbidding those who had left Belgium to re-enter the country. It demanded the registration of individual Jews and Jewish firms and restricted the rights of Jews to sell their possessions. Non-Jewish administrators were appointed to Jewish firms; Jewish concerns were obliged to display trilingual posters specifying their Jewish character; Jewish holders of stocks and shares and bonds were obliged to deposit them, and so on. A special clause ordered the confiscation of radio sets belonging to Jews.

The situation changed again on 22 June 1941 with the German attack on the USSR, and a great many important Communists and Communist sympathisers were arrested. Jewish Communists were arrested for their politics.

Meanwhile, Professor L. Flam's attempts to organise armed Resistance groups among his students and followers at Antwerp proved a failure, and others who followed his example fared no better. It was not the intervention of the Gestapo that caused this setback but disagreement between the Jewish leaders. Certain Zionist leaders regarded Flam's ideas as particularly audacious, some going as far as to accuse him of provocation; but it was obviously too soon to take action.

However, other militant Communist Jews from Borinage and even more from Charleroi participated directly or indirectly in the great strike at Liège and Borinage in May 1941. The Broder couple, Makowski, Katz and several other militant Communist Jews began to show their mettle, especially the Broders, modest travelling tradespeople who peddled their wares round the fairs and markets. Having suffered anti-Semitism in their native Poland they nursed few illusions even during what could be called the euphoric period when the directives of the Sixth Army still applied.

Nevertheless, it is elsewhere that we must look for illustrations of the individuality — and the successes — of the Jewish Resistance in Belgium.

One of its most striking features was in a way its Jewishness, or rather its Jewish motivation. And this is not a question of vain repetitiveness.

Belgium was the only country of the West to have formed a Resistance movement or rather a committee of Jewish Resistance fighters who, despite the fact that they belonged to every possible political and anti-military discipline, or to none at all, felt the absolute need to group themselves together in close-knit union and oppose the threat of Nazism. Drawn from every conceivable background and from all corners of the earth, they succeeded in setting up an efficient relief network for the Jews and for most others who called for their aid.

The setting up of this network did not mean that they renounced their political and religious convictions, nor did it quench a perfectly natural desire to share these with their fellow combatants, especially with those of not-too-firmly-fixed convictions; and despite the tight compartmentalisation imposed by clandestinity, they managed to co-ordinate their action with other Resistance duties, such as the mission which in their eyes was most urgent: that of saving the men, women and especially the children, condemned to death simply for being Jews.

Among the militants of this *Comité de Défense des Juifs* was Abouch Werber, one of the leaders of the Zionist Socialist movement, the left-wing *Poalei-Sion*, which between the two wars was firmly entrenched to the extreme left of Zionism. In Belgium, its militants co-operated closely with the Belgian Communist Party and when the elections came round voted, and encouraged others to vote, Communist. Since the signing of the Germano-Soviet pact the adhesion of the two groups had slackened, but personal links had not been altogether severed.

Between the end of 1941 and the beginning of 1942, Werber realised that the situation of the Jews was rapidly deteriorating and once more got in touch with the Communists, Jewish and non-Jewish, his idea being that the Jews should link themselves with the Resistance while acting on their own behalf. In order to do this they would need the support of the Belgian Resistance movement and to Werber it seemed natural to enlist the aid of his former political allies.

The Communists to whom Werber put his case listened attentively but gave no immediate answer. They did not forget him, and some time later he received a visit from Ghert Jospa, who up to then he had only known by repute for his long-standing political activities.

This young engineer, Bessarabian by birth, had only been in Belgium ten years or so but he had gone a long way in that period, and as a Communist had taken a very active part in the Spanish Civil War.

When the enactment of 28 October 1940 came into force Jospa did not register as a Jew, which to him seemed an extremely dangerous thing to do: as an experienced militant Communist, he knew that any measures imposed by the Germans only served to further their own interests; nor did he wish to give the German police the slightest clue as to his whereabouts. His wife, of course, followed his example, as did the welfare worker Ida Sterno and Roger Van Praag, who was just over thirty-four years of age when he gave up his post with the Belgian broadcasting service to dedicate himself to the Resistance.

Maurice Bolle, a Dutchman, was brought up in an environment deeply attached to the Jewish religion and Jewish traditions, but did not share these convictions to the same extent. He had sized up the destructive plans of the Nazis long before the war and had taken action against them by means of articles in the press and the circulation of propaganda leaflets. As a well-known industrialist Bolle was obliged to register himself as a Jew, but this did not prevent him and his friends from establishing an escape channel from Holland to France and Spain, across Belgian territory, reserved at the outset for Dutch military purposes, but later used to dispatch a large number of Jewish refugees and military allies. Fifty years old in 1940, Bolle was one of the oldest of the Jewish Resistance fighters in Belgium.

His close companion and aide was a younger man, Benjamin (Benno) Nykerk who took up Resistance activities on a large scale in 1941, on his thirty-fifth birthday.

Maurice Heiber, a business man from Galicia, also aged thirty-five, had spent his formative years in Britain and Vienna. He had entered business at a very early age and managed to conciliate his commercial activities with a deep interest in literature. The birth of Nazism followed by the Spanish Civil War had a considerable effect on him, and he flung himself into various relief actions in aid of the German refugees and of republican Spain though he did not join any particular welfare or political group, Jewish or Belgian.

Some of the Resistance fighters had ideological Zionist tendencies. Among these were Abouch Werber, Menachem Konkowski, known under the *nom de guerre* of Molière, Izgour, Lewkowicz, and Domb. Others such as Edouard Rotkel, Hungarian by birth but educated in Vienna, held strong Jewish religious convictions.

These men and women formed part of the *Comité de Défense des Juifs* when it was formed in 1942, people of cultural backgrounds, origins, and ideals who, in all probability would never have had occasion to work closely together but for the war and the Resistance movement, but who did so most successfully.

Of all the Jewish Resistance organisations the CDJ had the most remarkable record of success, though a large number of its members were lost at the hands of the enemy, or during deportation; many simply disappeared without trace. Even so the losses did not exceed a quarter of the total number of militants, while out of the 52,000 or so Jews actually living in Belgium in 1941, only about half escaped deportation. Once again resistance had paid off even where the personal security of the fighters was concerned.

The *Comité de Défense des Juifs* was dependent on the *Front de l'Indépendance*, which organisation, one of the principal bodies of the Belgian Resistance, officially came into being as a structured formation around September 1941. Its way had been carefully prepared.

The Belgian *Front de l'Indépendance* was similar in many respects to the *Front national français*. The Communist Party played a very important part in it, although it certainly did not have nearly so much influence as its French counterpart had in the *Front national*. The Belgian Communist Party was far smaller than the French one; and again many prominent non-Communists — Liberals, Socialists and Catholics — joined the Belgian organisation and held leading positions within it.

The journalist Fernand Demany was leader of the Belgian *Front*. A nondescript individual, he had been appointed to the post for this very reason[3].

The first meetings with a view to creating the *Front* were held as early as March 1941. The Communist Party was involved from the beginning and in May published a lengthy resolution entitled *Pour l'indépendance du pays*. A local group,

Front wallon, sprang up in Liège and by its very composition foreshadowed the *Front de l'Indépendance.* It united the Communist Party as such, the *Comité de vigilance des intellectuels antifascistes,* where the Communists played a preponderant role, the free *Wallons,* the so-called anglophiles, and others. This *Front wallon* gave its backing to the strikes of Liège and Borinage in May 1941.

Ghert Jospa was one of the founder members of the *Front de l'Indépendance.* A powerfully built six-footer, strong as a bull, he had a dream which he put forthwith to the leading members of the FI—Demany, Bolland, and Marteaux, a doctor, and a Socialist turned Communist. Jospa maintained that as the Belgian Jews were singled out for a special type of persecution, they ought to provide their own defence measures, and that in order to encourage as many Jews as possible to join the Resistance movement more flexible methods were required, better adapted to the situation.

Jewish individuality, which even today is at the roots of innumerable problems in Communist movements all over the world and in the USSR most of all, created difficulties for the Belgian movement as well. As far back as 1900 Lenin had taken the lead in a very heated dispute with the Jewish Socialist Party, *Bund.* In 1913, Joseph Stalin, then a mere militant Bolshevik on a local level, wrote a pamphlet devoted to Marxist and national affairs which was no more nor less than an analysis of the Jewish problem. The four characteristics by which Stalin defined a nation were selected in such a way as to leave the Jews bereft of any national characteristic whatsoever. These were the ownership of territory, a common language, culture and economic life. If even one of these characteristics was lacking in a group then, according to the individual cases, it become a people, a nationality, a national group etc. On this basis the Jews did not constitute a nation, and anyone insisting that they did was labelled a bourgeois nationalist. This thesis paved the way for Stalin to lump together Jewish Social Democrats, religious Jews and Zionists, etc.

Communist parties all over the world, with the possible exception of Asia, were faced with the same problem, since the Jews had played an important part in all of them from the start. The proportion of Jewish Communist Party members was — and remains — markedly higher than the percentage of Jews in the population of each country. And this does not apply to Europe alone, but to the Near East, North Africa — one need only recall the number of Jews in Communist parties and organisations in Morocco, Algeria, Tunisia, Egypt, Iraq, etc. — and even in Latin America. One of the three organisations that grouped together to form the Cuban Communist Party in the twenties was a Jewish youth movement, of Eastern European origin.

It was no easy task, but in the end Jospa managed to convince his comrades of the need to create an individual Jewish organisation, and Emile Hambresin, the non-Communist leader of the coalition against anti-Semitism in Belgium, gave his support to the scheme.

The next move was to gain the co-operation of Jews other than the *Solidarité juive* whose participation was assured, and here the biggest problem was how to win over the non-Communist and even the anti-Communist Jews.

At the end of 1941, having first assured himself of the co-operation of Professor Perelman, Jospa began putting out feelers in Jewish circles.

Chaim Perelman was a particularly brilliant young man, professor of philosophy at the independent University of Brussels. Although Polish born he was already at twenty-eight, one of the most promising academics there. The statute of 28 October 1940 had brought him his share of problems. Some of his colleagues hoped that he would resign gracefully 'so as not to create a fuss', but he could see no reason for doing so. In the end, the problem was 'solved': while not guaranteeing that his lectures would take place, Perelman continued to draw his salary, and this im- mediately proved a very valuable contribution to the cause, and remained so up to the Liberation; while Perelman's wife, Fela, another brilliant academic, spent freely to finance the founding of a primary school for Jewish children whom the Germans had driven from the public schools.

The professor, his wife and his sister were Zionist militants in the fullest sense of the word. Perelman's intellectual standing won him unanimous respect not only among the Jews, but also in non-Jewish circles: an exceptional situation in any country outside Belgium.

Jospa, Hambresin and Professor Perelman met for the first time in the latter's home in Uccle, south of Brussels, where Perelman was impressed by the sincerity of the two men and agreed to join them, and with his co-operation assured, it was possible to go ahead.

NOTES

1. He was to get personal proof of this in 1957 when he went on a business trip to Cologne and was refused entry into the German Federal Republic. The Bonn authorities had forgotten to strike his name off the list of undesirables . . .

2. In the special directions (*Sonderbestimmungen*) of the German Sixth Army, prepared with typical German meticulousness seventy-two days before the invasion of Western Europe, we read under section II (*Behaviour towards the population*), paragraph *d*: 'Refrain from bringing up the *racial question* (underlined in the text), for this could convey the impression that our intention is to annex the country. The mere fact that an inhabitant of the country is Jewish must not be used as a pretext for applying special measures in his case'. Appendix I of these special directives is devoted to the general orders for Army Group B (General von

Bock) describing how the German soldiers should conduct themselves in the ter-ritories to be occupied. It is expressly ordered in point 8 of this directive: 'Do not interfere with the Jews in occupied territory (*Juden im besetzen Gebiet sind unbehelligt zu lassen*).'

3. Later Demany joined the Communist Party, but he left it again around 1950.

CHAPTER 17

REVERSAL OF A JUDENRAT

THE period of the constitution of the *Comité de défense des Juifs* was a particularly difficult and dangerous one for Belgian Judaism. The Germans had decided to set up a *Judenrat*, a strictly official organisation of which every Jew in the country automatically became a member. This *Judenrat*, known as the *Association des Juifs de Belgique* (AJB), was set up by the Germans to ensure that the anti-Jewish measures they introduced were carried out. They chose an organisation of this type to enforce these measures, rather than relying on the Belgian authorities, whom they rightly suspected of wishing to sabotage them.

Faithful to their tactics, the Germans tried to find illustrious Jews to place at the head of the AJB, but since there were very few of these left in the country they were obliged to fall back on a second choice; people whose only claim to notability was that they were extremely rich. Several leading Resistance fighters also managed to get appointed, hoping to use their official duties in the organisation as a front for their anti-German activities.

The Germans made a point of including some of their own Jewish henchmen in the AJB: not obviously, the sort of Jew who was openly disposed to play the part of assassin to his own kith and kin. There were a few of these around, but very few: less than ten, in fact, worked directly for the Gestapo outside the AJB; and the henchmen employed in the AJB were Jews who obeyed German orders to the letter in the hope of saving their own skins.

The affair of the yellow stars, for which a decree was passed on 27 May 1942, gives a very clear idea of the sort of role the AJB was expected to play.

There were however, some unforeseen cases of non-co-operation: the burgomasters of the urban centre of Brussels, for example, unanimously refused to distribute the yellow stars, and the burgomasters of Uccle, Saint Gilles and Brussels, Herinckx, Diederich and Cools did not hesitate for a moment to present themselves in delegation at the *Oberfeldkommandant* on 5 June 1942, in support of their colleagues, adding that they were ready to face the consequences of their action, whatever these might be.

This firm stand by the burgomasters was preceded by an urgent call paid by Professor Perelman and his wife on Jean-Marie Herinckx, burgomaster of their district in Uccle, when they informed him in detail of the legal implications of the measure imposed by the Germans. Herinckx took the initiative in the proceedings, and on 30 July he was dismissed. The Germans already nursed a few other grievances against him. On one occasion they had ordered him to warn the population against writing pro-British slogans on walls. The burgomaster saw to it that enormous bills to this effect were pasted up on the walls of the parish, but the warning was embellished by inscriptions such as 'V' and *VIVE LA RAF* in enormous block letters that completely dominated the rest of the bill.

To by-pass the non-cooperation of Belgian authorities and the unenthusiastic response of the military administration, the Gestapo decided to resort to the AJB, which consequently received the order to distribute the stars, and obeyed.

At the same time preparations were in full swing for the deportation of the Belgian Jews, and on 11 June, a meeting in Eichmann's office settled how many Jews would be in the first deportations to leave Western territories: 10,000 from Belgium, 15,000 from Holland, and 100,000 from France[1].

In Belgium, the operation took place in two stages: the first in June, when several thousand young Jews were sent to do hard labour in the northern coastal zones and the Pas-de-Calais; the second on 4 August, when the first trainload of deportees was dispatched from the Dossin barracks to Auschwitz. There were 1,000 Jews in this batch: 525 men, 395 women and 80 children under sixteen years of age[2].

At the request of the Gestapo, the AJB had drawn up an appeal to the Belgian Jews asking them to follow Gestapo instructions and proceed to the Dossin barracks in Malines, where they would be 'given work'. The Association made themselves personally responsible for the distribution of these 'summonses', hiring a number of young people for the purpose and dispatching them to deliver these invitations to death.

The Belgian Resistance movement, and the Jewish Resistance fighters, in particular, did their utmost to dissuade the Jews from answering the summonses. They organised a vast propaganda campaign, mostly door to door, but it was not nearly so successful as they had hoped. The call was aimed primarily at the young people and it was set forth very clearly what would happen to their families if by chance they did not respond to the request; and no one knew at this point what lay in store for those who obeyed.

By the summer of 1942, however, people were beginning to suspect that something was not quite as it should be, and that the time had come to take action.

Four Jewish partisans were responsible for the first violent reaction. Two rigged themselves out in Gestapo uniforms, while the other two armed themselves with bottles of petrol. At about four o'clock in the afternoon of 31 July the four forced their way into the headquarters of the AJB in the Boulevard du Midi, and while the pseudo police officers assembled everybody in one office, the others set fire to the registration cards and lists of the Belgian Jews. All four managed to slip away without incident.

This was a serious setback to the Germans, who had made every effort to ensure that the Jews were deported speedily and with the minimum of fuss; but it came too late for those Jews who had already answered the summons and five more train-loads, 4,992 Jews in all, left in August; five more in September (5,793 persons); and six in October (4,940 persons). Then winter called a halt — while the battle of Stalingrad gave the Reich other ideas of how the rolling stock might be used.

Meanwhile, the Jewish Resistance movement had brought off a master stroke which was to seriously disrupt the plans of the Gestapo.

On 6 August 1942 one of the leaders of the AJB, whom we shall call X., was officially instructed by the Gestapo to take charge of the 'Jewish Labour' section. In other words this man was assigned the task of seeing that the deportations ran smoothly and above all that a sufficient number of Jews was available for each departure. Since the Jews were dispatched by trainloads of 1,000 per week, X. undertook to supply a weekly turnover of that number.

We do not know what induced X. to accept this responsibility. Perhaps he was completely ignorant of the fate that awaited the deportees, and really believed he was 'setting the Jews to work' for he took great pains to dissuade the Gestapo from deporting the sick, the old, and any unaccompanied children. For obvious reasons the Gestapo often acceded to the demands of X.

So where, thanks to the efforts of X., 5,992 Jews were deported in August 1942, again thanks to the efforts of X. an unknown number were exempt from deportation. The balance hung very much to the other side.

X. disappeared at 6.30 p.m. on 29 August 1942. He was enjoying a stroll with his wife when a young man approached him and asked him if he was X. Satisfied, it seems, with the response, the young man drew a revolver and shot X. at point-blank range. He then ran and hid himself in a friend's home where, it appears, he was seized with a fit of remorse. This young Jew had just joined the Resistance movement. He himself was shot a few months later.

After the murder of X., the local committees of the AJB vanished into thin air. From then on the Jews refused to pin their faith on the promises of the Gestapo, even though some Jews agreed to stand surety for them.

The death of X., the destruction of the files, and the growing distrust of the Jews, who no longer rushed headlong into the lion's mouth, spurred the Gestapo to make itself responsible for arresting them. A German observer, Herr von Bargen, delegate of the Ministry of Foreign Affairs of the Reich attached to the German Military Governor in Brussels, cabled on 24 September to his chief, Ribbentrop:

'. . . the Jews, for the most part, presented themselves (voluntarily) for work when summoned to do so, but later the police had recourse to raids and individual arrests as a large number of Jews ignored the requisition orders. Many of them . . . left their homes and tried to seek refuge with the Belgian Aryans. These efforts were supported by a considerable number of Belgian people. Other problems arose out of the fact that a great many Jews were in possession of false Belgian identity cards[3] . . .'

The AJB in the Belgian capital had not the same difficulties to cope with as the provincial AJB, for four-fifths of the Belgian Jews were already gathered together there[4]: over 30,000 at the end of September 1942, the other 10,000 or so having already taken the road to Auschwitz. Also, the presence of a number of institutions which the Nazis had placed under the control of the AJB prevented those members who would have liked to sabotage the Council from doing so. These institutions consisted of a number of orphanages and old people's homes which had been created long before the AJB came into being. In theory, at least, they were respected by the Gestapo, reputedly due to a promise made by Hitler, but perhaps also because the German military administration had to provide itself with an alibi in face of Belgian public opinion. These charitable organisations were nevertheless under strict Gestapo surveillance, while they undertook to send there any abandoned Jewish children they found: children whose parents had been deported or who had been separated from their families for quite different reasons.

In fact, the institutions were virtually prisons, which could just as easily become traps should the occasion arise, so that the Jews in charge of the children's homes and old people's homes found themselves faced with a cruel alternative: if they kept on these homes they ran the risk of one day seeing all the inmates deported, as happened in both Holland and Occupied France; if they closed them down, sending the inmates into hiding and going into hiding themselves, they condemned a number of children and old folk to deportation whenever the Gestapo stopped giving them preferential treatment.

Maurice Heiber, already mentioned, was in charge of the 'children's' section of the AJB and, at the end of 1940, agreed to be responsible for one of the orphanages. In the summer of 1942 he received a telephone call from Emile Hambresin and the two men met. Heiber did not know his companion, but Hambresin seemed to know quite a lot about Heiber's position and activities in the AJB and proposed that he should join the *Front de l'Indépendance*, mentioning at the same time that there was a special political section within the organisation for the protection of the Jewish people, the *Comité de Défense des Juifs*.

Thus the CDJ secured a position at the very heart of the AJB on the eve of the large-scale deportations and rapidly acquired others, not so much at executive level, but among the ordinary staff and welfare workers: in other words among those who had no direct contact with the Germans and who had nothing to do with power politics. For the overriding logic of the AJB and, for that matter, of all *Judenräte* insisted on the 'ruling strategic policy' being always and necessarily one in the Jewish spirit, aimed at cutting the losses; while as far as the Germans were concerned, it was a matter of applying what they called 'salami tactics'. Those Jews who allowed themselves to be drawn into the inhuman logic of the *Judenrat* were induced to sacrifice more and more of their fellows in the illusory hope of saving a few — the number of which, naturally, grew smaller and smaller. The Germans on the other hand, simply helped themselves almost without lifting a finger. The difficulty from their point of view was to get their 'enemies' to yield just once. The first time was the most difficult; the second a little less so; and so on. The Jewish Resistance fighters in Belgium knew that the only solution lay in repudiating the logic of the *Judenrat*, and launched a two-pronged attack against it.

They forged their own tool, the *Comité de Défense des Juifs*; and they neutralised the *Judenrat* by assassinating X. From then on — and this was their goal — the members of the AJB were as much afraid of the Resistance movement as they were of the Gestapo. The two fears cancelled each other out and some members felt that, as it were, their Jewish heart had begun beating again[5]. Nazi terrorism now had much less effect and sometimes none at all.

NOTES

1. Nevertheless, in a note sent on 22 June to Franz Rademacher, specialist in Jewish problems at the Ministry of Foreign Affairs of the Reich, Eichmann quotes different figures: a total of 100,000 Jews for the three countries, that is 50,000 from France, 40,000 from The Netherlands, and (still) 10,000 from Belgium.

2. The Belgian Ministry of Public Health, which was responsible for the deportees, notes that out of this number six men and one woman returned.

3. We must point out that the diplomatic career of Herr von Bargen was by no means over after the liberation of Belgian territory. He was appointed to the Ministry of Affairs in Bonn. There were protests, but these affected Herr von Bargen's *cursus honorum* as little as they had affected Dr. Hans Globke's. At this moment both these gentlemen are enjoying what they both consider a well-merited retirement, and it is an exceedingly comfortable one.

4. Antwerp had had more Jews than any other Belgian city before the war, but there were very few left, and these lived in hiding. The reason was that the Gestapo was more active there than in Brussels and had also managed to enlist the support of a local Fascist group. In 1941 a decree expelled a large part of the Antwerp Jews to the province of Limbourg. Some were later able to return to the city, but the majority took good care not to, especially as the local Fascist elements had desecrated the city's synagogue.

5. After the war, thanks to the processes of auto-suggestion, these men were even convinced that they alone, or almost so, saved everybody. They still believe so and are upset to discover that this opinion is not always shared.

CHAPTER 18

THE RESCUE OF THE JEWISH PEOPLE

THERE was no single supreme leader at the head of the *Comité de Défense des Juifs*; several men shared the responsibilities. Those of the Communist Ghert Jospa, for instance, were divided between maintaining liaisons between the CDJ and the *Front de l'Indépendance*, which he did until his arrest in June 1943, and heading the Communist Jews. There was no question of his being a chief, however; he was simply a *primus inter pares* who exerted a strong enough personal influence to disarm even the Zionist militants of the CBJ, anti-Communists *par excellence*, who trusted him implicitly.

Chaim Perelman, another type altogether, also held a high place in the general esteem, but unlike Jospa, whose responsibilities in the FI activities were on a national scale, and who consequently could not devote his energies to the CDJ alone, Perelman's activities from the summer of 1942 were confined to the Jewish sector. More than once he had to act as a sort of one-man band. Heiber, Bolle, Werber, Van Praag, and later, Ferdman and Orbach were the other leaders of the CDJ.

Its principal branches of activity were: press and propaganda, both clandestine; finance; false papers; the rescue of children and adults.

Clearly the first three branches of activity were all destined to culminate in the fourth, for the security of the children and adults depended first of all on persuading the Jews to reject passivity, to stop blindly obeying German commands, in whatever devious way they might be transmitted. Then a minimal amount of money and the most essential false papers had to be made available. Only when these three conditions had been met could the wheels be set in motion for a rescue operation.

The best form of propaganda was obviously by word of mouth, and this was practised on a large scale from the instant the AJB began distributing summonses to Malines. This CDJ propaganda campaign, urging the Jews not to obey the call occasionally took unexpected forms. Fela Perelman, for instance, one day received a farewell visit from a friend who was about to depart for Malines. When the visitor remained deaf to all her warnings Fela locked her up for several days — just long enough for her to come to her senses. The fact that she is alive today is due to this 'sequestration'.

Shortly afterwards a series of clandestine newspapers saw the light of day. There was the French *Le Flambeau*, which Jospa helped to publish up to his arrest, then Flam, assisted by Perelman, published the Dutch paper *De Vrije Gedachte* ('Free Thought'). This paper, of which ten editions or so appeared, had the good fortune to have several non-Jewish notabilities among its contributors, one of them the future Socialist senator Molter. There were also two newspapers in the Yiddish language, *Unser Wort* ('Our Word'), of Zionist leanings, the left-wing *Poalei Sion*, and *Unser Kampf* ('Our Combat') veering more towards Communism.

The first of these Yiddish newspapers, with which the name of Abouch Werber is associated, was issued more or less regularly once a month during the whole period of the German Occupation. *Le Flambeau*, of which only a few editions survive, was usually duplicated, although thanks to the efforts of Albert Wolf, one issue of it was printed at Liège. Wolf printed a whole series of clandestine newspapers in the course of the war, such as *La Meuse*, organ of the FI in the area around Liège, and various publications for the Communist Party and Belgian Soviet *Amitiés*. He was also responsible for typographical work of another sort: false papers and ration cards, for instance.

It would hardly be fair to conclude this short list without mentioning a quite unexpected tribute paid to the efficiency of the CDJ propaganda activities by Herr von Bargen, whom we have already met. In a report devoted to the development of anti-Jewish action, *The Jews in Belgium*, directed to his ministry, he says:

'First of all, a "work order" was delivered through the medium of the Jewish Association to those Jews selected for deportation. However, since immediately afterwards the work order was ignored because of rumours concerning the massacre of the Jews and so on, the Jews were rounded up by means of a series of raids and individual arrests.'

To convince the Jews of the truth of the 'rumours concerning the massacre of the Jews' took a great deal of time, trouble and effort on the part of the CDJ, who, before it could even begin to convince others had first to ascertain the facts for itself.

Leopold Flam did glean some information about the Eastern European Jews in Antwerp, where he learned of the mass executions perpetrated in occupied Soviet territory. There were other rumours circulating but no positive facts.

In October 1942, Jospa contacted a young non-Jewish sociologist, Victor Martin, like himself a member of the *Front de l'Indépendance*, and entrusted him with a particularly dangerous mission. It involved paying a visit to Germany, and exploring Silesia and Upper Silesia, in order to see at first hand what the fate of the deported Belgian Jews really was. The name of Auschwitz was already on people's lips; some had even received postcards raving about the almost idyllic conditions that existed there.

Martin was just the right person for the job; before the war he had been to

Germany to make a sociological survey on the distribution of labour, and had visited the universities of Münster and Cologne. When he applied to one of the many 'cultural centres' opened by the Germans he was well received and given all the necessary documents immediately and without question. He departed for Cologne, where he got in touch with his former professor and colleagues, among them the sociologist Leopold von Wiese, and set to work on his research. Then on the pretext of requiring to analyse a question more deeply, he applied for and received, still without difficulty, a letter of recommendation to a well-known sociologist in the university of Breslau.

Breslau being the chief town of Silesia, Martin was right on the doorstep of Upper Silesia, and after a few meetings intended primarily to strengthen the scientific pretext for his trip, set off one morning by train for the town of Sosnowiec, a former Polish town which had been annexed to Germany in 1939 and still boasted a large Jewish population, since the liquidation of the Jews of Sosnowiec and of its twin town of Bedzin were not to take place until the summer of 1943. Jospa had given Martin letters of introduction to a couple of Jewish families there. Sosnowiec was only a few miles from Auschwitz, but the only definite information Martin obtained was that the old people, the children, the sick and, generally speaking, those unfit for work were sent there and disappeared without trace.

Pushing his investigations further, Martin paid a visit to the neighbouring town of Katowice and got talking to a group of French workers employed in the *Buna* synthetic rubber factories of Auschwitz-Monowitz. They invited him to visit them in their hutments just outside the camp of Auschwitz. There Martin saw and heard many things then unknown in Western Europe, but about which today we have more than ample information.

Martin set off on his return journey to Brussels, but was not able to proceed beyond Breslau where the *Sicherheitspolizei* was waiting for him. They had had wind of his trip to Auschwitz and had attributed it to an attempt at industrial espionage. He was placed under guard for fifteen days at Breslau, then transferred to Katowice, where an investigator, a specialist in the field of industrial espionage, interrogated him; but the scientific blind which Martin had provided himself with proved effective and a few weeks later, without any charge having been brought against him, he was released. He was not altogether free. His passport was taken from him and he was transferred to a camp of voluntary workers, where he might have spent the rest of the war had he not caught the train for Aix-la-Chapelle as soon as he got his first wage packet into his hands. It was a reckless move, for he had no longer any identity papers and there were frequent checkpoints, but luck was on his side and he reached Malmédy another town annexed to the Reich, without mishap. Since he was familiar with the region, he had no difficulty in crossing the 'new' Germano-Belgian frontier and reaching Brussels, and shortly afterwards the leaders of the CDJ were listening attentively to his report.

Martin continued his invaluable work in the Resistance as regional chief of the FI at Charleroi until he was arrested by the Germans. They did not connect the Auschwitz industrial spy with the Resistance leader of Charleroi and happily Martin survived the war. The salient points of his report were passed on to London and put to full use by the propaganda section of the CDJ.

The vital financial section of the CDJ had two complementary tasks: to find money, and to spend it. The first was difficult, but less dangerous than the second, although it cost one treasurer of the CDJ his life. Naturally the money-collecting operations covered a smaller area on the whole than those of distribution.

For a long time, the national CDJ was far too poor to give support to the regional budgets, and the local sections had to get along as best they could by their own means, usually by making insistent applications to wealthy Jews. Collections, and the market in false papers also brought in a little money, but all in all it did not amount to very much.

On a national scale, the treasurer of the CDJ, Benno Nykerk, managed secretly to obtain quite large sums of money from certain Jews as well as generous loans from some Belgian banks, and some municipal corporations, that of Brussels, for example, released money from their strike funds and donated them to Jewish workers who were forced to live in hiding. The welfare services of the city of Brussels helped, too, by paying the board and lodging of the large number of children in hiding. Even the Ministry of Finance, under cover of the AJB and thanks to friends within it, transferred a credit to the CDJ, originally destined for Jewish refugees in Germany, which had been entered into the budget of the year 1940 but had never been utilised; but all this was no longer sufficient to meet the needs of what now amounted to thousands, if not tens of thousands, of Jews, and Nykerk decided to take a trip to Switzerland and solicit funds from foreign Jewish institutions, in particular from the *American Joint Distribution Committee*. He was, in effect, handed letters of credit in the form of microfilms, against which the Belgian banks released substantial sums. Nykerk paid a further visit to Switzerland. His trips were also linked with the activities of the *Dutch-Paris* section of the Dutch Resistance movement.

On 20 March 1944 he was arrested in Paris and deported under the false identity of Bernard Smits, Dutch Calvinist. He eventually disappeared at Neuengamme.

The disappearance of Nykerk, who was very well known in financial circles and was a surety in himself, posed very serious problems. His place had been taken even before his arrest by Roger Van Praag, for Nykerk had already been picked out by the Gestapo for his Resistance activities. Van Praag took over the duties of treasurer provisionally during the summer and autumn of 1943 until his arrest in the spring of 1944 when Jacques Pels was appointed treasurer and was able to carry on until the Liberation.

At the beginning of 1944 the CDJ received a share of Belgian funds parachuted into Great Britain and a special committee was set up to keep an eye on these operations, which were wide open to abuse, though in fact, there were only very minor incidents. This committee consisted of the treasurer of the CDJ and two others: Madamoiselle Y. Nèvejean, head of the National Children's Society, and David Ferdman, later known as the Jewish James Bond.

David Ferdman was, and still is, a dyed-in-the-wool Communist. He was a first-class businessman who refused to let the war interfere with his activities even though, as a Jew, normal business channels were closed to him.

His responsibilities increased in 1943 following the successive downfalls of Heiber, Jospa and Van Praag, and Perelman's passing into total clandestinity. At one period responsibility for the entire children's Section of the CDJ rested on him alone.

When Ferdman was told by 'well-intentioned informers' that the Rexists were planning to kill him, instead of going into hiding, he discovered the name of his potential assassin and contacted him. He was thus able to satisfy himself that the information relayed to him was true, and the ideological convictions of this sinister individual quickly crumbled at the sight of money.

Ferdman did not stop there but kept up this valuable contact and was able to warn prominent Belgians suspected of belonging to the Resistance of intended attempts on their lives. At this time, there was a wave of counter-terrorist actions launched by Belgian Fascist organisations, which may or may not have had the backing of the Germans, and Ferdman was able to save a number of marked men: lawyers, magistrates, former and future ministers. With one exception these people took him at his word, left their homes and went into hiding. The one who disregarded him was shot.

But these were only means to an end. The object was to save the lives of as many Jews as possible, who had to be helped to find a place and to be fed and supported behind the backs of the Germans and their accomplices.

But first the children's rescue operations had to be separated from those of their parents: the children must be taken away from their parents. To have kept the families together would have increased the risks a hundredfold. Thanks to a willing chain of helpers, it was a relatively simple matter to find shelter for the children among non-Jewish children, in schools, children's homes, in convents and in private homes; it was the adults who were the problem.

All sorts of institutions threw open their doors to the Jewish children. They were hidden in Catholic and Protestant children's homes; healthy children were hospitalised in schools for blind and tubercular children, others in institutions patronised by the most illustrious names in Belgian society. The protection of Elizabeth, the Queen Mother, Cardinal Van Roey and others, including the exiled government, ensured a place for a child in any convent. Yvonne Jospa, wife of Ghert Jospa, and as staunch a Communist as her husband, had no difficulty whatsoever in obtaining from Mothers Superior and titled women all the places she needed for 'her' children — and she needed a great many.

Other children were housed with private individuals, either as foster children that is to say for a consideration — and the CDJ was in a position to pay a modest but adequate sum for their keep — or gratis.

With very few exceptions, the entire children's rescue operation passed off without any serious losses; but there was the tragedy of a private school in Brussels run by the Ovart family where seventeen Jewish children and 13 adults were hidden. A Gestapo raid ended in the arrest and deportation not only of the Jews, but also of Monsieur and Madame Ovart. Not one was ever seen again.

One episode, a tragi-comic one ended happily, but only by the merest chance. One afternoon at the end of May 1943 the Gestapo swooped down on the Convent of the Little Sisters of the Poor, Avenue Clemenceau, in Brussels-Anderlecht, where an informer had been at work. True enough, the French nuns had about fifteen Jewish children hidden there whom the Gestapo had no difficulty in ferreting out. Since the police officers had not sufficient means of transport for them all, the Mother Superior, Marie-Amélie, persuaded them to leave the children in the convent overnight so that they could be fed and dressed and generally prepared for their departure. The Gestapo withdrew after warning the nuns what would happen to them if, by some unlucky chance, the children were not there next day. Immediately the Germans had departed the Mother Superior got in touch with a priest, who sent urgently for Maurice Heiber.

Heiber swiftly assembled all the available members of the CDJ at a council of war, where it was decided to appeal for help to the Belgian Partisan Army. Heiber himself was urged to go into hiding, but refused.

That same evening, a group of armed and masked Partisans broke into the convent, 'to the great relief of us all' the Mother Superior was to write later. While some of them cut the telephone wires others swept up the children and took them to a place of safety. The squad withdrew after having bound and gagged some of the nuns.

Maurice Heiber's hopes that the Gestapo would be satisfied if they got him, and even his wife, without pushing their investigations further were to be fulfilled.

By dawn on 21 May, German police officers were already knocking at his door. He must answer a few questions at the police station, they said: a mere formality. After cooling his heels for a time in the cellar at Gestapo Headquarters, Heiber was taken before an SS Officer who accused him of aiding and abetting the surprise attack carried out on the convent, for only a Jew could have the effrontery to perpetrate such a sacrilegious act as to attempt an armed raid on a convent of nuns. Obviously the Gestapo raid the evening before constituted neither effrontery nor sacrilege.

The Heibers were transfered to the Dossin barracks in Malines where they promptly joined the local Resistance group. They managed to establish contacts with the outside world, and within a few months, thanks to influence in high places, they were released. Incidentally, the Gestapo officer who knew the Heibers best and hated them most, the SS Hauptsturmführer Kurt Asche, had been 'transferred'. He was discovered to have filched Jewish belongings, not for the Gestapo, but for his own personal benefit. This cost him a discharge from the SS and sixteen months in prison.

The children's homes of the AJB of which there were seven, although they were not all in operation at the same time, housed an average of 500—600 youngsters, the number of 'illegal youngsters' being in the region of 3,000, and were subject to regular visits by the Gestapo. There was only one instance where the Gestapo seized all the children, around sixty of them: in the Wesembeek-Opham Home. The teachers and their assistants were invited by the Gestapo to clear out but refused to abandon the children and insisted on accompanying them to Malines. As these chaperons were not all Jewish, the Gestapo was embarrassed. Moreover, Heiber got wind of events as the raid was taking place and was able to contact the FI and raise the alarm. Before proceedings could be instituted the Gestapo backed down and within a few days the children left Malines and returned to Wesembeek. The personal intervention of Ferdman and the sum of money he disbursed had a great deal to do with the unexpected turn of events; this was obviously only a postponement. There was absolutely no guarantee that these Jewish children's homes would not suffer the same fate as the Belgian ones raided on the night of 3—4 September, 1943. Something had to be done to save the children; and the matter became more and more urgent during the summer of 1944 at the approach of Liberation. The German front in Normandy was only just holding out when the Gestapo evacuated Breendonck and the Belgian prisons. At this stage the drama of the Convent of the Little Sisters of the Poor was re-enacted, but on a much larger scale, in all the children's homes of the AJB, as well as in the old people's homes. Armed squads evacuated the children despite the protests of certain leaders of the AJB who feared for their own lives but were not prevented from taking credit for the operation when the war was over. As for the old people, they flatly refused to budge.

The adults were Perelman's responsibility up to 1944, when he was obliged to pass the flag to J. Orbach and go into hiding. In the course of his duties Perelman had to call on the assistance of a band of volunteers who visited people who knew and trusted them. The Jewish tradition of a wide circle of god-parents and god-children proved to be a blessing, for most people could find someone to turn to.

The distribution of the false papers and ration coupons followed the same pattern.

Even the armed Resistance, led by the CDJ, was closely linked with the rescue of the Jewish population. Its most vital missions were to get rid of informers in the pay of the Gestapo and to rescue the Jews threatened with deportation.

Helping Jewish prisoners to escape was particularly difficult, and the affair of the twentieth deportation train was without precedent in the history of the Resistance.

Circumstances were relatively favourable. In the first place, the SS were so sure of themselves that they informed the Malines prisoners in advance of the date of their departure to the east, so that the local Resistance organisation knew exactly when the train would be leaving and who would be on it, while there was a strong Resistance group in the camp itself which was in almost constant communication with the outside world.

At last word came that the SS were planning to dispatch a large number of Resistance fighters in this their twentieth deportation train which was due to leave Malines on the evening of 18 April 1943.

There had been quite a few successful escape attempts from the Malines deportation trains, which consisted of nothing more nor less than a string of cattle trucks — rather the worse for wear from continual use. All that was required was a few enterprising men among the occupants of the truck, or even just one, provided he had a tool of some sort, and it was the easiest thing in the world technically speaking, to open one of the sides, or to make a hole in the floor. The difficulties were much greater on a psychological level, for no one in his senses relished jumping from a moving train, especially when that train was heavily guarded and added to this was fear of the reprisals that could involve the escapee's parents, friends, and comrades.

The sixteenth deportation train alone, which left Malines on the evening of 31 October 1942, had at least thirty escapes to its credit.

M. H. Dumonceau de Bergendael, of the Belgian Ministry of Health, made a close study of escape attempts. Here is the summary of an investigation he carried out on 9 January, 1957 at 42 Rue Bonne-Femme, Grivegnée:

'Subject: Lewenkron Albert, born in Nancy on 14 June 1924.

'On the request of the "Documentation" department I questioned the above named in order to find out how he had fared during the 1940—1945 war.

'M. Lewenkron . . . told me that he had been arrested at Liège on 1 August 1942 and sent to the Dammes-Camier camp in the north of France.

'On 31 October 1942 he was taken to Malines so that he could be put on the 17th deportation train bound for Auschwitz. On 1 November 1942 he was fortunately able to jump from the train near Tirlemont and return to Liège by the normal service.

'He was given shelter in the bishop's palace at Liège and hid there for several months. Then he joined the ranks of the Army of Liberation. Finally, he took to

F

the maquis at Wandre and at Beyne-Heusay and was there until the liberation.

'He was recognised as an armed Resistance fighter on 13 December 1948.'

The twentieth deportation train was the subject of a series of subversive actions, among the most successful of which was that of a group of Polish Jews affiliated to the National Belgian Movement (MNB), under the leadership of Roger D. Katz, which smuggled tools to one of their members imprisoned in the Dossin barracks in Malines enabling him to force the locks of his truck and jump from the train on the outskirts of Tirlemont. All the other occupants of the truck appear to have followed his example.

One of the survivors, Jacques Cyngiser, writes:

> We were made to get into the goods wagons, fifty of us to each wagon. Immediately afterwards an officer marched along the train ordering everybody to descend and line up in front of the wagons. That done, young Henri Dobrzynski, looking like death, and livid with bruises, was paraded in front of us, flanked by Gestapo officers, who were closely regarding both him and the assembled prisoners to see if they could detect the least sign of recognition or complicity. In this way the Gestapo hoped to betray any armed Partisans in our ranks. The young man conducted himself admirably; nothing was discovered. Shortly afterwards (on 11 July 1943) he was shot by the Nazis. He was just seventeen years old.
>
> Once Henri and his torturers had disappeared the order was given to get back into the trucks. I had a small saw in my possession and once the train had started we attacked the sliding door of the truck. We managed to saw a hole in it and through this we were able to reach the bolt which locked the door from outside. The train was not going too fast and outside it was pitch dark. Monik jumped first, followed by the others. When it came to my turn I jumped, too, and fell flat on my face on the gravel of the railway ballasting. Once the train had gone, I was rejoined by P. and Monik. We took to our heels across the fields and were eventually given shelter by an old woman, who patched up my split lip with a makeshift dressing.
>
> Next morning, at dawn, we made our way to the station at Louvain. The stationmaster saw us approaching and signalled to us to slip onto the platform through his office. That same day, we were in Brussels . . . We learned afterwards that the train had been attacked just ten minutes after we had jumped off it.

The CDJ had also been informed of the impending departure of the convoy and Bolle, Heiber, Perelman, Nykerk and Jospa devised a plan whereby somehow or other they would manage to stop the train in open country, then, while one formation created a diversion to distract the attention of the German guards, the others would open the doors of the trucks, give the occupants some money and send them on their way.

Jospa naturally contacted the armed Partisans for military support and according to Raoul Balligand, then leader of the Brussels sector, two groups, one from Brussels and the other from Louvain, were accordingly dispatched, consisting of about thirty men, including a number of Jews.

Bolle also got in touch with the *Groupement général de Sabotage*, better known as Group G, which finally agreed to supply four militants.

The action was in fact carried out by not more than two or three Partisans, who survived the action itself but were arrested afterwards. None survived. Among them was a Jewish doctor Georges (Joura) Livchitz, who had 20,000 Belgian francs in small notes to be distributed among the escapees.

Shortly after the escape of Jacques Cyngiser's group, a member of Group G took up a position on the side of the railway track running between Louvain and Tirlemont, swinging a red lantern. The deportation train stopped dead and Livchitz and his comrades dashed towards the trucks and forced open the doors, Livchitz even having time to distribute a few of the precious notes.

The Germans showed no immediate reaction, since it was a slow train which stopped frequently, usually to give troop trains priority, but suddenly the guards realised that something was wrong and opened fire, killing at least twenty-nine Jews.

Nevertheless, over 200 got right away, while about 100 were recaptured.

The attack on the twentieth convoy took place on the night of 19—20 April 1943. At the same time, about twelve hundred miles further east, the survivors in the Warsaw Ghetto were living out their first night after the battle. They had been grappling with the Germans since 6 o'clock that morning and were still undefeated.

At the two extremes of Europe, in Warsaw and in Tirlemont, armed Jews, tragically few and tragically ill-armed, made a brave stand against the enemy.

In Warsaw the battle was about to recommence. In Belgium, another action was imminent, the purpose of which was to save eight gravely wounded men transported to the Tirlemont hospital by the Germans, for whereas the uninjured or only slightly injured Jews had been sent to Malines, to be duly deported from there, these eight men had been deposited at the nearest hospital.

The CDJ leaders, Van Praag, Bolle and Jospa, had hastily devised a plan to save them.

They succeeded in moving one of the wounded from the hospital in a Red Cross ambulance commandeered by the armed Partisans. The driver, Yvonne Limagne, willingly took part, only asking to be bound and gagged at the end of the operation, but a grave error of judgement was committed in the choice of the second ambulance driver, who was to pick up the rest of the wounded men. The Resistance men had approached a certain Romanovitch, a White Russian who professed to be a Resistance fighter but was in reality a Gestapo agent, and instead of taking the wounded to the assembly point, dumped them at the Dossin barracks.

The same Romanovitch, who was a contact of Georges Livchitz, also of Russian origin, contributed to his arrest on 14 May. Livchitz escaped next day shooting one of the guards, but was arrested a second time on 2 June and condemned to death. In the report of his trial we read:

> He was the leader of a band of terrorists and participated in the attack (sic) of 19 April 1943 against the Jewish deportation train. The accused admits that after his flight he shot at the soldiers who pursued him. He was arrested for the first time on 14 May 1943 but succeeded in seizing the revolver of a guard in the cellar of a local police office. He grievously wounded the guard and managed to escape. On his subsequent arrest he was sent to Breendonck.

It was at Breendonck on 17 February 1944 that Georges Livchitz fell before a German firing squad, five other Belgian Resistance fighters falling beside him.

The same fate befell Jean Burgers, national head of Group G, executed at Buchenwald on 6 September 1944.

Other leaders of the CDJ who fell into the hands of the Germans spent varying periods at Breendonck until, in the summer of 1944, they too were dispatched to Buchenwald. Among these were Jospa, Roger Van Praag, M. Bolle and L. Flam. On their arrival at the camp they followed the instructions of the interior Resistance movement and promptly became Gentiles. As their dossiers had still not caught up with them, what with the speed of events and the hasty withdrawal of the *Wehrmacht*, the strategy succeeded. Some became Catholic, others Protestant, Jospa turned into a Free Thinker. All four owed their lives to the clandestine Resistance movement.

They were more fortunate than a relative and namesake of Roger Van Praag, nicknamed Maxime, leader of the national Resistance movement *Zero*. Arrested by the SD in July 1944 and later deported he was never seen again.

When an *Amicale* of CDJ veterans was set up twenty years later, all the survivors, Jews, Catholics, Protestants, Communists, Socialists, Zionists, believers and non-believers, eagerly grasped the opportunity to get together once more.

A military formation on the fringe of the CDJ, which included a large number of militants of that organisation, was the 9th Brigade of the National Belgian Movement, called *Molière* after the *nom de guerre* of its leader, Menachem Konkowski. It was almost entirely composed of Jews. This brigade had planned to go into action as the Allies were nearing the Belgian frontier, but was unable to keep up with their rapid advance into Belgium.

The Communist Jews, whether or not they were members of *Solidarité juive*, supplied the Resistance movement with a great number of armed combatants. 'Commander Albin' (Jakob Gutfränt) led an all-Jewish detachment, while another well-known Resistance fighter, known as 'Commander Marcel' and 'Oscar', among other names, became deputy leader of sector 0.4, the Brussels sector of the Belgian Partisan Army, and commander of his own 'special squad'. His duties included the disagreeable task of doing away with Gestapo informers.

René de Lathouwer was very closely linked to the Communists on an operational level although he never became one himself. His Resistance activities covered a wide field, and were particularly well known in Nemur.

The contrast between the wartime situation in Belgium and Holland, countries so similar in other respects, was particularly striking.

In Holland the first wave of German repression in some way anaesthetised the Jewish community's biological instinct of self-preservation. The Germans put all the early organised resistance out of action practically at one fell swoop. After this shock, the resilience of the community was broken and it made no attempt whatsoever to get rid of the bogus protectors the enemy had imposed on it.

In Belgium, on the other hand, the Jewish instinct of self-preservation did come into play. From the outset the Jews were determined to survive, mothers even severing themselves from their children to this end; and the Jewish Resistance had near perfect conditions for its activities.

The Belgian Resistance, like the Dutch Resistance, was on the whole on the side of the Jews. There were two reasons for the final results being much more bloody in one country than in the other: German repression was much more brutal in Holland than it was in Belgium, and the Jews in the two countries reacted in different ways.[1]

NOTES

1. There were less than 3,000 Jews in Luxembourg and half of these dispersed immediately after the German invasion. Others were expelled to France where they managed to take refuge, or went into hiding. A thousand were deported and never came back. The Luxemburger Jews who joined in the struggle against Hitler did so outside Luxembourg, mostly in Belgium and France, but also in the British-based Belgian army.

CHAPTER 19

THE DUTCH DRAMA

THE historian M. Presser, in his analysis of the events that led to the destruction of Judaism in The Netherlands, dedicates only a very short passage
of his monumental work, *Ondergang*,[1] to the Jewish Resistance there. According
to him, the number of Jews engaged in the struggle against Hitler was proportionately as high as the number of non-Jews. This seems a rather rash assertion when
out of 140,000 Jews living in The Netherlands more than 110,000 were deported
and more than 105,000 died; and this in a country where the great majority of the
population was anti-Nazi and pro-Jewish. Holland was the only German-occupied
European country to organise a general strike as a protest against German anti-
Jewish measures.

Of all the German-occupied countries of the West, Holland was the only one
that had a German civil service administration over and above the German occupation authorities. The fanatical anti-Semites to be found in all grades of this civil
service considered the deportation of the Jews to be one of their first tasks.

At the head of this administration was the *Reichskommissar* Dr. Artur Seyss-
Inquart, former Viennese lawyer and ex-clandestine leader of the Austrian Nazis,
who by the grace of Hitler became Prime Minister of Austria a month before the
Anschluss. Just after the occupation of the country, in October 1939, Seyss-
Inquart began exercising his talents in Poland. He played a prominent part in the
sinister *AB-Aktion*. The choice of code names gives an idea of the Nazis' warped
sense of humour which was concerned with arresting and destroying as many Polish
intellectuals and scholars as possible, hoping by so doing to reduce the Polish people
to the rank of slaves in perpetuity.

Seyss-Inquart arrived in The Netherlands immediately on the surrender of
its army, his entourage consisting of a number of prominent individuals who, like
himself, had taken part in the Nazi movement in Austria; notably the *SS.
Brigadeführer*, later *Obergruppenführer*, Hans Albin Rauter. He received the
double title of *Höhere SS-und Polizeiführer*, that is to say Commander-in-Chief
of the SS and of the German police in The Netherlands, and Superintendent of the
security police in The Netherlands. He was responsible in his first capacity to
Himmler; in his second to Seyss-Inquart. This divided allegiance did not cause
friction between the two men, in fact in the field of anti-Jewish activities it was
actually welcomed. The Austrian Nazis, by which we mean the true Nazis and not

the opportunists — and there were some of those, for the percentage of Nazi Party members was decidedly higher in Austria than it was in Germany itself — were fiercely anti-Semitic. Like Adolf Hitler their anti-Semitism was their principal reason for becoming Nazis: a contingency that was not so frequent in Germany.

Under these conditions, the delegates to The Netherlands in Adolf Eichmann's service IVB played a more unobtrusive role than elsewhere, for the good reason that the leaders of the German administration in the country instigated the most radical anti-Semitic measures themselves[2]. Thus men like Zoepff or Aus den Fünten, both Eichmann delegates on different levels, had no need whatsoever to stimulate anti-Jewish action in The Netherlands as their counterparts had to do in Paris, Brussels and elsewhere. Theirs was an active role in the truest sense of the word and it must be admitted that they played it to perfection, Dutch Judaism being the one to suffer, in round figures and in percentage, the worst blood-letting of the whole of Western Europe.

The first anti-Jewish measures, very swiftly introduced in The Netherlands, followed the usual pattern. By August 1940 registration of the Jewish population was already under way. This was stricter in Holland than anywhere else, since not only were the Jews as such registered, — in conformity with the Nuremberg laws — but also the half-Jews, and even the non-Jewish partners in marriage. There followed in quick succession measures forbidding the employment of Jewish government officials and teachers; the exclusion of Jewish students from universities; and finally the so-called 'economic Aryanisation' measures.

Since the Dutch Jews were deeply rooted in the country, these measures seemed perfectly odious to the population. Besides, it was difficult to swallow the role played by the indigenous Nazis who were few in number but all the more arrogant for this, knowing perfectly well that with the protection of the Germans no one could harm them. On 26 January 1941, according to a report of the *Höhere SS-und Polizeiführer* Rauter, the Catholic Church of The Netherlands published a pastoral letter forbidding the administration of the Holy Sacrament to the Dutch Nazis. The Calvinist Church was equally severe in the expression of its disapproval; and even Nazis who belonged to neither of these churches were conscious of the nation's condemnation: The Netherlands wanted nothing to do with them.

The black-uniformed WA, an organization similar to the SS, decided to put up a show of strength to the population of Amsterdam and on 19 February 1941, they marched through the streets of the town, molesting the Jews as they went along as well as any Dutch who showed hostility towards them. Although the WA were protected by the Germans the people fought back vigorously and a number of them were wounded, some fatally.

That evening the WA made a raid on the Jewish quarter of the town where an unwelcome surprise awaited them in the form of groups calling themselves *Knok-ploegen* (combat groups). These groups were composed mostly, though not entirely, of Jews, and reflected both the number of inhabitants in the quarter — which was rather poor, with a large, predominantly Jewish, population of labourers and artisans — and its political colour. In the opinion of the country's historian B.A. Sijes, who participated in the movement and is one of the few survivors, the major-ity of the members of the various *Knokploegen* were Socialists, with a small num-ber of Communists and a few Zionists.

Surprised by the violence of the reaction, the WA beat a hasty retreat, but two days later forty or so of them tried to march through the streets of the Jewish quarter. They had cause to regret their action for the *Knokploegen* and the population in general responded by attacking them. About twenty members of the WA were wounded, one fatally, three seriously.

The Germans retaliated swiftly, but they did so in stages. First of all, a number of important Jews were summoned by the Occupation authorities and called upon to set up immediately a Jewish Council (*Joodse Raad in Dutch*). They were also instructed to see that all weapons belonging to the Jews were confiscated. The *Joodse Raad* published an announcement to this effect and its leaders, under German surveillance, called a public meeting in front of the headquarters of the Council and reiterated the command.

Thus the very first manifestation of the *Joodse Raad* assumed the character of demobilisation and capitulation. Since it was a body created by the Germans for their own ends, the fact is scarcely surprising, but the proclamation further reflected the profound conviction of the members of the Council that German reprisals would be terrible.

At the same time as they set up the *Joodse Raad*, the Germans isolated the Jewish quarter, and Amsterdam's peculiar topography made their task easy: all they had to do was to erect a few bridges, and barricade a few existing ones. To all intents and purposes the Jewish quarter in the centre of Amsterdam became a ghetto.

On 15 February 1941, three days after these incidents, unexpected opposition flared up in quite a different sector of the city: about 2,200 Amsterdam shipyard workers went on strike against the German decision to send some of their number to work in Germany. Taken completely off guard by the strike the Occupation authorities shelved their plans.

The atmosphere in the city was becoming more and more tense and the Dutch Nazis did nothing to ease the situation, but continued to make public demonstrations, this time in the residential quarters in the southern part of the city where the most prosperous Jews lived. Their reaction was as vigorous as that of their less fortunate counterparts, for they too had set up defence groups. At the same time the Dutch people began to take action, by attacking the homes of prominent Nazis.

Faced with the repeated defeats of their protégés the German police tried direct intervention. It knew that defence groups had been set up among the Jews and was well aware of the probable consequences. Late on Wednesday evening, 19 February, the police made a surprise raid on the ice-cream café *Coco* where it expected to find one of the headquarters of the *Knokploegen*.

When an SD patrol burst in about 10 o'clock the proprietors, Ernst Cahn and Alfred Kohn, Jewish refugees from Germany, and their customers, retaliated against this Nazi scum. A more or less exact account of the event is found in the bill of indictment brought against the proprietors of *Coco* and six other persons: three Jews and three non-Jews. As far as weapons were concerned the *Knokploegen* gathered in *Coco's* had a syphon containing sulphur dioxide, or according to another version, ammonia, used in the manufacture of ice-cream and therefore perfectly legitimate. It might serve as a useful weapon against hooligans, but certainly not against a heavily armed police force. There were also some truncheons, an axe and a pistol. The lights in the café had been put out and this unequal battle was fought in the dark.

The eight accused were tried by the special tribunal of the *SS-und Polizei* on 27 February. Ernst Cahn was condemned to death and shot four days later, the first inhabitant of The Netherlands to be executed for a Resistance action.

It goes without saying that the Germans did not stop there. Several hundred young Jews were arrested and deported to Buchenwald and Mauthausen. At the end of the war only one deportee remained out of the 660 or so arrested: approximately 430 in February and 230 in June 1941.

The Germans had achieved their purpose: the backbone of the Jewish Resistance was snapped, and although many Dutch Jews participated in the Resistance, there was no longer any organised group capable of openly fighting the enemy, and in Holland itself, the Resistance dwindled practically to nothing.

Some Zionist groups, mostly German refugees living on farms, were preparing to emigrate to Palestine. These groups comprised 820 persons in all, the majority of them in hiding, many of whom had already succeeded in leaving The Netherlands but got no further than France. Others established escape channels from Holland to Switzerland, Spain and Britain.

One Resistance group in which the Jews played a prominent part was that led by the young neurologist Geerit Kastein, or Kastijn, veteran of the Spanish war and dedicated militant Communist. His group is credited with the execution of the Dutch general Seyffardt, one of the few senior Dutch officers to side with the Germans, even to the extent of recruiting a Netherlands Legion of Volunteers similar to the FLV.

Kastein himself shot Seyffardt, and assassinated other collaborators, among them the former minister Posthuma, before he fell into the hands of the SS for the simple reason that he was linked with the victims of the notorious *Englandspiel*.[3] Fearing that he might be forced to talk, he committed suicide to avoid arrest. His death did not prevent the group from being disbanded and the members were tried on 30 September 1943 by a police court martial, under the auspices of the *Höhere SS-und Polizeiführer Nordwest*, Hans Albin Rauter. The 29 accused were condemned to death and executed on the following day, among them the 20-year-old Jewish medical student Leo Frida, and the 24-year-old half-Jewish student of biology Hans Katan. There were also three brothers, Louis, Gideon, and Jean-Karel Boissevain, of Huguenot descent, whose ages ranged from 20 to 23 years.

The trial and the execution of the 19 combatants were the subject of an article in the German-controlled Dutch press, where Frida was blamed for aiding and abetting the execution of General Seyffardt and for having personally assassinated several collaborators. He was also accused of laying bombs on railway tracks and causing serious damage and of having placed incendiary bombs in cinemas in The Hague reserved for the *Wehrmacht*.

Another group of Jewish Resistance fighters in The Netherlands, executed for acts hostile to the German police in the German *Bekanntmachungen* included Benedictus Hijmans, shot on 20 January 1943; Eliezer Pachter, shot on 29 June 1943, for possessing and using firearms; Jacob Boekman, a Jew, and his companion Adrianus Nas — both 'Communist terrorists'; and Max Werkendam, also a 'Communist terrorist', shot on 22 April 1944.

Three more Jews were shot on 29 February 1944, having been condemned to death the day before by the same SS tribunal that had tried and passed the sentence of death on Frida and his companion. They were 47-year-old Leo Fischer, 33-year-old Karel Keizer, and 25-year-old Heinz Löwenstein. These 'full-blooded Jews of ill-repute', according to the evidence at the trial, were members of the non-Communist group *Oranje Vrijbuiters* (Orange guerrillas). Like all groups that bore the name of Orange they must have been Resistance fighters claiming to be defenders of The Netherlands dynasty.

The trial resulted in 20 death sentences followed by 20 executions. The 20 accused were blamed for the assassination of a considerable number of collaborators and for the theft of a great many ration books. There was an element of hysteria in the charges, such as the claim that the theft of the ration books reduced the population of The Netherlands to starvation level.

The German Jew Gerhard Badriaan fell in action on 30 June 1944. With his German education, it was easy for him to disguise himself in SS uniform and rescue Jewish and non-Jewish Resistance fighters who had fallen into enemy hands.

One type of action the Jewish Resistance fighters of the Netherlands shied away from was a direct attack on the *Joodse Raad*. Unlike the Jews in Belgium and, in a different way, those in the South of France, they never attempted to sabotage, or even to interfere with, the deadly activities of this Council which were so opposed to their own. Council members actively discouraged those who consulted them from resisting; and it was the most elementary form of individual resistance that they opposed: their instructions were on no account to assume a false identity and certainly never to ignore a summons from the Gestapo.

On 20 June 1943 the hour of destiny rang for the *Joodse Raad*: a large proportion of its members were arrested. The delegate of the German Ministry of Foreign Affairs in The Netherlands, Bene, points out in his report of 25 June 1943 that the Jews found it difficult to conceal their delight at finally seeing members of the Jewish Council arrested and deported in their turn.

NOTES

1. See Bibliography.
2. Seyss-Inquart was sentenced to death at Nuremberg for his activities in The Netherlands and was duly hanged.
3. The *Englandspiel* was a standard example of radio piracy. Having forced Dutch radio stations of the British SOE to broadcast under its control, Major Giskes of *Abwehr III F* managed to link up with London. This enabled him to capture most of the paratroopers dropped by the British on Holland and to identify the Resistance fighters who were in liaison with them.

CHAPTER 20

THE DANES TO THE RESCUE

HOLLAND was the only country in Western Europe where Jewish losses could be compared with those of Eastern Europe. In Belgium, half the Jews were saved by the action of the Jewish Resistance movement. In Denmark the situation was altogether different.

None of the 8,000 or so Danish Jews took a direct part in the Resistance, but the mere fact of their being there encouraged the Danish Resistance movement to organise itself and, in the end, to save almost all of them.

The German occupation of Denmark on 6 April 1940, was peaceful on the whole. King Christian IX continued to occupy his palace and the Danish government remained in office, and for over three years, up to the summer of 1943, the Germans scarcely interfered in Danish home affairs. There were even free elections in which the Danish pro-Nazi party only obtained 1 per cent of the votes. No anti-Semite measures were imposed, even upon Jewish refugees of German origin. On the other hand, there was little Jewish resistance.

In the summer of 1943 there were manifestations of open resistance in the form of strikes and sabotage. The measures the Germans took to repress them were as nothing compared to those taken in Russia or even in France; but the Danish government disappeared and at the same time the decision was taken to deport all the Jews.

In an unprecedented response, General von Hannecken, military commander of Denmark, let it be known that he could put no soldiers at the disposal of the German police in their campaign to arrest the Jews, nor could the Danish police take part. The Gestapo were so outraged that the affair reached the ears of Marshal Keitel and Hitler himself, with the result that Hannacken received categorical orders, which he chose to ignore.

Seeing that things were not going as smoothly as he would have wished, Eichmann sent his assistant Gunther to Copenhagen and also provided a ship for the transportation of the arrested Jews, but at this stage certain German officials stationed in Copenhagen and in professional contact with important Danish people deliberately allowed the news of the imminent deportation of the Jews to leak out, and Jewish leaders in Denmark were informed by their Danish friends of the fate that lay in store for them, though it took the Danes much time and effort to convince them of the truth.

King Christian IX, of whom it is said that he threatened the Germans that he would hoist the yellow flag himself if it were introduced into Denmark, reacted with extreme courage. Although he had made it a matter of principle to look upon himself as a prisoner in his castle and to have no contact with the Germans, he sent for Dr. Werner Best, *SS-Brigadeführer* and proconsul of Denmark and protested vehemently at the measures to be taken against the Jews that very day.

The Danish Resistance movement, which was still in its early stages, took it upon itself to remove the Jews to a place of safety, and several thousand were secretly transported in small boats to Sweden. The operation was financed not by the Jews, but by the Resistance movement itself, and went off without serious incident. It was the first Resistance action of a great number of Danes and the first time they had found themselves faced with a real challenge.

Eichmann's men only arrested about 500 Jews, mostly old people who had been unable to undertake the journey across the Belt and the Sund. The Danish authorities kept up their protests, urging the Swedish diplomatic service to do likewise, and as a result the Jews deported from Denmark were sent to Theresienstadt. Only one of them was sent from there to Auschwitz, and he went voluntarily so as not to be separated from his sweetheart. All the deportees returned to Denmark after the Liberation, apart from those who died natural deaths — and there was a woman of 102 among these.

Norway was less fortunate. Of the 1,700 Jews there, half were deported to Auschwitz where more than 90 per cent perished. The remainder took refuge in Sweden.

Part Six

The Ghetto Uprisings

CHAPTER 21

THE EASTERN EUROPEAN JEWS

THE greatest concentration of Jews was to be found in Eastern Europe, where they had been for centuries. Up to a thousand years before most of them had lived in the former Tzarist Empire and the Polish section of the Austro-Hungarian and Germanic Empires, but neighbouring zones, such as Romania, and even the areas bordering Poland in the Hungarian part of the double monarchy, Sub-Carpathian Russia, Maramourech, Northern Transylvania, also harboured dense Jewish populations, the most usual form of Jewish settlement then being the 'Jewish village', the *shtettel*. These villages were often entirely Jewish; some had even been founded by Jews, probably the local land-owners. They lived there in almost complete isolation, closely linked with other Jewish communities, near and far, but having little to do with their immediate non-Jewish neighbours — whether these were Polish or Lithuanian Roman Catholics, Graeco-Catholic or Greek Orthodox Ukrainians, or the exclusively Greek Orthodox Romanians.

There was a decided change of attitude in the nineteenth century when the emancipation of the Jews in the various Central and Western European countries, the lure of the United States and other countries as lands of settlement, and the redoubling of anti-Semite violence in Tzarist Russia and Romania, all contributed to the drift of the Jewish population to Western and Central Europe, and to the Americas. At the beginning of the twentieth century the Zionist movement began to attract Jews to Palestine.

The growth of the middle class in all those countries with a large Jewish population resulted in the Jews having difficulty in maintaining the social standing they had previously enjoyed, when they themselves were the middle class among largely agricultural populations.

One thing that remained unchanged far into the twentieth century, and was particularly noticeable just before the Second World War, was that large communities of Jews in Poland, Romania, sub-Carpathian Russia, Lithuania, and to a lesser degree in Eastern Slovakia, continued to live in a closed circle. They went to Jewish primary and secondary schools, and the Jewish lycées, especially the Hebrew-speaking ones, were excellent; Jewish shopkeepers catered for Jews; Jews mixed socially with Jews. Even Jewish intellectuals rarely ventured outside their own milieu.

167

The non-Jews were not wholly responsible for this invisible barrier, even though they might greet any friendly advance with reserve. The Jews themselves distrusted those of their own kind who tried to strike up a relationship with 'the others', and there was always that underlying fear of losing substance. In Western and Central Europe the Jews were largely assimilated, but in Eastern Europe 'assimilation' was a dirty word, as it is today among the Israeli Jews.

Although communications between Jews and non-Jews improved slightly with time, on the eve of the Second World War the majority of them still hardly knew the Gentiles among whom they lived and who knew the Jews even less, neither side feeling any need to communicate.

Accounts written by the Jews of these regions show all too clearly how much alone the Jews were in their hour of need, and alone to the point of not knowing a single Christian to whom they could turn even for advice. More often than not, the Christians who rescued the Jews were complete strangers to them.

Relations between the Poles and the Jews, to cite only one example, bore no comparison to the relations between the French and the Jewish immigrants, the French treating the immigrants as such and making allowances for them, while in Eastern Europe the Jews were anything but immigrants: they were populations who had resided in the same country for centuries in compact masses, jealously guarding their individual national characters. Moreover they spoke a different tongue and practised a different religion. So there resulted a definite barrier, very noticeable in the Jewish quarters of the cities, and in the villages, where there was often a strong Jewish element, or even a Jewish majority. Again, the Jewish people were the 'people of the Book'. In Eastern Europe especially the Jews as a whole were well read and more attached to cultural, literary and spiritual values than the neighbouring peoples whose literature was chronologically-speaking still in its infancy and where illiteracy was the rule rather than the exception.

Progress had been made in that field, too, since the turn of the century, with many Jews producing literary and artistic works in the language of the country of their adoption, but for the great majority of Jews these were exceptions which had nothing to do with Jewish culture[1].

In 1939, there were about three million Jews in Poland. The previous census dates as far back as 1931 and during the next eight years there had been widespread emigration; but the demographic balance being constant, the size of the Jewish population in Poland in 1939 presumably remained more or less static.

Around the beginning of 1938 there were approximately 800,000 Jews in Romania; about a quarter of a million in the Baltic countries; and one to two million in the Soviet territories of the West.

In the non-Socialist countries of the period the Jewish communities were on their guard. They knew perfectly well that their future was far from promising. Driven from their traditional economic positions, the Jews suddenly found themselves with no real prospects and with no way out other than emigration, and this was true of the mass of artisans and tradesmen, as well as the intellectuals and professionals. It was true also of the students who, the moment they entered university, came up against a quota system that was applied more or less throughout Europe, justifiably or not. Anti-Semitism, not to be confused with Nazi anti-Semitism which was a later innovation, was extremely powerful and virulent. For example, the 'doyen' of the Romanian anti-Semites, the university professor A. C. Cuza, was proud to recall that he had given his first anti-Semitic address in the year the Führer Adolf Hitler was born, in 1889. This was true, but anti-Semitism was flourishing in these countries long before Cuza was born.

The natural reaction to this state of affairs was the growth of extremist movements, first of all Communism and Zionism, with their numerous minority groups ranging from an extreme left pro-Communist group to one that sympathised with Mussolini and Italian Fascism, and another profoundly orthodox and clerical.

The Jewish Communists, relatively numerous in these countries, were strongly represented in the Communist movements and parties, which were illegal in Romania, the Baltic States and Poland. Since the regimes of these countries questioned the right of the Jews even to go on living, many saw the Communist solution, involving the total destruction of these regimes and their replacement by a Socialist society, as a solution to the Jewish problem itself.

The large proportion of Jews in Communist movements was not such a good thing for the movements in the long run, since they might give the impression that they were appealing more to national minorities than to any other section of the community; and the fact that the Polish and Romanian Communist Parties had a large Jewish membership did not attract the majority populations, most of whom tended towards anti-Semitism[2].

The Zionist movement, on the other hand, was going through a grave crisis, since it realised that it was not in a position at this stage to solve the Jewish problem. Its advice to Jews that they should emigrate to Palestine could only be taken up by a very small minority, as the mandatory power, Great Britain, strictly limited the influx of Jews into Palestine by insisting on immigration certificates; and hardly one Zionist leader of that period — and these included Doctor Chaim Weizmann, the quasi-permanent president of the Zionist executive — saw any prospect of mass immigration. Up to 1939 the number of immigrants had not exceeded 30,000 per annum which meant that, at best, and limiting emigration to Palestine to the Polish Jews alone, it would have taken a century to absorb them.

Only one Zionist leader, Vladimir Jabotinsky, head of the right-wing Revisionist movement, grasped the true situation, and gave the signal for the evacuation of the

Jews of Eastern Europe. It is interesting to speculate on the final outcome had the other leaders followed Jabotinsky's example; in fact they did not come round to his way of thinking until the war was well advanced[3].

A third policy accepted the fact that the Jews must continue to live in the heart of the larger populations, and tried to turn this situation to account. The Polish Jews could be placed in this category as members of the former *Bund* that had been the subject of the bitter controversy with Lenin around 1902. These Socialist Jews had certainly more affinity with the Polish Socialists than with certain 'bourgeois' Zionists whose solution was quite foreign to them in that it implied 'class collaboration'. As for the Bolshevist 'solution', the fate of their comrades living on Russian soil was sufficient to show how much that was worth.

At the opposite side of the political chess-board, but still in the same category, could be ranged the more or less liberal, more or less democratic, militants who were doing their best to improve Jewish conditions on a legal and juridical level.

While Zionists and non-Zionists sometimes joined forces, the Jewish Communists usually went alone; and only two left-wing Zionist groups had occasion to collaborate with the Communists.

When the Nazis occupied Poland, they discovered that the Jewish sector was fragmented into a great many political movements having only one thing in common besides their Jewishness, and that a history of failure. The Communists, Zionists, bourgeois non-Zionists, the non-Zionist Socialists of *Bund* had all made a mess of things.

At the defeat of France in May—June 1940 there was no question of the vanquished leaders, political or military, re-entering the fight; the Jewish leaders in Occupied Poland, defeated even before the German onslaught, were barred from taking their place at the head of the Resistance, and though the movement certainly recovered, its leaders and officials came into their own elsewhere.

The situation of the Jews varied according to where they happened to live. In conformity with German-Soviet agreements in 1939, Germany occupied only half of Polish territory. The eastern part of the country, where the number of Poles was proportionately very small, especially in the provinces, was incorporated into the USSR. The territory of Vilna, which Poland had seized in 1920, was restored to Lithuania at the end of 1939; but in the summer of 1940, Lithuania and the two other Baltic States, Latvia and Estonia, voted by plebiscite — in the presence of the Red Army — to become part of the USSR. Shortly before this, on 27 June 1940, following a Soviet ultimatum, Romania had restored Bessarabia, former province of the Tzarist Empire, to the Russians, together with the northern part of Bukovina, former territory of the double monarchy.

The situation of the Jews in the USSR up to 1941, the year of the invasion of

Russia, was entirely different from that of their fellows in the neighbouring coun-tries of Eastern Europe. Generally speaking they had made the most of the October Revolution, though some had acceded to the bourgeoisie, or to the professions, or to membership of political parties other than the Communist Party, and these had tended to emigrate. The great majority of Jews, however, had benefited from the abrogation of anti-Jewish measures: the theory of equal rights had actually been put into practice and they were free to settle anywhere they wished — a right which had previously been denied to them. They took full advantage of this pri-vilege and followed the universal practice of Jews in moving from the villages to the towns and, if they could, to the cities, preferably to the capital.

While the courts that conducted their trials in Yiddish were not tolerated for long, the Moscow Jewish Theatre rapidly acquired international renown. Anti-Jewish measures were not introduced until after the war had begun, for although there was a very large number of Jewish victims in the purges of 1936—1938 they were condemned not as Jews but as militants. Subsequently, the Soviet Commun-ists had removed most of the Jews who held leading positions within the Party[4].

The Jewish situation in the Polish territories annexed to the USSR in 1939 was just as contradictory. Following the Soviet occupation, the left-wing and extreme left-wing elements found themselves smartly in the Soviet Communist Party or in one of its peripheral organisations, while a great many intellectuals and pro-fessionals, who were looked upon as pro-Polish, were simply dispatched to the interior of the Soviet Union — the term 'interior' covering Central Asia, Ouzbek-istan, in particular, and the far north. The unexpected effect of this was that those categories classed as dispensable from the Soviet point of view, escaped the consequences of the Nazi invasion, while up to 95 per cent of their fellows left behind in occupied territory were annihilated.

When, at dawn on Friday 1 September 1939, the columns of the *Wehrmacht* crossed the Polish frontiers, they were closely followed by very special units, later to be seen in action in Yugoslavia and the USSR, who always followed in the wake of the proud *Wehrmacht*.

These *Einsatzgruppen*, or task forces, were directly responsible to Himmler in his capacity as *Reichsführer SS* and chief of the German Police, and their actual command was in the hands of Reinhard Heydrich, Head of the Security Police and the SD. The *Einsatzgruppen*, each consisting of not more than a thousand men, were divided into *Einsatzkommandos*.

These armed units operated immediately behind the front lines but were not directly dependent on military command, which had the right to permit or forbid access to the zone, but could not order any specific action. It was a strange arrange-ment, without precedent in the history of the German Army, and German soldiers were envious of these command units, especially those in the front line, who were not answerable to the local military command or to the High Military Command, but only to the Chief of the Gestapo.

Their orders were extremely specialised: to seize all archives and documents in any way connected with the 'ideological enemy', and with enemies of the Reich in general, that is to say the archives of police departments, political parties and organisations, Jewish organisations of every kind, and those of masonic lodges.

All armies of occupation had special services charged with this far from savoury mission. Another branch of the *Einsatzgruppen* activities, the one that conjures up death whenever the historian comes across the most trivial document or the least allusion to these notorious units was, in their own words, 'putting the enemies of the Reich out of harm's way'. More often than not, this meant quite baldly putting them to death, and cases of simple arrest were rare.

The expression 'final solution of the Jewish problem' (*Endlösung der Judenfrage*) does not seem to have been in current use at the time of the conquest of Poland, and it is not known that Hitler had decided to put all the European Jews to death when the time was ripe to strike a hard, swift blow at the Jews.

Before the Polish campaign ended on 21 September 1939, Heydrich was busy collecting around him the leaders of the *Einsatzgruppen* and his principal collaborators, as well as certain officers of more modest rank chosen for their specialist knowledge of Jewish matters. Among these was Adolf Eichmann.

The minutes of the meeting mention Heydrich only by the code letter C, and some of his former collaborators, among them Schellenberg, head of the Department (*Amt*) VI, in charge of foreign espionage, noted this idiosyncrasy of their leader, who liked to be known simply as Chief, or C, thinking in this way to put himself on a level with the big chief of the Intelligence Service with whom he had a love-hate relationship.

The following are C's proposals concerning the Jews:

> The Jewry of the towns shall be gathered together in ghettos under surveillance to facilitate eventual deportation [Abschub]. The most urgent matter is to get rid of the Jews isolated in the country. This must be done within the next three or four weeks. When the country Jews are tradesmen, the Wehrmacht will indicate how many should be left behind to meet the needs of the army. The following skeleton orders have been issued:
> 1.   The Jews — into the towns as quickly as possible;
> 2.   The Jews of the Reich — to Poland;
> 3.   The 30,000 gypsies still resident in the Reich, likewise to Poland;
> 4.   The Jews from the German provinces to be systematically dispatched in goods trains[5].

On the same day, Heydrich sent a written directive to the leaders of the *Einsatz-gruppen*, regarding the Jewish problem in occupied territories:

> *With reference to the meeting which took place this day in Berlin, I again stress the fact that the comprehensive measures (that is to say the final aim) must be kept strictly secret*[6].
>
> *Distinction must be made between:*
>
> *1.   The final goal (which will need more time) and*
>
> *2.   The stages of the realisation of this goal (which will rapidly be put into operation).*
>
> As a preliminary measure, in view of the eventual goal, the first step must be to concentrate the country Jews in the towns[6].
>
> *This measure must be put into force without delay. Distinction must be made:*
>
> *1.   Between the territories of Danzig, Western Prussia, Poznan and Eastern Upper Silesia;*
>
> *2.   And the rest of occupied territory.*
>
> *As far as possible the territory mentioned under 1 must be cleared of the Jews; or, if the worst comes to the worst, only a small number of concentration towns should be set up.*
>
> *In the territories mentioned under 2, there must be as few concentration points* [Konzentrierungspunkte] *as possible to facilitate later measures. Bearing these in mind, arrangements should be made for the concentration points to be in towns situated at a railway junction, or at least served by a railway.*

Heydrich then devoted a long exposition to the Jewish Councils which he calls 'The Council of Elders'[7]:

> *3.   The Jewish Councils will register all Jews in their district according to sex and age groups — a) up to 16 years old; b) above that age — in addition subdividing the latter according to their professional status.*
>
> *4.   The Jewish Councils will be duly informed of the dates and the time-limit for the transfer* [of the country Jews] *and the proposed itinerary. They will be held fully responsible for the departure of the Jews from the country. To justify concentrating the Jews in the towns it can be pointed out that the latter played a prominent part in guerrilla attacks and were guilty of pillaging.*

The directive then went on to enumerate the measures that would come into play in the ghettos so formed (the word 'ghetto' is written in block capitals). These measures — which did in fact come into operation — entailed confining the Jews to the ghetto, the imposition of a curfew, etc.

In retrospect, it is possible to read between the lines and see what was to become only too clear: that this was nothing more or less than a deferred death sentence, but it was not possible at the time to see through 'ruses' as equivocal as the decision to stop the manufacture of kaftans, the customary garb in these regions of traditional Jews.

It does appear that, originally, the dispersal of the Jews was not necessarily intended to be the preliminary to large-scale extermination. Other methods were considered preferable. Even the Gestapo did not envisage exterminating the Jews by technical means.

Much has been written, in Yiddish and Hebrew especially, on the subject of the Jewish Councils. The very name *Judenrat* brings a blush to the cheek of the average Jew, and there is no doubt that in most cases their reputation is well deserved. We must re-examine the *Judenrat* system if we are to understand the problems the Councils had to face in Poland.

The American historian Jacob Robinson[8], himself a Jew, is among those who have displayed the greatest understanding of the *Judenräte* and their members, and he gives a rough indication of how its leaders' minds worked.

In the beginning the majority of them were confident that Nazi Germany would lose the war. They were equally sure that an Allied victory, and only an Allied victory, would save the Jews from Hitler's persecution.

That being so, all that had to be done was to survive until the Allied victory, though it was impossible to count upon all Jews living to see the Liberation.

Once this idea had sunk in, there naturally followed the question: which of them — individual, groups, categories — was it imperative to save come what might, and that decided, how was one to set about it?

The answer to the first question was far from sure since almost without exception, the relatives and friends of the members of the various *Judenräte* were given priority. Then came those who could afford to buy the necessary protection. Then — and this varied from one *Judenrat* to another — it was the turn of the intellectuals, or Rabbis, or children.

The mechanics of survival inevitably became more and more distressing as time went on. In the earlier period, before the deportations to the death camps, the privileged were given the best rations, priority in employment, and living conditions of a rather more bearable standard than the rest, the prosperous Jews buying these benefits for cash. When the Germans requisitioned men for hard labour the poorest members of the community were the first to go, when it was not possible to bribe the Nazis to cancel the requisition.

Once the death march began the situation became more delicate. From now on, the Germans simply got in touch with the *Judenrat* and ordered it to hand over either a given number of Jews conforming to certain norms — age, profession, or the lack of it, etc. — or those belonging to a specific category; or all those living in a given sector. The *Judenrat* had the far from enviable task of drawing up the lists of the condemned. In consenting to do so they sentenced innocent people to death; if they refused, they signed their own death warrant and also risked the lives of the most valuable categories: Rabbis, scholars, young people of promise who would have assured the future of Israel, etc.

Faced with such an uncompromising situation the reaction was more or less what one would expect. There were certainly some top men of the *Judenräte* who did refuse and who asked the Germans to shoot them in place of others. Jacob Robinson mentions a few: Ovsej Itzikson in Baranovichi, other leaders in Mlawa, Stanislawow and Kolomya, but inevitably such cases were the exception. Some, like Adam Czerniakov in Warsaw, committed suicide when they realised where this policy was leading them; and there were a great many who gave up their posts in the Jewish Councils, or were driven out by less scrupulous members, when they realised that they could not help their fellow Jews by holding office there; while their participation in the Councils gave them an unjustified guarantee of security.

The extent to which members of the *Judenräte*, and of the Jewish police were stigmatised can be estimated by the fact that immediately after the war in the Displaced Persons' camps, which at one time housed more than 200,000 Jews, the mere fact of having belonged to one of these institutions was considered as sufficient grounds for suspicion in itself; and those concerned had to give proof of good conduct. A large number of them disappeared without trace and those who remained were in no hurry to make themselves known.

The Jewish police, recruited from within the ghettos and more often than not among unemployed intellectuals and professionals, were subjected to the same harsh treatment and treated with equal or greater suspicion. Certainly a few of the ghetto police behaved correctly towards the Jews, but these were even harder to find than irreproachable *Judenräte*. There was Kovno, Riga and to a lesser extent Bialystok, and that was about all.

It is difficult to see how the Resistance movement was ever set up, let alone how it operated within the ghettos, yet almost every ghetto had its organisation once the inmates accepted the fact that the Germans would end up by killing everybody anyway.

The Resistance operated wherever the Jews were, and as the Jews were not allowed to settle, its operations extended throughout Eastern Europe. It functioned in three stages: first of all in the ghettos; when the destruction of the ghettos began, in the forests, where some Jews took refuge, and where they did what they could to set up autonomous detachments, or to join already existing non-Jewish ones.

The third stage, which has been compared with the inner circle of Dante's *Inferno*, was that of the extermination camps, where the majority of Jews eventually found themselves, and from which a remarkable élite had the amazing good fortune to emerge.

Although the period of the mass deportations to the death camps began at the outbreak of the Germano-Soviet war, mass assassinations did not take place immediately in the camps specially equipped for that purpose. For months and months shooting was the only method of execution; and although later the gas lorries, and the gas chambers were in constant use, the shootings only ended with the end of the Third Reich.

When the Germans invaded the USSR, the *Einsatzgruppen* sprang up again; four in number: A, B, C, D, with the notorious subdivisions: *Einsatzkommando* (operational commando), *Sonderkommando* (special commando) and the secondary subdivisions *Teilkommando* (partial commando).

Each *Einsatzgruppe* numbered just under a thousand men, recruited from the ranks of the Gestapo and the SD, but also including men from the *Waffen-SS* and the *Ordnungspolizei* (regimented constabulary), all of whom were directly or indirectly responsible to the SS. The leaders of the four *Einsatzgruppen* were top level men in the SS hierarchy: Stahlecker (A), an experienced SS man, had been Chief of Police in Vienna. Arthur Nebe leader of Group B, was chief of the Reich Crime Squad, a criminologist of high repute and writer of detective stories, who ended by conspiring against his Führer and was executed on 20 July 1944 after his attempted assassination. Nothing more is known about the chief of the *Einsatzgruppe C*, a person called Rasch. The leader of *Einsatzgruppe D*, Otto Ohlendorf, was a special case. Thirty years old or so at the time, and besides being chief of the service SD-Inland, charged with sounding German public opinion, but not with taking any action inside Germany, he was also professor of political economy, and director general of the Ministry of Economy of the Reich.

The statute of the *Einsatzgruppen* had been drawn up in deliberately vague terms by Hitler in his famous directive number 21 (*Barbarossa*) which foreshadowed the attack on the USSR.

In this directive, dated 13 March 1941, paragraph 2b was written by Hitler himself:

'The *Reichsführer SS* has been asked to undertake special duties for the Führer in the field of operations of the land forces, with a view to preparing the political administration for certain tasks. These arise from the need to put an end to the struggle between two conflicting political systems. The *Reichsführer SS* will operate independently and holds all responsibility for the execution of these tasks. Moreover [*sic*], the executive power entrusted to the commander-in-chief of the land forces and delegated by the latter to his subordinate services will not be questioned. The *Reichsführer SS* will ascertain that [military] operations will not be impeded by the execution of his own tasks.'

What in fact did this tortuous language mean? Simply that the *Einsatzgruppen* subordinate to the *Reichsführer SS* were instructed to seek, arrest and execute on the spot the following persons:

— political commissaries;

— senior-grade officials of the Communist Party and the Soviet Union, including any lower-grade ones who were well-known activists;

— all officials of Komintern;

— all politically active Communists;

— commissaries of the people (Ministers);

— Jews holding office in the Party and in the State;

— All other radical elements (saboteurs, propagandists, guerrillas, agitators, etc.)

The directive continues:

'The main thing, as far as is necessary in the individual cases, is to extract political and economic information vital for future police security measures and for the economic reconstruction of occupied territories.'

The later directive came from Heydrich and was dated 2 July 1942. The written instructions were more detailed than those already given verbally. The Jews, *all* Jews, were to be shot, as indeed they were.

The *SS-Standartenführer* Jäger, chief of *Einsatzkommando* 3 of *Einsatzgruppe A*, dresses the balance of his action in Lithuania on 1 December 1941. He totals up the executions as follows:

A. Jews: 136,421;

B. Communists: 1,064 (including a commissary, an *oberpolitruk*, 5 *politruks*);

C. Partisans: 56;

D. Mentally sick: 653;

E. Poles: 44; Russian prisoners-of-war: 28; gypsies: 5; Armenians: 1.

Total: *138,272*,[9] including 55,556 women, 34,464 children.

The first part of the *Standartenführer* Jäger's report runs to six pages, which record day by day, town by town, person by person, category by category, the death-throes of Lithuanian Judaism. The second part gives an insight into Jäger's personal views, and the moral difficulties he and his men had to face:

I am able to confirm today that the ultimate goal, the solution of the Jewish problem in Lithuania, has been accomplished by the EK 3. There are no longer any Jews in Lithuania with the exception of the Jews working for the Germans [Arbeitsjuden *in the original*] *and their families. Of these, there are approximately 4,500 in Schaulen, 15,000 in Kovno, and 15,000 in Vilna.*

I would have destroyed these Arbeitsjuden, *too, and their families along with them had the civil administration* [the Reichskomissar] *and the* Wehrmacht *not bitterly opposed me and in the end prohibited me from doing so. It is evidently against the law to shoot these Jews and their families.*

Our purpose, to make Lithuania judenfrei *might not have been achieved had it not been for a mobile commando unit of picked men led by the* SS-Obersturmführer *Hamann, who made my aims his own and managed to co-ordinate his work with the Lithuanian guerillas and the competent civilian services.*

The accomplishment of these actions was primarily a question of organisation. Whenever the decision was taken to purge a district of Jews, it was necessary to plan each move meticulously and study the conditions of that particular district. The Jews had to be assembled at one or several points. Taking into account the number of men at our disposal, a place had to be found for the burial pits and these had to be dug. The average distance from the assembly point to the graves was 3 to 4 miles. The Jews were transported to the place of execution in groups of 500, at least one and a half miles apart. The difficulties this entailed in labour and nervous exhaustion can best be illustrated by a random example:

At Rokiskis, 3,208 men had to be transported 3 miles before they could be liquidated. In order to complete this work within twenty-four hours it was necessary to fall back on at least 60 of the 80 Lithuanians at our disposal. They were made available for transport and supervision. Only the smaller number remained here with my men to finish off the work. Lorries were scarce . . . But because no time was wasted, at times it was possible to fit in up to five trips in a single week[10].

The *Einsatzgruppe A*, as a body, also delivered an undated report, probably written at the beginning of 1942, since it indicates that the mass executions had to be suspended, the frozen ground preventing the mass graves from being dug, that officially records the execution of 229,052 Jews, including the 136,421 mentioned by Jäger. *Einsatzgruppe B* had already reported the execution of 45,467 Jews up to 14 November; *Einsatzgruppe C*, 95,000 up to the beginning of December 1941; *Einsatzgruppe D*, 92,000 up to 8 April 1942. There is a personal report from

Himmler to Hitler which accounts for a further 363,211 executions; and this between August and November 1942 in the regions of Bialystok, the Ukraine, and South Russia alone, with the exception, therefore, of Bielorussia.

But these are only recapitulary documents and there are further reports from these *Einsatzgruppen*, for other periods, which mention many executions not included in the above totals. By adding up all the figures we reach a grand total of well over a million Jews executed.[11]

A large part of what had been Poland before 1939 became Soviet territory in the summer of 1941 and it was in those regions that the *Einsatzgruppen* began their massacres. Lvov, Dubna, Pinsk, Baranovitchi and Vilna, were some of the large agglomerations where the Jews were assassinated by the thousands.

The *Einsatzgruppen* succeeded in getting rid of the Jews in the numerous towns and regions of the USSR conquered in the autumn of 1941; but for all their efforts things did not run so smoothly in the former Polish territories, for the simple reason that the *Wehrmacht* had plunged too quickly into the East, and ghettos were set up throughout what had formerly been Eastern Poland, as well as in a number of towns in the Baltic countries: Vilna, Kovno, Shavli in Lithuania, Riga and Labau in Latvia, and less frequently in the USSR itself.

The second wave of violence began in 1942, and the killings were no longer confined to occupied Soviet territories, but extended to the whole of Poland. When it became clear that the on-the-spot executions practised up to then were inadequate against the whole mass of Polish Jews, the Germans fell back upon the installations in the extermination camps.

There were a few 'small' extermination camps, where the Jews were simply shot; Ponary near Vilna, Trostyanets near Minsk, Izbica near Lublin, Kayserswald near Riga, the 9th fort of Kovno, etc. With the exception of Ponary, all these camps dealt not only with the Jews in the neighbourhood, but also with Jewish deportees from the whole of Europe.

The next stage was the setting up of permanent extermination camps equipped with gas-chambers, and these were invariably situated in the relative vicinity of towns with a large Jewish population, which were to supply the first victims. Belzec, for example, near Lvov; Sobibor and Treblinka, linked to Warsaw; Chelmno, near Lodz. There were also mixed camps, with sections for 'ordinary prisoners', who were not always Jews but none the less shared their miserable existence, with sections for extermination equipped with gas-chambers and crematoria. Auschwitz, and Maidanek, near Lublin, were the best equipped. Auschwitz, originally set up to serve Silesia, soon became the extermination camp *par excellence* for Jews deported from the rest of Europe, although the Polish Jews were always in the majority.

The appearance of these extermination camps, immediately after the executions

in the ghettos, gave birth to the idea of fighting the assassins. The battle could be
carried on in the ghettos, in the forests, even in the death camps themselves. And
that is exactly what happened.

NOTES

1. Even in the mouths of Jews who had been resident in Berlin or Vienna for
generations, the word *Ostjude* was not complimentary. They, too, treated the
'Jews of the East' with suspicion, and for a variety of reasons. In common with all
Jews who had been assimilated into Western European countries and had adopted
their habits, they were afraid of being compromised by their presence. These
Eastern Jews, '*Ostjuden*', who dressed differently, lived differently, were willing
to work harder than they did, and who still betrayed a profound and visible
attachment to the faith of their ancestors, reminded them of what they themselves
had been one or two generations earlier. This shameful behaviour — and they were
often the first to feel ashamed — frequently took the form of rational argument.
They declared that they feared an insurrection of anti-Semitism. So their charity
organisations put pressure on the newcomers in two ways. On the one hand they
gave them large subsidies to encourage them to settle elsewhere. On the other hand,
they urged them to assimilate as quickly as possible.
2. The Polish Communist Party had been dissolved by the *Komintern* in 1938,
apparently on Stalin's orders. A number of its leaders were the victims of Soviet
purges.
3. Jabotinsky motivated other policy keynotes which were subsequently adopted by
the Zionist movement. But neither Jabotinsky's group nor succeeding groups,
as he died in 1940, reaped any political benefit. The Israeli party *Herouth* which
took over from Jabotinsky now represents only about a tenth of the electoral body
of Israel. It is situated more to the right and couples a very liberal home policy
with an extremely activist foreign policy, especially towards the Arab States.
4. In the spring of 1939, the Minister of Foreign Affairs, Litvinov, who favoured
a *rapprochement* with Western democratic countries and the SDN, was replaced
by Molotov. No doubt Stalin had decided that at this period such a move might
well lead to war with Germany, a war in which the Western democracies would
play only a passive role. Whether this analysis was true or false, the fact remains
that to follow his own policy, one that involved at least temporarily, close relations
with Nazi Germany, he chose a non-Jewish collaborator.
5. Later we become aware of C's ever-smouldering resentment against the regular
soldiers who prevented him from doing what he wanted: 'There will be no shooting
except in the case of legitimate defence or attempt to escape. All other offences
must be tried by court martial. The courts martial must be inundated with dossiers

to prevent them from dominating the situation. C asks that all trials not terminating in the death sentence be referred to him.' It is heartening to read the last lines of the summary, which show that the morale of the Jews was high. 'Discussions were continued during lunch which all those who had taken part in the conference attended.'

6. Underlined in the original.

7. See also page 13.

8. *And the crooked shall be made straight. A new look at the Eichmann Trial* (New York, 1965).

9. Underlined in the original.

10. One must not get the impression, however, that M. Jäger was utterly bereft of human feelings. On the contrary, he was indignant about the insanitary conditions in the Lithuanian prisons. There were far too many detainees in these prisons whose presence could not be satisfactorily explained. As a man of action, Jäger simply (in his own words) had the most suspect among the suspects shot and let the others go free. Nor did he neglect to address them, or have them addressed, publicly, explaining that unlike the Bolsheviks, the Germans did not shoot its prisoners — or at least not straight away — but were content simply to keep an eye on them. In the last sentence of his report, Jäger declares that this extreme generosity had been so well received by the population that the members of his *Einsatzkommando* had to struggle to free themselves from the embraces of the Lithuanians (sic).

11. These reports are the only existing Nazi documents in which the question of Jewish executions is öpenly discussed. There is no circumlocution whatsoever, though frequently the writers of the reports feel obliged to offer 'justification' for the executions. These 'justifications' range from the danger caused by Jewish Partisans, Jewish agitators, and the black market, to the risk of disease; mentioning in passing the difficulty of feeding the Jews, whom they consequently preferred to shoot.

CHAPTER 22

THE FIRST GHETTO UPRISINGS

THE ghetto populations in the East fluctuated enormously. For instance, soon after Heydrich's directives came into force on 21 September 1939 a number of small ghettos disappeared altogether, their inhabitants being dispatched to larger ghettos or simply done away with, while many others succumbed to the combined effects of the conditions of transport and starvation.

It is estimated that in Warsaw alone, 25 per cent died of hunger or disease before organised extermination had even begun, and in other ghettos the situation was little better. It was reckoned at the beginning of 1942 that even without help from the Germans, the inhabitants of the Warsaw Ghetto would disappear within two or three years as the result of starvation and disease; and when the Nazis launched their extermination campaign it did little more than speed up the process. There was resistance potentiality everywhere in the form of Zionist, Communist and Bundist-type youth movements, which did occasionally become linked with the Resistance movement, *stricto sensu*. All Resistance groups had to surmount enormous obstacles merely to survive, and they were not always successful.

Every ghetto was under the strict surveillance not only of the Gestapo and its auxiliaries, but also of the local police, who worked in close co-operation. Another difficulty in most ghettos was the presence of 'moderate', 'realistic', 'reasonable' elements in the Jewish population; members of the Jewish Councils, and others.

We cannot even excuse these moderate, realistic, reasonable Jews on the grounds that they were *non compos mentis*, or even insane. This was not so. People whose duty it was to advocate armed retaliation would have no part in it. Dr. Ignacy Szyper, the well-known historian of Polish Judaism, is a case in point. One would have thought that a historian would understand the value of taking arms against the oppressor, not only from the point of view of those immediately involved, but for the sake of future generations of Jews. In fact Dr. Szyper, a militant political Zionist of moderate views, opposed the Warsaw Ghetto rising, and, after the revolt was crushed and he was deported to Maidanek, continued to maintain that the armed uprising had been a tragic mistake.

A great many ghettos had to choose where they would fight. Ought they to stay where they were and await the arrival of Germans, only opening fire on them then with any weapons they had managed to lay their hands on in the meantime? Or ought they to send the young men into the forests to set up Partisan formations there, or to join up with those already in existence? Would that not have entailed weakening the ghettos to an unjustifiable extent? Who would be left to face the Germans? Only the women and the children and the old people?

The eventual solution to these problems varied from ghetto to ghetto.

Lachwa, a tiny ghetto of a few hundred families, had only become part of the USSR in September 1939, with the result that, psychologically, the inhabitants still conducted themselves like Polish Jews. They were so isolated that they were unable to obtain weapons from other Jewish centres and when the decisive moment came they armed themselves with bludgeons, kitchen knives, clubs and iron bars.

The Jews, numbering 2,000 or more, represented about a third of the local population. As a community, there was little to choose between this and dozens of others scattered about the Russo-Polish zone. There had been no mystical union of the Jews, but practically all the Zionist youth movements were represented, from *Betar* on the right, to *Hachomer Hatzair* on the extreme left, but as happened in a number of small towns, the petty divergencies that separated the various Zionist movements were insignificant beside the Zionist ideal itself.

The Jews greeted the entry of Soviet troops into Lachwa on 17 September 1939 with indifference; but when Germany attacked the USSR on 22 June, 1941, an icy fear gripped the community. The Red Army withdrew from the region on 3 July; the *Wehrmacht* did not occupy it until 8 July 1941. In the interval pogrom risks were kept at bay by bribing the potentially most dangerous ring-leaders.

The arrival of the Germans brought with it the usual succession of anti-Jewish measures: hard labour, looting, violence and brutalities, preference for this treatment being given to the elderly and to the Rabbis, while the non-Jewish population of the region, at the best of times never very sympathetic towards the Jews, grasped every opportunity to manifest its anti-Semitic feelings.

The ghetto was set up on 1 April 1942: 43 houses in two streets. Any children who dared to wander beyond the perimeter in search of food — and near famine prevailed — were shot as an example and their bodies returned to the Jewish Council.

The last straw was when the Lachwa Jews learned that, early in August, the entire Jewish community of the neighbouring small town of Mikaszewice had been exterminated, and realised that it would soon be their turn.

In numerous ghettos there were many Jews only too willing to fight, but not knowing how to set about it. Lachwa was an exception in that it had an organised Resistance movement. This was headed by young Icchak Rochczyn.

Rochczyn had no illusions about the fate that awaited him and his fellow Jews, and knew perfectly well that nothing could be done to avert it. In his opinion, however, it was better to go down fighting. At least in that way they could make sure that as many of their assassins as possible would die with them, and something

G

would have been done to restore the dignity of the Jewish people, even if in the immediate future this dignity would consist of little more than the right to choose their manner of dying.

On the ethical side, the Jews had to be made to understand that all the future held for them was death, and death alone. Next, the young men capable of fighting had to be mobilised. Most important of all, weapons had to be found.

The population was convinced, the young men mustered forces, but it was impossible to get hold of a single automatic weapon. A quantity of makeshift weapons, axes, knives, iron bars, pitchforks and clubs, took their place.

The plan adopted by Rochczyn and his companions was a simple one; when the Germans and their auxiliaries arrived to lead the Jews to the slaughter, the first thing to do was to set fire to the ghetto, then they would break down the surrounding palisade, and make a dash *en masse* for the nearest forest. Once there they would try to get in touch with the Partisans or organise themselves into autonomous groups.

The signal was given on 27 August 1942, when it was discovered that pits were being dug in the vicinity.

The ghetto was besieged on the night of 2 – 3 September. Early in the morning five lorry-loads of SS, fresh from the slaughter of Jews in the neighbouring locality of Kozangrodok, drew up in front of the Lachwa ghetto. They did not enter immediately but took time to eat and rest before they began the siege, firing in all directions as they advanced. To their astonishment they were greeted with a hail of blows from axes and pitchforks. Some of their men fell.

At this point the small Resistance group led by Rochczyn gave the order to set fire to the ghetto. Rochczyn decapitated one German before he, too, was killed. The Germans fled, dropping their weapons as they went, and these were swiftly seized on by the Jewish fighters.

Leaderless as they were, the Jewish combatants stuck to their plan of action, and taking advantage of the general disorder caused by the fire and their surprise attack, forced open the gates of the ghetto and sped off in the direction of the forest. Several hundred of them succeeded in reaching it, while back in the ghetto, the bodies of some hundreds of their companions lay strewn about the streets.

The troubles of the six hundred survivors were far from over. They were treacherously attacked by irregular Ukrainian soldiers and by the peasants of the locality, including some of their former Lachwan neighbours, and only a handful survived.

Lachwa was the first known case of organised physical resistance (we can hardly call it armed resistance) in a ghetto. It could not serve as an immediate example, for the facts were not known until the Liberation, when the survivors, painfully few, bore testimony to it.

In the Tuczyn ghetto, also within the Russo-Polish borders, in the former Polish Ukraine, and about 180 miles south of Lachwa the Jews in the ghetto drove back their assassins with the aid of primitive weapons. The outcome was identical, even to the massacre of the ghetto survivors by the irregular Ukrainian soldiers.

Many other ghettos followed its example.

Moshe Damaszek was a subaltern in the Polish Army; Shalom Cholawski is today *spiritus rector* of an Israeli institute of historical research on the Jewish tragedy of the last war. Both were resident in Nieswiez. Both lived through 'the action' of 30 October 1941 which cost 4,000 Jews of the locality their lives, the survivors being shut up in another ghetto.

Together they set up a Resistance group and provided weapons for it, including a Bren gun they found in the forest. Two young women, Rachel Kagan and Leah Ducker, who worked in the German barracks, procured ammunition for them at great risk to themselves.

The plan of action was more or less the same as that at Lachwa and Tuczyn, apart from the fact that the Nieswiez combatants had firearms. They, too, planned to set fire to the ghetto and to escape *en masse*.

When word came that the ghetto was to be liquidated on 21 July 1942, Resistance fighters installed the Bren gun on the roof of the synagogue under cover of darkness, drenched the houses with petrol and cut through the barbed wire entanglements surrounding the ghetto.

At 6 o'clock in the morning, German lorries escorted by the SS drove up to the entrance to the ghetto. A loudspeaker barked out: 'Everybody into the lorries!'

Damaszek, Cholawski and their comrades shouted: 'Don't!'

On that the Bren gun opened fire on the Germans. The houses burst into flames. The palisade was forced. And a large number of the Jews of Nieswiez escaped.

The clandestine Polish press reported the Nieswiez rising and the news swiftly reached the Warsaw ghetto, arriving just as the 'major operation' of deportation was taking place, but it failed to ignite the fuse of armed resistance. The time was not yet ripe. When the fuse was finally lit the resulting explosion was to be like a thunderbolt.

Other communities set fire to their ghettos, not only to allow them to escape, but because they were determined to leave nothing for their assassins.

The fire in the Opole ghetto, a small town situated on the western side of the Bug, is mentioned in a report dated 2 January 1943, which was sent to Himmler only a few days before the first Warsaw Ghetto uprising. Also on 2 January, 'bandits' attacked a labour camp at Grabowice, in the region of Lublin, freeing a number of Jewish prisoners. Immediately afterwards, a 'band' led by a certain Szmul — a common Jewish name — attacked police stations in the neighbourhood of Lasczow. This same band had made its presence felt before Christmas 1942.

Reports sent to Himmler say that the 'bandits' in this region were Communists. Nazi propaganda had no compunction in lumping all the Resistance fighters together, speaking of 'upholders of Judaic-Bolshevist capitalism', and there were many variations on the same theme; but in their reports to Himmler, which were not for publication, evasion was hardly necessary, and it could well be that the 'bandit' attacks were in fact the first actions of the Communist-inspired People's Guard in the Lublin region.

On 13 June an SD formation garrisoned at Baranovichi set off on the march for Naliboki, north of the Pripet Marshes, with the intention of killing the Jews there, but they were ambushed on the outskirts by Partisans who wiped out practically the whole unit, including the chief. There were three survivors.

The killing of an SD chief was certainly no petty crime, and the SS-und Polizeiführer in Bielorussia, Carl Zenner, added his own alarmist report to those sent in by the civil authorities[1].

The reprieve of the Naliboki Jews lasted only six months. Between Christmas and the New Year, the Germans returned and all those who had not had the good sense to make their escape in the meantime were put to death.

A group of thirty-two of them, men, women and children, had taken refuge in a large hole they had dug. After the pogrom, they began to emerge from the hole, a few at a time. They had to cross an open space, crawl through the barbed wire entanglements that surrounded the ghetto, get out of the village, cross a 3-mile stretch of open country before they could finally reach the forest.

It was mid-winter. Those who reached the forest began to wander aimlessly about in it, not knowing where to go in the strange locality. Their food supplies rapidly gave out. Soon there were only thirteen of them left.

One evening, in desperation, they knocked at the door of a peasant's house. The man was a Baptist and comparatively well off. He took them in. As some of the members of the group asked his permission to eat some potatoes he was about to give to his pigs, he kept the fugitives for the night, only asking them to depart before dawn, for he was afraid that the Germans would arrive. At the same time he drew a rough map of the locality on which he marked the farms where the fugitives had a chance of being well received and those they had better avoid. They discovered later that he had sent them to other Baptists.

They went on their way, hiding here one night, there another. Even so their numbers continued to dwindle. Those who remained wished to return to Naliboki, but one of the friendly peasants dissuaded them from doing so, warning them that they ran the risk of falling upon those who, rightly or wrongly, considered themselves their 'beneficiaries'. The latter usually would prefer to denounce them to the Germans.

Later, the survivors discovered a secret fortified encampment which 150 Jewish fugitives from the near-by ghetto of Mir had set up for themselves in the forest. The latter obviously considered themselves too poor and in too dangerous a position to be able to help anyone else. According to Pnina and Haim Schlossberg, they requested the newcomers in no uncertain terms to move on.

Naliboki, in the meantime, had been busy getting in touch with the Partisans. Their leader, a certain Vassilievitch, a friend of Haim Schlossberg, put the fugitives in contact with a Partisan brigade commanded by Zorin, a Soviet Jew from Minsk. So at long last, after eight months of aimless wandering, the refugee Jews found an organised movement willing to receive them.

Later they joined another Partisan brigade commanded by a Jew, Tobiasz Bielski. Reports of the German military command in Bielorussia early in 1944 often allude to 'the band of Bielski' and another brigade whose political commissar was a Jew known as Isaak Charin, who may well have been Zorin himself.

Today the Schlossbergs live in the Eilon kibbutz not far from the Israeli-Lebanese frontier. There are infiltrations of hostile commandos in the region from time to time, but the Schlossbergs are hardly likely to lose any sleep over those.

There were other fugitives in the Bielski brigade, survivors of a number of small ghettos and camps in the region, one of which was Koldyczewo. Once an enormous farm, it was converted first into barracks for the Red Army; then, by the German Army, into *Stalag 377*, and later into a training centre for the Bielorussian auxiliary pro-Nazi police force.

As usual, the drudgery was done by the Jews of whom a large number were employed in the camp as labourers, receiving little more than cuffs and blows and a miserable pittance for 'wages'. Others were used as targets for shooting practice.

Gradually the place became a regular concentration camp. It had a crematorium but no gas chamber.

As the military situation strengthened, the number of Jews diminished in the usual way. When there were no more than 95 left, they decided to escape. After all, having seen all their loved ones perish, they had nothing more to lose — moreover there would be no one left behind to harm.

The escape took place on 22 March 1944. The Jews had dug a tunnel from their hutments to outside the camp. They had taken the additional precaution of mining both the entry to the hutments and that of the tunnel. The next day, when the SS went to rouse the prisoners for work, a powerful charge of explosives destroyed the huts and caused the death of ten or so of them.

Most of the escapees joined the Bielski brigade.

As for the Jews from the Mir ghetto whom we last met in the forest encampment, they owe their lives to Oswald Samuel Rufeisen. This strapping fellow, blond with blue eyes, could have passed for one of the Aryan types that the Bavarian Heinrich Himmler, himself small and dark, so much admired. Rufeisen was born in Upper

Silesia and spoke German without the trace of an accent, in fact more correctly than the members of the SS who came from Bavaria, Austria or Hamburg.

When the German invasion took place in 1939, Rufeisen took refuge in what was to become the Soviet Zone. Some time after 22 June 1941 he was captured, but chose to pass himself off as a German[2], and was taken on without question by a German unit as interpreter.

This put Rufeisen in a position to help whomever he could. One day a Soviet commanding officer was brought before Captain Hein, the German for whom he acted as interpreter. The man had just been picked up. Rufeisen took an attitude which delighted his chief and completely stupefied the prisoner, who, having been recognised as a Russian officer, had been badly knocked about before being taken into their presence. But according to Rufeisen's interpretation the man was merely a peasant who had got drunk the night before and had beaten his wife and children. And he, Rufeisen, was going to teach him a lesson.

'Very well, now let me show this pig how we treat drunkards!'

Rufeisen beat the Soviet officer black and blue, dragged him from the room and whispering in his ear that the Partisans were only ten miles away, sped him on his way with a hearty kick.

On his return, Hein slapped him on the back:

'Oswald, old fellow, you are a true German. You know how to communicate with these Russian pigs in the only language they understand: a good hiding!'

Hein's unit was sent to Mir. Only about 800 Jews had survived and their days were numbered. Desperately searching for a way to save them, Rufeisen was surprised one day to recognise among them Ber Resnik, one of his former comrades in the Zionist youth movement. The latter, of course, would not have shown any recognition, even had he dared to raise his eyes and look at the black-uniformed German.

Rufeisen sought him out in his squalid quarters, and, learning that there was a Resistance movement in the ghetto, took it upon himself to provide arms. The combatants had intended fighting in the ghetto, but Rufeisen dissuaded them, advising them rather to flee to the forest.

As the day of liquidation drew near, he confided his plan to the combatants. He had the Partisans raise a false alarm, which called all the police to another sector of the region. The Jews grasped the opportunity, forced their way through the barbed wire and the palisades, and tore off in the opposite direction.

However, the next day, the one intended for the liquidation of the ghetto, the Germans still found a good half of the Jews, those who had been unable physically or morally to join the Partisans. Rufeisen was deeply shocked.

He received a second shock when Hein bustled in bristling with indignation and told him that a Jewish fugitive who had just been brought before him had claimed that it was he, Rufeisen, who had organised the mass escape and worse, that

Rufeisen himself was a dirty Jew. This individual had paid for this outrage by being shot on the spot.

Rufeisen cried out that he *was* a Jew, and that his sole aim was to thwart the Nazis in their plans to murder the Jews.

After a moment's silence, Hein left the room, and returning shortly afterwards muttered something about not understanding, not remembering a word of what had just been said. The best thing for Rufeisen to do was to come and have lunch with him in the mess and put the sordid affair out of his mind.

Rufeisen, who after all was still a very young man, had come to the end of his tether. He replied quite frankly that it was impossible for him to continue to play at being a German. Hein took him by the arm and made him sit down at the table and eat his lunch. Everybody else was eating peaceably. Suddenly Rufeisen got up and left the building.

He had just time to get out of the town before the alarm was raised, and when eventually he heard the patrols approaching, he hid in a heap of hay and fell soundly asleep. Then he wandered for three days. On the fourth day he knocked at the door of a convent and was invited to come in. Within three months he was converted to Catholicism.

Twenty years later, at the end of 1962 the Rufeisen affair was to become a celebrated lawsuit in Israel. The name that some believed to belong to history, if not to legend, was once again on everybody's lips.

Rufeisen was still a Catholic, and was known as Father Daniel, but, in 1956, at the time of the big Jewish exodus from Poland when President Gomulka came to power, he too decided to leave the country.

Father Daniel followed the normal procedure laid down for Jews who wished to leave Poland and return to their own country, and was given a travel permit when he officially renounced his Polish nationality. In 1958, his Order permitted him to return to Israel, to a monastery on Mount Carmel.

It was in Israel that his difficulties began.

Father Daniel wished to be recognised as a citizen of the State, in conformity with the Israeli law of The Homecoming which allowed every Jew arriving in Israel the privilege of becoming an Israeli citizen *eo ipso*, while non-Jews had to apply for naturalisation.

As it happened the Israeli authorities at that time in charge of the immigrant problem belonged to a party of religious extremists, considered particularly retrogade by their adversaries. They refused to accept that Rufeisen was a Jew but recommended that he be rewarded for saving the lives of hundreds of Jews even though he was not a Jew himself. Rufeisen rejected this compromise and took legal action. The whole of Israel was agog. The burning question was *who* was Jewish.

The Minister of Home Affairs, whose duty it was to deal with questions of nationality, made a point of informing Rufeisen that he himself would have willingly accepted him as a Jew, but that he could not claim to have jurisdiction over the Rabbinate.

Finally the Supreme Court of Israel decided by one vote that Rufeisen was an honourable, courageous man who had served the Jewish cause well in saving hundreds of Jewish lives; but that as a Carmelite Father he was not, and never could be, a Jew.

Despite all this, Father Daniel now lives peacefully in Israel and vigorously opposes anyone who tries to criticise the State of Israel by bringing up the 'Rufeisen affair'.

NOTES

1. Zenner, who had to his credit the assassination of tens of thousands of Jews in the various ghettos of Bielorussia, would not have been arrested after the war but for his greed, for no one bothered about him until he decided to apply to the West German authorities for a pension as former brigadier of police and *SS-und Polizeiführer* in Bielorussia; whereupon his dossier, which was certainly known of but which no one had looked into until then was brought to light.

2. Tens of thousands of Germans or people of German origin resided in the Ukraine and Bielorussia.

CHAPTER 23

THE WARSAW GHETTO

I T is extremely difficult to find words to describe the Warsaw Ghetto and its uprising. Countless books, ceremonies, discussions, lectures, papers, symposia, studies and articles have been devoted to the subject, and no doubt will continue to do so for some time, for the Warsaw Ghetto uprising has caught the whole world's imagination.

The ghetto was set up on 2 October 1940, when Ludwig Fischer, German governor of Warsaw and its immediate vicinity, published a decree effecting the constitution of a Jewish quarter (*Judisches Wohnbezirk*) in the town. The non-Jewish inhabitants had to leave the area, while the Jews who lived outside its precincts, a much larger number, were forced to take up residence inside. Later the Jews who lived in the market towns or large villages on the outskirts of Warsaw, and again there were large numbers of them, were turned out of their homes and confined in the ghetto. In 1942, it was reckoned that in theory the density of the ghetto occupation was thirteen persons to a room, which was double the density of the worst Warsaw slums before the German Occupation. In fact tens of thousands of Jews, and there were 450,000 in the ghetto, had not even a roof over their heads, and many more existed in reception centres or in overcrowded, improvised dormitories.

On top of all this the Jews had to put up with the hostility of certain sections of the non-Jewish population, and ran the constant risk of being rounded up for some petty offence by German soldiers, policemen and civilians, to be sentenced to who knows what drudgery.

Few of them felt the full import of the decree: the feeling of being cut off from the community, the majority considering themselves lucky to be together with their own people; and many of them could quite easily have procured false identity papers and continued to live in the 'Aryan town'. They did not wish to do so.

A series of official and officious actions ended in the more or less total confiscation of the possessions of a great many Jews, even inside the ghetto. Not that everybody shared this misfortune: far from it. A great many had no possessions to lose. Deaths for psychological reasons, even to the extent of self-starvation, were widespread. Tens of thousands starved to death and a still greater number died of typhoid fever and other diseases, which they might have resisted had they been able to get proper nourishment.

It was the Germans themselves who were chiefly responsible for this state of affairs, deliberately allowing only very meagre quantities of foodstuffs to reach the ghetto. Germans resident in Warsaw had rations equivalent to 2,310 calories per day; foreigners, non-German and non-Polish, were allotted 1,790; the Polish people 634; the Jews 184, and although there were non-rationed foodstuffs in circulation, these only reached the ghetto in the form of contraband. In fact, it was said in the ghetto that the unknown smuggler without whose aid all the ghetto community would have died of starvation deserved to have a monument erected in his honour. History did not share this view.

Once inside the ghetto all wage-earners and most intellectuals, professional people and officials found themselves out of work and penniless, apart from any money they might make from the sale of such personal possessions as the Nazis had not appropriated in the meantime.

Then Jewish bank and savings accounts were blocked, while the Germans saw to it that all credits were made chargeable to them. Jewish industrialists had their businesses confiscated; merchants had their stocks seized; artisans' machinery and tools were appropriated, while Jews were obliged to surrender foreign currency, gold, jewels and precious stones — though here, again, there were countless irregularities — and any stocks and shares they might have, Polish or otherwise, first blocked, were then confiscated.

There still remained a small section of well-off, even rich Jews, mainly people who knew the ropes, and knew how to turn the circumstances to their advantage. Smuggling, both into and out of the ghetto, helped to save the lives of a great many people and was also extremely profitable for those who organised it. There were naturally many non-Jews among these but also Jews from the ghetto. The black market, particularly in foreign currency and especially in the dollar, had its headquarters in the Warsaw Ghetto where two distinct types of business enterprise existed, most of them of an artisan rather than an industrial character. Certain astute Germans had obtained permission from the German authorities, first from the *Wehrmacht*, then from the SS, to set up small-scale industries in the ghetto with the aim of supplying the armed forces of the Reich. Schutz and Toebbens are among the best known of these, but there were others, all of whom grew rich overnight. It is not difficult to understand how. They had an assured market and extremely cheap, very well qualified, skilled labour, who, far from making claims of any sort, clung to the place of work as their only guarantee of survival.

A number of small-scale Jewish enterprises were also working for the German Army, in what were known as 'shops'. The lot of the workers in these was little better.

The Jewish Council with its various subdivisions and affiliated organisations, nursing homes, hospitals and other welfare institutions, was by far the biggest employer in the ghetto, if one discounts another very special type of employer: the various German services in Warsaw and elsewhere that requisitioned thousands of Jews from the ghetto for hard labour. If the work was carried out in Warsaw or its vicinity, they left the ghetto every morning under escort and returned there in the evening. Others were sent to work in labour camps far removed from Warsaw and did not return for several months at a time — if they ever did return.

A second institution, found also in other ghettos but which took on a particular form in Warsaw, was the Jewish ghetto police force. Originally known as *Judisches Ordnungsdienst*, it was composed mainly of unemployed intellectuals, but the quality of its members swiftly degenerated. In theory, it was responsible to the Jewish Council; in practice it became much more powerful. Szerynski, and later, Szmerling, were two of the unprepossessing individuals in command.

Under these conditions the Jewish police of the ghetto came to be detested as much as the Gestapo. Far from trying to put down criminal actions and black-marketeering, its members practised these on their own account, and corruption was rife.

The deportations from the Warsaw Ghetto to the extermination camps began on 22 July, most of them destined for Treblinka. The Jewish police of the ghetto were responsible for gathering the deportees together and packing them into the trains and promptly discharged this task by rounding up all the Jews they could lay hands on. This 'major operation' came to an abrupt halt on 13 September 1942 when about 310,000 Jews had been deported. By an irony of fate, the last train-loads were mostly made up of members of the Jewish police themselves, with their families. They were pitiful victims, perhaps even more wretched in that they were hand-in-glove with the enemy, who had not considered this sufficient grounds for sparing them.

It is only fair to mention that the first shot fired by a ghetto Resistance fighter was directed at one of the chiefs of this police force, and that this shot was swiftly followed by others, so that one can say that it was the Jewish Resistance fighters of the Warsaw Ghetto who wiped out the blot of the Jewish ghetto police.

The idea of armed resistance did not spring spontaneously to mind in the Warsaw Ghetto, nor anywhere else for that matter. The insurrection of the ghetto on 19 April 1943 preceded by more than fifteen months that of the rest of the town, although conditions both politically and otherwise were much harder there. It is interesting to note in passing that Paris rose up sixteen months to the day after the Warsaw Ghetto and Prague twenty-five months later.

Not that we are trying to establish any sort of Jewish pre-eminence in the field of heroism or courage. The towns we have just mentioned launched their insurrections at what they considered to be the right moment for them. In both cities there were powerful Allied armies close at hand and the purpose of the uprising was not to allow them to advance and liberate the city in question, but, if possible, to liberate it before their arrival. In such uprisings there was hate for the German invader but also mistrust of the liberator: there was always the chance that he would turn into a protector. All the same he was there should the need arise.

Not so in the Warsaw Ghetto uprising. There was not even a 'small' near-by ally. The combatants of the ghetto could only count on getting minimal help from the non-Jewish Resistance movement, a miserable contribution not only in relation to the strength of the Nazis but also in relation to what could have been given. The fact remains: the Resistance fighters were completely alone.

According to German sources there were about 2,000 Jewish combatants; the Jewish estimate is slightly less.

When the ghetto uprising took place there were about 60,000 inhabitants left. The final report of the SS General Stroop, whose responsibility it was to put down the rebellion, puts the number of Jews killed and deported at 56,015, adding that several thousand perished in fires. Adding to that the several thousand who succeeded in escaping to the Aryan quarter of the town, a much smaller number than those burned to death, we reach the sum total of just under 70,000 Jews, which means that the combatants represented 3 per cent of the population.

The Germans involved were not very numerous. Stroop mentions a total of 31 officers and 1,983 men; but the difference in equipment was enormous. The number of combatants more or less corresponded to those of the FFI who took part in the armed combat to free Paris, and indeed the two operations are comparable apart again from the question of arms, which were vastly superior in Paris.

When the Warsaw Ghetto was set up in October 1940, the political sections comprised the whole range of Zionist parties, the non-Socialist party *Bund*, and a few rather disorientated Communists not grouped together in any party. The Polish Communist Party (Polish Workers' Party — PPR) did not come into being until January 1942 in Poland itself, a month later in the Warsaw Ghetto.

Side by side with the Zionist parties were youth movements, largely autonomous offshoots. Apart from the Communists it was these youth organisations, and not the political parties, that supplied most of the combatants when the big moment arrived[1].

The political movements and parties, including the youth organisations, offered a somewhat orthodox type of resistance right from the start, seeing to it that clandestine newspapers were published more or less regularly, and these gave a fairly accurate picture of how the ghetto population lived, and of the dreams they dreamed.

By 18 April 1942 most of the clandestine newspapers had disappeared. The Gestapo had arrested and shot the principal editors and distributors. Time was when they had quarrelled among themselves; now death had united them.

This surprise operation was obviously meant to prepare the way for the deportation of the ghetto Jews. Up to then there had been no armed Resistance movement in that quarter; but the Nazis preferred to forestall events by doing away with those most likely to instigate one.

The Resistance found it very difficult to recover from this blow.

The idea of armed resistance was envisaged at the beginning of 1942, perhaps a little earlier and seems to have originated in Vilna and Bialystok. It came into being when it became known that the Jews were being systematically exterminated in Soviet-occupied territories.

Divide and rule was the guiding policy of the Germans who applied it everywhere in their anti-Jewish campaign, and found it extremely effective. It was meant to play upon a characteristic trait of the Jewish population, the philosophy of this ancient people, inured to facing and overcoming all sorts of trials and tribulations: the feeling that somehow or other the Jew will always pull through.

Well aware of this trait the Nazis played on it at every opportunity, and usually with excellent results. In Warsaw, they let it be known that whatever might happen 'far to the East in the steppes of Russia' — actually only 135 miles away — could not possibly happen in a large, civilised capital city like Warsaw. In Russia they were battling to destroy 'Judaic-Bolshevism', but things would be quite different in Warsaw: whether or not the Warsaw Jews shared the same fate as their fellows rested entirely with them.

This sort of propaganda was not likely to encourage the actions of those who found it imperative to take up arms and defend themselves from what they believed to be both inevitable and imminent extermination.

The Warsaw Jews deserve great credit for uniting the principal Resistance movements of the ghetto, including the left-wing Zionist groups, into a single anti-Fascist bloc. The Polish Communist Party, as we have seen, was set up outside the ghetto in January 1942, and inside in the following month. Lewartowski and Andrzej Szmidt, the most important figures at this period, did not contemplate taking up arms in defence of the ghetto, but concentrated rather on intensifying sabotage action behind the German front line.

It was the left-wing Zionist movements, *Dror, Hachomer Hatzair*, and *Poalei Sion* that united with the Communists to create the anti-Fascist bloc. It did not strike the Zionist moderates that any sort of immediate danger hung over the ghetto, and they feared the consequences of any ill-considered action[2].

Their irrefutable argument was that the Germans had just been defeated outside Moscow and had obviously other fish to fry; but in this sphere the Germans were inconsistent. The so-called Wannsee Conference on 20 January 1942 guaranteed the extermination of the Jews. It was even decided to accede to the suggestion of the Secretary of State of the German General government, Joseph Bühler, who wished to speed up the extermination of the Jews in Poland, since they were more numerous there than anywhere else, and nearer the places of execution. So the reasoning of this individual was irrefutable, too. The Zionist moderates of the Warsaw Ghetto knew nothing of the declarations of Bühler, and their conservative bourgeois minds were incapable of grasping the sort of reasoning Hitler went in for. Their attitude was consistent with the general pattern of Jewish behaviour, at least the sort that had prevailed since the unleashing of Christian anti-Semitism in Europe. Refraining from making oneself conspicuous was the beginning of wisdom.

As for the Orthodox Jews, they naturally put their trust in God, knowing that He would not only assure their personal salvation but would guarantee the continuity of His chosen people.

The first concern of the anti-Fascist bloc was to procure arms, and this is where their difficulties began. These difficulties were to grow and multiply until they reached their climax at the time of the ghetto uprising.

The Communist Party, promoter of the bloc, naturally turned for assistance to the Resistance organisation it had created: the People's Guard (*Gwardia Ludowa* — *GL*). The only problem was that the People's Guard had been founded at the same time as the Communist Party itself and, as a result, was still desperately short of men and equipment.

There were other Resistance organisations in Poland, mostly in and around Warsaw, and the majority of these were allied to the exiled Polish government and formed part of what was to become the principal non-Communist Polish armed Resistance organisation, in Poland, embracing all other organisations: the famous *Armja Krajowa* (Home Guard — AK).

Now these Polish political movements, claiming to be linked to the government in exile in London[3], with the possible exception of the Socialists, contained a high percentage of anti-Semites, some of whom, when confronted with the German Occupation and the crimes committed by the Nazis against the Jews, changed their attitude and even went to the aid of the Jews. But these were only a tiny minority[4].

The combatants of the Warsaw Ghetto quite naturally turned to the AK for weapons, but the bitter and brutal truth is that the *Armja Krajowa* gave them hardly any. In a report that came to light long after the fall of the ghetto, and mentioned by Michel Borwicz[5], it is recorded that late in 1942 a minute quantity of arms was received from the AK: ten pistols in bad condition and a negligible amount of ammunition.

At the same period, the People's Guard (GL) managed to contribute only a single revolver — a fact that has been cited time and time again by the official Polish historians, as proof of the sort of assistance the Polish Communists provided.

The anti-Fascist bloc naturally had to have a mouthpiece, and this took the form of a clandestine newspaper, *Der Ruf* ('The Appeal'), which only ran to three editions. One example of the first edition has been preserved[6]. Dated 15 May 1942 it contains the following appeal:

'Jews! Jewish workers! Jewish intellectuals! Jewish youth!

'Unite and join the fight. Let us face Fascism as one man in a united anti-Fascist front.

'Only the destruction of Hitler's war machine by the Anti-Fascist armies, and by the mass of the people subjugated to it, will put an end to our slavery and lay the foundation of the entire social and national liberation of all Jewish peoples.

'The Jewish people must join forces and strive for this one goal: let us fight on for freedom and liberation, and not relinquish the fight until victory over the Fascist enemy is assured.'

Despite these fine words the writer did not seem to have a very clear idea of the dangers that lay ahead. Nothing in the newspaper, at least in the sections quoted by Bernard Mark, the historian of the Warsaw Ghetto, hints that the editors had the least idea of what lay in store for the ghetto population, or they would have tempered their brave words with some practical advice. Unless the newspaper editors, Communists for the most part, judging by the style and tone of the appeal — and Mark mentions among them Lewartowski, Communist delegate, and Sagan and Tennenbaum, left-wing Zionists — genuinely believed it possible to create a single united Jewish and non-Jewish front in the spring of 1942, and that such a united front, besides fighting the Germans and helping in the Soviet war, would also attempt to save the Warsaw Jews.

The editors of *Der Ruf* perished without exception.

The anti-Fascist bloc did not last very long, and was destroyed by the enemy in a bitter attack against the Communists inside, as well as outside, the ghetto. One of the leading Jewish militants, Andrzej Szmidt (Pinhas Kartun), former combatant of the International Brigade, was given the task of organising armed resistance nuclei. He was shot by the Gestapo on 30 May with his comrades, Meretik and Wlosko. The circumstances of his death give us an idea of the 'strength' of the Polish Communist Party at this period: Szmidt and his comrades were in the process of delivering a small printing-press to their Communist comrades in the Aryan quarter of the city, a gift from the PPR section in the ghetto. The first appeal to the Polish patriots was launched on 15 May 1942, on the day the anti-Fascist Jews sounded their call to arms.

The first crucial test took place on 22 July 1942, when the mass deportations from the Warsaw Ghetto began, more than 310,000 Jews being deported in the space of six to seven weeks.

During this whole period, there was not a single act of armed resistance, if one discounts some indirect uncorroborated evidence regarding a revolver-shot fired at an indeterminate moment by an unidentified person at an unknown target with unconfirmed results.

The wave of deportations brought with it an unexpected victim. Adam Czerniakov, President of the Warsaw Jewish Council, noted and esteemed for his moral integrity even by his fiercest antagonists on the Council, took cyanide. During the whole period since he had assumed what he considered to be an onerous responsibility: that of saving the Jews from what he considered to be the real peril, the engineer Czerniakov had honestly done all that he could.

He was only human and had his failings. One of them, it seems, was an inability to choose decent, upright collaborators. He could not even detect the real aims of the enemy.

No doubt Adam Czerniakov shared the view of most of the Jewish Council leaders; that while an Allied victory was assured it was certain that not all Jews would survive to see it; the important thing, therefore, was to save as many of them as possible, especially the ones they considered to be most precious.

It is in this perspective that one must judge the twofold policy pursued by Czerniakov while he was President of the Warsaw Jewish Council, when he took into the Council's administration as many Jewish intellectuals as he possibly could; and he went to the aid of children in the ghetto, especially the waifs and strays, endeavouring thereby to save the élite on the one hand, and to take care of the future on the other.

It is in this perspective also that we must try to understand why Czerniakov committed suicide. On 23 July 1942, the second day of what was later to be called the 'major operation', two members of the SS came to his office. When they left, he rang for a glass of water. A few minutes later his colleagues found him dead. Written in his diary was the figure 9,000[7].

Adam Czerniakov had realised that his policy had failed and that all his efforts had only led to what would shortly be the total annihilation of those for whose lives he was responsible. Faced with this atrocious reality he felt incapable of suggesting any alternative either to his masters or to his protégés, and he chose to die.

Czerniakov has been blamed for not launching an appeal for revolt; but he was not a man who believed in armed revolt. His death had at least one positive consequence: the moral authority of the Jewish Council, already crumbling, collapsed altogether, and later, when the Jewish Resistance movement came into its own, it had no trouble at all in substituting its authority for that of the *Judenrat*.

Early in the month of August 1942 a particularly dramatic meeting took place in the ghetto. Present at this meeting were representatives of every political tendency, from the ultra-religious *Agoudat-Israël* to the Communists, who called themselves left-wing trade unionists. The Communists and the left-wing Zionists — in other words, the members of the anti-Fascist bloc — maintained that the Nazis were preparing to exterminate all the Jews in Warsaw and that the time had come to take armed action. The religious representatives voiced the opinion that such behaviour was hardly in keeping with Jewish tradition and that it was much better to die for the Sanctification of the Name of the Almighty. As for the moderate elements, they, like the religious elements, maintained that there was no positive proof that any deportees had in fact been put to death.

It was then that the partisans of the armed Resistance fell short on two counts. In the first place, they failed to impose — and if need be to enforce — their point of view.

They had not succeeded in arming themselves. Their delegate Arieh Wilner (Jurek in clandestinity) had had great difficulty in establishing contact with the AK and in the end he got nothing, but he was used to this type of operation and was not too dismayed. A few months previously he had succeeded in smuggling into the ghetto twenty to thirty pounds of chemicals, intended for the manufacture of explosives, as well as a quantity of hand-grenades, flick-knives, and American knuckle-dusters[8].

The future Resistance fighters also needed automatic weapons, apart from those bought from the Poles, and from German or foreign soldiers passing through Poland, which were just a drop in the ocean.

The second failure was the decisive one. A great many partisans in the Resistance refused to believe that deportation was really synonymous with the gas-chambers and were only too ready to fall in with the point of view of the conservative elements.

It is easy to criticise the blindness of the people in the ghetto from the vantage point of thirty years later. It is rather more difficult to try to put oneself in their place. They had seen their nearest and dearest depart. They had begun pondering the question, turning events over in their minds, and drawing their own conclusions, but none of them really *knew*. They were certain of one thing, however: that any sort of resistance would bring with it bloody reprisals, far more bloody than any they had experienced up to then; and they knew that the first victims would be the deportees, who as far as was known were still alive.

A clandestine pamphlet published by the AK at the end of 1942, gives one possible explanation of the attitude adopted by the representatives of the Jewish organisations:

By deliberately overstepping the limits of what is imaginable for

> *a man of sound mind, the Germans are knowingly acting with the*
> *ignoble hope that the world . . . will refuse to believe the extent of*
> *their bestiality . . .*

At the time, in fact, the world did refuse to believe, as it sometimes still does, that such bestialities ever took place. The victims themselves refused to believe it all too often.

There were a great many members of the youth organisations among the 310,000 deportees: those organisations that were to combine later in the Jewish Combat Organisation; there were also heavy losses among the Communists. Lewartowski, for instance, vanished in the turmoil; no one knows how or where.

When the deportations came to an end, the historian Ringelblum dedicated some poignant pages to the events that had just taken place. In them his grief for his fellow Jews is sometimes eclipsed by the shame he felt in knowing that they had gone passively to their deaths.

In more recent times a young Franco-Jewish writer was reproached for employing the well-known Jewish expression used when referring to this death march: 'like lambs to the slaughter', but the phrase was employed by Ringelblum long before then — and he took it from the Bible[9]. Ringelblum wrote:

> *Everyone is saying the same thing: one ought not to allow oneself*
> *to be deported; far better to fight in the streets, set fire to every-*
> *thing, scale the walls. . . . The Germans would have wreaked their*
> *vengeance, certainly, and there would have been tens of thousands*
> *of victims — but never 300,000! This must never happen again.*
> *The whole world must forbid it.*

Similar sentiments are expressed in a manuscript written by Jochoua Perle. We cannot help wondering, however, if in both cases the reaction was not a little belated. Spontaneous mass action had never taken place and is never likely to. What was lacking in the Warsaw Ghetto in the summer of 1942 was not courage on the part of the Jewish people as a whole but vigorous leaders who knew what they wanted and knew how to get it. Men like these could have gained the sympathy of the masses and given clear directives. Even if the ghetto had been better armed, the rising would not have taken place, for the eventual leaders of the revolt were still morally unprepared and the population would probably not have followed them. When, at the end of August, Israel Kanal, a young Jewish Resistance fighter drew his pistol and struck down Szerynski, the loathsome chief of the Jewish police, without managing to kill him, his gesture was not immediately imitated.

The Jewish Combat Organisation, known in Warsaw under the initials ZOB, was officially set up in December 1942, when Mordekhai Anielewicz, a militant from the extreme left-wing Zionist movement *Hachomer Hatzair*, took command. At twenty-three he had already seen eight to nine years of militant action in his own movement and had become its commander-in-chief.

According to Emanuel Ringelblum, who knew Anielewicz well and admired him enormously, despite a twenty-year difference in age, it was not until 1942 that the latter saw armed resistance as the only possible solution. He envisaged its taking place in the Warsaw Ghetto and had no illusions as to what lay in store for the combatants. The important thing, in his view, was to fight for the honour of the Jewish people.

He was no mystic, nor was he ignorant of military matters, which had always absorbed him. Before the German invasion he had attended a pre-military training school. He realised that neither the Jewish masses nor even the combatants could manage to get out of the ghetto and fight outside it. In 1942, there was no Polish Partisan movement in the vicinity of Warsaw, and the local inhabitants on the whole were very unfriendly towards the Jews. Resistance fighters in other ghettos, in Bielorussia and Lithuania in particular, had an alternative: to fight to the death in the ghetto; or to flee to the forests and continue the fight as Partisans, in so doing abandoning the ghetto community, including relatives and friends of the combatants. By the time the Warsaw JCO was founded the second alternative no longer existed.

In 1942 Anielewicz secretly toured the several towns where his movement had branches and managed to establish that the rumours in circulation concerning the extermination of the Jews were based on fact. He then set up local autonomous sections of the ZOB in a number of the towns, the most important of these in the ghetto of Czestochwa.

The Jewish Combat Organisation had both a military and a political leadership. Mordekhai Anielewicz was the commander-in-chief, with Itzhak Cukierman (pseudonym: Antek) from the Hechaloutz movement as his deputy; Berek Sznajdmil was later replaced by Marek Edelman as head of Intelligence (both were members of *Bund*); Hersz Berlinski, from *Paolei-Sion*, was in charge of Finance, and then there was Michel Rozenfeld (PPR).

Anielewicz was also one of the political leaders, as was Morgenstern. There were delegates from *Bund*, such as Abrum Blum, and PPR Communists such as Edward Fondaminski.

Arie Wilner (Jurek) was responsible for liaisons with the Aryan quarter. When he was put out of circulation he was replaced by Itzhak Cukierman. Wilner later returned to the ghetto to fight, and die, in the uprising.

Outside the ZOB, but closely linked with it, was Itzhak Giterman, former representative of the American *Joint*, who helped enormously on the financial side.

A number of Polish men and women: personal friends of the ghetto combatants, Polish patriots, or simply ordinary individuals shocked at the way the Jews were being treated, offered their services. Particular reference must be made to Irina Adamowicz, former member of the Girl Scouts, who had been linked with the Jewish Scouts before the war and was a long-standing friend of Anielewicz. She risked her life daily to maintain liaisons between the ghettos of Warsaw, Vilna, Kovno, Shavli and Bialystok.

Other Poles, particularly the members of the ZZW, and the AK, gave their support to the ghetto combat by helping to procure arms, and this in spite of opposition from some of their leaders. The volunteers from these groups were pathetically few — and deserve all the more credit for that.

The ZOB was not the only fighting organisation in the Warsaw Ghetto. ZZW, the Jewish Military Union (JMU), an emanation of the Zionist-Revisionists, was, ideologically speaking, situated further to the right than any other group represented in the Jewish Combat Organisation. It was also smaller, comprising little more than 400 combatants, compared with 700—800 in the JCO, but two factors largely compensated for its numerical deficiency: a large proportion of the members were seasoned ex-soldiers; and its right-wing political leanings were very useful in establishing direct liaisons with Polish right-wing Resistance groups through whom they obtained a large quantity of arms — large, that is to say, compared with the JCO. Later, just before the uprising, the JMU handed over part of its stock of weapons to the JCO, but unfortunately, the political exigencies of the JCO prevented the two organisations from fusing.

The first armed actions of the Jewish Combat Organisation had strictly material objectives. The organisation needed funds and applied first of all to well-off individuals — and there were still some of these left, because the richer people found it easier to escape deportation — but most often to the Jewish Council itself. To lend weight to their request, the militants of the JCO kidnapped the son of one of the principal members of the Council. This individual was heartily disliked in the ghetto and his son even more so. The *Judenrat* paid over the ransom with a good grace. This was in a way the final abdication of the Jewish Council, and shortly afterwards, when Lichtenbaum, Czerniakov's successor to the leadership of the Council, was asked by the Germans to say a few words in the ghetto, he had to reply that it would serve no purpose since the Council no longer carried any weight and the actual authority was in the hands of the JCO.

As we have seen, the Jewish police did not escape deportation, and when its chiefs, Szerynski and Lejkin, were shot by the JCO, it ceased to exist as an active body.

Besides the chiefs of the police, the JCO did away with a number of informers and Nazi accomplices, even pursuing its efforts outside the ghetto and shooting several Polish informers; but spying did not disappear completely. Anti-Semitism was too firmly rooted for that, and blackmailing those Jews who tried to hide away in the Aryan quarter of the town was far too lucrative a business to be lightly abandoned.

NOTES

1. In Warsaw, in fact, there was soon a more and more pronounced split, if not a complete separation, between the various parties and their respective youth organisations.

2. Because of their liaisons with the Polish Socialists, the Bundist militants found it impossible to integrate with the anti-Fascist bloc where they would have been classed as Communists; they preferred to remain autonomous. This did not prevent them from co-operating closely with the other members of the Resistance.

3. This London government was based on a coalition of the principal pre-war Polish political parties, both legal and illegal. These ranged from a moderate left wing to a more or less extreme right wing. There were no Communists, and the latter certainly did not recognise the government. Polono-Soviet contentions, temporarily in abeyance while the contested territories were occupied by the Germans, were certainly not of the nature to improve relations between the Polish Communists and the militants of other political tendencies.

4. Anti-Semitism continued to be professed in Occupied Poland, not only in the official press, in other words that under German control, but also in much of the 'clandestine' and consequently 'Resistant' press.

5. In *L'Insurrection du ghetto de Varsovie*, Paris, Juillard, 1966.

6. *Der Ruf* came out at a period when, as we have seen, the clandestine press of the ghetto had been more or less reduced to silence by the execution of its publishers and distributors. We do not know how many copies were printed, but one copy is in the archives of Ringelblum, part of a collection of clandestine newspapers that is used for reference today.

7. Adam Czerniakov, *Warsaw Ghetto Diary*, Yad Vashem, Jerusalem, 1968, p. 328 (in Hebrew).

8. This remarkable man was seized in the course of a round-up in Warsaw a few days before the meeting but managed to escape from the deportation train in which he had hidden, to avoid being shot on the spot.

9. Jeremiah, chapter 11, verse 19.

CHAPTER 24

THE SYMBOL

THE year 1943 opened with an unexpected visit that left the Jews in Warsaw in no doubt that their days were numbered.

On 9 January, two tanks followed by a Mercedes drove into the ghetto, two more tanks bringing up the rear. All four tanks had their guns levelled. The man in the Mercedes was none other than Heinrich Himmler, *Reichsführer SS* and Chief of the German Police. He had come to see the ghetto with his own eyes, or rather to see it again.

Himmler had officially requested back in 1942 that the ghetto should be liquidated, but pressure from the *Wehrmacht*, who wished to hold on to their source of military supplies, had forced the Gestapo to shelve its plans. In 1943, Himmler at last managed to impose his point of view: the threat the Jewish workers constituted to the Reich was far more urgent than the exigencies of war production.

The visit of such a personage could hardly go unnoticed.

The two fighting organisations, the JCO and the JMU sent out appeals for action in view of the big demonstration on 22 January, when it was planned to seize all the remaining members of the Jewish police, confiscate their uniforms and make a public example of them. The affair could lead on to still more serious incidents.

But fate decided otherwise. On 18 January, the *SS-und Polizeiführer* of the Warsaw district, Sammern-Frankenegg, launched a large-scale round-up in the ghetto.

Much to the Germans' surprise, they were received with a shower of bullets. That was how the first battles of the Warsaw Ghetto began.

The most striking feature of these battles was the complete contrast of the two sides, the Germans and the Jewish community: they had absolutely nothing in common.

While the Germans were powerfully armed, the equipment of the Resistance fighters was positively ludicrous. Not only that. The Germans had decided to use all the means at their disposal to attain their ends, for they had no need to take any precautions against killing or wounding civilians. And since they had orders to deport all the Jews in the ghetto willy-nilly, and to kill any who offered violent resistance, they could fling aside all restraint; so that when the Jewish snipers stationed on the rooftops began to inflict damage, they simply set fire to the houses, and even to entire blocks of houses. If a few non-combatants were roasted in the process, so much the better.

Since the large-scale deportations in the summer, the ghetto was no longer a single territorial area. A great number of streets, in some of which the inhabitants had been completely wiped out, had been abandoned, creating a sort of no-man's-land, where the 'illegals' lived.

There were two types of these: those who by good luck or good management had succeeded in avoiding being rounded up; and the others, less numerous, who had escaped from deportation trains, or even from Treblinka. There were about thirty thousand or so of these 'illegals', that is about the same number as the 'legals' who lived in the vicinity of the factories and workshops where they were employed; each of these constituting a more or less self-contained unit.

Strange to say, one of the plagues of the ghetto had disappeared since the deportations. No one starved to death any more, for despite the extensive looting, official or otherwise, there still remained the stocks of foodstuffs that had belonged to the deportees, and these were swiftly seized by the temporary survivors. After September 1942 there is no mention of famine in any of the ghetto reports and eye-witnesses have confirmed these facts.

The German operation officially began a few days before 18 January but in the Aryan sector. The helpless victims of this preliminary onslaught were the Jewish workers in the labour camps.

At half past seven on the morning of 18 January, 200 German police accompanied by 800 Latvian and Lithuanian auxiliaries, as well as several detachments of the Polish police, hurled themselves at the ghetto. The *SS und Polizeiführer*, Ferdinand von Sammern-Frankenegg, personally directed operations.

The Jews were called upon by loudspeaker to come out into the street and to proceed in single file to the *Umschlagplatz*. A very small number obeyed.

The Jewish Combat Organisation had no intelligence service and was caught unprepared. Its leaders had just time to launch a brief appeal:

> *The German occupying forces have just begun the second stage of extermination.*
> Don't go to your death without a fight!
> *Stand up for yourselves!*
> *Get hold of an axe, an iron bar, a knife — anything, and bolt the doors of your houses!*
> Dare them to try and take them!
> *If you refuse to fight you will die.*
> *Fight! And fight on!*

It was a young woman called Emilia Landau, who worked in the carpentry shops of the *Ostdeutsche Baustelle*, who had the honour of launching the Jewish counter-attack. When the Germans forced their way in, she tossed a hand grenade among them, causing the death of some and panic among the rest; but they quickly pulled themselves together and in the unequal fight that followed Emilia Landau was struck down.

A bigger skirmish was taking place at the Niska Street intersection where the *Hachomer Hatzair* combatants commanded by Anielewicz, attacked the SS as they were escorting a string of Jews towards the *Umschlagplatz*. There were two hundred Germans. The Anielewicz group had five hand-grenades, five pistols, a few Molotov cocktails made in the ghetto and a collection of iron bars and clubs.

The Jews' only advantage was that their attack was a total surprise. The Germans were ready for anything except to have Jews directing grenades and bullets at them. The members of the master race did not know which way to turn, and the Jews took advantage of the fact to make themselves scarce.

Another fight took place in a house in the same vicinity where a group led by the Communist porter Mosze Czompel defended themselves to the last bullet. The battle against the *kibbutz* Dror,[1] aided by a reinforcement of *Gordania* combatants, was won by the Jews.

Next day at ten o'clock the Germans arrived and set about ransacking the house. The combatants remained hidden and held their fire until the Germans had gone upstairs, when they suffered serious losses of men and equipment.

Other battles took place on the *Umschlagplatz* itself, lasting for three days and leaving only a handful of survivors.

In the Schultz and Toebbens German workshops in the heart of the ghetto, Jewish Resistance fighters, even less well armed than their comrades, put up a desperate fight. The three detachments led by Lejbgot, Jadworski and Kanal, possessed between them two revolvers, a hand-grenade and a few homemade bombs. The Germans beat a retreat, but the Jews had lost most of their combatants.

In the course of these four days of fighting, from 18 to 21 January, a large number of Jewish militants perished. Even so the Germans deported 6,500 Jews, which was far less than they had expected[2]. The combatants who survived were able to say that like the last of the Jews, the Germans died under fire, and had even beaten a retreat: mortals like the rest and not immune to fear. If there was an insult the Jews of the Warsaw Ghetto had never been able to stomach it was the taunt; 'Vile Jews, cowardly Jews![3]'.

There were glowing reports of the January combats in the underground newspapers, and there is no doubt that it was the courage of the Jews rather than their tragic fate that impressed the non-Jews.

That same month, an illegal Polish newspaper, *The Sword and Plough*, run by the local Fascists, not only attributed to Jewish propaganda the avowed intention of saving the rest of the ghetto by inciting a Polish revolt but forecast a Judæo-German alliance against the Polish citizens.

Without going as far as that, it seems that the Polish Resistance movement, particularly the non-Communist movement, which was only just beginning to arm itself in earnest, feared above all that it would be dragged into precipitate action which could only result in a crushing defeat and heavy losses, not only among the Jews, but equally among the Polish Catholics.

On the other hand the veiled conflict between the Polish government in London and the USSR made the Polish Resistance fighters suspicious. Germany was certainly the principal enemy, but it was not the only one[4].

Curious though it may seem, the Germans did not learn the lesson from the January events and three months later, the same scenes, more or less, were repeated.

After the 'operation' of January 1943, it was clear to the ghetto community that the end was near, and taking advantage of the brief respite, the insurgents set about organising themselves as best they could and pursued their unending quest for weapons; but the wheels of war had not stopped turning.

On 2 February the battle of Stalingrad was more than 300 miles from Warsaw, but even so the effect of this crushing German defeat made itself felt, not as far as equipment was concerned, nor even the morale of the soldiers or the SS, but inversely on the morale of the Jews. It began to dawn on them that some of them might survive after all.

Not surprisingly, relations between Communists and non-Communists on the Polish home front were not improved by events. The Germans were happy to be in a situation which at last gave them an opportunity to denounce the 'atrocities' of their enemies, and they took full advantage of the occasion.

As for the Jewish combatants, they made a clean sweep in the ghetto. The Jewish Military Union liquidated some members of a group of *agents provocateurs* placed there by the Gestapo, as well as several SS. The JCO executed a few Jewish Gestapo agents, among them a seventy-five year old German Jew, Dr. Alfred Nossig. There was one man at least who regretted his passing. *SS-Obersturmführer* Konrad stated at his trial that Nossig had placed himself at the disposal of the Germans. After the January combats, he had taken it upon himself to write a six-page memorandum in which he advised the Germans how to go about organising future deportations, using peaceful means and not violence. According to Konrad, this memorandum contained interesting pointers on the JCO.

There were a few so-called expropriation operations, then the Germans practically ceased to show themselves in the ghetto by day, and never came at night. The curfew was lifted.

On 3 March the JCO issued a proclamation listing all the executions of traitors and informers and the crimes committed by each one. The organisation added that it possessed the complete list of German accomplices and that these would be done away with when the time came. Members of the Jewish police were requested not to hinder the JCO in its work. The JCO also cautioned the overseers of the 'shops' who attempted to persuade the Jews to have themselves 'transferred'.

Two episodes that took place around this time could be taken as proof of a *de facto* recognition of the JCO by the Germans. Late on the night of 30 January 1943 a handful of JCO men raided the safe of the Jewish Council to get funds for their organisation. The following day the members of the Council reported the matter to the German authorities, who went to the scene of the crime and reported it. No further action was taken. It was the last blow but one delivered to the authority of the Council, the final one being the execution of the Gestapo agents, and the conditions forced on the members of the Council.

The second episode took place in March. The German civilians in charge of the 'shops', types like Schultz and Toebbens, observed that their workers refused to believe in the benefits of 'voluntary transfer', and had posters printed warning the people of the ghetto and especially their own workers against the 'bogus protectors and adventurers' of the JCO who pretended to succeed where all the armies of Europe had failed.

The Germans did not remain inactive, however — far from it. On 16 February 1943 Himmler sent an order to the SS General Kruger, *Höhere SS-und Polizeiführer* (commander-in-chief of the SS and of the police) of the General Government of Poland:

> For security reasons I order the destruction of the Warsaw Ghetto following the setting up of a concentration camp. Before this is carried out we advise the removal of all equipment and transportable materials.
>
> The destruction of the ghetto and the setting up of a concentration camp are of paramount importance, otherwise we shall never succeed in restoring peace to Warsaw, for it will be impossible to stamp out crime so long as the ghetto exists.
>
> We advise that a general plan for the destruction of the ghetto be drawn up and submitted to me. It is vital that this be designed in such a way that the area occupied up to now by 500,000 of this sub-species, which will never be utilisable by the Germans, will disappear off the surface of the earth and that the millionaire (in inhabitants) town of Warsaw be reduced in size.

The same day another letter from Himmler was directed to the SS General Pohl, head of the SS Central Bureau of Economy:

> 1.   I order the setting up of a concentration camp in the ghetto of Warsaw.

2. All Jews resident in Warsaw will be transferred there. It will be forbidden for Jews to work for private firms.

3. Private business enterprises at present operating in the ghetto will be transferred to the camp.

4. The concentration camp as a whole, including the businesses and the prisoners must be transferred as speedily as possible to Lublin and its locality so as not to impede production in any way.

Thus the destruction of the Warsaw Ghetto was decided on, and all that remained was to settle the date and the details.

The combat organisations were ready, or nearly so. The 22 JCO detachments (compared with 50 preceding the January combats) comprised 5 *Dror* detachments, 4 *Hachomer Hatzair*, 5 detachments drawn from other Zionist youth organisations: *Akiba, Hanoar Hatzioni*, the left-wing *Paolei-Sion CS*, and *Gordonia*; 4 *Bund* detachments and 5 Communist detachments.

According to Stroop, there were 20 to 30 combatants in each of these.

Only one of the 22 detachment leaders survived: the Bundist Marek Edelman. All the others fell at their posts.

The 400 or so JMU combatants were divided into 3 groups, each consisting of several detachments which were smaller than those of the JCO but better equipped, each possessing one or two machine-guns.

Most of the members of the JMU were either former soldiers or militant Zionist Revisionists, while the various detachments of the JCO were mainly made up of militants drawn from widely varied movements, but a large number of combatants in both organisations simply wished to fight the Nazis and to do so joined the first organisation they could find.

Beside the organised detachments others formed up more or less spontaneously, and these left no documentary traces apart from declarations given by Stroop and his adjutant Karl Kaleske, who insisted at their trial that there were between 1,500 and 2,000 Jewish combatants in the ghetto, whereas the total official figure of JCO combatants seems not to have exceeded 1,200.

The Resistance fighters had a number of bunkers fitted out, the principal one at 18 Mila Street being the general headquarters of the JCO. It appears that this bunker had originally been built for a less worthy cause by prosperous smugglers who had taken the precaution of providing several carefully camouflaged exits. It was discovered by the militant Communists who offered it to the leaders of the JCO.

The other bunkers had originally been constructed on the pretext that they were to be used as air raid shelters, so that the ghetto was given official permission to obtain large quantities of cement.

As well as fitting out a large number of bunkers, the combatants built a network of connecting tunnels, some of which even went under the wall and into the Aryan sector of the town; and around this time efforts were made to re-establish contact with the Polish Resistance groups outside the ghetto. Personal relations improved a little, but the actual material aid offered was still very small.

Himmler now ordered the SS General Stroop to return to Warsaw and attend to the liquidation of the ghetto in place of his colleague, Ferdinand von Sammern-Frankenegg.

According to Jürgen Stroop's report, he had the following formations at his disposal:

Waffen-SS

3rd battalion of armoured grenadiers	4 officers and 400 men
A cavalry detachment	3 officers and 381 men
Wehrmacht	
A DCA artillery detachment	2 officers and 22 men
A detachment of engineers led by Rembertow	2 officers and 42 men
14th battalion of engineers led by Gora-Kalwaria	1 officer and 34 men
Armed Constabulary	
Two battalions of the police regiment number 22	6 officers and 228 men
Technical aid	1 officer and 6 men
Polish police	4 officers and 363 men
Polish firemen	166 men
Gestapo (Sipo)	3 officers and 32 men
One Trawniki battalion[5]	2 officers and 335 men

Beside the above there were about 7,000 SS. These were not actively engaged in the fight but constituted a sort of strategic reserve force, which could be called upon if the uprising chanced to spread from the ghetto to the town. In the event this proved unnecessary.

General Stroop had experience of Partisan combat, mostly gained from his activities in the Nikolaievsk region. General von Rossum, military commander of the Warsaw Ghetto, seems not to have been informed of the action in hand, for his direct co-operation was not sought. Nevertheless he had to supply Stroop with some additional artillery, the *Waffen-SS* battalions and the police regiments being deficient in these, as well as engineer troops to set fire to the blocks of houses. The *Waffen-SS* and the police regiments had managed to set fire to the Soviet villages, but the procedure was not quite the same in a large town with more solid constructions.

There were several phases to the fighting, the first lasting for some days, with the ghetto combatants offering organised resistance.

During the second phase, which marked the beginning of the systematic burning of the ghetto, several pockets of resistance continued to fight. This phase ended on 8 May with the collapse of the bunker headquarters of the JCO.

The third phase was more of a massacre than a battle. There were only a few scattered pockets of resistance left and some of these consisted of no more than a single combatant. The period from 8 to 15 May marked the end of organised resistance and the beginning of flights to the Aryan quarter of the town and to the near-by forests.

During the whole of that summer of 1943 occasional shots could be heard coming from what had once been the ghetto, fired by isolated gunmen holding out in their hiding-places in the ruins. No survivor of this period is known.

During the night of 18 to 19 April 1943 the German troops took up their positions. Powerful contingents of SS men, police and foreign auxiliaries surrounded the wall of the ghetto. Machine-guns were placed in firing position every few yards along the wall. Roads in the immediate vicinity were closed off.

Sammern-Frankenegg still nursed bitter memories of the January and March operations, and had seen to it that the units taking part in this operation were given a swift training in street combat. The General had orders to pass the command to Stroop in the course of the day, but he was responsible for launching the offensive and hoped to deal such a crushing blow that resistance would be shattered immediately, leaving his colleague with little more than the rather tedious task of rounding up and deporting the victims.

Ferdinand von Sammern-Frankenegg led his troops at 6 o'clock in the morning of 19 April to the Nalewka gate, the main entrance to the ghetto. His men had orders to take over the principal streets, arrest all those they found there and swiftly cut short any show of resistance.

Sammern-Frankenegg took the extra precaution of forcing the last survivors of the Jewish police, requisitioned the day before, to act as a vanguard. Any who refused to carry out this extremely unpleasant task were promptly shot. Loudspeakers relayed a message to the Jews recommending them to allow themselves to be transported to the 'labour camps' without offering any resistance.

This two-fold psychological action, the employment of the loudspeakers and of the Jewish police, suffered a two-fold defeat. The Jewish police marched in without incident, but the Germans following behind them were greeted with a volley of fire, hand grenades, Molotov cocktails, and sniper bullets, from the detachment of the JOC commanded by Artsztajn, Zylberberg and Rojtblat. The German column scattered and fled leaving several of their supermen sprawling in the road. The Jews suffered no losses.

A second wave of Germans surged forward, this time wisely covering their advance with automatic weapons. They might have spared themselves the effort, for they, too, were driven from the ghetto.

The fighting had lasted two hours. At 7.30 a.m. Sammern-Frankenegg reported to Stroop that his men had not been able to enter the ghetto and that word must be sent to Kruger requesting him to supply bombers. Stroop could hardly conceal his pleasure at the discomfiture of his predecessor. He kept calm, and did not call Kruger, but simply ordered his unhappy colleague to relinquish his command immediately and to leave Warsaw. Sammern-Frankenegg complied[6].

Jürgen Stroop, a dedicated Nazi, had joined the Party and the SS in 1932, before Hitler came to power. He had begun life as a civil servant, but had swiftly climbed the hierarchical ladder. In 1939 he was already *SS-Oberführer* and colonel of the police. He had behind him two long administrative affairs, the first concerning the changing of his Christian name from the Jewish-sounding Joseph to the more Germanic Jürgen, and the other concerning the liquidation of his rights to retirement in the little *Land* of Lippe. It appears that he won both cases in spite of legal and statutory provisions.

The war took him to the Poznan district where he was responsible for massacring more than 2,000 Polish patriots. When Russia entered the war he was chief of the police and the SS at Nikolaievsk. After short periods in the Balkans and Lvov, he came to Warsaw where he accomplished his bloodiest and most notorious mission. Since his Nikolaievsk period he had become *SS-Brigadeführer*, brigadier of the Police and the *Waffen-SS*. In the space of less than ten years he had moved from the ranks to become a general. It was a rapid promotion and not undeserved[7].

On 19 April 1943, Stroop reported:

> *The moment we set foot inside the ghetto, the Jews and the Polish bandits began to offer armed resistance and managed to beat off the attack of our forces, including the tanks and armoured cars.*

Stroop had all his daily telegraphic reports bound in leather. They were preceded by a sort of introduction which purported to be a general history of the Warsaw Ghetto but was no such thing. There was an iconographic section consisting of 53 stills from a film taken in the Ghetto during the battle.

Unfortunately for Stroop this report was found in his home after the war, and he was hanged on his own written evidence.

It is a most valuable historical document on the battle of the Warsaw Ghetto, and without it a great many details would have been lost to us. Stroop pays an involuntary compliment to the Jewish combatants when he pointedly refers to the strength of his forces and the equipment he had to bring against the enemy, whom he repeatedly refers to as 'sub-species' and 'scum'.

His daily report includes what has been called the 'body-count': the number of

Jews killed and the number deported to Treblinka, which the writer calls 'T.II'; and he records every firearm seized, every building burned down.

Stroop had an exalted idea of his role in history, thinking of himself as a sort of second Titus 1,873 years on and such pretensions hardly endeared him to the majority of his compatriots.

Had his report not been found the SS would have had to shoulder the responsibility for the whole affair. Since Nuremberg, they had been the scapegoats for all that had happened in the Third Reich, including the breaches of honour of some, the renunciation of others, and the cowardice for the great majority[8].

The first ghetto engagements had by no means come up to German expectations. Stroop reports on 20 April 1943:

> *The tank and the armoured cars engaged were attacked with Molotov cocktails. The tank caught fire on two occasions. The units retreated immediately under the counter-attack of the enemy. We lost 12 men (6 SS and 6 Trawniki).*

On 19 April, following up the information given him by his predecessor, Stroop went to the Jewish position at 29 Zamenhof Street, and launched the assault at 8 a.m. A few hours later, the Resistance fighters were forced to abandon the building.

Jewish accounts of this second engagement report heavy enemy losses: dozens killed and two tanks set on fire. The battle lasted six hours. As the insurgents retreated, they set fire to the German depots in the *Werterfassungstelle*, where valuable personal effects, the belongings of deportees, were stored.

A second theatre of operations in Muranowski Square, was held mainly by JMU combatants, better armed than their comrades in the JCO, since they had just received a stock of arms from their Polish friends in the KB resistance network which was affiliated to the AK, and commanded by Captain Henryk Iwanski. A Polish group of six men, led by Joseph Lejewski, was responsible for delivering the arms, and joined their Jewish friends when the ghetto battles began. They were assigned to Jan Pika's detachment and took part in the struggle. Later, Lejewski and a seriously wounded companion managed to get back into the Aryan sector. The other four fell to the enemy. This, one of the few occasions when Poles took an active part in the combats, did not escape the notice of Stroop, who mentions in his report armed opposition by 'Jews and criminals'.

The insurgents in Muranowski Square flaunted the white and red Polish flag along with the blue and white Jewish one struck with the star of David.

Thanks to the machine-guns, this position held firm for the whole of that day and the following day, when Stroop had the anti-aircraft artillery brought in, which had a far wider range than machine-guns. Even so Stroop's men suffered heavy losses before they were able to seize the position, and at the time of his trial, Stroop recalled the death of his deputy and friend, the *SS-Untersturmführer* sub-lieutenant Dehmke, 'a brilliant officer', who perished in this battle.

The sector of the 'shops', some distance from the main centre of action, was also fighting a desperate battle, and succeeded in driving back squads of German police. The Jewish 'garrison' of this sector was composed of several groups commanded by Geller, Nowodworski, Kawa, Szwarcfuchs and others. When at one point a mine failed to explode at the passage of a Nazi column, a few Molotov cocktails were flung at the leading tank instead, and the remainder tossed over the ghetto wall onto a passing Nazi platoon.

But on 20 April the principal zone of combat was centred in the brushmakers' quarter, and here an episode took place that gives a clear indication of the sort of relations that existed in Warsaw between the immured humans of the ghetto and the non-Jewish population. The Germans launched their assault on the Jewish positions, and the Jews prepared themselves to fight to the death.

According to Professor Bernard Mark:

> The Jewish combatants shouted to a number of Poles who happened to be passing on the 'Aryan' side: 'Brother Poles, watch out, take shelter! We are about to open fire on the Germans.'

Sixteen months later, these 'brother Poles' themselves became the victims, when the Germans — and perhaps the same Germans — destroyed the 'Aryan' city of Warsaw.

Nevertheless, on 20 April a detachment of the Communist People's Guard (GL) led by Franciszek Bartoszek, and including the Jewish woman combatant Njuta Teitelbaum, attacked an anti-aircraft defence battery that was firing on the brushmakers' quarter. The battery was reduced to silence. Bartoszek, an artist by profession, was an experienced Partisan. Another GL group silenced a nest of heavy machine-guns by shooting all the gunners and putting the artillery out of action.

The AK, for their part, tried to launch a diversionary attack in the direction of the ghetto with the aim of blowing up the surrounding wall. This task was entrusted to a detachment composed mainly of workers and schoolboys from the Praga quarter. The German patrols caught up with the combatants before they were able to reach the wall of the ghetto, and in the course of the ensuing battle each side lost two men, and several Germans were wounded. The Germans also lost an armoured car[9].

The battle of the seven Jewish groups in the brushmakers' quarter on 21 April lasted the whole day. One of the survivors, Simha Rotam-Rathauser, seventeen years old at the time, and now living in Israel, was able to turn his 'Aryan' appearance to some account. Here are a few extracts from his report:

The first day, 19 April, was calm in our sector, but the following day two armed German soldiers and a civilian appeared on the scene. (The latter was in charge of the workshops of the quarter.) They began shouting to the Jews inside the houses to come out and assemble in the streets promising that if they allowed themselves to be peacefully transferred no harm would come to them. When they drew level with the positions of our combat groups, the latter opened fire. The three Germans immediately turned tail and fled. Their place was taken by an SS formation which, as far as I could gather, numbered about a hundred men. Whenever I spotted them I raised the alarm by a prearranged signal (the ringing of a bell). My comrades immediately took up their assigned positions.

Several months earlier, we had dug a hole under the street and filled it with explosives. As the SS passed over it we blew the charge. Several were killed and the rest beat a hasty retreat to reform their ranks. An hour later they advanced again, this time in the direction of the building where I was stationed. When they attempted to enter the house we greeted them with a shower of rifle and pistol bullets, hand grenades and Molotov cocktails. It was perfectly obvious that they had not expected such a show of resistance.

From then on they stuck to the usual military tactics. We managed to set fire to one of them, however, with the aid of a Molotov cocktail. His companions retreated to outside the ghetto and began to bombard us with heavy gunfire and incendiary bombs.

The house where we were positioned burst into flames and our group was forced to find refuge elsewhere. I had succeeded in getting hold of an SS uniform and took command of the group. The only risk I ran was that my own side might fire on me. In fact, when I reached the bunker held by some of our men the sight of SS jackboots and uniform was greeted with a string of invectives. Happily, I managed to convince them of my true identity. Soon it became clear that we would have to abandon that position as well. We managed to find another more solidly constructed bunker. Our comrades there welcomed us with open arms. Then we tried to establish contact with other combat groups and in doing so stumbled on the bodies of several comrades, among them the well-known Bundist Michal Klepfisz

H

When night fell there were 80 to 100 persons in the bunker. Six or seven detachments, with 15—16 men in each, were operating in the sector. That evening each of the groups gave a report of that day's events in his own sector. As there were still a considerable number of men missing, we formed reconnaissance and search patrols of which I took command. I had no need to select men for these patrols — the volunteers were so numerous that I was embarassed by the choice.

. . . One of our most difficult tasks was to link up with central command. Eventually, after a great deal of effort, we succeeded. Gradually we were able to form a rough estimate of our numbers. We were surprised to find that our losses were relatively small compared with those of the Germans.

From then on there was no longer any real contact between the different sectors, but each of them submitted reports and these all presented much the same picture: German attack, Jewish reaction, some deaths inflicted on the German side, return of the Germans with reinforcements, retreat of the Jewish survivors — when there were any.

On 23 April, a peremptory message arrived from Heinrich Himmler himself. He was quite obviously angered by the moral defeat of the Germans, for in the meantime the whole world had begun to talk about the Warsaw Ghetto since the news was broadcast on all Allied radio stations — Western as well as Eastern:

'The round-ups in the Warsaw ghetto must be carried out with relentless determination and in as ruthless a manner as possible. The tougher the attack the better. Recent events show just how dangerous these Jews really are.'

Stroop immediately complied with the order and changed tactics. His first orders had been to save as much as possible of the ghetto's general equipment, raw materials and confiscated belongings. Now he had one house after another systematically set on fire. The combatants replied by setting fire to everything that could possibly be of use to the Nazis.

On the day Himmler's message was received, the JCO published an inspiring proclamation, which was distributed mainly in the Aryan quarter of the town. It did not contain a single direct appeal for support or assistance, but once again the brave 'Promoter' (Chrusciel) of the AK, who had already been in action the day before, led an attack on German positions at the entrance to the ghetto. Two other AK groups, commanded respectively by Major Lewandowski and Lieutenant 'Klimek', harassed a number of Polish police stations and several Baltic Fascist units.

The same day, Anielewicz addressed a sort of testament to a friend in the 'Aryan' quarter. It read:

Several of our detachments have managed to rout the enemy. Our losses in manpower have been minimal. The whole affair is a success . . . And the dream of my life has become a reality. The Jews in the ghetto are defending themselves at last and their vengeance has taken a positive form. I bear witness to the superb and heroic battle being fought by the Jewish insurgents.

From then on the battle was localised around the various bunkers. The Germans still did not dare to move about in the ghetto alone during the day; and for several months they had even been avoiding doing so at night. German planes circled above. Sometimes they dropped pamphlets calling on the Jews to give up their senseless resistance — after all no one wished to do them any harm! Sometimes they dropped incendiary bombs.

The conflagrations began to get the better of the less hardy elements of the Resistance movement, not so much combatants as civilians. The SS, and the gapers of Warsaw, had another choice spectacle: they could feast their eyes on the terrorised inhabitants jumping out of their blazing houses and dashing themselves to death on the ground below. Sometimes these poor creatures were living torches; occasionally they remained suspended by their clothes from the balconies. One of Stroop's photographers must have considered the photogenic qualities of such a scene to his liking for he sent a copy of it to his leader, who incorporated it in his album.

It did not even occur to the insurgents to capitulate. Instead they decided to change tactics and, according to Anielewicz, follow the Partisans' example. They only ventured out at night, often dressed in German uniform, and killed as many Germans as possible under cover of darkness.

On 26 April, a final communiqué reached the outside world from the ghetto:

We are now in the eighth day of our fight to the death . . . The Germans have suffered heavy losses and were forced at one point to beat a retreat for two days. They returned with reinforcements: tanks, armoured cars, heavy guns, planes, and began systematically to lay siege to the ghetto. The number of Jewish losses, victims of the shooting and the fires (in which men, women and children perished) is enormous. Our days are numbered. However, so long as we can hold a weapon, we will resist and oppose them and fight on. We have rejected the German ultimatum calling upon us to capitulate.

Since we see our end drawing near we beg of you: Do not forget!

The day shall come when the innocent blood spilt will be revenged Help those who manage to escape from the enemy so that they may continue the fight.

The following day, several of the most important bunkers succumbed to the relentless pressure of the SS. A fiercer battle, with Jews and Poles fighting and dying together, took place in the vicinity of Muranowski Square. Survivors of the JMU, including the leader Apfelbaum, and Lopata, managed to re-establish contact with their Polish friends, among them Captain Iwanski, who, with his group, was smuggled into the ghetto by Jews, who had already made the journey in the opposite direction. A desperate battle took place. Captain Iwanski's brother was killed and his son seriously wounded, but the rest of the Poles managed to withdraw, taking their wounded with them. They wanted to take Apfelbaum with them, but though he was mortally wounded he refused. He died the following day.

The insurgents began to explore the sewer system in preparation for an escape to the Aryan quarter. But Stroop's men had had the same thought and had sealed all the gully-holes. Engineer units set off explosive charges, smoke bombs, and chemical bombs inside, and this, added to the flooding of some of the sewers, made them extremely hazardous to negotiate; but there was no other way out.

On 8 May a German column marched to 18 Mila Street, and stationed themselves outside the entrance of the bunker headquarters of the JCO. The hundred or so combatants in the bunker were called upon to surrender, but preferred to perish by their own hands. One of these was Mordekhai Anielewicz.

At the last moment, someone found an undiscovered exit, and twenty-one of the combatants got away before the Germans gained access to the bunker with the aid of heavy gunfire and dynamite and destroyed it completely, the bodies with it.

On 10 May, a very daring operation conducted by Rathauser enabled a number of the combatants who had escaped through the sewers to be evacuated by lorry across the German lines. A second attempt failed because the organisers were denounced by a Polish woman.

It is interesting to compare Rathauser's account of events with the report drawn up by General Stroop:

> This morning at 9 o'clock a lorry drew up at the sewer in the Prosta quarter. One of the men in the lorry exploded two hand grenades as a signal for the bandits waiting within. The bandits and the Jews armed with rifles and various other firearms, including a Bren gun, got into the lorry, which immediately set off for an unknown destination. The last of the band stationed on sentry duty outside the sewer was captured ... Investigations concerning the fate of the lorry proved fruitless ...
>
> Because we are on good terms with the Wehrmacht, the Engineer group has managed to get reinforcements. We have been given an even larger supply of explosives.

In his report of 16 May, Stroop was able to declare:

> *The former Jewish quarter no longer exists: An explosion (for which the Jews, themselves, were responsible) destroyed the Warsaw synagogue. The* Grossaktion *is terminated.*

The ghetto combatants had fought for their honour more than anything else. They found themselves in a situation where there was no longer any hope of their surviving; so they had decided to choose their manner of dying, ensuring that as many Germans as possible died with them. At the same time, they hoped that their sacrifice would serve as a lesson not only for the Jews but for all freedom-loving peoples.

That lesson has been learnt.

More than 56,000 Jews, combatants and non-combatants, of both sexes and all ages, had either been killed during the uprising or deported to Treblinka or Maidanek.

Some combatants had managed to reach the forests; either the near-by Puscza Kampinoscza forest, or that of Wyszkov, where they set up Partisan detachments bearing significant names like *Anielewicz*, or *The Avengers of the ghettos*. These detachments managed to equip themselves and were lucky enough to receive parachuted Soviet arms. Two heroes of the ghetto, Abraham Szwarcfuchs and David Nowodworski, were among the members.

There were few Polish Partisans in the forests at that time, but the situation soon changed. When rumours of the Jews' activities reached the ears of the Russian prisoner-of-war camp, number 333, in the Wengrow district, there were a great many successful escapes. The Russians joined up with the Jewish combatants, knowing that they had a better chance of being well received by them than by the Poles and they fought side by side. A great number of railway systems were sabotaged, including the Warsaw—Malkinia—Vilna line serving Treblinka.

All these detachments ended up by being attacked by the Germans; in one case, by Ultra-Fascist Polish partisans of the NSZ movement. Few of their members survived.

At the time of the ghetto rising, Antek-Cukierman was the principal JCO liaison agent in the Aryan quarter of Warsaw and was to remain so until the Polish insurrection exploded in its turn in August 1944. The few remaining members of the JCO rallied together and bravely took their place at the side of the insurgents. Other Jews participated in this national Polish uprising, and not all of them were Polish.

Himmler's orders for the total destruction of the Warsaw ghetto having been carried out, a concentration camp was set up. For security reasons, and even the most dull-witted of the SS knew what these were, it was not the Warsaw Jews who were imprisoned there, but detainees from Auschwitz, Dachau, and other camps.

When the insurrection took place in 1944 one of the first engagements involved the liberation of almost all the 2,000 prisoners in the camp, most of them Jews, who then set up combat groups among themselves, the Greek Jews taking the lead.

The surrender of the Warsaw insurgents led by General Bor-Komorowski had the paradoxical result that the several thousand Jews hidden in Warsaw were confused with the Polish masses. Their security was further assured when they were scattered throughout Poland.

The battle of the Warsaw Jews was over.

NOTES

1. Some time before the various youth organisations had created *kibbutzim* in the ghetto itself. The use of this name may seem surprising. The Hebrew word *kibbutz* (plural *kibbutzim*) means a gathering, a group, a community. The members of each community lived together in one or two buildings, according to the principles that still govern the Israeli *kibbutzim*. Up to 1939 the Jewish *kibbutzim* were made up of groups formed abroad, whose members had acquired the habit of living together. In the very special circumstances of the ghetto the fact that the young people had experienced life in barracks was to be very useful. In 1942, however, the size of the *kibbutzim* was limited by the equipment and arms at their disposal.

2. Mark (op. cit.) wrote that he had anticipated deporting a first batch of 16,000 Jews, and the remainder at a later date.

3. Most of the non-Jewish Poles were firmly convinced of the innate cowardice of the Jews. Less than three weeks before the January 1943 combats, the Polish general Grot-Rowecki, Commanding Officer of the AK, reported in a message to his government in London that at the request of 'Jews of various small groups' he had tentatively supplied them with a dozen or so revolvers, but that he was not at all sure if they would use them.

4. These misgivings were not unjustified, as history was to prove in August-September 1944, when the Polish insurgents of Warsaw fought the Germans themselves — and were beaten. The time — had it only occurred to them — was ripe for an insurrection. The Germans were beating a retreat. The Russians were at the gates of Warsaw, and the combatants expected to seize the capital without too much difficulty and themselves welcome the advancing Red Army. They were proved wrong, for the Germans halted their retreat, after having carried off a major tactical victory in the vicinity, and the Red Army had to delay its advance. Once

the insurrection was under way the Soviet soldiers were less eager than ever to seize Warsaw. It will long be disputed as to whether they were unable, or simply unwilling, to come to the aid of the combatants. In our opinion it was better for them to wait until all their troops were assembled before Warsaw. But they certainly did not speed up the operation. In any case, the situation in 1942 and 1943 was much less favourable for a general uprising than was the case in August 1944; and that operation failed at the cost of a great many human lives, though fewer than were lost in the ghetto.

5. This last unit was made up of non-German volunteers from various East European countries, Latvia, Lithuania and Ukraine, who wished to become SS.

6. He fared even worse a year later in Croatia where a Partisan's bullet put an end to his days.

7. After his Warsaw 'victory' he was transferred to Athens, where he was made *Höhere SS-und Polizeiführer* of Greece. Having displayed his talents in Greece, he was appointed *Höhere SS-und Polizeiführer* in the Westmark — a region in the Rhineland comprising the German Palatinate, Luxembourg, and even the French department of Moselle. Following his usual practice he had a great many hostages shot. When the war ended, Stroop was sentenced to death first by a British military tribunal for the crimes he had committed in Greece, and again on his extradition to Poland. He was finally executed in July 1951.

8. No doubt some Germans, and the former SS in particular, rebelled against this manoeuvre. But they did not get very far, even in Federal Germany, for they were too valuable as scapegoats. When the situation worsened, they tried to keep their distance from those among them who were too compromised, secretly helping them at the same time.

9. Other detachments went into action during the next two days. A group commanded by Bartoszek sabotaged the railways, thus delaying deportations. The general quartermaster of the GL, Bonislawski, was killed while trying to deliver supplies to the ghetto. An armed attack by an AK detachment led by Richard Wieckowski in the Muranowski Square district allowed a group of Jewish prisoners to make a getaway. The ghetto combatants were not unaware of these manifestations of solidarity.

CHAPTER 25

BOMBS AT CRACOW

THERE were three large ghettos in the south-west of Poland: one in Cracow, 'capital' of the General Government of Poland, another in the industrial centre of Czestochowa, and a third in the twin cities of Sosnowiec-Bedzin in territory annexed to Germany.

All three possessed small Resistance groups, which had managed to link up with the Warsaw Jewish Combat Organisation. The ghetto Resistance fighters belonged to the same Zionist youth movements as their Warsaw compatriots. There were also a few Bundists, mostly in Czestochowa and Cracow. There do not seem to have been many Communists.

It was the members of the Cracow group who gave most trouble to the Gestapo, even though there were only a few dozen of them. It had two branches: one in the capital, where some of the members lived in the ghetto and some, under false identities, in the Aryan quarter; and the principal one about a hundred miles away in Wisnicznowy, near Bochnia.

A farm in the locality had been leased by the authorities to serve as an agricultural institute for young Jews. It may seem surprising that the Gestapo had authorised the setting up of such an institution late in 1941, at a time when Jewish emigration was forbidden and the 'final solution' had already been adopted in principle.

One possible explanation is the communication problems between Berlin and the provinces of occupied territory; more probably it was a Nazi ruse to gather all the young Jews together so as to facilitate their capture when the time came.

Adolf Liebeskind, one of the first of the Cracow Jewish Resistants, maintained liaison between the farm and Cracow from April 1942 onwards. His 'official' duties in a philanthropic institution gave him reasonable coverage for his other activities and he managed to establish contact with the Warsaw JCO as well as with a number of young Cracow Jews. Among the most important militants were Leibowicz-Laban and Tennenbaum in the Bochnia group; Simon and Gusta-Justyna Draenger, Feldhorn and Joseph Wulf in Cracow itself.

All these young people were Zionists. They did not believe there was the slightest chance of their surviving and left a letter destined for their comrades in Palestine, so that they might know, after the war, that they had not died without defending themselves.

In the autumn of 1942, Liebeskind tried to set up an underground movement in the vicinity of Cracow. This venture was both rash and premature. Of the six young men sent into the forest, armed with two revolvers, all died immediately. This was their first engagement.

The failure of this attempt led the Resistance to look for other methods of combat, and they now began to concentrate on railway sabotage, on the one hand, and urban terrorism on the other.

Several members of the group had managed to get hold of uniforms and documents which enabled them to pass as either Polish policemen or Polish, and sometimes German, employees of the Reich railways. The number of people working in complicity with them in Polish and even in German circles was such that before very long the Resistance fighters had an adequate supply of funds and weapons.

Between November and December 1942, the combatants liquidated a number of individual Germans in various quarters of the town; but their most dramatic attack took place on 23 December 1942.

On that day a group of Jewish combatants tossed hand grenades into the *Cyganeria*, one of Cracow's most elegant cafés, frequented solely by German soldiers and civilians. Other combatants did the same thing in German-patronised cafés throughout the city.

The German authorities in Cracow were more sensitive to urban terrorism than were those in other Polish towns since it was the capital and administrative centre of the General Government. They had suffered serious losses and their reaction was swift and effective. By evening most of the assailants, including Leibowicz-Laban, found themselves under lock and key.

On the following evening a powerful Gestapo detachment formed a cordon round a certain house in the 'Aryan' quarter of the town, allegedly a hostel for railway employees. The hall porter was arrested and a group of police officers descended to the cellars. They were greeted by revolver fire. Intense shooting followed, but the police had the advantage. Both Liebeskind and Tennenbaum fell on that Christmas Eve in 1942.

The Gestapo found 3 revolvers and 45 unfired bullets on their bodies. They also found, hidden in the cellar a typewriter, a duplicating machine, a small printing press, a radio set, 200 dollars, 10,540 *zlotys*, a Polish police uniform and a German railwayman's uniform.

The police attached a great deal of importance to this capture and the central headquarters of the Berlin Gestapo was notified immediately. At 2.25 p.m. on Christmas Day, *SS-Gruppenführer* Muller, chief of the Gestapo, sent a teletype to *SS-Obergruppenführer* Wolff, at the Führer's headquarters, informing him of the great victory won by his men. Wolff, who had long been personal deputy to Himmler, was at this time personal representative of the *Reichsführer SS*, attached to Hitler himself. Presumably Hitler took a close interest in the affair; otherwise it is difficult to see why such a message was transmitted on Christmas day to Wolff in his current capacity.

Hitler had his full share of military problems at that point. His Sixth Army had been blockaded in Stalingrad for over a month. The counter-attack designed to release it had failed. The Red Army had already penetrated the Don front and threatened to encircle the relief detachment as well. Yet the Führer had to be informed that two dangerous Jewish terrorists had been put out of action in Cracow.

Within a few weeks all the members of the two sections of the group, in Cracow and Wisnicznowy, had been captured. Gusta Draenger managed to write her memoirs while she was in prison and these were discovered after the Liberation. It appears that she made an attempt to escape before she, too, vanished in the turmoil. Her husband shared the same fate. Leibowicz-Laban made a last, vain bid to escape as they were leading him before the firing squad.

Joseph Wulf, the future historian, was luckier: he was shut up in Auschwitz, but not as a deportee. He was a *Schutzhäftling*, that is to say a prisoner by virtue of a prison mandate, on which it was clearly stated that the person concerned was to be kept at Auschwitz to await trial.

There was no trial, since from 1943 onwards the German police were wholly responsible for the punishment of the Jews. Nevertheless, one of the many paradoxes of Auschwitz was that those who had been imprisoned there because of what they *had done* had some chance of survival, while those who had been deported because of what they *were* had scarcely any. After the Liberation, Joseph Wulf had the unexpected joy of finding his wife and son again. Thanks to the complicity of Polish peasants, they had lived for more than two years in a dug-out in a cave.

In Sosnowiec and in the industrial centre of Czestochowa young Jewish Resistance fighters who tried to oppose deportation by force were defeated. Their failure to mobilise the mass of Jews in the two ghettos was due not to lack of effort but to lack of numbers: there were only a few dozen of them in all.

They did, however, have one successful operation to their credit, when they succeeded in smuggling a few of their best and most courageous militants into Slovakia and even though this mission failed when the decisive moment came, at least they were able to pass on tidings of the Jewish combatants[1] to the outside world.

The Resistance groups in Cracow, Sosnowiec-Bedzin and Czestochowa had very little contact with the Polish Resistance movement, although Joseph Wulf mentions a liaison with a militant Communist, Gola Mirer. The Communists were in the process of establishing themselves and the Cracow region was not one where their efforts were most swiftly or most easily rewarded.

One of the great disadvantages of the Jewish combatants in this part of the country was the absence of those Jews or Poles with close contacts dating back before 1939, though at this period, there were Jewish and Polish militants in the Polish Socialist Party (PSP) who were closely united not only politically but also on the personal side. To mention two of them: Josef Cyrankiewicz future prime minister of Poland was very friendly with Maksymilian Boruchowicz, who later became the writer Michel Borwicz. While JCO were operating in Cracow both of them were in prison; Cyrankiewicz for his action in the Polish Resistance movement, and Borwicz for having been caught prowling around the Lvov (Lemberg) ghetto where he was trying to organise a Resistance movement[2]. Rather than be shot on the spot, he confessed to the police that he was a Jew and was shut up in the Lvov concentration camp, 'the Janow camp', a small-scale one, containing fewer prisoners than Buchenwald or Treblinka, though it compared very well as far as maltreatment was concerned and is said to have been a training ground for SS guards.

Borwicz had a remarkable military record. A sub-lieutenant in the Polish Army, he happened to be in Switzerland on 1 September 1939, when war was declared. With no thought for anything but his duty he crossed half Europe — skirting Germany — in order to reach Poland and arrived just as the Polish retreat was in full swing. Unable to find his own unit, he joined another, as a lieutenant, and flung himself into the fray. Captured near Zamosc, he managed to escape across the Soviet frontier. There the fact that he was a Polish officer, as well as a writer of Socialist—Zionist leanings did not exactly facilitate his relations with the Soviet authorities. Nevertheless, although a great many resident militant Zionists from Lvov, or those who had sought protection there, had been 'transferred' to Central Asia or to the labour camps in the far North, Borwicz managed to remain where he was until the Nazi invasion caught up with him.

In the Janow camp, Borwicz was subjected to particularly brutal tortures. He was even hanged, and survived because the rope broke. The SS commander, shaken by the event, spared his life[3].

Borwicz escaped shortly afterwards but only after he had prepared the ground for others to follow his example.

He returned to Cracow under the guise of a Polish railwayman, and within a few weeks became military commander of the Polish Socialist combatants in the Cracow region. He later took command of the national *Armja Krajowa*.

He contacted the JCO survivors of Warsaw: Cukierman, Cyvia Lubetkin, Rathauser, and a few others, who were living in hiding in the Aryan quarter, and also took part in the work of the Jewish Rescue Committee which had been set up in Poland through the good offices of the exiled Polish government.

This committee, working against tremendous odds and in a very trying psychological climate, helped to save the lives of thousands of Jews living in hiding. The mere fact that it existed, and that it let the population know of its existance, was enough to encourage a great many Polish people to risk coming to the aid of the Jews.

The head of the committee, the Socialist leader Julian Grobelny, was struck down by an enemy bullet, but his deputy, Sofia Kossak, survived.

Borwicz, with his heavy military responsibilities in the AK, had a Jewish counterpart, Gustave Alef Bolkowiak, who exercised similar functions in the Communist-orientated AL, functioning in the Lublin region where there were a great many Jewish fugitives from the labour camps. The AL movement in the Lublin zone, almost exclusively Jewish, suffered very heavy losses but was never completely wiped out.

NOTES

I. This group suffered very heavy losses in Slovakia and later in Hungary.
2. However, at the time of the liquidation of the ghetto, the Germans had, in their own words, 'to take brutal action right away' (*von vornherein brutal*) in order to protect themselves.
3. Some twenty years later, this same SS was tried in Federal Germany for his crimes and had the surprising idea of citing Borwicz as witness for the defence.

CHAPTER 26

NO TO RESISTANCE IN VILNA

T HE area covered by Central and Eastern Europe has often been described as a zone of international conflict. The close proximity of the two sections, indeed their cohabitation, continues to cause particularly distressing problems, especially since the deterioration of international relations on a world scale, and if there was one region where these conflicts had overstepped the limits of endurance, it was Vilna.

In the Middle Ages, Vilna was the capital of the Grand Duchy of Lithuania, a much larger country than the independent republic, with its miserable 33,664 square miles, set up by the Treaty of Versailles. The Grand Duchy extended up to Smolensk, and across to Brest-Litovsk, covering the whole of Bielorussia and, at certain periods, stretching down as far as the Black Sea. It was later swallowed up by Poland, and subsequently annexed to Russia.

When Lithuania regained its independence in 1919 it recovered the Lithuanian-speaking countries even though these had been minority regions, and also its capital. At this time Vilna could scarcely have been described as a truly Lithuanian city, since there were far more Poles and Jews than Lithuanians, and a large number of Bielorussians, Russians and, Latvians, though there were no Germans.

In 1920, a Polish column commanded by General Zeligowski brazenly violated the peace by crossing the Lithuanian frontier and seizing Vilna, when the Lithuanian Vilnius became the Polish Wilno. The little country of Lithuania, incapable of withstanding this Polish *coup de force*, burned with resentment and longed for the day when it could take its revenge.

On 17 September 1939 'in response to an appeal by the Ukrainian and Bielorussian peoples' — the German armies were laying siege to Warsaw at the time — the Soviet troops conformed with the Germano-Soviet pact of 23 August 1939 and crossed the Polish frontier. Reaching Vilna two days later they promptly took up their positions along the Lithuanian frontier.

Shortly afterwards, the Soviet Union exacted from its Baltic States, Lithuania, Latvia and Estonia, the right to set up naval air bases on their territory, but in order to ensure the good graces of Lithuania, Stalin restored Vilna.

The intermission ended with the fall of France at the end of June 1940, when Stalin simply overthrew the governments of the three Baltic States, and had the people vote by plebiscite to join the USSR. Vilna became Russian.

But Vilna was also a very ancient cultural and spiritual Jewish stronghold — a sort of Lithuanian Jerusalem from which great Jewish philosophical movements had sprung. In more recent times, towards the end of the nineteenth century, it had been the scene of intense political activity, notably among the various Socialist parties: the Russian Social Democrats, who later split up to become Bolshevists, Mensheviks and Bundists; Zionist Socialists; and the non-Socialist Zionists. There were also militant trade unions.

Estimates of the number of Jews living in Vilna in 1939 vary between 60,000 and 80,000 out of a total population of just over 200,000 inhabitants, or between a third and two-fifths of the population.

The most prominent figure in the drama that was to disrupt Judaism in Vilna was the Pole Isaac (Itzic) Wittenberg. He was thirty-four years old in 1941 when the Germans conquered Vilna. Two years later he was dead.

As soon as he was old enough, Wittenberg had joined the Polish Communist Party. A shoemaker by trade he was an active trade unionist. It was the only field where a Communist could legally militate at that time, since the Communist Party was officially banned. In 1936 Wittenberg was appointed president of the skin and fur trade union and member of the town's Trade Unionists' Council. He thus became an important member of the Jewish community and a prominent citizen as well.

His position probably saved his life in 1938 when Stalin announced the dissolution of the Polish Communist Party and took the further step of liquidating a number of its leaders. Wittenberg, senior city official as he was, did not dream of surrendering to the USSR, but remained at his post, and became more active than ever after the entry of the Red Army and the transformation of Lithuania into a Soviet republic. However, he stayed on in Vilna which once again had become the capital of Lithuania, but was no more Lithuanian for that.

When it was the turn of the *Wehrmacht* to occupy Vilna after the invasion of the USSR, Wittenberg was well aware that he was earmarked for arrest and execution. Growing up in the tradition of clandestinity he immediately took to the underground. In common with many militant Communists in occupied Soviet territories he planned to organise a Partisan war.

The Jewish population suffered terribly in the early months of the German occupation of Vilna, as the few survivors have testified[1]. *SS-Standartenführer* Jäger gives the following figures of executions in Vilna from the time he took up his duties on 9 August 1941 to 1 December 1941.

12—8					
to 1—9	425 Jews	19 Jews		total	444
2—9	864 Jews	2019 Jews	817 children Jewish	total	3700

12—9	993 Jews	1670 Jews	771 children Jewish	total 3334
17—9	337 Jews	687 Jews	247 children Jewish	total 1267
4—10	432 Jews	1115 Jews	436 children Jewish	total 1983
16—10	382 Jews	507 Jews	257 children Jewish	total 1146
21—10	718 Jews	1063 Jews	586 children Jewish	total 2367
25—10	718 Jews	1706 Jews	812 children Jewish	total 2578
27—10	946 Jews	184 Jews	73 children Jewish	total 1203
30—10	382 Jews	789 Jews	362 children Jewish	total 1533
6—11	340 Jews	749 Jews	252 children Jewish	total 1341
19—11	76 Jews	77 Jews	18 children Jewish	total 171
25—11	9 Jews	46 Jews	8 children Jewish	total 64

Jäger points out that the executions on 2 September constituted a *Sonderaktion* because Jews had opened fire on German soldiers.

The day after this *Sonderaktion*, which for a long time was the most devastating single action ever to take place in Vilna in the course of a day, Dr. Marc Dvorjetski, a Vilna physician, and chronicler of the ghetto, received a surprise visit. It was from a frightened-looking woman with a bandaged arm, carrying a bunch of flowers. He had the greatest difficulty persuading her to explain what had brought her to him; but eventually she managed to stammer that she had come from Ponar.

Ponar was at that time considered to be a somewhat strictly disciplined labour camp. Everybody knew that people were sent there, but no one ever heard what happened to them afterwards, until the woman, Pessia Aronovitch, described her eventful journey to Dr. Dvorjetski. She and her two children had been taken along with others to Ponar where all of them had been shot, her two children included. She alone had survived, and when darkness fell she had climbed out of the death-pit and on the advice of a passing peasant had picked a bunch of wild flowers to act as a blind, so that the Germans took her for a peasant woman and let her pass.

Dvorjetski's first reaction was that he had a mythomaniac on his hands until he opened the dressing on the woman's arm and found a bullet wound, and small insects such as one would find in the forest.

He sent the woman to hospital and informed the other Jews that Ponar was not a labour camp but an extermination camp. No one believed him.

Meanwhile, Pessia Aronovitch had found employment in the ghetto as a dressmaker. The doctor went to see her again and asked if she had related her experiences to her companions. She had not. She was afraid that the Gestapo would get wind of the affair and try to shoot her again, and do the job properly this time.

Dr. Dvorjetski's conclusion was: 'She was a rejected witness.'

She was not the only one. Motel Gdoud, nineteen years old at the time, had a similar adventure. He and thirty-four other Jews were taken to Ponar in a police van. On arrival there they were greeted by the Nazi Schwannenberg, — known to ghetto survivors as Schweinenberg. This individual made the Jews undress, then beckoned them forward one after another and shot them in the back of the neck. Gdoud fell to the ground just as the bullet left the gun, so that he heard it fired, heard it whistle past, but lay there unharmed.

The following day Gdoud returned home, took his father aside and told him what had happened. He was not believed.

In the ghetto the number of inhabitants grew smaller and smaller yet life tended to go on as usual. Everyone felt death hovering over them and knew that there would be other victims, but what could they do? At least as long as they worked for the Germans they would have some sort of security. Or would they? One day thousands of workers failed to come home.

The Germans imposed a Jewish Council on the Vilna Jews and promptly shot some of the members. A second Council suffered a similar fate.

Jacob Gens, *der stolzer Jude*, 'the proud Jew', as the Germans called him, now became chief of the Vilna police, and incidentally chief of the ghetto.

Gens was a militant Zionist with Revisionist leanings. A reserve officer of the Polish Army married to a Lithuanian, his qualities had probably impressed the Germans. Whether he really collaborated with them or really wished to save as many Jews as possible is not known.

Gens was shot by the Germans on 15 November 1943, more than two years after the setting up of the Vilna ghetto.

It appears that Gens saw himself as something of a Maecenas. Speaking at a literary soirée in the ghetto, he declaimed:

> *Many of you look upon me as a traitor . . . It was I, Gens, who blew up the underground hideouts of the Jews, but at the same time I took infinite pains to procure papers and employment for the ghetto people. We are compatible in our Jewish blood but not in our Jewish sense of honour. When I am asked to deliver up a thousand Jews, I do so, otherwise the Germans would help themselves, and it would not be one thousand, but thousands they would take. By offering a hundred Jews, I save a thousand; by offering a thousand Jews, I save ten thousand.*
>
> *You who devote yourselves to spiritual matters are not implicated in the corruptions of the ghetto. If you are lucky enough to escape, you escape unsullied . . . If I, Jacob Gens, do, I shall be defiled, my hands dripping with blood. Nevertheless I would offer myself for trial, I would stand before the Jewish judges and I would say to them: I have done everything in my power to save as many Jews as pos-*

*sible. But that certain Jews might live I was obliged to lead others
to their death. In order that some Jews might keep a clear conscience,
I was obliged to act without conscience.*

Jacob Gens did not escape; and did not have to account for his actions before
a Jewish court. Dr. Dvorjetski, whom we have to thank for the above, did not
substitute himself for the judges whose sentence Gens accepted in advance but
contented himself with the apparently modest role — how much more formidable
in reality — of witness.

We do not intend setting ourselves up as Jewish judges either. We merely point
out that Gens himself, even at that period had recourse to spiritual protection. He
consulted the Rabbis of Vilna — and Vilna was a city famous for the wisdom of its
Rabbis. The Rabbis told him that his reasoning was wrong. They told him in no
uncertain terms that he had no right to hand over Jews to the Germans, for religious law forbade it. They reminded him of the response given seven centuries
ago by the great Maimonides: 'If the pagans ask you [Jews] to deliver up one of
your numbers so that he might be killed, for otherwise they would kill you all,
you must have everyone killed and not deliver up a single Jewish soul.'

Jacob Gens, the 'false Messiah', as Dvorjetski calls him, contravened Jewish
religious law. He soiled his hands. Nor is there any evidence that by his action
he saved even one of the Vilna Jews.

Gens is convicted on his own confession.

Wittenberg was the anti-Gens. Not that he had the least tendency to look
upon himself as a Messiah. He claimed no miraculous solution, nor did he promise salvation for all. All he had was experience in the field of political struggle.
He knew how to make a cool assessment of the situation without allowing his emo-
tions to get too involved. He was also a disciplined Communist. Stalin had given
the go-ahead for the Partisan war, for battle to commence in occupied territories.
But Wittenberg would have acted whether Stalin had spoken or not.

He contacted his Communist comrades and the organised Zionist youth move-
ment. To mention only a few: Abba Kovner — one of the few survivors —Glasman,
Resnik, Frucht, and a little later, Khwoinik. There was also Mordechai Ten-
nenbaum-Tamarov of the Bialystock ghetto, about half way between Vilna and
Warsaw, who tirelessly maintained communications between the two ghettos, and
Frouma Plotnicka, who assisted him.[2]

Two groups sprang up and swiftly joined together to form the United Partisans
Organisations (UPO). Like other ghettos they were faced with a difficult alternative: whether to fight on the spot or try to escape to the forest? Wherever there
were sufficient Communists to have their motion carried, the forest solution prevailed, at least in theory, for it was one of those paradoxical situations so fre-

quent in the history of the Jewish Resistance and especially in Eastern Europe: those who favoured defence within the ghetto distinguished themselves in the battles of the neighbouring forests, while Ilya Scheinbaum who was the leading advocate for combat in the forests fell while engaged in more or less single-handed defence barricade in the ghetto.

Visits paid to the Vilna ghetto by Tennenbaum-Tamarov, Frouma Plotnicka, Irena Adamowicz, the young Polish Girl Scout, and the young Polish Scout Heniek, had stimulated the spirit of resistance in the various Zionist-orientated youth movements.

It is here that we must mention Corporal Anton Schmidt of the *Wehrmacht*. A Viennese born in Bohemia and a paint shop proprietor in private life, he served, like all Austrians, in the German Army; but unlike most of his fellow soldiers, Anton Schmidt was outraged at the massacre of the Jews and decided to oppose it with all the means at his disposal.

He had already had occasion to come to the aid of some Jews in Vienna in 1938 and 1939, in the early stages of Nazi persecution; not openly, for that would have earned him the concentration camp and probably his death, but in a practical fashion by finding 'illegal' work for the Jews and keeping them from the brink of starvation.

In Vilna he went a step further, driving combatants to and fro between the ghettos so that they could form liaisons. He also supplied them with foodstuffs and arms. He was eventually caught, sentenced to death, and shot. Father Kropp, today a teacher in the Catholic *Lycée* of Ansbach in Bavaria, was present at the moment of his execution. Unfortunately, Schmidt left no last message for posterity, and there is no knowing what led him to act as he did.

The inaugural meeting of the UPO took place on Christmas Eve 1941. There were the usual heated discussions, but they ended in firm decisions. A leadership of three was chosen, headed by Itzik Wittenberg (Leon), with his deputies Abba Kovner (Ouri) and Joseph Glasman (Abram).

They decided to adopt combat structures: groups of five and sections of four groups. The entire UPO consisted of 2 battalions, each comprising several sections. Kovner and Glasman had a battalion each. Sectional leaders were Sonia Madejsker, Baroukh Goldstein and Samuel Kaplinski. The combatants had taken as their rallying cry 'Lisa calls us', in memory of Lisa Magoun, the young Vilna Jewess who had smuggled herself into the neighbouring ghetto of Cszmania. When she reached the square she had begun to harangue the Jews at the top of her voice imploring them to flee from the Germans, or to fight the Germans but never, never to allow the Germans to take them to Ponar. She was identified and assassinated, but a number of Cszmania Jews owe their lives to her.

The meeting of 24 December 1941 also led to the publication of an appeal for resistance circulated in the Vilna ghetto. Abba Kovner, who was hiding at the time in a Benedictine convent on the outskirts of Vilna was apparently responsible for this.

The appeal, which could not have been plainer or more to the point, did not attempt to conceal the harsh realities from the Vilna Jews, but endeavoured to put them in their true perspective:

> *Let us not go to our death like lambs to the slaughter. Young Jews, I appeal to you, do not believe those who wish to do you harm. Remember there were once 80,000 Jews in Vilna, now there are no more than 20,000.*
>
> *We have witnessed the slaughter of our parents, our brothers and our sisters. Where are the hundreds of men rounded up by the police allegedly for work? Where are the naked women and children led out of the ghetto on the night of the provocation[3]? Where are all those who were rounded up on Yom Kippur? Where are our brothers of the second ghetto[4]?*
>
> *Those who have been taken from the ghetto will never return. All roads lead to Ponar, and Ponar is death.*
>
> *Throw away your illusions; I assure you, your children, your wives and your husbands are no longer with us. Ponar is not a labour camp. Everybody there has been shot. It is Hitler's plan to annihilate all the Jews in Europe — we are the first.*
>
> *Let us not go like lambs to the slaughter! It is true we are weak and alone. But the only answer worth giving to our enemy is Resistance!*
>
> *Brothers, far rather die fighting than live by the grace of the slaughterer. Let us defend ourselves to our last breath.*
>
> *Vilna, 1 January 1942, in the ghetto.*

Jechiel Scheinbaum headed the UPO on the political side. Arms were smuggled into the ghetto, usually through the sewers. The ghetto chimney-sweeps were persuaded to help, for being the only ones in Vilna they were allowed to circulate freely in the town.

Like all ghetto organisations, the UPO had heated discussions as to exactly when the uprising should take place. When one reads the appeal of 1 January it is immediately apparent that the insurrection was only conceivable as a last resort and many had still not reached that stage.

The Jewish Resistance fighters decided not to give the official go-ahead for the uprising until the very last moment but to begin anti-enemy operations on their own account without delay.

Baroukh Goldstein brought in revolvers concealed in the bandaging of a wound.

Sixteen-year-old Zalman Tiktin stole handgrenades and smuggled them into the ghetto. He was caught but not searched and later managed to blow open the door of his cell and escape, but was shot before he got very far.

In February 1942, Wittenberg got in touch with Soviet parachutists dropped in the Skrabouchany forest. He was officially recognised by the UPO. Shortly afterwards an urban committee of the Communist Party was set up in Vilna headed by another Jew, Berl Cherechniewski, living in hiding in the Aryan quarter of the city. Wittenberg made Vilna his headquarters and took up his duties as military leader of the UPO, while Sonia Madejsker headed the youth organisations. There was a Bielorussian, Korablikov, and a Pole, Przewalski on this committee, but not a single Lithuanian.

A young woman, Vitka Kampner, set about organising the sabotage of the railways. Wittenberg and Isaak Matzkievitch, a Jew who had taken the identity of a Tartar, put the plans into operation. A train loaded with arms was blown up on the Vilna-Novo-Vilejka line, and the local peasants and the Partisans divided the considerable booty between them.

The ghetto suffered no reprisals, for the simple reason that no one was caught. It would not have crossed the enemy's minds that the saboteurs might have been Jewish.

In April 1942 the Vilna Resistance organisation tried once more to get in touch with stronger and more powerful ghettos. It was a question of convincing the Jews of Bialystock and Warsaw that their fellow Jews in Vilna were on the brink of a precipice and that they themselves would soon be in the same position. The sisters Sarah and Rose Silber reached Bialystock and Warsaw to launch the appeal. They were scarcely listened to. The Silbers did not return to Vilna, for a Nazi patrol intercepted them at Malkinia, a main station on the Warsaw-Vilna line, from which a branch line ran to Treblinka.

Others left on the same mission: Elie (Edek) Boraks, who participated in the Bialystock insurrection and lost his life doing so; Haika Grossman who accompanied him but escaped. Gessia Glaeser (Glezerit) managed to establish liaisons with the Partisans but was caught and shot.

The ghetto, weak and dispirited, was called upon to help the Communist organisation of the 'Aryan' quarter of the city, just as the Warsaw combatants had been, which speaks volumes for the popularity of the Soviet régime in Vilna, at least in 1942. It was a ghetto printer, a member of the UPO called Kowalski, who had the task of procuring a clandestine printing press for the city Communists. He did this by stealing equipment piece by piece from the State printing works where he was employed as a technician. Once the operation was completed, and it took many days, he began all over again and assembled another printing press, this time for the ghetto.

The UPO had set up an intelligence service. Members of the special section assigned to procuring false papers and uniforms also took indirect action in local police organisations, German and Lithuanian. Some of them were seconded to the ghetto police directed by Gens, to keep an eye on him, probably with his knowledge.

Little by little the combatants made their presence felt in the ghetto, a force to be reckoned with, even if they were not capable of fighting Gens on an equal footing, for Gens had the ghetto police at his disposal, armed with revolvers as well as truncheons; not only this: Gens had a much more effective weapon in the trust of the great majority of the ghetto inhabitants. When he promised to do his utmost to save as many of them as he could, they took him at his word: their belief never wavered.

The mortal blow was to be struck in July 1943. The liquidation of the ghetto had already been decided on in that summer which saw the end of all the existing ghettos with the exception of Lodz, which was to last a year longer.

But another drama was to be enacted at Vilna before the end. It began with the breaking up of the urban Communist organisation and the arrest of the two non-Jewish leaders, Witos and Kozlowski. All equipment was seized and Wittenberg was identified. Someone had talked.

Kittel, the Nazi in charge of the ghetto, ordered Gens to hand over Wittenberg.

When the leaders of the UPO were summoned to Gens' office on the evening of 15 July 1943, they obeyed the call but took the precaution of posting an armed guard outside the *Judenrat*.

Discussions had hardly begun between Gens and the UPO leaders when the ghetto police officers burst in and seized Wittenberg. When they tried to take him to the ghetto prison UPO militants fell upon them and freed their leader.

Wittenberg went into hiding and the UPO was ordered to mobilise at once.

The next morning there was pandemonium in the ghetto. Aided by the ghetto police acting for the occasion as spokesmen for the crowd, Gens delivered a message from his balcony to the people below: the Gestapo had arrested a Polish Communist in the town who had declared that he was in contact with a certain Wittenberg, whom Gens know very well, but he was careful not to admit it. The Gestapo wanted Wittenberg; it wanted him without delay. If Wittenberg was not handed over immediately, the Gestapo would have the ghetto bombed.

What Gens was careful to conceal was that someone had already tried to call off the search by producing Wittenberg's death certificate. A ruse which had not tricked the Gestapo.

Gens reiterated his appeal. Was the ghetto, with its 20,000 inhabitants, to be destroyed for the sake of one man?

Put in this way the question could have only one answer, but to be doubly sure, Gens' deputy, Dessler, sent some of his own men to mingle in the crowd and to shout for Wittenberg to be handed over.

'Yes, give up Wittenberg! Save the ghetto!'

Gens then besought his hearers to find Wittenberg, while the ghetto police went from house to house encouraging the inhabitants to search out any stranger among them who might be he.

That day Dr. Dvorjetski received a visit from two of his patients: Wittenberg's wife and son. Madame Wittenberg begged him to hide her and her child and he led them to his own hideout. The ghetto was riddled with these places, either cavities walled in or hideouts specially dug and then concealed in various ways. Everybody, including the police, knew of their existence, but it was impossible even for the Germans to discover all of them.

Dvorjetski's hideout was already crammed full, and its occupants showed no enthusiasm at the sight of the new arrivals, whom they did not recognise. They knew that the ghetto was in danger and that the Gestapo wanted Wittenberg, and their principal concern was to know if he had been found. Madame Wittenberg whispered in the doctor's ear:

'They are all just waiting for my husband's death, I can see it, they all want him to die. I don't think he will last the day!'

At this point she knew nothing of the latest developments: that at that very moment her husband, having escaped from the ghetto police, was fighting for his life against his fellow combatants, his own followers. The battle was entirely dialectic but the arguments were the same as those of Gens. Wittenberg had found an absolutely secure hiding place where the Germans could not possibly find him; he even had a machine-gun, but his colleagues, even his closest allies, considered it impossible to launch an attack against the Germans unless the whole ghetto was behind them.

Wittenberg kept calm. He considered that come what might the ghetto was to be liquidated, that it was only a question of weeks, if not days. He saw through the Germans' plan. They were hoping to seize their most dangerous opponent and in so doing divide the ghetto against itself.

At that stage neither Wittenberg's comrades nor the rest of the ghetto could see his point.

Dr. Dvorjetski, who was not one of the leaders of the UPO, wrote later that the three members of the military staff of the UPO, Kovner, Glasman and Sonia Madejsker asked Wittenberg to give himself up to Gens. Souzkever, another member of the UPO wrote that Wittenberg intended to commit suicide but that his comrades dissuaded him since the Gestapo demanded him alive.

Abba Kovner, writer and poet, Wittenberg's deputy at the time, later his successor, brought up the Wittenberg affair on 4 May 1961 when he was called as a witness at Eichmann's trial[5]. He described the meeting with Gens on 15 July and the circumstances of Wittenberg's first arrest and told how he had Wittenberg put in a place of safety, and then circulated a printed pamphlet which declared that the German threat to destroy the ghetto if Wittenberg was not handed over was all bluff. Kovner had since recognised that this claim was unfounded. With Wittenberg's backing the writers of the pamphlet called on the members of the UPO to mobilise along with them.

At this moment events took an unexpected turn: the whole ghetto came out on the streets to oppose the UPO. The Jewish combatants found themselves faced with a painful alternative: if they wished to defend their leader they had to fight and even to kill their own fellow Jews, the people they were out to defend.

Kovner and his men ended up by joining Wittenberg in his hideout. Wittenberg was ready for anything. His revolver was lying in front of him and he asked his comrades what they wished him to do. Should he give himself up? There was a moment's silence, then Kovner spoke:

'Look, the Jews are in the street. Those are the ones we must fight. Give us the word and we shall fight them.'

It was Wittenberg's turn to be silent.

The Jews of Vilna thought that by delivering up Wittenberg they would save their own skins. They had a reprieve of ten weeks. On 23 September the ghetto was liquidated. Most of the inhabitants took the road to Ponar; the remainder were deported to concentration camps in Latvia and Estonia. At the approach of the Red Army the Jewish prisoners who had escaped being put to death and had survived the maltreatment were deported by sea to Germany. There are only a handful of survivors.

Rejecting resistance had not saved the ghetto.

The liquidation of the ghetto was not a straightforward task. A group of UPO Partisans led by Ilya Scheinbaum took up arms against the Latvian police detailed to evacuate certain streets in the ghetto. Scheinbaum was killed. Evacuation was interrupted for a time.

There was more opposition when the time came for the Jews to embark for Germany, and a growing number of escapes. Sonia Madejsker fell into the hands of the Gestapo; Chwoinik, young Assia Big, and Jacob Kaplan were captured but not without putting up a good fight; others managed to escape to the forests. A first group, led by Glasman, suffered heavy losses and Glasman himself was killed. The following groups were luckier. Abba Kovner, Wittenberg's successor as leader of the UPO, ended up with several hundred Jewish Partisans under him.

Several UPO groups united in a brigade headed by Jourgis (Georges) Ziminas in the Roudnicki forest, about twenty-six miles from Vilna, and this brigade is mentioned in the communiqués of the German High Command in Bielorussia (*Wehrmachtbefehlshaber Weissruthenien*) in the months of February, March and April 1944.

Abba Kovner commanded a detachment which took the name of *The Avengers* while Samuel Kaplinski commanded another; *To Victory*. Two other formations, exclusively Jewish in the earlier stages, *Combat* and *Death to the Fascists*, fought under Berek Cherechniewski. As the number of Partisans increased, its formations integrated with mixed groups, though not without some hesitation on the Jewish side. All these fought with a courage born of the thirst for vengeance. Haim Lazar, future doctor and Israeli politician, did not stop fighting when he lost his right hand in a mine explosion.

The Red Army recaptured Vilna on 17 July 1944, a year to the day after Wittenberg died.

NOTES

1.   The reader would do well to consult Dr. Marc Dvorjetski's remarkable book. *La victoire du ghetto*, Paris: France-Empire, 1962.

2. Tennenbaum-Tamarov was to fall during the Warsaw Ghetto uprising. Frouma died fighting a little later at Bedzin in Upper Silesia.

3.   2 September 1941.

4. Suppressed on 29 October 1941, its inhabitants ended up at Ponar.

5. The truth is that neither the tribunal nor the public prosecutor had any special desire to be enlightened on this point. Kovner supplied the information spontaneously and even at times against the wishes of the tribunal who considered — not without reason — that however moving the facts were, they bore no direct relation to the trial of Adolf Eichmann.

CHAPTER 27

KOVNO: A POET'S JOURNEY

THE city of Kovno, situated on the Niemen, had always been looked upon as a Slav, or rather a Russian stronghold. It had been the capital of Lithuania between the two wars.

When Lithuania won its independence, Kovno become Kaunus, and in 1920, when Poland seized Vilna, it became the capital of the tiny new state.

Before 1939, a good quarter of the city's 120,000 inhabitants were Jews. Kovno differed from most other Polish towns in that relations between its two communities were relatively good, perhaps because the Jews had sided with the Lithuanians against the Poles and had contributed in large measure to the struggle for independence.

Kovno was occupied two days after the German attack. No battle was necessary to secure the city since the Soviet forces, defeated at the frontier, had beaten a rapid retreat. The German army was given an enthusiastic reception by the city's inhabitants.

Feelings gradually changed as people came to realise that the Germans had come not to liberate the city but to conquer it. However, it took the citizens some time to recognise the true state of affairs. The Fascist and pro-Nazi elements in the city — and there were quite a number — decided that they had to prove themselves in the eyes of the Germans, and that the best way of doing this was by killing and pillaging the Jews, a task which they set about with enthusiasm, forming themselves into groups of what the Germans called 'Lithuanian partisans', which were in fact more or less regimented irregular soldiers. During the first few days of the German Occupation they shot or clubbed to death several thousand Jews.

SS-Standartenführer Jäger's report gives no figures of the number of Jews massacred more or less 'spontaneously' by the Lithuanian 'partisans', only indicating that there were two mass executions, on 4 and 6 July 1941, in fort number 7 in 'Kauen': 416 Jews and 47 Jewesses on 4 July; and 2,514 Jews on 6 July. Jäger reports that these executions were 'carried out by partisans in compliance with my directives and my orders'.

This second series of executions brought the total number of 'official' deaths to 2,974 — to which can be added nearly 4,000 who though not officially recorded as dead, were dead all the same.

Next day five prominent Jewish citizens were taken to the Gestapo headquarters of the city. They were introduced to an unidentified SS general, probably Franz Stahlecker, who informed them in Jäger's presence that they had been chosen to set up a Jewish Council, and that the immediate task of this Council was to gather together all the Kovno Jews in the suburban district of Slobodka (also known as Viliampole). The general pointed out that in a way it was for their own safety, for the Lithuanians could no longer bear the sight of a Jew, and slaughtered them in public, causing serious disruption to public order. That said, the general made it clear that he did not hold this against the Lithuanians since the Jews were all Communists anyway.

His hearers cannot have quite grasped the true situation for they tried to convince the general that the Jews were *not* Communists, and when he retorted that Marx and Stalin were Jewish, the Jews pointed out that Stalin, for one, was Georgian. This argument did not impress Stahlecker for he declared that whatever Stalin was, all his relatives were Jews. It was, in fact, the 1941 version of the fable of La Fontaine: *Si ce n'est pas toi, c'est donc ton frère* (If it is not you, then it must be your brother).

The following day the Jews had to appear before Jäger, and state how they intended to carry out the general's instructions, and a curious dialogue took place between the two parties.

The Jewish delegation declared that it felt itself compelled to obey orders but that it wished to make a few observations. Jäger indicated that he was disposed to listen to them and, encouraged, the Jews went on to say that the time allowed for the move was too short and that since the interests of the Lithuanians were at stake, they should be consulted in the matter.

When Jäger refused to consider any joint programme the Jews fell back upon another line of defence: the area allocated for the ghetto was too small; would it not be better to include the old quarter of Kovno which was more or less entirely populated by Jews anyway?

Jäger did not appear to be against this second suggestion: 'This can all be discussed when you have proved that you are capable of organising the move to the ghetto. When you have done that we shall decide where the limits are to be.'

Jäger struck the delegates as being a cold, impassive man. They certainly could not foresee the manner in which he intended to solve the problem of space in the ghetto.

Executions at fort number 7 are mentioned in Jäger's report of 9 July, that is to say the day he was calmly discussing matters with the Jews, and on 19 July; 43 Jews in all. Then, on 2 August another 205 Jews were shot, followed by 534 on 9 August, and 1,812, including 711 intellectuals, on 18 August, as reprisal measures. These executions took place in fort number 4. In the same fort 1,608

Jews, men, women and children, were shot on 20 September for medical reasons, Jäger mentioning the threat of an outbreak of contagious disease.

In October, another fort, number 9, was appropriated for the execution of Jews: 1,845 were killed on 4 October, as a reprisal measure and finally 9,200 on 29 October. This was described as 'ridding the ghetto of useless Jews'. Thus SS Colonel Jäger dealt with the problem of overcrowding.

On 25 and 29 November, the execution equipment of fort number 9 was ready to play its part in solving the Jewish problem in Germany: a total of 4,934 Jews, 1,852 men, 2.755 women and 327 children, deported from Berlin, Munich, Frankfort, Breslau and Vienna, were annihilated. On 29 November, 18 local Jews were included in the massacres, also one German of the Reich (*Reichsdeutsche*) found guilty of the supreme crime: he had been converted to Judaism and had even studied in a rabbinic school. For good measure 15 'terrorists', members of the Kalinine group, were also shot.

To sum up, in the second half of the year 1941, 16,394 local Jews, duly accounted for, 4,000 others, not accounted for, and 4,934 Jews of the Reich, were all put to death.[1]

What was the reaction of those Jews who remained in the ghetto? Jäger reckoned there were 15,000 of these at the end of 1941. A Jewish report, based on a census taken in November 1941, lists 17,412 survivors of the 'actions' of 1941.

Kovno, like other towns, had its Jewish Council, which bore the name of *Aeltestenrat* (Council of Elders). It also had a Jewish police force. It differed from other ghettos, however, in that most members of the Council and the police felt it their duty to use all the means at their disposal to save Jewish lives.

More than once, the Jewish police received orders from the Germans to ransack the Jewish houses that had been separated from the ghetto when their occupants had been sent to their death, and to get rid of any Jews who might be hidden there. The Jewish police obeyed, but not quite according to plan, smuggling arm-bands and police helmets to the hidden Jews thus enabling them to return, so to speak officially, to what was left of the ghetto. Had they remained where they were they would certainly have starved to death.

The Jewish police officers were able to cover up their action by presenting the Germans with the bodies of Jews who had committed suicide, or had died of hunger. There were enough of both categories to keep the Germans from becoming suspicious.

The ghetto was not immediately suppressed because the *Wehrmacht* had to have a large and more or less skilled, undemanding labour force, and here, as they were well aware, the Jews were the ideal choice. Knowing that the ghetto inhabitants owed their survival to the needs of the enemy, rather than to humanitarian considerations, the Jewish Council did its utmost to keep this vital force of the

Jews inside the ghetto and thought nothing of using the most 'illegal' inducements to encourage the setting up of bakeries — even of a flour mill — within the ghetto.

The ghetto of Kovno remained as it was, isolated from the whole world, until the spring of 1942, when it received a visit — an illegal one of course — from the indefatigable, heroic Irina Adamowicz. Irina could only offer the outcasts a few words of consolation, and even these were far from optimistic, but her visit was a breath from the outside world. When she had gone, a few daring Jews fitted up a radio receiver which they hid in the cellar of the pharmacy. Up to now there had not been a single radio in the ghetto and the inhabitants were forbidden, under penalty of death, to read the local newspapers.

From the autumn of 1943 the ghetto of Kovno changed character. The population was housed in barracks; workmen, and especially those the Germans employed, for example, the navvies preparing the Kovno air-strip, were obliged to move with their families to huts near their place of work.

On Christmas Eve 1943 a sensational escape took place at Kovno, 64 Jewish prisoners fleeing from fort number 9.

The task these Jews had been given was to empty five enormous communal graves, packed with nearly 50,000 Jewish and non-Jewish corpses, and to burn the bodies so that no trace of them remained. This was part of a large-scale operation launched by Himmler, embracing all those regions where massacres had taken place, most of the victims being Jewish.

The *Sonderkommando* men of fort number 9 were locked up at night in cells and sent to work during the day with their legs shackled. At the same time, these highly specialised workers were extremely well fed and received generous supplies of tobacco and alcohol.

About half the *Sonderkommando* of Kovno was composed of Judæo-Soviet prisoners of war who, for one reason or another, had not been killed straight away. Their leader was a captain called Vassilevsky, who had been captured while attempting to rejoin the Partisans.

The Kovno escape plan was relatively simple. The first scheme, which involved the digging of a mile-long tunnel, had to be abandoned for lack of tools. The prisoners then discovered a passage leading from their cells to the exterior wall. This tunnel was closed off by a metal gate, and was full of logs.

Using penknives and saws, the prisoners made a hole in the door. Since part of their task was to strip the bodies of non-Jewish victims who had been shot fully clothed, parcel up garments, seize gold teeth, wedding rings and all other valuable objects, they took advantage of this to procure tools and build up a collection of spoils.

The escape took place during the night of Christmas Eve 1943, when the Jews expected the guards to get so drunk that they would neglect to do their rounds. Everything went to plan, and all the 64 prisoners escaped.

Only one or two were retaken. The rest got right away. Thirteen sought refuge in the Kovno ghetto where the Jewish Council and the Jewish police did their best to disguise them. All the escapees' garments, which gave off a stench that hung in the atmosphere for hours, were burnt, and they were given clean clothes, shoes, and identity papers: all items that were extremely difficult to come by in December 1943 in an isolated ghetto. After a few days they were directed to the neighbouring forest where they got in touch with the Partisans. It was then that their leader, the poet Haim Yellin, made his last journey[2].

The aim of the struggle was to escape from the ghetto, ideally smuggling out arms as well, cross the German lines, and set up groups of Partisans — or join existing ones. Like most Eastern European ghettos that had belonged even temporarily to the USSR, Kovno had a large Communist contingent, who launched a strong campaign urging the young to 'take to the forest'. The only difference was that in Kovno, the 'official' authorities, in other words the Jewish Council and the Jewish police, discreetly but effectively supported the action although they did not wholly agree with it. This was one of the rare occasions when the tables were turned on the Germans in one of those institutions they had specially created, the better to dominate the Jews.

From September 1941 onwards, a number of Jews from Kovno, Raseiniai and other northern and western Lithuanian localities managed to band together in the forests of northern Lithuania. Thanks to the arms abandoned by the Red Army during its hasty retreat in the summer of 1941[3], the Partisans were able to protect themselves against the irregular Lithuanian soldiers acting for the Germans, and persuade the peasants to sell them foodstuffs, paying for them in kind with watches, clothing, and other articles. Occasionally, weapons were used as a final persuasive measure.

The mass exodus from the Kovno ghetto to the Soviet Partisan groups did not begin until 1943. There were four such groups in the region up to then, and the distance to Bielorussia was too great.

In Kovno, it was the Young Communists, with Haim Yellin, the 30 year-old Yiddish-speaking poet, at their head, who took the initiative in these escapes. There were quite a large number of poets in the East European Jewish Resistance.

Yellin had managed to contact the Communist organisation of the 'Aryan' quarter, which put him in touch with the Soviet Partisans. He also had the support of such men as Dima Halperin, and Simon Ratner who was employed in the labour exchange of the Jewish Council. The Council, or at least its principal leaders, were perfectly well aware of these Resistance activities.

Despite their opposing political views, the Communist Jews readily joined up with the Zionist combatants. For example, both Zvi Levin and Moshe Levin, who held an important position in the ghetto police, belonged to the Zionist Revisionist movement, which normally would have been considered by the Communists —

among others — decidedly Fascist, or at least pro-Fascist. Itzik Serebnitzky was a
member of the majority party *Poalei Sion*. Y. Zoupovitz and I. Grinberg, deputies
to the chief of police of the ghetto, belonged to the moderate Zionist movement
Hanoar Hatzioni. The journalist Valsonok, who had greatly assisted the work of
the Jewish Council, was nearer the Communists.

It would be an exaggeration to say that the two factions, Communists and
Zionists, were able to resolve their ideological differences and mutual mistrust
straight away; the wonder is that they eventually succeeded in doing so in Kovno,
Warsaw, Bialystock and elsewhere. In Kovno, credit for this achievement is due
primarily to Haim Yellin. The Communists may not have been the majority party
in the ghetto, but they represented Soviet power, and however the Jews regarded
this power as individuals, it was the only one that offered them a chance of survival.
Also, the Partisans they intended to join were Soviet Partisans; so when Leib
Garfunkel, former militant Zionist and vice-president of the Kovno Jewish Council,
paid homage to Yellin for having prepared the way for the Zionist youth movements
to unite with the Partisans, this was no mean tribute, especially when one considers
that the author lives on in Israel and that Haim Yellin fell in Kovno.

The young Kovno Zionists, like their counterparts in other Eastern European
cities, lived together in a *kibbutz* inside the ghetto, and they made their exodus
from there. The Kovno *kibbutz*, known in the ghetto under the Russian name of
kolektiv, was a centre of spiritual resistance of the highest order.

In August 1943, Yellin slipped out of the ghetto and travelled 100 miles to the
Roudnicki forest near Vilna to establish contact with the Soviet Partisans who
had settled there in large numbers.

On his return to the Kovno ghetto, Yellin enlisted a group of about 80 young
men and set off for Suwalki-Augustow in the south-west to meet a group of Partisans supposed to be based there. They were intercepted and most of them were
killed. The only two who managed to reach the rendezvous found it deserted.

They went east and finished up by uniting with the Partisans in the suburbs
of Vilna, joining the detachment of nearly three hundred Partisans called *Death
to the invaders*, of which a good third were young women.

The false papers which described them as 'Jewish *kommandos* for hard labour'
were issued by the labour exchange of the Jewish Council and carts supplied by the
Council facilitated the escapees' journey.

Yellin himself did not live to see the Liberation, nor even to rejoin the Partisans. On 6 April, he was recognised by a Gestapo informer and arrested, after an
exciting chase during which he shot down several of his Nazi pursuers. He was
never seen again, and it is not known how he died.

A few more groups managed to escape from the ghetto, or what was left of it,
during the month of April 1944. The movement was dissolved practically at the
same time as the ghetto itself.

In November 1943 the ghetto acquired the status of 'the Kauen concentration camp'. The day of its liquidation was drawing near. At the time of Yellin's capture it no longer even had its police. On 27 March 1944 an SS *kommando* appeared in the ghetto and summoned the police 'for inspection'. The 140 Jewish police officers were taken to fort number 9 where they had to make an agonising decision. They were asked to reveal the exact location of all the ghetto hideouts[4], and also to tell what had happened to a Gestapo informer who had disappeared a few days earlier. This man had been identified, discreetly killed, and buried. All 140 police officers pleaded ignorance, knowing perfectly well that in doing so they signed their own death warrants. They were all shot.

On that day and the next, the Nazis seized all the children and old people remaining in the ghetto — a total of nearly 1,500. Some of them were sent to Auschwitz; some to fort number 9. There were no survivors.

The Jewish Council ceased to exist on 4 April 1944. For several days the Germans had been searching the ghetto for Ratner and Levin, who had formerly belonged to the Council. They had not been found. On 3 April the Council held its last meeting at which the president, Doctor Alkes, urged his assistants to go into hiding. He himself preferred to remain at the disposal of the Germans in case they might require a scapegoat. The two assistants refused to abandon their president, who then drew out an envelope containing cyanide and divided it between the three of them. They knew how precious it might become.

The next day the three leaders of the Council and eight of their colleagues were arrested and taken to fort number 9. Two days later they were all released with the exception of Goldberg and Garfunkel who were kept in prison for a few days longer.

The end of the Kovno ghetto came in July 1944, when, in face of the Soviet advance the Germans decided to evacuate its occupants and destroy it.

The city was liberated by the Red Army on 1 August. A few days later about 600 Jews who had managed to keep out of harm's way, either in their hideouts or in the homes of Lithuanians, were united once more among the ruins of the ghetto in a free Kovno.

Kovno-the-Jewess had survived.

NOTES

1. In the years that followed up to the liberation of the city, tens of thousands of Jews from Lithuania and from every part of occupied Europe (even from Paris) were slaughtered in Kovno, mostly in fort number 9.

2. Another Galician *Sonderkommando* known under the code number 1005, and similarly employed, escaped around the same time but under slightly different

circumstances. The members of this *kommando* first obtained arms, then set about slitting the throats of the SS guards. The latter did not only see to the destruction of the corpses, but kept the *kommando* supplied with work, as it were, by slaughtering Jews, resistance fighters, Poles whose land was wanted, and all sorts of other undesirables (and there were a great many) living in Galicia. See Leon Welliczker, *Die Todesbrigade* (East Berlin); and by the same author — his name spelt Léon W. Wells — *Pour que la terre se souvienne* (Paris, Albin Michel, 1962).

3. This group held out until just before the end of the occupation, when it ran into a German unit and suffered such heavy losses that it completely disintegrated.

4. These individual concrete hideouts that the Jews built in their homes were called *malines*. The ghetto chroniclers confess their ignorance of the etymology of the word (pronounced as it is written), although some suggest it could be Lithuanian slang. Our guess is that it was originally a French word that had acquired a special meaning. Sometimes the *maline* was a filled-in stairwell; sometimes a wall with a false bottom built in the middle of a room; occasionally it was underneath the cellar or attached to it. Bunkers were also built in the courtyards or under the streets — wherever there was room for one. Generally speaking there were two types of *malines*: those in which people could hide for a brief space of time, for example during a round-up, and those that were constructed to last. A number of these *malines* were never discovered by the Germans, with the result that several hundred Jews in Kovno, and an even larger number in Vilna, managed to survive.

An operation to destroy the *malines* was launched immediately after the mass escape from fort number 9, but it was not successful, perhaps because the Germans entrusted the Jewish police of the ghetto with the task. The latter only managed to 'discover' one *maline* (an unoccupied one at that) and a number of abandoned cellars.

CHAPTER 28

BIALYSTOK: DEFEAT OF A TECHNOCRAT

T HE three cities of Warsaw, Vilna and Bialystok all belonged to Poland up to 1
September 1939, but they were to have different regimes in the course of the
war. We are already familiar with what happened in Warsaw and Vilna. Bialystok
was situated more or less halfway between these two cities.

In 1939 the region of Bialystok was incorporated into Bielorussia, that is to
say into the USSR. Two years later, on 27 June 1941, the Germans occupied the
city, but instead of placing Bialystok and its region under the *Ostland* administration, they integrated it directly into the German province of Eastern Prussia.

Bialystok was an industrial centre, especially important for its textile industries, which gave employment to most of the large number of Jews resident in the
city.

Like other cities, Bialystok had a *Judenrat*, set up just after the German Occupation. The Council held its first meeting on 8 July. Several thousand Jews had
already been shot, but there were still 50,000 left — perhaps more, for there had
been a continual influx of Jews from the neighbouring villages and market towns[1].

The fact that there had been no pogrom of any size in the city from the second
half of the year 1941 up to 1943, had lulled the Bialystok citizens into a feeling
of security.

Unlike those of most other Jewish Councils, the members of the Bialystok
Judenrat were prominent Jews who genuinely represented the Jewish community.
The most active of these, the engineer Efraim Barash, was what one would now
call a technocrat. He shared the view of his colleagues in Vilna, Lodz and Upper
Silesia, that the Nazis considered the Jewish workers first as workers, then as
Jews and therefore flung himself enthusiastically into the task of re-establishing
workshops and small factories, calling upon Jewish skilled workers everywhere.
This policy seemed to work, and early in 1942 Barash even managed to organise
a Bialystok ghetto industrial exhibition for the benefit of the Germans, which seems
to have impressed them enormously.

Barash was neither a toady nor a coward. He did not hesitate for a moment
to give financial aid to the militants of the Zionist movement *Hachomer Hatzair*,
knowing perfectly well that they were preparing for armed resistance, which he
himself thought useless. He did everything in his power to ensure that the ghetto

would be spared by the Germans and considered that militant action would either be ineffectual or have tragic results.

There were not many Communists in Bialystok, as most of the Jews massacred just after the Occupation had been drawn from their ranks. Those who remained firmly opposed the *Judenrat*: a purely bourgeois Council was hardly likely to inspire them with confidence. Despite this, the members of the *Judenrat* seemed to be well-intentioned and efficient and remained so for a long time.

The *Hachomer Hatzair* movement was quite powerful in Bialystok, especially after it received reinforcements from Vilna. Later, young Zionists from Slonim, Baranovichi, and other smaller localities turned up to swell the numbers. Barash gave cover to them all, considering that the young above all must be saved.

The *Hachomer Hatzair* militants managed to establish a sort of common platform with a view to co-operating with the Communist-inspired anti-Fascist bloc. One of their leaders Elie (Edek) Boraks, who had come from Vilna, tried to link up with what was called the 'Second Bloc', comprising the other Zionist groups and the Bundists, but the link was not made until July 1943, just before the ghetto was destroyed, and then was largely due to the efforts of Mordechai Tamarov-Tennenbaum.

The decision to destroy at least part of Bialystok was made known on 16 December 1942. According to the orders of the Gestapo chief Müller, 30,000 Jews were to be evacuated from the region. Barash's German 'friends' had solemnly promised to warn him if ever the enemy planned to liquidate the ghetto, but they failed to do so.

The schedule of special trains, dated 16 January 1943, and issued by the German Railways' administration (*Deutsche Reichsbahn — Generalbetriebsleitung Ost*), details a series of trains called PJ (*polnische Juden* — Polish Jews), whose destination was Auschwitz or Treblinka.

We read that at 9 a.m. on 5 February, a train bearing 2,000 Jews was scheduled to leave Bialystok, bound for Auschwitz, where it was due to arrive at 7.57 a.m. on the following day. It was to leave again empty for Bialystok on 7 February. At 9 a.m. on 9 February, it was scheduled to transport 2,000 more Jews to Treblinka, the arrival being set for 12.10 p.m. By leaving for Bialystok that same evening at 9.18 p.m. (arriving at 1.30 a.m.) it was able to set off again for Treblinka on 11 February at the same time as the previous day.

Eight trains were scheduled to transport a total of 16,000 Jews, either to Auschwitz or Treblinka, between 5 and 12 February 1943, but in fact there were only 10,000 deportees. When the SS entered the ghetto on 4 February, the day before the first train was to leave, they were faced not with organised resistance, but with individual reactions, like that of the chemist Isaac Malmed who sprayed them with sulphuric acid. Malmed went into hiding, but when the Germans informed the Jews that unless he gave himself up the ghetto would be demolished, he surrendered and was hanged.

By this time some of the young Jews had already got away. There were three factions: one in favour of escaping to the forests; another consisting of Tamarov and a few Communists, was firmly against doing this; and a third favoured setting up armed detachments outside the ghetto, ready to come to the aid of the inhabitants when it was threatened with destruction. The last group won the day, and between December 1942 and March 1943 enough young men left the ghetto to set up a powerful Partisan detachment called *Forois* (Forward).

The young men of the Bialystok ghetto lived together in communities similar to those in the Warsaw ghetto, having formed their own *kibbutzim*, one to each movement. During the lull they flung themselves into agricultural work, cultivating as much as they could of the land that vaguely belonged to the ghetto. The *Judenrat*, and the engineer Barash in particular, provided the necessary funds. Some young women and a smaller number of young men who looked like Aryans — Tamarov-Tennenbaum being one of the rare ones who had no Jewish characteristics — hoed the turnips between Bialystok and the Warsaw, Vilna and Grodno ghettos, but so much movement finally led to their arrest, one by one, and the links they had forged were gradually severed. Already the disappearance of the Austrian corporal, Anton Schmidt, had made moving about much more difficult. We are already familiar with the part he played in Vilna and it was thanks to him that other ghettos were able to contact Bialystok. Those envoys who were not killed as they travelled from ghetto to ghetto perished when their own ghettos were liquidated.

One young woman, Bronia Winitzki (now Klibanski), like Tamarov-Tennenbaum a member of the *Dror* movement, left Grodno in 1942 to settle in Bialystok. On Tamarov's instructions she took up residence under a false identity in the 'Aryan' quarter of the town, and immediately after the action of February 1943, took charge of the ghetto records. Unfortunately, these records were only begun at a very late date, in 1942 or 1943, when Tamarov was ordered to keep them by Emanuel Ringelblum. Though the information they contain is therefore incomplete, they are much more detailed than those of other ghettos.

Tamarov, and Moszkowicz, one of the leaders of the Communist Jews, took the bull by the horns and set up an organisation of 500 combatants inside the ghetto, using all the means at their disposal to procure arms, but when on 15 August 1943 the moment arrived for the liquidation of the ghetto, they possessed in all 25 German rifles, a single machine-gun, a few submachine-guns, about a hundred revolvers and one or two hand grenades.

The Germans had at least learnt something from the Warsaw uprising, and launched a surprise attack that very swiftly succeeded in driving the Jews into a corner of the ghetto.

The 500 combatants tried desperately to break through the encircling SS and their Polish auxiliaries, but failed, while the *Foroïs* had been overpowered by the Germans and were unable to play the part assigned to them.

The ghetto combats lasted a whole week. In the end Moszkowicz and Tamarov committed suicide to forestall their executioners.

The Jews of Bialystok were no more: it took more than an industrial exhibition to make the Nazis abandon their plan to annihilate all Jews.

Just before the incursion, Mordechai Tamarov-Tennenbaum wrote the following appeal to the ghetto:

> *BROTHER JEWS!*
>
> *Agonising days are upon us. We are not only threatened with yellow armbands, hate, perfidy, insult and humiliation, now death itself is hanging over us. Our wives, children, mothers and fathers, brothers and sisters, have been sent to their death before our very eyes. Thousands have been led to their doom and thousands more will follow.*
>
> *In these days that decide whether we live or die we issue the following appeal: first, I would have you know that five million European Jews have already been killed by Hitler and his executioners. Barely ten per cent of the Jews in Poland are still alive. More than two million Polish Jews have been subjected to every conceivable form of torture in Chelmo, Belsen, Oswiencim, Treblinka, Sobibor and other death camps.*
>
> *I assure you that whoever is taken from the ghetto is going to his death!*
>
> *Have no faith in the Gestapo's tempting propaganda based on alleged deportees' letters. These are the brazen lies that pave the way to the giant crematoria and the burial pits in the heart of the Polish forests; all of you are doomed to die.*
>
> *We have nothing to lose!*
>
> *Do not deceive yourself that work will save you. The first 'action' will be followed by a second, the second by a third — right to the last Jew! The division of the ghetto into different categories is nothing but a perfidious enemy manoeuvre to ease their task by sowing false illusions among us.*
>
> *JEWS!*

Our destination is Treblinka. There we shall be gassed, then burnt like mad beasts. Do not go like lambs to the slaughter! We may be too weak to save ourselves, but we are strong enough to defend our honour as Jews and as human beings, strong enough to show the world that even though we are in chains, we are not conquered.

Do not go meekly to your death. Fight for your lives to your last breath. Stand up to your slaughterers with your teeth and nails, with axes and knives, with vitriol and iron bars. Extort from them blood for blood, a life for a life.

Do you intend hiding in rat holes while they take away your nearest and dearest to humiliation and death? Will you sell your wives, your children and parents, and your souls for a few more weeks of abject slavery? Rather let us ambush the enemy, kill him, seize his weapons; let us oppose the murderers and if need be let us die heroically and gain immortality by our death.

We have nothing to lose but our honour!

Let us not sell our lives cheaply! Let us avenge the annihilated communities! When you leave your house set fire to it! Set fire to the factories, demolish them! Do not allow our assassins to be our beneficiaries as well!

Young Jews, follow the example of generations of Jewish fighters and martyrs, the doers and the dreamers, the pioneers and the builders. Arm yourselves and fight!

Hitler will lose the war. Slavery and oppression will be wiped out, leaving the world purged and purified. With such a radiant future before you why die like dogs! Escape to the forests and join the partisans.

But do not flee from the ghetto unarmed for you will certainly perish. Do your duty by your country, opposing the destruction of the ghetto and escape with arms to the forest.

All you have to do is to seize one weapon from every German in the ghetto.

Be strong and courageous.

The Bialystok combatants responded to Tamarov's appeal. They sold their lives dearly. The SS suffered considerable losses, while all the industrial and workshop equipment, all the stocks of raw materials, went up in flames.

Barash allowed himself to be taken away like the other 40,000 ghetto Jews. No doubt he could have saved himself, and probably his family as well, but he made no attempt to do so.

NOTES

1. Practically all the Polish Jews who had fled the ghettos or managed to escape from the extermination camps — sometimes even from the pits where they had been taken to be shot — eventually returned to their own ghettos, or sought refuge in another. There they found a handful of survivors enjoying what amounted to a stay of execution. Why did they return? Simply because they had nowhere else to go.

CHAPTER 29

THE COMMUNISTS ALONE AT MINSK

M INSK, capital of the Soviet Socialist Republic of Bielorussia, was the nearest Soviet city to the pre-1939 Polish frontier, little more than a mile or two away. It was a traditional Jewish stronghold. After the 1917 revolution, the Minsk Jews, like their fellows in other Soviet cities, had largely integrated into the economic, social and political life of the country. The percentage of Communist Party members among them was very high.

Minsk was no different from other USSR towns in that there was no Jewish structure outside the Communist Party and its fringe organisations: no Jewish community life, no organised religious body, much less any Jewish non-Communist political movement, Bundist or Zionist, although the Bundists had been very powerful in the region up to the time of their forced disbandment in the early twenties.

Unlike those in the other occupied Soviet towns the Minsk Jews were not executed *en masse* immediately the Germans captured the city. Their captors were content to shut them up in a ghetto, following a decree dated 20 July 1941. Instructions were also given to set up a Jewish Council, to be responsible for seeing that German orders were carried out.

In Poland, the Germans had chosen prominent Jews for the Jewish Council, but none were available in the USSR and especially not in Minsk. Since there was no organised Jewish life, the only Jews likely to be looked upon as 'notables' were influential members of the hierarchy of either the Communist Party or the Soviet state; and not only were both these categories anathematised, but, on *Einsatzgruppen* orders, on their arrest, members were to be shot on the spot.

On the other hand the Jewish Councils set up in Soviet territory were not, to the German way of thinking, intended to play the same role as their forerunners in Poland, for the good reason that in the meantime Hitler had decided to annihilate the European Jews immediately on the invasion of Russia.

Hersz Smoliar, head of the ghetto Resistance organisation, has written a report on the Minsk ghetto describing the summary manner in which the Germans set up its Jewish Council. In the course of a round-up, the Nazis lined up the Jews and ordered those who spoke German to step forward. As no one made a move the order was furiously repeated. Elie Mushkin then stepped forward and said that he knew a little German, and was immediately nominated president of the Jewish

Council and instructed to appoint the other members. He and his Council had subsequently to set up the ghetto, which was not at first encircled with barbed wire.

The Minsk ghetto started off with thirty or forty thousand inhabitants[1], but was reduced in size by stages, and was finally liquidated along with those occupants who had not managed to escape.

According to Smoliar's report the members of the Council set up by Mushkin were recognised by the militant Communist Jews, but later the Gestapo eliminated members favourable to the Resistance and replaced them with more dubious elements, sometimes even traitors, whom the Resistance had to do away with; but the Communist Jews of Minsk did not consider the Jewish Council as an intrinsically treacherous institution.

In August 1941 an embryo Resistance organisation sprang up in the ghetto. None of the participants had practical experience of Partisan warfare for few, if any, remained of those who had taken part in secret resistance work before the October revolution. Smoliar mentions none. The organisers intended setting up a propaganda network which would be active outside as well as inside the ghetto. The inaugural meeting was held in the immediate vicinity of the Jewish Council.

Pamphlets printed in the ghetto were taken out by the Jewish labourers who worked outside the ghetto every day and were then distributed among the Bielorussian population. These pamphlets made no mention of the fate of the Jews, but were simply military communiqués taken from the Soviet radio[2].

A youth organisation was also set up and became responsible for forming liaisons with the Partisans: an extremely difficult task since at that time there were hardly any organised groups and those that did exist had no fixed headquarters. On the other hand, the Communist Party attempting to set up a clandestine organisation in the city of Minsk, succeeded in doing so only with the greatest difficulty; thanks to an efficient ring of informers one after another of the networks was broken up by the Gestapo, leaving the Communists back where they started. The local chief of the Gestapo, Strauch, was *Kommandeur der Sipo und des SD* (Kd S) in Minsk from 1942; until then the *Einsatzgruppen* had assumed the authority of the Gestapo.

One of the principal local auxiliaries of the Gestapo, Gorodetski, made several round-ups in the ghetto, shooting down people at random. One of the first victims was a participant of the August meeting, Zhasha Kirazheski. The Resistance fighters took extra precautions, holding their meetings in the hospital for contagious diseases, knowing they could trust its director Dr. Leib Kulik and well aware that the Germans were terrified of infection.

In the middle of the month of October 1941, the Nazis took it into their heads to reduce the area of the ghetto by cutting off the Niemen and Ostovski streets, and warned the inhabitants that they would have to find alternative accommodation. Some did; others were less successful, for the ghetto was already overflowing and there were a great many involved, about a third of the inhabitants living in the two streets. On 2 November, encouraged by Gorodetski, the Nazis evacuated 200 skilled workers from the quarter and imprisoned them in the Shiroka Street concentration camp. The rest of the inhabitants were put to death at Touchinka, on the outskirts of the town. According to Smoliar some 12,000 Jews perished that day, and the houses thus made available were used mostly to accomodate Jewish deportees from Hamburg and other German towns.

In this way two separate ghettos were set up in the town, and there is no hint in any of the survivors' reports or testimonies, or in any German documentation, that there was the slightest liaison between Eastern and Western European Jews. Both categories were slaughtered in the end, but while the German Jews survived they could at least count upon an occasional kindness from some German official or police officer, whereas the Soviet Jews received no such concession. The *Gauleiter* Wilhelm Kube, general commissary in Bielorussia, was by nature a dedicated anti-Semite, but he seems to betray a hint of regret when he states that Jews 'of German culture' even 'holders of the Iron Cross', to use his own words, were treated exactly like any Eastern Jew. He saw no reason to object to the massacre of the Soviet Jews, but he did manage to postpone the massacre of certain German Jews.

Kube was killed in 1943 by Soviet Partisans, who slipped a bomb under his bed.

Jewish writers reacted variously to the death of Wilhelm Kube. Gerald Reitlinger and Raul Hilberg were almost inclined to deplore it; Jacob Robinson goes to the extent of writing of the dead man that 'for a Nazi he was exceptionally humane'; whereas the Jewish writers with Communist leanings — closer intellectually and in feeling to the Eastern Jews — bracketed Kube with the worst Nazi criminals and greeted his assassination as a great victory for Soviet Resistance. Some of them even claimed that there was Jewish participation in the affair. According to Kahanovitch, the Jewish Partisan leader David Keimach was directly involved in the operation. On the other hand, General Erich von dem Bach-Zelewski of the SS corps, a friend of Kube, declared in the course of his interrogation at Nuremberg that Kube had fallen out of favour at the time of his death. According to Himmler, if the Soviet Partisans had not killed him, he, Himmler would have been forced to shut him up in a concentration camp.

Kube had been a *Gauleiter* in the Berlin region in 1933. His dismissal from that post was not in any way connected with pro-Jewish sympathies. He was accused of drinking too much and of having spread the rumour that the wives of certain of his political rivals were Jewish or under Jewish influence. So we do not really know whether or not Wilhelm Kube could rightfully claim extenuating circumstances[3].

Thanks to the Resistance network centred in the hospital, the Russian ghetto of Minsk became a medical base for the Soviet Partisans in the vicinity. Sick and wounded Partisans were taken into the ghetto and given false Jewish identities for the duration of their stay. Many an Ivan became Yankel, and many a Piotr, Pessach. Hersz Smoliar became Efim Stolierovitch.

The task of the Resistance became more difficult after the arrest of the president Mushkin and the subsequent disbanding of the Jewish Council. From this point on the Council was much more circumspect, although its members continued to do everything they could to protect Efim Stolierovich until his eventual escape. When the Gestapo ordered the ghetto to hand over Stolierovich, threatening it with the worst reprisals if it did not, the president of the *Judenrat* had a set of identity papers prepared in Stolierovich's name. He dipped them in blood before handing them over to the Gestapo, explaining that they had been discovered on the body of a man shot dead. This explanation was accepted and Efim Stolierovich disappeared officially from circulation[4].

Mushkin was replaced towards the end of February 1942. On 2 and 3 March another massive execution took place in Minsk. According to the Gestapo report of 9 March 1942 (*Erreignismeldung UdSSR Nr. 178*), 3,412 persons were exterminated in this *Judenaktion*.

Shortly before the massacre, the Jewish Council received orders from the Germans to draw up a list of 5,000 Jews 'not productively employed' who 'would be put to work elsewhere'. The list might include the names of children and old people. This last detail was sufficient reason for the *Judenrat* to refuse to obey Gestapo orders — but the massacre took place all the same.

The same report mentions three young Jews responsible for keeping in touch with the Partisans who were captured by the Gestapo and a Jew called Bronstein who directed a Partisan recruitment network. These are not included in Smoliar's report. On the other hand the *Einsatzgruppen's* monthly report for March 1942 points out that the printing press of the Minsk Communist Party, mounted by a Georgian Jew called Delikurdgly, had been dismantled. The headquarters of the Soviet Partisans of the region was destroyed at the same time.

Smoliar, extremely discreet about the whole affair, limits himself to pointing out that at that period a number of non-Jewish Communist militants sought refuge in the ghetto. He is also careful not to disclose the name of the 'well-known Jewish painter and sculptor' who was arrested by the Gestapo in March 1942, charged with spying. This artist approached a great many important Germans in the town on the pretext of painting their portraits and in this way managed to procure much valuable information.

In the course of its existence, the Minsk ghetto succeeded in sending about 10,000 persons on their way to the Partisan lines. A great many exclusively Jewish units were formed in this way, among them 'family detachments', a phenomenon peculiar to Jewish Resistance fighters. Unlike the non-Jewish Partisans, the Jews were convinced that if their families fell into the hands of the Germans, they would inevitably be put to death, and took their families with them when they left the ghetto despite the serious difficulties this created.

One of the most courageous combatants, and one of the best liaison agents between the ghetto and the Partisans, was Michel Gebeliov. He was eventually arrested and killed.

A number of fugitives from the ghetto were drafted to the *Frounze* and *Lazo* Partisan brigades; others to the *Boudienny* detachment. Later the *Family Detachment 106* 'sprouted', and became the reservoir for the *Zhukhov* brigade.

With the destruction of the Minsk ghetto Jewish Partisan action alternated between success and failure. Just before the liberation of their region they participated in the great 'rail battle'. This took place in Bielorussia around 23 June 1944, at the time of the Russian offensive that ended in the annihilation of the German *Mitte* army groups: a greater disaster for the Germans than even Stalingrad.

Of the 10,000 or so men, women and children of the Minsk ghetto who took part in various ways in the Partisan war, around half survived, while of the thousands of German Jews in the ghetto only thirty of forty lived to see the end of the war.

NOTES

1. Smoliar reports 50,000 — even 80,000; but this figure seems exaggerated.
2. Pamphlets played a very important role in the USSR, since radio sets were forbidden. The people of occupied France were allowed to keep theirs and continued to listen to 'enemy' broadcasts despite being strictly forbidden to do so. In Nazi Germany, strong repressive measures were taken to prevent the same thing happening, but the radios were there and it was possible to use them. In occupied Soviet territory the only possibility was to risk infringing the law by keeping a radio and not declaring it.
3. His immediate superior, Hinrich Lohse, commissioner general of *Ostland*, (the administrative region comprising Bielorussia and the Baltic countries) was left more or less in peace after 1945 and died recently in his bed. Legal proceedings were begun against him, but the court ended by dismissing the charge. The only excuse Lohse's friends could offer for him when he died was that he had become senile and was incapable of defending himself.
4. After the Liberation, Efim Stolierovich, who had become Hersz Smoliar again, returned to Poland and played a prominent role in Jewish political life. He remained, politically speaking, the militant Communist he had always been and took over publication of the Yiddish Communist newspaper *Volksstimme* in Warsaw. Nevertheless, in April 1968, he was publicly declared a 'Zionist' by his non-Jewish comrades in the Polish Workers' party. In fact, a few years before, Smoliar had expressed his solidarity with the Israeli Communist Party.

CHAPTER 30

THE PARTISANS' WAR IN THE EAST

T HE difficulty in relating the true facts of this chapter of the Second World War lies mainly in the distorted public images of the opponents. A Partisan is usually depicted as a cross between a modern Chevalier Bayard (the knight without fear and beyond reproach) and Till Eulenspigel, while his adversaries are shown either as insignificant dwarfs or loutish and brutal giants.

What is more, the Partisan's enemy is always shown as a German whether in his civil, military, or police form. True the German was a powerful and inexorable enemy, but he was not the only one.

The SS general Erich von dem Bach-Zelewski, German commander-in-chief of the war against the Partisans (*Chef der Bandenbekämpfungverbände*), was indeed a formidable enemy; but so was General Famine, and had long been so. The Partisans also suffered heavy losses at the hands of his colleagues: General No-Arms, General No-Medicines, General Treachery, not to mention the one who came into his own after all the others had launched their attacks, General Disorder.

But first, let us destroy a very widely held fallacy: the USSR had absolutely no hand in preparing the Partisan war. In other words Soviet strategy of 1941 cannot be likened in any way to that of Kutusov, who, a hundred years previously, had tried to entice Napoleon and his *Grand Army* into the heart of Russia. If the Soviet regime had had to depend on this sort of propaganda, it would never have been able to hold out. On the contrary, its propaganda asserted that if an enemy was insane enough to strike a blow at the USSR the Red Army would retaliate with such violence that it would be wiped out on the spot.

But even though neither the Red Army nor the Soviet state foresaw a Partisan war, there was no doubt that the Russian people themselves had enormous experience in this domain, for Russian history abounds in tales of their adventures. As far back as the Middle Ages the almost uninterrupted conflicts between the Russian seigneurs and the Mongols, then centuries of battling with the Tartars, made guerrilla warfare second nature to the people of the future Union of Soviet Socialist Republics. Although the Tsarist Empire remained more or less stable during the 15th and 16th centuries, a number of invasions, mostly in the west, brought about the rebirth of guerrilla warfare. The invasions of the Crimean Tartars and the Cossacks, followed by the immense peasant revolts, kept up the spirit, or rather the tradition, of this type of warfare, which reached its climax in 1812 when

Napoleon's *Grand Army*, glorious victor on so many battlefields was finally harried to near decimation by guerrillas, aided in their task by the harsh winter conditions.

Much more recently, in October 1917, during the several years of civil war that followed the socialist October Revolution, Red and White Partisan detachments faced each other more or less throughout the land. There were a number of pitched battles, but it was the Partisan war and the Bolshevist guerrillas that finally forced the enemy's hand. All in all, these Bolshevists had much more difficulty in overcoming the resistance of the 'white' Turkestan and 'black' Ukrainian Partisans, the anarchists of the Ottoman Makhno, than they had in driving out the Denikine or Koltchak armies.

In 1941, even though the civil war had been over for about twenty years, it remained engraved in the minds of the Soviet people. Historically speaking, it was nearer to them than the days of August 1944 are for the Parisian today. A great many former Partisans are still alive.

These facts explain the Soviet people's approach to guerrilla warfare, their vivid recollection of past events serving as an antidote to the dreadful shock of the shatteringly unexpected German invasion.

On 3 July 1941, the twelfth day of the German invasion, Joseph Stalin spoke on the Soviet radio. It was one of the greatest speeches of his political career — one that will go down in history — and contributed enormously to strengthening the people's will to resist.

It was in this speech that Stalin announced the keynote of his policy: the creation of Partisan detachments:

> *Partisan units must form up on the occupied territories. Diversion groups must attack enemy troops and spread war throughout the country by demolishing and destroying roads and bridges, and cutting communications; by setting fire to forests, enemy depots and transport convoys. Conditions in occupied territories must be made intolerable for the enemy and his accomplices by unrelenting assault and destruction.*

In fact, some Russians had already chosen this line of attack, but they were few and far between. There were, for example, the stranded soldiers and officers who had been left far behind the front line by the swiftness of the *Panzerdivisionen*'s advance. There were also a large number of high-ranking and not so high-ranking Communist leaders who had chosen to escape from the enemy fully aware that the *Kommissarbefehl* had ordered the immediate execution of all Party officials.

In certain areas, particularly in Bielorussia, the whole Party machine from a certain grade upwards took to the forest. Sometimes, but not very frequently, they managed to build up stocks of arms, food and clothing before the Germans arrived, but the swiftness of the retreat did not always allow enough time for such preparations[1].

Yet the Partisans had to have food. Regular military forces are provisioned in two ways: either they have food supplies sent from their various bases; or they live on the country. The Partisans had no choice: they had to depend upon local resources.

The patriotism of the local Soviet peasants is unquestioned but the Partisans' presence weighed heavily upon them. All the more so since the Germans, too, demanded supplies and the amount they required grew and grew. They had established a network of auxiliaries which also had to have their 'due'. Moreover, the Germans had no compunction in burning the homes and even the entire villages of those who were suspected of collusion with the Partisans. Needless to say the 'guilty ones' were publicly hanged.

The Partisan movement, beginning in a small way in 1941, had expanded enough in 1942 to justify the setting up of central headquarters. Besides, the Germans had committed so many atrocities that the people had turned against them. The mass assassination of the Jews, in particular, seemed to augur the worst. Small wonder that Soviet propaganda put the question, 'Today, the Jews. Tomorrow?' German requisitions, and especially the massive recruitment of forced labour for Germany, did the rest, and as the people realised they had nothing more to lose the Partisan ranks began to swell, reaching a peak in 1943[2]. Up to this time the Partisans had had to depend almost entirely upon their own efforts, receiving only a few officers, tradesmen, radios, and a meagre supply of arms from the free world. Now things took a new turn: not only did the Partisans receive large quantities of arms, explosives, foodstuffs and medicine; they were even able to get reinforcements and were given some help in evacuating their wounded.

The 'free zones', or 'Partisan republics', had also increased in number and covered a wider area, and Partisan activities continued to expand.

Jewish participation in the organisation took a particular form for various reasons.

We have already explained why the Jews could not join the Partisan ranks *en masse*. In the East European occupied territories, that is roughly east of the 1939 Polish-Soviet frontier, the Jews were massacred before they could even consider taking such an action. When the first Partisans appeared in the regions of Smolensk, Gomel, Chernigov, Zhitomir and Kiev, there was not a single living Jew left. It was the same in the Crimea. The case of Vladimir Weissmann, a member of the *Partisanskaia Iskra* detachment of the Krymka village, in the Nikolayiev region on the Black Sea, is quite exceptional.

However, even in these regions a number of Jews managed to take to the Resistance. Adam Aron Shazanov, from the district of Klimovichi, was sixty years old when he formed a detachment. Besides being a dedicated Communist, he was, more important still, a veteran Partisan.

In 1942 Jewish-led detachments sprang up also near Mohilev on the Dnieper (Benik's for example); others in the same zone near Gomel (Samuel Rakhlin's). It was the survivors of the first Jewish Partisan groups of the region that the *Polizeiregiment 14* identified in September and October 1941.

The Jewish Partisans were more numerous further west, especially in the western part of Bielorussia, which had once belonged to Poland. When the first massacres took place in the autumn of 1941, only a small proportion of the Jews were suppressed, and large-scale massacres did not take place in the region until 1942, continuing into 1943.

Not all the Jewish survivors who reached the forests were physically capable of fighting, for there were children, old people and expectant mothers among them. The able-bodied men and women either set up conventional Partisan detachments of their own or joined forces with other detachments. There were also what were known as 'family camps', typically Jewish structures that were officially recognised by the Soviet administration of the Partisan war.

Since these camps sheltered a proportion of non-combatants they were allotted very meagre food supplies and the leaders of the sectors preferred them to be situated as far off as possible, in the heart of forests or marshes. The camp guards themselves were too poorly equipped to carry out such 'economic' operations as sending armed men into the surrounding villages to obtain food supplies, while the Partisan combatant detachments considered that as fighting men they should be served first; naturally they were better armed.

The Partisan leaders were not ready to take responsibility for such camps, and the Jewish inhabitants tended to interpret this attitude as a mark of anti-Semitism — not unknown, it seems, among the Soviet Partisans; but in this particular instance, the real reason appears to have been concern for security, many Partisan leaders fearing that the 'family camps' would only serve to attract the attention of the Germans, especially since the occupants of these camps did not always know the safety regulations, and therefore failed to respect them.

The names of Zorin, Tobiasz Bielski, and his brothers Zosia and Assael Zorin, acquired a symbolic value for the Jews of the various regions to which their activities led them both during and after the war.

The Bielski brothers were unusual in that they had never lived in a ghetto. Coming from the village of Stankevich, in the province of Novogrudok, they had taken to the forest immediately the Germans arrived, and set up detachments there which received the survivors of the ghettos of the Novogrudok and Lida regions.

Moshe Kahanovich, himself a former Eastern European Jewish Partisan and historian of the movement, praises the breadth of spirit of Bielski and those few other Partisan leaders, not all of them Jews, who accepted responsibility for the 'family camps'[3].

The mortality rate in these camps was terrifyingly high: famine, sickness, and especially contagious diseases, took a heavy toll of the Jews who had sought refuge there: all this in addition to the round-ups sprung on them every now and then by the Germans.

Nor were the able-bodied men who took part in 'economic operations' always certain to return safely to base, for even if they managed to avoid the Germans and their accomplices — the police and the militia — they might meet with a cold reception in the villages. What was more, they ran the risk of coming up against other armed Partisans after the same 'economic products'. Kahanovich mentions a number of appeals for arbitration submitted to the upper hierarchy of the Partisan movement. The Partisans were not all of the same political colour: in the Ukrainian districts (Volhynia, Podolskiy) were to be found the more or less Fascist-orientated 'white' Ukrainian nationalists who were certainly anti-Semitic, blaming the Jews for attempting to establish Soviet power; the attribute 'Judæo-Bolshevist' was constantly used in both Polish and Ukrainian vocabularies.

The round-ups are explained by the fact that most German leaders, whether they belonged to the military or to the police, considered it an essential part of their duty to clean up regions particularly infested by Partisans. In this case it was the SS general Erich von dem Bach-Zelewski who had to mass the troops at his disposal — police regiments, *Waffen-SS* squadrons, local auxiliaries and even regular units of the *Wehrmacht* — and launch them against the Partisans. Among these units were a number of questionable ones, even by Nazi standards, such as the Dirlewanger Regiment which later became an SS brigade and then a division. Its leader, Oskar Dirlewanger, Doctor of Law and SS colonel had been the subject of legal action in his own country before the war on a matter of immoral practices involving young boys.

The war journal of the *Höhere SS-und Polizeiführer für Ostland* for 22 August— 21 September 1942, gives us some information about one apparently large-scale round-up.

The headquarters of this *SS-Obergruppenführer* and police general, Friedrich Jeckeln, were in Riga but for the purposes of the operation he had installed himself in Minsk. The operation, given the code name *Sumpffieber*, (swamp fever, malaria), had as its objective the 'total destruction of the so-called Partisans and bands of brigands' (*sogenannten Partisanen und Rauberbanden*) in White Russia.

To this end Jeckeln assembled:

The 1st infantry brigade of the *Waffen-SS*, partially motorised, comprising 2,300 officers, non-commissioned officers and men;

two police regiments and a number of Lithuanian auxiliaries, partially motorised; total strength 3,570 men;

32 officers and 244 non-commissioned officers, together with troops drawn from the Minsk Security Police and the SD;

350 Lithuanian auxiliaries and 100 Russian auxiliaries.

During splendid summer weather, in the words of the journal, Jeckeln's men struck — mostly in thin air, for the Partisans had an excellent intelligence service and managed to avoid any confrontation. On 26 August, 32 Partisans who had been unable to escape, perished. On 29 August, we are told, the villages of North Kormsha and South Kormsha were destroyed 'along with their inhabitants'.

On 3 and 4 September, Jeckeln moved on to the forest of Naliboki. He managed to seize five abandoned camps and enough booty to warrant a mention: three rifles and three horse-carts laden with kitchen utensils. This particular operation ended, we are told, with the shooting of 204 persons suspected of sympathising with the Partisans and the evacuation of 1,217 others.

The operation then moved on to Kossov and Baranovichi, still without coming to grips with the Partisans, apart from taking 19 men on 8 September and 3 the day after, near the Lake Bobroviki. On 13 September, the journal reports a counter-attack at the spot where the Oginski Canal runs into the Lake Vigonovski: *Hauptsturmführer* Liebram's *SD Kommando* was ambushed by the Partisans and completely wiped out, Liebram included.

The final result of the operation according to the journal was 389 Partisans killed in battle, 1,274 suspects shot, and 1,217 evacuated. The report adds, however, that 8,350 Jews were executed, although no details are given as to where and when. Presumably these Jews belonged either to 'family camps', or to the few ghettos situated outside the immediate field of action, and the Germans had decided to liquidate them in the same operation.

The Partisans must have been relatively well armed considering the extent of the German booty at the end of the operation: three anti-tank guns, five machine-guns, a quantity of rifles, mines and ammunition, a walkie-talkie and other items (including 42 bicycles, 62 horses and 5 cows).

Similar operations took place at other periods, and we continue to find the same disproportion between the number of Partisans and the number of civilians (or Jews) killed. *Sumpffieber*, however, was the operation that made the biggest haul of weapons and other booty.

Jeckeln's journal reveals that when events took a dangerous turn the Partisans could evade the enemy and go into hiding, taking up the fight again later on, whereas the civilians had no such escape, and risked being executed as suspects; and the Jews, whose movements were further hampered by the nature of their family camps, were consequently a prime target.

The Second World War was an exceedingly cruel war; that of the Eastern European Partisans the most barbarous of all. Human life had no value whatsoever, and no one had any compunction about sacrificing his neighbour's life to save his own skin. What seems particularly significant in the circumstances is that the comradeship of the Partisans held firm, and that scattered family camps still managed to subsist; and credit for this must go not only to the Jewish Partisans, but also to the Soviet leaders who, although they did not attach great importance to these camps, on many occasions had them protected. The fact that half the refugees in the 'family camps' managed to survive is significant.

Although the Jewish or mainly Jewish Partisan units were mostly found in western Bielorussia and Lithuania, there were also a great many Jewish Partisans in other regions of the USSR who fought in non-Jewish detachments and regiments[4].

The legendary Partisan commander Sidor Kovpak had a great many Jews in his brigade. At the beginning of 1943 he made an incursion, more like a long march, several hundred miles behind enemy lines, from the Pripet Marshes to the Carpathians, in the course of which he caused considerable havoc, and inflicted heavy losses on the enemy. He seized the Skalat locality near Tarnopol and freed the Jews imprisoned in the small concentration camp there. The able-bodied men joined up with Kovpak; the others remaining behind, for an army on the march could hardly encumber itself with non-combatants.

Finally, it is interesting to note that in the great majority of Partisan units almost all doctors and nurses and other medical personnel were Jewish. According to official Soviet testimonies, without the devotion of these doctors who tended the wounded for months at a time, relying solely on their medical or surgical skill, with neither hospitals, nor instruments, nor medicines to help them, the Partisans would have lost tens of thousands of men.

But it was not only his medical skill that distinguished one of the best-known Jewish Partisans: Doctor Atlas.

In 1942 Yehezkel Atlas was thirty-two years old and had been a qualified doctor for three years. He lived in Lodz, in what was to become the *Reichsgau Wartheland*, and not caring to have the Germans at too close quarters, he took refuge with his family in the eastern part of Poland, settling in Koslowszczyna, near Slonim, which later became part of the USSR.

When the Germans occupied the country, and Atlas was wondering which way to turn, the Germans made the decision for him. In May 1942 an *SS Kommando* from Slonim — mostly Lithuanians under German command — descended on the locality and wiped out all the Jews, with the single exception of Yehezkel Atlas, whose life was spared because doctors were scarce in the region[5]. Transferred to the neighbouring village of Wielka Wola, he found he was the only Jew in the Polish and Bielorussian community; the Germans no doubt considering that for the local inhabitants a Jewish doctor was good enough.

Atlas decided to avenge himself. He was not sure what form his vengeance would take for there were no organised Partisan groups in the region. There was no lack of forests, however, and these were full of men who for one reason or another dared not be seen in the villages: isolated Soviet soldiers, villagers who had not handed over the requisite measure of grain, Communist militants, and even a handful of Jewish survivors.

At the end of July, Atlas got in touch with thirty or so Jews from Derechchin, some eighteen miles from Wielka Wola, who told him that their ghetto had been liquidated on 24 July and that they were the sole survivors.

Atlas managed to procure arms for them, and the *Atlas* detachment was born. He surprised himself by becoming an extremely able commander, resolving problems of organisation and provisioning and even displaying some expertise in public relations. His detachment began to assert itself over the peasants of the locality, who had the reputation of not being overfond of Jewish fugitives. No doubt an armed detachment commanded more respect than a pack of beggars.

The first operation of the *Atlas* detachment took place in Derechchin in August 1942, the target being the German and Lithuanian garrison. It was a surprise attack and a successful one and very few of the enemy escaped with their lives. Forty-four SS and Lithuanians were shot on the spot where so many Derechchin Jews had perished.

Atlas, whose medical and military experience had made him particularly astute, warned his men that they must accept the fact that they were enjoying nothing more than a temporary stay of execution. They had really perished on 24 July, and their reprieve was simply to give them time to avenge themselves on their assassins.

Men spurred on to battle on these terms were particularly deadly adversaries.

All aspiring Partisans were asked the same question: 'What do you want?' the requisite reply answer being: 'I want to die fighting.' But some of Atlas's men survived, and grew in strength when they joined the survivors of various small ghettos in the forests of Lipitchanssk, the ghetto of Zdzieciol (*Jetel* in Yiddish) providing the *Atlas* detachment with the largest number of combatants.

Atlas was the first Partisan to derail a train in the region, having replaced the detonators of two unexploded shells he had found. This operation, which took place near Roshanka station, was followed by similar ones. Atlas also perfected a special technique for destroying bridges.

After a series of attacks on German garrisons, some successful some not, Doctor Atlas fell on 21 November 1942, while leading his men.

Although his detachment had only been fighting since August it was fully inured to combat and had sufficient stocks of arms and provisions; and it was able to continue the battle by uniting with Soviet regiments.

Together his comrades kept up the tradition established by 'the little doctor'.

This 'quite handsome, slim fellow with blue eyes, dressed in a homespun shirt and high Russian boots, with a revolver stuck in his belt' — the description given of him by his former nurse and comrade Bella Hirschborn — has a place in Jewish medical as well as military legend.

Of all the small Jewish groups that left the ghetto and took part in the struggle, that led by Misha Gildenman deserves special mention, for it operated in Ukrainian territory where relations between the Jews and the local population were even more strained than they were in Bielorussia or Poland.

Misha Gildenman was born in Korets, in Volhynia. He took to the forest along with sixteen companions in September 1942. Their first armed action was directed at a patrol of police officers who had been ordered by the Germans to round up the young Jews for forced labour in Germany. Six of the police officers were killed and the rest beat a hasty retreat, and Gildenman was thus able to arm and equip his men. This action also earned him the sympathy of the local Ukrainians.

Various police headquarters in the region were later destroyed by the men of *Diadia Micha* (Uncle Misha), whose detachment grew rapidly in size as first dozens and later hundreds of Jews wandering in the forests attached themselves to it.

Uncle Misha, who settled in Israel after the war, and died there a few years ago, describes in his memoirs some of the characters he had under him: extraordinary Partisans indeed. There was, for example, a carter from the village of Jarevitch, a pious Jew if ever there was one, who never forgot to recite the benediction before departing for some mine-laying expedition, and offered an extra-special benediction when he was ordered to blow up a trainload of German airmen on the night of Pourim, the feast day of Queen Esther. It is customary for Orthodox Jews to exchange gifts on this day, called *Chlakhmoness* (sending of presents), and this was the name given to the mine destined for the *Luftwaffe* pilots. No doubt as he prepared for his departure, he thought nostalgically of the wonderful Pourim celebrations of better days, his thoughts lingering on his mother and his father, his wife and two children, and how the Germans had killed them all.

Motele, a musical prodigy, was twelve years old when patiently, over the course of several weeks, he succeeded in winning the trust of the German officers of Ovruch. This gave him the opportunity of placing a bomb in the officers' mess. Motele had been found by Uncle Misha's men asleep in the forest where he had been wandering exhausted for days, having escaped being massacred with his family. Before he fell into the hands of the enemy he covered himself with glory on several occasions.

Some Jews assigned to forced labour were delivered to Uncle Misha on the eve of their execution.

Uncle Misha was received by Marshal Voroshilov after the liberation of the Zhitomir region. His only request was for permission to continue to fight as an officer of the Red Army since he wished to avenge his wife and daughter; and he finished the war as a captain in German territory.

One of his assignments was to liberate an internment camp for women at Torgau on the Elbe, and he later participated in the Battle of Berlin.

That is a general outline of the actions engaged by Jewish Resistance fighters in the zone of the ghettos. There were certainly others, but they have left no trace, no witnesses. There was a small Jewish group in Estonia, for example, calling itself 'The Red Guard'; a Resistance network in the Riga ghetto, made up of Jewish deportees from Germany and native Jews; then some unidentified Galician Jews of whom SS-Brigadeführer Fritz Katzmann complains in a report, describing how they had bought Italian arms and had no hesitation in using them. And dozens and dozens of other groups, large and small.

In the Rohatyn ghetto the Jews dug underground bunkers, three of which — Stalingrad, Sebastopol and Leningrad — were discovered by the SS. Katzmann reports indignantly that the Jews had the audacity to shoot at the police, who were forced to burn them out — the few, that is to say, who survived.

Likewise, the SS-und Polizeiführer of Galicia mentions a group of Jewish Partisans headed by a certain Horowicz, leader of the Polish Communist Party, that had formed up in the Brody region, north-east of Lvov. There were a number of Rabbis in this group and they had no scruples about using firearms. Katzmann reports that 53 'Jewish bandits' were struck down on 13 May 1943, both on the way from Lvov to Brody and on the outskirts of this town. He also mentions a fierce armed skirmish at Rava-Russkaya, to the north of Lvov, on 21 May; another in the forest of Busk, in the same region, on 31 May, and finally one with a group in Lvov itself on 2 June 1943.

From his report a general picture begins to emerge: the Resistance movement seemed unable to get a real start until German terrorism had shown its true face; and this peculiarity was not confined to the Jewish Resistance alone: in all occupied countries the Resistance took some time to come into its own, the period of quiescence varying from country to country, according to circumstances.

For the Jews, and especially those who lived within the Soviet frontiers of 1941, the first manifestation of Nazi terrorism was also the last, since it signalled their mass execution.

The survivors of the first wave of executions had enormous difficulty in regrouping themselves, the astonishing thing being that they eventually succeeded in doing so — astonishing, too, that they even went to the extent of staging revolts in the death chambers of the Nazi extermination camps.

NOTES

1. The first partisan groups were not all partriotic-minded; they included quite a number of anti-Soviet nationalist detachments. These were very swiftly 'roped in' by the Germans. The same thing happened in the Ukraine, at least in the beginning. Later, when the Ukrainian nationalists realised that Germany had not the slightest intention of giving the Ukraine its independence, that its real aim was to transform the country into a colony, many of them had second thoughts. They did not go to the extent of fighting the Germans, however, but continued to combat the Soviet regime and its equivalent in the German-occupied territories — the Red Partisans.

2. The weekly report of the *Kommandeur* of the Security Police and of the SD in Minsk devotes several pages to describing Partisan attacks that took place early in 1943 (allowing about three lines for each). The nature of these attacks hardly ever varies: mining of railways, mining of roads, destruction of the pro-Germans' livestock, execution of the village leaders appointed by the Germans, attacks on isolated German barracks or those of German auxiliaries. Taken singly, these actions were not very important, but they had the cumulative effect of undermining the enemy psychologically, and caused adverse results on the military side as well.

3. Moshe Kahanovich, *Milhemet Hapartizanim Hayehoudim Bemizrah Europa* (The War of the Jewish Partisans in Eastern Europe) Ayanoth, Tel Aviv, 1954, 435 pp. (in Hebrew).

4. Moshe Kahanovich's book gives the names of one hundred and forty East European regiments, detachments, brigades, and other Partisan units in which the Jews fought.

5. Heydrich himself forbade the immediate shooting of Jewish doctors from July 1941 onwards 'except when absolutely necessary', simply because there were no others available.

Part Seven
Revolt in the Death Camps

CHAPTER 31

THE VICTORY OF SOBIBOR

THE Sobibor extermination camp was situated practically on the banks of the River Bug about 114 miles east of Warsaw, in a thickly wooded part of the Lublin region. The 'stable' population varied from 600 to 2,000 prisoners, and the camp was equipped to 'handle' batches of between 1,000 and 2,000 Jews.

For a certain time — roughly from the second half of 1942 to the beginning of 1943 — Sobibor received a weekly trainload of prisoners from The Netherlands, more than 30,000 Dutch Jews ending their days in the Sobibor gas chambers.

Transports were also directed there from Czechoslovakia, Germany and other countries, but the majority of the victims came from Poland itself and from the territories reoccupied by the USSR in 1939, Sobibor lying more or less on the 1939 Germano-Soviet line of demarcation.

According to the estimates of the Warsaw Institute of Jewish Historical Research, the number of Sobibor victims reached as many as 350,000: that, during a period of seventeen months and six days.

On 8 May 1942, the camp was open to receive its first victims. On 14 October 1943, it ceased to exist, the occupants having escaped after systematically disposing of most of the officers and SS non-commissioned officers. There were 600 prisoners in the camp at that time of whom one-third survived.

At Treblinka the uprising was the outcome of lengthy preparations by veteran prisoners, but the Sobibor revolt — and victory — was led by a young Red Army officer, Alexander (Sasha) Pechorski, who had been in the camp for no more than three weeks.

Certainly the Germans in Minsk made a fatal blunder when they dispatched to Sobibor a group of prisoners which comprised not only the usual contingent of women, children and old people destined for the gas chamber, but also some Soviet prisoners of war, 'selected' because they were Jews — and among them a junior officer, Pechorski, then thirty-four years old.

Mobilised in June 1941, Pechorski had been captured in October of the same year; an escape attempt resulting in his being sent to the reprisals camp of the Minsk ghetto in Sheroka Street. When this camp was liquidated on 18 September 1943, the 100 Jewish prisoners of war, together with 500 skilled Jewish workers and their families, were piled into a train about to leave for Sobibor.

Their route led across the dangerous regions of western Bielorussia where a large number of Partisan detachments operated.

On reaching their destination five days later, the prisoners noticed that flanking the name of Sobibor, printed in Gothic letters, there was another, similarly printed, *Sonderkommando*, which did not mean anything in particular to them. They got out of the train to find themselves faced with a 'reception committee' of eleven SS men armed with whips. The *SS-Oberscharführer* (regimental sergeant-major) Gomerski, a former Berlin boxer, who was in command, barked out a brief order: 'Carpenters and cabinet-makers without families, step forward.'

About twenty-four men, most of them prisoners of war, stepped forward. They were led away to a hut and integrated into the Sobibor camp. The other prisoners were given the usual treatment.

Pechorski swiftly made friends with one of the 'veterans' of the camp, the tailor Barukh, and discovered the sort of place he had come to and what lay in store for him and his companions. He was seized with an agonising fit of despair which he found very difficult to shake off, but on the following day he began to make notes about the camp, and managed to conceal them, which in itself betrayed an unusual determination.

Unlike most of the other prisoners, the majority of them Polish Jews, Pechorski did not speak Yiddish. In fact he could hardly speak Russian, which the Polish Jews might perhaps have understood. One of his companions, Shlomo-Leitman, acted as interpreter for him, while others, the German, Czechoslovak and Dutch Jews, had no difficulty in communicating.

On 26 September, Pechorski was busy chopping down a tree along with other prisoners when one of these, a rather elderly Dutch Jew who was having some difficulty in being equal to his task, was promptly encouraged by a few strokes of the whip, administered by Franz, one of the SS chiefs of the camp. When Pechorski showed his disapproval, Franz stopped whipping the Dutchman, and approached Pechorski. He ordered him in broken Russian to chop down the tree within five minutes, adding that if he was successful he would be given a packet of cigarettes; if he failed his reward would be 25 strokes of the whip.

Pechorski set to work on the tree. When he had felled it, Franz came up to him with a packet of cigarettes in his hand: 'Four and a half minutes. A promise is a promise.'

Pechorski replied: 'Thank you, but I do not smoke,' and carried on with his work.

Franz left him without a word. But about twenty minutes later he returned with a chunk of bread and some margarine:

'Here, Russian soldier, have this'.

'Thank you, but my rations are quite adequate,' the young officer replied.

'So you don't want it?'

'No, thank you, I am not hungry.'

Later, the other prisoners told Pechorski that at Sobibor Jews had been killed for much less.

Reports of the incident rapidly spread among the prisoners and Sasha the Russian soon became the talk of the camp.

The next day, one of Pechorski's travelling companions, Shubayev, confided in him that he intended to escape. Pechorski replied that single escape attempts would bring reprisals on those who remained behind and suggested they should escape *en masse*. In fact, that very day, the arrival of another batch of prisoners warned everyone that time was running short.

To digress for a moment, one small detail struck the imagination of the Soviet prisoners. The SS kept several hundred geese for fattening for the table. These creatures served another useful purpose: when a fresh batch of prisoners arrived and the women and children were led away to the gas chamber, prisoners were ordered to release the geese and chase them so that their honking might drown the cries of the human victims.

Boris Tsilbulsky, one of Pechorski's Minsk friends, pointed out that winter was approaching and that it would be more difficult to escape when the Germans could follow the imprints in the snow.

Like all concentration camps Sobibor was divided into sections separated by barbed wire and at Sobibor there were four. Pechorski and his comrades had been the first to occupy the north section and were busy enlarging it. Section, or camp I, contained the workshops and living quarters of the carpenters, cabinet-makers, tailors, shoemakers and locksmiths. Camp II consisted of depots where the clothing of the victims was sorted. The women chosen for this task lived on the premises. The 'baths' and disposal pits were situated in camp III. The Russian camp, the north camp, was separated from the first two camps by the restricted area of the gas chambers and crematoria.

The quarters of the SS, mostly Ukrainian guards, and the SS military installations were all situated within the camp boundaries, and were marked by a series of barbed wire entanglements and a mined zone, all surrounded by yet another barbed wire entanglement.

On 28 September, Barukh helped Pechorski and Leitman to get into the women's huts. The 150 detainees there were eager to meet this Sasha they had heard so much about and hoped to be given his personal assurance that their tribulations would soon be over. Leitman acted as interpreter. One of the prisoners asked him the crucial question:

'Tell me, since there are so many Partisans why don't they attack the camp and rescue us?'

'The Partisans have enough to do. No one can do our work for us.'

In the next few days a number of prisoners told Sasha of their intention to escape, inviting him to join them. Each time he gave the same reply: 'We must find a way of escaping altogether. If you want to go it alone, good luck to you. I shan't stand in your way but don't count on me.'

Here was exactly what the prisoners needed: the tone of a leader whom they felt they could trust. Escape attempts had already taken place. One, by a group of 72 Dutchmen led by an army captain, ex-combatant of the International Brigade in Spain, ended in failure. Whether or not they were denounced, the fact remains that the plot was discovered and the 72 men executed.

In the first place, a close eye had to be kept on the *kapos*. One of these, a certain Brzecki, made a direct approach to Pechorski.

According to Pechorski, Brzecki was not a very attractive character. He always carried a whip and had no compunction about unremittingly whipping and insulting the prisoners. When he spotted a woman prisoner who attracted him, he had to have her. All the same — and on this point all the prisoners agreed — he was not an informer and had never denounced anyone.

Brzecki came straight to the point. He was well aware that Pechorski was preparing an escape attempt and going about it very cleverly, too. In fact, the young officer had become very friendly with an eighteen-year-old woman of the Dutch group called Luka. She was actually a German Jew whose Communist father had been run to earth in Hamburg. From this point on, Pechorski was never seen about the camp without this young woman, who served as a sort of camouflage. Brzecki realised what was going on and said to Pechorski:

'I have been informed of your remark that "no one else can do our work", and could have had you shot for that alone. I am well aware that you don't trust me but I haven't come to justify myself. Anyway, rest assured I shan't say a word to the SS about it.'

'Go on. I am all ears.'

'Sasha, include me in your plans. If we work together it will make things so much easier for both of us. We *kapos* can move about freely in the camp and speak to anybody without arousing suspicion. You are probably wondering why I am making this proposition to you, but that is easily explained: I do not believe that the Germans will keep their promises. At the moment the *kapos* are privileged, but it is perfectly obvious that they will eventually be killed like everybody else.'

'I know you are aware of what is going on, but why tell me?'

'Because you are the leader, and my colleague Genick and I want to join you.'

'And what about the other *kapo*, Schmidt?'

'I have no idea. He could be swayed.'

After a moment's silence, Pechorski bluntly demanded:

'Tell me, could you kill a Jerry?'

'I don't know. If it was a matter of life or death, I suppose I could.'

'And could you kill simply for the pleasure of it, as they do?'

'I have never thought about it.'

'Very well. It's late. Let's sleep on it.'

Pechorski knew just how valuable the co-operation of the *kapos* would be. Brzecki's replies seemed sincere. If he had been an *agent provocateur* he would certainly have declared that nothing would have given him more pleasure than to kill a German, whereas his reply had been exactly the one a Jew would have made in similar circumstances.

11 October was just one more day of bloodshed. A batch of new arrivals, already naked, attempted to escape just as they were about to enter the gas chamber. They had left it too late and were all caught and dispatched.

The next day, having consulted his Minsk friends, Pechorski sent for Brzecki and entrusted him with a dangerous and vital mission.

The operation was scheduled to take just over an hour, the plan being that at 3.30 p.m., two days later, Brzecki and three men chosen by Pechorski from among the Soviet prisoners would enter camp II. Barukh would persuade the SS to go to a certain hut, where the Soviet prisoners would dispose of them with axes. Immediately afterwards — at any rate, before 4 o'clock — the telephone wires would be cut. At 4 o'clock the same operation would be repeated in camp I: the mission would be completed by 4.30 p.m.

The two *kapos* Brzecki and Genick, would then assemble the prisoners as though they were taking them to work, putting the Soviet prisoners at the head of the column. When they reached the armoury they would seize it by force, killing the guards and if necessary attacking the watch-tower.

In the event of the plan's failing, Pechorksi had prepared an alternative one which entailed getting out via the SS quarters near the boundaries of the camp. On this side the ground was only slightly, if at all, mined and the prisoners could throw stones ahead of them to explode any mines that there were.

D-day was fixed for 14 October.

At 2 o'clock in the afternoon, with zero hour drawing near, came the first *contretemps*. The SS officer Ryba called Brzecki and three other men away. It seemed that the plan was wrecked, or at least that an alternative way of smuggling the men into camp II must be found. Pechorski summoned the other *Kapo* Genick, and passed the assignment on to him. Genick tried to get out of it by saying that he was not officially allowed to enter camp II, but Pechorski insisted that any excuse would do, since he must replace his absent colleague, and Genick duly set off for camp II accompanied by Leitman, Tsibulsky, and two others.

Just around that time, the *SS-Unterscharführer* Berg dismounted from his horse and entered the tailor's hut in camp I to try on a suit he had ordered. As he took off his belt and holster Shubayev struck him a violent blow with the flat side of his hatchet, swiftly followed by a second that silenced him for good. The *SS-Unter-scharführer* was bundled in thick cloth and pushed under the bed so as not to scare away his colleagues who were shortly due to arrive for their fittings. The tailor had just time to deliver Berg's pistol to Pechorski before his second 'client', the leader of the guards, Helm, appeared.

At 4 o'clock precisely, the commander of camp III, big chief of the gas chamber, Goettinger, entered the shoemakers' hut to try on a pair of boots. He had just time to tell the shoemakers what he had come for.

At 4.45, Tsibulsky returned to camp II and announced 'Mission completed': the four SS had been put out of harm's way. He had been preceded a quarter of an hour earlier by Brzecki and his men. The summons had been a false alarm: the SS officer had simply wanted them to supervise the unloading of some timber. Another SS, Haulstich, passed by and Leitman called him into the hut. Haulstich entered. The *kapo* Schmidt was about to follow Haulstich when Brzecki stopped him. He told Schmidt that most of the SS had already been killed and that he himself had no choice but to co-operate — unless he preferred to be killed, either by the rebels or by the German reinforcements which would certainly turn up eventually.

Further off, in the garage, SS Walter Ryba met his destiny in the form of Engel, the mechanic from Lodz. That left only Franz to be disposed of. But Franz was not destined to die just yet, but survived to be tried in Hagen, in the Ruhr, almost a quarter of a century later.

The rebels were now much better armed than they had been at the outset, the women having ransacked the living quarters of the SS and helped themselves to their arms, and the locksmiths having found several rifles.

Finally it was decided not to wait for Franz any longer. The column, headed by the Soviet prisoners responsible for attacking the armoury, was completely dis-organised by the stampede when the departure signal was given. As the unruly crowd reached the gate of camp I, the commander of the guards, a German from the Volga region, rushed forward saying that the whistle had been blown and they must fall into line. He had not grasped what was happening and was quickly dis-patched under a rain of blows from the prisoners' axes. The Ukrainian guards beat a hasty retreat, most of them taking the opportunity to desert.

Forcing the gate of camp I, the column met up with the women escapees from camp II. These humble creatures, bowed under the yoke of the SS, had just seen their executioners have their throats slit — and the heavens had not fallen. The shock was overwhelming.

Making the only possible decision Pechorksi cried: 'Forward, comrades!'

The crowd hurled themselves at the door of the armoury, but it held firm, and the SS, who had had time to recover, sprayed them with machine-gun fire.

Those who had come in by the main entrance to the camp, however, passed through without difficulty, attacking the guards with rifle and revolver fire, and pelting them with stones. The rebels were free. The battle of Sobibor was won. Apart from those who had fallen during the assault on the armoury, all the prisoners got away to the forests.

It was an outstanding operation, conceived by a junior officer, and carried through to success within the space of three weeks and thanks to him, 600 un-armed prisoners, including a large number of women, had braved several dozen SS and 200 or more of their Ukrainian and Polish auxiliaries.

The German reaction to this mass escape was violent, but not immediate, for the insurgents had taken the precaution of cutting communications, and had an extra stroke of luck when a woman telegraphist in Chelm delayed Franz's appeal for reinforcements for more than four hours.

The camp was now annihilated, no doubt on direct orders from Berlin. Since its very existence had to be kept secret, the fact that several hundred witnesses were now at large was embarrassing, and like Treblinka, Sobibor was razed to the ground.

The prisoners, dispersed throughout the neighbouring forests, met with varying fortunes. Pechorski speaks of 'three Dutch Jewesses', Selma Weinberg, Ursula Stern and Katje Gokkes. In fact Ursula Stern was of German origin. These three had climbed over the barbed wire with the help of a ladder conveniently placed there. At the time they regarded this contingency as something of a miracle, but later realised that the 'miracle' had been carefully prepared.

Ursula and Katje joined up with a Polish woman called Edda, who helped with the language difficulty, and after a period spent wandering in the forest eventually fell on a group of Jewish Partisans who received them well.

A few days later this detachment walked into an ambush laid by a much larger detachment of Polish nationalist Partisans, belonging to the *Armja Krajowa*. According to Ursula Stern, these Poles detested Jews, Russians and Germans in that order. They had a further reason for bearing a grudge against this particular detachment, for the men led by Michal had discovered a stock of arms in the forest and had appropriated them. These arms came from London and had been parachuted specially for the *AK*, who were finally content to take what they considered to be their property and let the Jews go. Later the two young women joined and fought with a mounted Russian detachment.

Ursula is now married to another Dutch Resistance deportee, Horst Buchheimer, and lives in Ashquelon in Israel. She has Hebraised her name to Ilana Safran.

Pechorski himself managed to rejoin the Soviet Partisans a couple of weeks after his escape. He resumed active service and was wounded on several occasions before the war ended. Most of his companions fell later in the ranks of the Red Army.

In spite of the indisputable heroism of his exploit, Pechorski received no extra-ordinary distinction. This was indirectly advantageous to him for it meant that he was 'forgotten' during the latter period of Stalin's life, a period marked by ruthless persecution of the most prominent Jews.

Another of Pechorski's companions, Simon Rozenfeld, a Soviet prisoner of war like himself, managed to hide for several months, then resumed service in the Red Army and fought as far as Berlin. Wounded several times, he ended the war in front of the Reichstag building.

At the Hagen trials, where several former SS guards from Sobibor were tried and sentenced — to the usual paltry terms of imprisonment — it was the evidence of the rebels, the testimony of those who ought not to have survived, that settled the argument.

CHAPTER 32

THE POETRY AND TRUTH OF TREBLINKA

O
N Monday, 2 August, 1943 the extermination camp of Treblinka, 60 miles
or so north-east of Warsaw, staged an uprising. Several hundred prisoners,
all that remained of several hundred thousand, succeeded in killing some of the
guards and getting through the barbed wire entanglements to freedom. A large
number of them managed to survive the year that was to pass before the arrival
of the Red Army.

Under the title of *Treblinka — la révolte d'un camp d'extermination*, the young
French writer Jean-François Steiner published an intense, impassioned book[1]
which is neither a history nor a documentary — not even a novel; it is a work which
in our opinion belongs to the category Goethe called *Dichtung und Wahrheit*, poetry
and truth.

Here we have the testimonies of men who participated in the uprising, and survived. Collected at various times from 1943 onwards, as far as we can gather they
are all, from a rather modest category of individuals. There is not a single testimony
from the instigators of the revolt, for the simple reason that they all perished. The
evidence therefore is fragmentary, the witnesses failing sometimes to distinguish
between hearsay and fact.

There were, on one hand, the realities that they themselves had witnessed and
lived through; there were also the facts that they had heard repeated over and over
again until they assumed the character of a legend, and one so strong that it has
acquired the status of the collective memory of the group.

Many of the survivors of Treblinka have since settled in Israel, and the Israeli
institutes of historical research have naturally made every effort to collect their
testimonies. An important Israeli research institution, Moreshet, published a
number of them, in its journal number VIII, for example, but these contained a
great many contradictions which the publishers have not tried to explain away.

Having chosen to follow the technique of *Dichtung und Wahrheit*, Steiner can
therefore rest assured that his account strays no further from the truth than do
certain others, and now that the controversy over his book has died down we find
that what happened in Treblinka is easier to understand in the light of events in
Sobibor.

The Sobibor uprising occurred sixty-three days after that of Treblinka. There
was no contact between the rebels of the two camps. Although the insurrections had

something in common, there were a number of contrasting situations which decisively influenced the results.

Treblinka was to have been the extermination camp for the Warsaw Jews and those of central Poland, but matters connected with railway administration brought quite a number of Jewish transports to Treblinka from other occupied countries, batches of prisoners coming from as far afield as Greece, Yugoslavia, Czechoslovakia and Germany.

However, most of the normal complement of prisoners, that is to say those who were not put to death on arrival, were Polish. To achieve anything at all, the first essential was to survive the selection ritual that usually took place on the arrival of the deportation trains — not invariably, however; some batches of prisoners were completely exterminated. The very small proportion of Jews left alive had then to survive maltreatment, famine, disease, subsequent selections and, perhaps the most difficult of all, deadly lassitude and nervous exhaustion.

When the revolt was launched at the end of the summer of 1943, the number of able-bodied men in Treblinka had been comparatively stable for several weeks, and it was these circumstances that made the uprising possible; but there were several setbacks.

Some individual resistance actions had taken place before the new batches of prisoners had even reached the selection and annihilation stage. One deportee from Warsaw, called Berliner, stabbed an SS guard the moment he set foot on the landing ramp of Treblinka station. Another deportee, who had managed to smuggle in a grenade, flung it at the first guard he saw. There were even cases where whole trainloads rebelled, either *en route*, or on reaching their destination. Finally, camp legend cherishes the memory of an unknown, very beautiful young woman who, on entering the gas chamber, seized the weapon of one of the guards and had time to shoot down several SS before she perished.

Treblinka, like all the other camps, was divided into several sections. A criminal detention camp where Polish peasants guilty of various misdemeanours were interned became Treblinka I. When it was decided to kill the Jews *en masse* Treblinka II was set up close by. Treblinka II, referred to in reports of the SS General Stroop as T2, was itself divided into sections. That set apart for exterminations — the gas chambers — was isolated from that of the Jewish prisoners assigned to forced labour. The tasks these were given varied from the upkeep and development of the camp to turning the mass massacres to account by retrieving the clothing, hair, gold teeth and rings of the victims and any valuables they might have brought with them. It amounted to a considerable booty.[2]

All identifying signs had to be taken from the victims' clothing. Anything that could betray where they came from like yellow stars or yellow armbands, had to be removed, and woe betide the unfortunate prisoner who overlooked some revealing sign.

Other work parties saw to the bullion, jewels and coins, and these prisoners were to play a vital role in the uprising, for the quantity of gold they had managed to hide away enabled them to buy arms, and also to survive after the uprising.

One of the first Resistance organisers, Doctor Chorazycki, employed by the SS as medical officer to the guard, was caught by the camp commandant, Kurt Franz, while he was hiding gold coins destined for the purchase of arms. Chorazycki failed in his attempt to kill the commandant and preferred to poison himself rather than risk breaking down under interrogation. The SS seized him just before he expired and tried to resuscitate him so that they could interrogate him, but to no avail.

When a new camp armoury was installed an armoured door was brought in from outside and the camp locksmiths were ordered to make a key. They managed to make a duplicate, which was to prove very useful later on.

Chorazycki's place was taken by the engineer Galewski. The Resistance group already had a few dozen members, as well as silver, gold, and weapons which Jewish labourers who worked outside the camp had managed to buy from the local peasants, behind the backs of the SS. But the group still lacked a real military leader. They eventually found one in Zelo Bloch, former captain in the Czechoslovak army and at that time thirty-two years old. Bloch was assisted by one of his fellow townsmen, Rudolf Massarek, 'a half-Jew' from Prague to whom some survivors and historians wrongly attribute a relationship with Thomas G. Masaryk, first president of the Czechoslovak Republic.

It can be seen that the Treblinka Resistance was far inferior in strength to that of Sobibor where the uprising was headed by a group of former Red Army soldiers commanded by Alexander Pechorski, whereas Zelo Bloch, captain though he was, had had no fighting experience and was not even supported by experienced fighters. Pechorski and his Soviet comrades had only been a few weeks in Sobibor when they launched their insurrection, while the military chiefs of Treblinka had been there for months.

Using the duplicate key to the armoury, the camp Resistance movement smuggled out a number of grenades, but these proved to be useless because the detonators were missing, and the operation had to be postponed.

During the enforced delay the Resistance fighters waged a merciless clandestine war against all those suspected of acting as informers for the SS, Treblinka having its share of these like all the camps, and many a case of 'suicide' was in reality an execution by the Resistance.

The Resistance fighters finally managed to recruit two young men who were acting as liaison agents for the SS and were therefore permitted to circulate freely inside the camp. When the crucial moment came, it was these young men who smuggled the grenades and rifles to the prisoners.

After several postponements, it was decided that the insurrection would take place at about 4 p.m. on 2 August 1943, choosing the hour when hundreds of prisoners who worked outside would be returning to the camp. A shot was to be fired as a signal for the revolt to begin.

Squads of prisoners were detailed to dispose of the Ukrainian guards in the watch towers, others were to cut the barbed wire. Some were armed with bottles of petrol to set fire to the camp. Others would shoot down the SS. The SS camp commandant was to be taken into the forest and tried. Any stocks of gold and valuables still remaining in the camp were to be loaded into lorries.

Things did not go off exactly as planned, mainly because the shot that was to serve as a signal was fired an hour too soon.

The enforced change of schedule meant that the several hundred prisoners still outside the camp were unable to participate; but most of the guards in the watch towers were effectively disposed of as were a large number of SS. Badly armed as the rebels were, with only twenty or so rifles, a slightly larger number of revolvers, and a few hand grenades between them, some hundreds of them managed to force the encircling barbed wire fence by cutting it in some places and climbing over it in others, more often than not over the dead bodies of their comrades who had been mown down. Bloch, Galewski and Massarek all perished.

Accounts differ as to the number of survivors, varying between several dozen and several hundred. At a preliminary examination at the trial of SS guards of Treblinka which took place in Düsseldorf between 1964 and 1965, as many as 58 former prisoners were called upon to give evidence, indicating that 22 years earlier there must have been a great many more.

Most of the installations had been set on fire. The Treblinka Jews were meant to vanish into thin air. Justice demanded that the fire be lit this time by a few of the intended victims, and it was Treblinka itself that was reduced to ashes.

NOTES

1. This book was awarded the Literary Prize of the French Resistance in 1966.
2. For example, files of the goods transport department of Treblinka station contain a note dated 13 September 1942 concerning fifty truck loads of clothes. And that was only one delivery.

CHAPTER 33

AUSCHWITZ AND ITS INSURRECTION

TODAY the name of Auschwitz is synonomous with gas chambers and crematoria, symbols *par excellence* of the concentration camp system, but between 1940 and 1945 this name meant different things to different groups of people.

Auschwitz was originally devised in 1940 as a concentration camp for rebellious Poles who refused to accept German domination, and was only later developed into a multiple-purpose complex:

the concentration camp for the Poles grew larger and larger;

political prisoners from all over Europe were sent there in ever increasing numbers;

sections for women were built;

special gas extermination facilities were established in Auschwitz II (Birkenau);

a third complex, Auschwitz III (Monowitz) was erected for the exploitation of prison labour;

emergency squads working outside the camp, but dependent on Auschwitz, operated in the same way as those attached to the Reich concentration camps;

there were other camps outside the boundaries of the main concentration camp (*Postenkette*), mostly occupied by British prisoners of war who were employed in German industry;

and, finally, in other parts of the region there were camps of foreign workers who were in Germany either by virtue of the STO or as free workers. In particular, there was a large number of French labourers, usually from labour camps, who had been transferred to Germany, more often than not, without a proper trial.[1]

Most of the Jews who ended up in Auschwitz had never seen the inside of the principal camp — Auschwitz I. Arriving by train at a special station, as they did at Treblinka, Sobibor and Belsen, the majority were led straight to the gas chambers. The selection was made on their arrival by SS men specially chosen for the task; these were occasionally assisted by SS doctors. It was a question of selecting from the mass of doomed Jews those who could be usefully employed. There are no reports of serious incidents on the arrival ramp. The SS went to a great deal of trouble on the public relations side: there was backgound music, lorries ready to transport women, children, and the infirm, while prisoners were at hand to act as porters; in short an atmosphere of relative welcome greeted the

283

Jews when they got out of the cattle trucks in which they had existed often for several days.

But all good things come to an end and the situation swiftly deteriorated. Most of the arrivals were passed on to the crematoria via the gas chamber. In the whole history of gassing in Auschwitz, it appears that there were only two bloody incidents when the crucial moment came. One is reported by Rudolf Höss, commandant of the Auschwitz camp, in his memoirs, written in prison while under sentence of death. He tells how on one occasion a few Jews managed to get hold of some weapons and use them on the guards, before being forced into the gas chambers. The SS suffered some losses but quickly regained control of the situation.

In the autumn of 1943, the Gestapo collected together a number of Jews in special camps — Vittel (Vosges) and Bergen-Belsen, in particular. These Jews had been arrested in places throughout Europe, mostly in Poland, but they were not of European extraction. Most of them were natives of Latin America. Very often the passports were false, even blatantly so, but the Gestapo paid no heed since these people were to be exchanged for German citizens interned in the New World.

But one day there was a counter-order. All those whose nationality was open to question were loaded into trains and dispatched to Auschwitz. In the history of the camp this was called 'the extermination of the Americans' although the only American thing about these unfortunates was their false papers. While being un-dressed, one of the 'Americans', a young woman, whose name has been lost to us, seized an SS officer's revolver and shot him. She killed several others before she died[2].

When the Auschwitz guards were tried in Frankfurt in 1963—1964, Hans Laternser, counsel for the defence, thought he could use a *de facto* argument. As several of his clients had been accused of having participated in the 'selections' in the course of which thousands of people were sent to their death, Laternser pointed out that his clients had in fact saved the lives of those they had selected since the Jews chosen temporarily were spared. The Frankfurt Assize Court did not follow the eminent jurist down this slippery path, but the accused received lighter sentences.

Auschwitz had a Resistance organisation, from which the Jews were initially excluded. It took the form of an international committee led by a Polish Socialist lawyer, Josef Cyrankiewicz, future Prime Minister of the Polish People's Republic.

It was not surprising that the committee should be headed by a Pole, since the vast majority of prisoners were Polish. Other leaders were German, Austrian, and Russian.

Contact was made between the committee and Polish Resistance outside the camp. Auschwitz was situated in Upper Silesia, a region with a predominantly

German population, most non-Germans having been expelled. Eventually, a Jewish Resistance group formed up in the main camp. Bruno Baum, a prisoner of Jewish origin who is now living in the Democratic German Republic, reports that a Resistance group was set up comprising three hundred Jews, all originally from the Ciechanow region north of Warsaw which formed liaisons with the clandestine leaders. He mentions among them Horst Jonas, who worked in Auschwitz-Monovitz, and whom we know from his past activities in Sachsenhausen.

Among the Jewish members of the Auschwitz Resistance committee was an Austrian, Hermann Langbein. A Communist at the time and former member of the International Brigade, he had earned high esteem with his comrades. Although a political prisoner and despite his Austrian nationality, Langbein enjoyed certain 'privileges' thanks to his ethnic origin, for besides being an Aryan, he was a *Reichsdeutsche*. Taking full advantage of his position, Langbein saw to it that Jewish doctors were employed in the *Revier* hospital, where previously this sector had been reserved for Polish doctors, chosen for their anti-Semitism. After the war, one of these, Doctor Dering, was the subject of grave accusations concerning the role he played in so-called medical experiments practised on Jewish victims. The British court in which he brought an action against his accusers delivered a rather subtle judgment, awarding nominal damages against his accusers. The fact that he chose a British court shows that he had reason to fear the justice of his own country; and it was probably on the same grounds that he chose to settle first in Somaliland then in Great Britain.

The Jewish doctors were now in a position to tend the sick Jews in Auschwitz. In this way Langbein's intervention — which gave the Jewish medical personnel the opportunity of working for their own race — saved the lives of some hundreds of Jews.

Other Jewish Resistance organisers were Israel Guttman, Szmulewicz, Farber, and others; but the hard core of Jewish Resistance was elsewhere: in the *Sonderkommando*.

In Nazi terminology the prefix *sonder* often has a sinister ring to it. *Sonderbehandlung* (special treatment) meant putting to death; *Sonderaktion* (special action) generally meant mass execution. *Sonderkommando* was the name of the special squad responsible for executions. In Auschwitz, however, this was not the case; the name *Sonderkommando* had been given to the team of Jews allocated to assisting the SS after the executions.

They collected the clothes of those who had gone stark naked to their death. Then they removed the bodies, extracted gold teeth, retrieved any jewels or coins that the prisoners might have managed to conceal in anatomical cavities, and piled up the corpses in the crematoria. When there were too many victims, funeral pyres were set up in the open. The *Sonderkommando* Jews were also responsible for these.

Here as elsewhere they had the right to more generous rations than the other prisoners. In Auschwitz, where there was a surplus of labour, the *Sonderkommandos* were periodically replaced, the SS doing away with all or part of the *kommandos* from time to time, dipping into the pool of prisoners for the necessary replacements. Many *kommando* prisoners could not stand the strain and either committed suicide or let themselves waste away, so that of all the doomed Auschwitz prisoners the *Sonderkommando* had the shortest expectation of life, and they knew it.

The camp Resistance committee planned to stage an uprising on the approach of the Red Army, if possible with the co-operation of the Polish Resistance movement. On 9 July 1944 the Red Army launched a major offensive which achieved brilliant results on most fronts, but north of the Carpathians they met with less success. Proceeding from the line Kovel-Lutsk-West Tarnopol, the Ukrainian 1st Front, headed by Marshal Koniev, later reinforced by the 4th Front under General Petrov, overwhelmed Galicia, destroyed a German corps at Brody and seized Lvov. It crossed the San and the Vistula, but was finally halted east of the Kielce-Tarnow line, just over 60 miles from Auschwitz. The front was stabilised during the second half of August.

That same month the Polish national insurrection in Warsaw ended in tragedy, traumatising the whole Polish Resistance movement in the process. The Resistance committee of Auschwitz was obliged to change its plans and postpone the uprising.

The *Sonderkommando* Jews themselves were in a much better position having managed to obtain ammunition and explosives from Jewish women working in the *Union* munitions factories in Auschwitz. The principal smuggler of this very special contraband was young Rosa Robota, a native of Ciechanów and member of the Zionist movement *Hachomer Hatzair* who also supplied explosives to the Resistance fighters of the main camp. She was in contact with Noah Zabludowicz, also from Ciechanów, Moshe Kulka, Israel Guttman and probably one or two others.

When the *Sonderkommando* Jews learned that the operation had been postponed they knew that their time was running out. Already the SS had withdrawn a number of their comrades from the *kommando* and taken them away to an officially unknown destination which was none the less easy to guess.

A few Communists exercised a strong influence in the *Sonderkommando*, particularly Jacques Handelsman, a militant of Polish origin deported from Paris, and his friend and fellow deportee Joseph Dorembus (Warszawski).

More isolated from the outside world than the committee, the *Sonderkommando* Jews found themselves alone and faced with a dilemma: should they allow themselves to be massacred without resistance, or should they act on their own, exposing themselves to certain death and running the risk of dragging the Resistance fighters outside the camp into the *débâcle*?

At the beginning of November 1944 fate took a hand. One of the most detested *kapos* appeared suddenly in the middle of a group of conspirators and threatened to denounce them. Knowing that the die was cast they quickly disposed of the *kapo* then attacked the SS guards in an attempt to fight their way out of the camp.

The battle continued for hours. The *Sonderkommando* Jews, most of them Polish or Greek, held their own in the unequal struggle and succeeded in setting fire to one of the crematoria, but in the end they were overpowered.

The Auschwitz *Sonderkommando* Jews, thrown together at the whim of their executioners, were perhaps the most unfortunate of all the unfortunate Jews in Europe. Yet they proved by their action that it was possible to dissolve international barriers and restore the unity of the Jewish people. Polish Jews, French Jews, Belgian Jews, Greek Jews, Hungarian Jews fought together and died side by side.

Besides this celebrated example of armed uprising, the Auschwitz Jews engaged in another form of Resistance activity, in which they revealed their faith in human nature, when they attempted to let the outside world know the true significance of Auschwitz. One of the leaders of the camp Resistance movement, Szmulewicz, brought off the *tour de force* of photographing an execution and several cremations in the open. With the help of contacts in the Polish Resistance movement he managed to get these photographs to London. Other Jews escaped to try and tell the world what was happening.

Two of these, Mala Zimetbaum, a young Belgian Jewess of Polish origin, and her friend, were recaptured as were most of the others. The Polish and German Jews had a slightly better chance of making a clear getaway because they spoke the language of the country; but those who returned to their home towns risked being recaptured, finding on arrival that there were hardly any Jews left. Charlotte Holzer recalls having met some of these in her concentration camp in Berlin.

Seven Czechoslovak Jews managed to escape. One of them, Lederer, returned to his own country and set about penetrating into the ghetto-camp of Theresienstadt in order to warn the *Judenrat* — and Theresienstadt was the only concentration camp to possess a *Judenrat* — of what was happening in Auschwitz. The *Judenrat* either could not, or would not, believe him; in any case it took no action whatsoever and went on drawing up the lists of deportees, and Theresienstadt Jews continued to be dispatched to Auschwitz.

Two other Jews of Czechoslovak origin, Wetzler (Vrba) and Rosenberg, managed to re-enter their country early in 1944. They got in touch with the Jewish community — which still existed — then contacted Rabbi Weissmandel and gave him an exact and detailed account of what they had seen and lived through in Auschwitz. Weissmandel made a careful note of all they said and even arranged a meeting between them and a delegate of the Papal Nuncio in Czechoslovakia. Moreover, he transmitted the news to Doctor Kasztner and his committee in Budapest early in March 1944, a fortnight or so before the German Occupation of Hungary. Needless to say, this did not prevent the deportation of half a million Hungarian Jews to Auschwitz[3].

Wetzler and Rosenberg then drew up a report which they dispatched to the West. Whether or not there were other such reports, we know that this one reached its destination and was received by the Vatican and in Switzerland, and later in London and Washington. Furthermore, early in the summer of 1944, both the neutral and Allied press began to publish extracts from the report giving the world the first details about Auschwitz: this was the first time the facts were publicised. The account of the two escapees, Wetzler (Vrba) and Rosenberg, had broken the wall of silence.

It might be more fitting to call it a deliberate deafness. News of the gassings had reached London just after they had commenced. The delegate of the Jewish World Congress in Switzerland, Gerhard Riegner, had sent a detailed telegram about the matter during the summer of 1942. The American diplomatic mission which he had asked to deliver his report certainly did so, but the document did not reach its destination until many months later. Soon after, the American State Department requested its mission in Switzerland not to send any more 'private messages'. The Jewish press in Palestine, which had received detailed information in the summer of 1942, that is to say around the time that Riegner was writing his report, hardly mentioned it for six long months; and when it did, all it had to say was that the information appeared to be extremely exaggerated: a good idea to be on the alert but there was no need to panic.

As for the Allied authorities, they knew exactly what was happening in Auschwitz as far back as 1942, thanks mainly to Szmulewicz's photographic 'reporting', and to various pieces of intelligence provided by the Polish Resistance. They had prevented previous publication of this information.

And now, at last, in 1944, people were beginning to write about it openly, and without concealing any facts. The Wetzler-Rosenberg report continued to serve its purpose for a long time and was produced at the Nuremberg trials as an exhibit (document L-022, case classification USA-294).

The publication of the report by no means put an end to the Auschwitz exterminations. On the contrary, this was the period when every twenty-four hours a train from Hungary would dump yet another human load on the camp ramp, and it was not until the beginning of November 1944, a few days after the crushing of the *Sonderkommando* revolt, that the gassings came to an end. The crematoria were blown up and the gas chambers demolished. Even though the advancing

Red Army was still about sixty miles east of Auschwitz, they had chased the Germans from half of Hungary and from the eastern part of Czechoslovakia. In the west, the front ran along the Vosges and the Siegfried Line. Aix-la-Chapelle was occupied by the Americans.

When it began to dawn on Himmler that the war might end otherwise than in victory for Hitler he ordered the gassing to be discontinued, though the massacre of the Jews went on on a lesser scale.

On 12 January 1945, the Red Army launched its new offensive. Six days later the evacuation of Auschwitz began. The last 50,000 prisoners were dispatched in trucks, on foot, or occasionally by train, to the concentration camps of the Reich, some taking advantage of the occasion to escape. They were soon to be liberated by the Red Army. Henri Bulawko and Raphael Feigelson, both former FFI, were among them, Feigelson even fighting alongside Red Army soldiers in the final combats. Others, like Karel Lagus, went straight into hospital. Erich Kulka and his son Dov, now a professor at the University of Jerusalem, were hidden by friends in Moravska-Ostrava. About 3,000 sick and infirm people who could not be moved were left where they were in the camp infirmary. A few months before they would certainly all have been liquidated. The distinguished Italian writer Primo Levi, then a chemist, was also left behind to help the doctor, De Benedetti, look after the sick.

Auschwitz was liberated on 27 January 1945, by the Soviet 60th Army, commanded by Marshal Koniev, which formed part of the Ukrainian First Front. The Red Army medical corps immediately took charge of the sick.

We have searched the *War Journal* of the High Command of the *Wehrmacht* (OKW) in vain for the smallest mention of the capture of Auschwitz by the Red Army. Hitler, however, was informed about it by General Heinz Guderian, Chief of General Staff, the following statement appearing in the report of the military conference held by the Führer on 27 January, 1945:

> *Fierce fighting took place in the Seventh Army sector. The attacks were checked right along the line from the dead ground of Richau to Auschwitz. However, Auschwitz itself was lost.*

NOTES

1. The correspondence of their leaders, who were appointed by Vichy, contains no allusion at this point to anything ominous connected with the name of Auschwitz.
2. It is interesting to note that there were never any incidents of this sort when non-Jewish political prisoners arrived at Buchenwald, Dachau, Mauthausen, or any of the other big concentration camps.
3. The action of the Budapest Committee is examined later on p. 323.

Part Eight

Contrasting Situations in Central Europe and the Balkans

CHAPTER 34

FROM THE FORTRESS OF THERESIENSTADT TO THE SLOVAK RESISTANCE

T HE Czechoslovak Republic, as an adjacent democratic state — over-populated by the addition of three million Germans foisted on Sudeten territory, and sanctuary of anti-Nazi refugees — was one of the first victims of Hitlerian Germany. Its existence was a challenge to National Socialism in every respect, and the Nazis had fought it from the very start.

A number of emigrant agitators were purely and simply assassinated by the SS commandos 'infiltrated' from Germany. Such was the fate of Professor Theodor Lessing, an anti-Nazi Jewish intellectual left-wing extremist. His murderers were never discovered.

This political action served its purpose: the mustering of the Sudeten Germans into the Germano-Sudeten Party (*Sudetendeutsche Partei* — SdP) by the local Nazis, followed by the support given to Slovak autonomy, then to the ultra-Fascist and anti-Semite factions of Abbe Hlinka and Monsignor Joseph Tiso undermined the young Czechoslovak Republic, which, as a matter of fact, was the envy of its neighbours.

In the autumn of 1938 the whole structure crumbled in Munich. Following its abandonment by Great Britain and France, Czechoslovakia lost all its frontier regions, its territories being seized not only by Germany, but by Hungary and Poland. Slovakia gained semi-independent status with Monsignor Tiso at its head, while the extreme eastern part of the country became the autonomous Republic of Carpathian Ukraine.

In less than six months this new structure foundered completely. Hitler annexed Bohemia and Moravia — the term 'protectorate' being nothing but a myth. Slovakia itself became 'independent' but asked for and received German 'protection'. Unlike the Czech countries it remained more or less autonomous, which meant, in practical terms, that whereas Bohemia and Moravia were under military occupation, Slovakia only had German 'counsellors', though a great number of them and of all grades. As for Carpathian Ukraine, which certain German elements hoped to use as a spearhead, or Trojan horse, against the Soviet Ukraine, it was left to its fate: Germany authorised its seizure by Hungary.

In the Czechoslovakia of 1937, the Jews accounted for barely 1 per cent of the population. Their situation varied from region to region. In Czech territory — and especially in Prague — they were largely assimilated, mainly with the Bohemian

Germans. There were several Jewish families whose Judaism went back no further than the Thirty Years War. During the Catholic counter-reformation which followed the Czech Hussite insurrection, and especially after the assassination of Wallenstein, whom a great many Czechs claimed as one of their own, a large number of Hussite and evangelical families rejected Catholicism in favour of Judaism. Some of Kafka's forebears belonged to this category.

The Jews of Slovakia were more successful in preserving their character. There was even a Jewish population in Carpathian Ukraine, or sub-Carpathian Russia, as the territory was called between 1918 and 1939. It was composed for the most part of peasants and shepherds, and was strictly Orthodox on the religious side and terribly retarded on the economic and social side, desperately poor, but buoyed up by its intense spiritual life.

The catastrophe of the Czechoslovak Republic was also the catastrophe of the Czechoslovak Jews whom the enemies of the republic insisted were 'the only Czechoslovaks', for the non-Jewish inhabitants were either Czechs or Slovaks.

The Jews in Czech territory were subjected to the same regime as the German Jews. Their fate was much worse than that of the non-Jewish Czechs, who were too afraid to come to their aid. Nearly 70,000 Jews from Czech territory died in deportation, barely a thousand escaping death by hiding in the country.

This did not mean that they took any less part in the Resistance, especially in the ranks of the Communist Party. The two Synek brothers, members of the Central Committee of the Party, were executed for doing so. A Gestapo report at the end of 1941 imputes the sabotage of a large part of Czech military production to an unnamed Jewish engineer. In Prague at the beginning of 1942, there was — still according to a Gestapo report — a nucleus of Jewish Communists in the very heart of the city.

The great majority of the Jews from Czech territory were imprisoned in the Terezin ghetto (Theresienstadt), an ancient Vauban fortress built in the time of the Empress Maria Theresa, from which the non-Jewish population had been evacuated. The Czech and other Jews, mostly from Germany, Austria, Holland and Denmark, lived there in particularly wretched conditions, which did not prevent the Nazis from considering this particular ghetto as a luxury camp to which they deported only 'privileged Jews', and indeed, the Jews imprisoned in Theresienstadt had no fear of being gassed — as long as they stayed there; but whenever the ghetto became overfull, the Gestapo 'jettisoned' some of the occupants, sending the surplus to Auschwitz and its gas chambers.

The ghetto had a Resistance organisation, but it never managed to achieve an uprising, though it did collect a certain amount of equipment and kept in touch with what was happening in the outside world by means of a radio receiver, hidden in the belfry of the disused church of Theresienstadt, while men like Karel Lagus and others succeeded in establishing contact with Czechs living in the neighbour-hood[1].

In Slovakia there were fewer Jews, but their fate was no more enviable, though their general situation was not quite as bad as that of their fellows in Bohemia and Moravia and they were able to take a more active part in the Resistance.

From 6 October 1938 onwards, the Tiso regime gave first priority to the per-secution of the Jews; the measures grew steadily more severe, coming to a head at the end of 1941 in the creation of concentration camps, the so-called labour camps, in Sered, Novaky and elsewhere. In 1942, at the request of the Germans, the Jewish internees of these camps were 'put at the disposal of the Reich for work' and were the first Jews living outside Germany to take the road to Auschwitz.

Some of the internees escaped and joined with non-Jewish Communist elements to set up Partisan nuclei in the mountainous region of eastern Slovakia. One of these groups was broken up after a fight with the Slovak police which cost one police officer his life. There were 25 arrests, including 18 Jews.

During this period several prominent members of the Slovak Jewry took parti-cularly bold action on quite a different level. Two names stand out: Rabbi Michael Beer Dov Weissmandel and Gisela Fleischmanova (better known under the name of Gizi Fleischmann). They got in touch with the man in charge of the deportation of the Jews from Slovakia, *SS-Hauptsturmführer* Dieter Wisliceny and offered him a considerable bribe. This individual, who was directly responsible to Eichmann and his delegate in Slovakia, enjoyed diplomatic status as police attaché for Jewish problems to the German Embassy in Bratislava. As such he gave practical 'guid-ance' to the Slovak Government on its anti-Jewish policy.

Before the deportations began there were about 55,000 Jews in Slovakia, but by 1942 about 32,000 had already gone. The movement was slowed down, however, when rumours concerning the fate of the Jews began to infiltrate into Slovakia: the Church was showing signs of concern, and Monsignor Tiso raised his voice in protest.

It was at this point that Wisliceny received the Jews' offer of a bribe on condition that he put an end to the deportations, and whether it was agreed, or because Wisliceny was prevented from deporting the Jews for some other reason, the deportations were halted. What is more, Rabbi Weissmandel set up a veritable life-saving campaign, known as *Europa-Plan*, to rescue all the Jews in German-occupied territories. It was simply a matter of finding the necessary money. During the following two years Rabbi Weissmandel sent request after request to the Jewish organisations in Switzerland, each one more urgent and more anguished than the last, begging for money, a great deal of money, and still more money.

The amounts he received were paltry. Fabulous sums were needed, and Switzer-land and the rest of the outside world did not really believe in the *Europa-Plan*.

Even if they had, it would have been impossible in wartime to hand over so many dollars without permission from the Allied governments, and this permission was refused.

Be that as it may, during those two years there were no deportations of Jews from Slovakia, so that the Slovak territory even came to be a sanctuary for those Jews who escaped from the camps and ghettos of Poland — some of them even from Auschwitz.

Incidentally, it was Rabbi Weissmandel who smuggled the Wetzler-Rosenberg report to the West at the beginning of 1944. This report, written by the two Auschwitz escapees, was the first published account of events in the extermination camp.[2]

The other Jewish militants in Slovakia did not sit twiddling their thumbs while Weissmandel and Gizi Fleischmann were negotiating with Wisliceny. Resistance groups were set up in the internment camps of Sered and Novaky and in the labour camps, directly subordinated to the Slovak army, and here they went to the extent of giving the prisoners secret military training. The Novaky camp group also got in touch with the Partisans in the Priedvize zone, where detachments directed by the Communists were being formed.

The Slovak national uprising began on 29 August 1944. The internal Jewish organisation had taken over the Novaky camp the night before, and 250 young men were assigned the task of looking after the goods and equipment stored there. Two hundred others formed a Partisan company under the leadership of Lieutenant Imrich Müller (Ivo Milen), which captured the German village of Sklene, and fought in the region of Upper Nitra. Following a German counter-attack, which pushed the rebels back into the mountains, the company withdrew to Martin in central Slovakia where it attached itself autonomously to the 8th battalion of the *J. V. Stalin* brigade, lead by the Soviet captain Jegorov. Later the Novaky group split into two and carried on the fight in the mountains.

The uprising gave other Jews the chance to distinguish themselves, but at that time the Novaky detachments were the only homogeneous ones. Two factors played a predominant part: as far as manpower was concerned there was the whole Slovak army, but the Slovak Communist Party supplied not only the political and executive staff but a large number of organised Partisan groups.

The fate of the man at the head of the Communist organisation was particularly tragic: Rudolf Slansky, then resident in Moscow, was sent to Slovakia with Jan Sverma to co-ordinate the uprising. Slansky was a militant Communist and a Jew, though not a particularly devout one. He was tried in 1952, on trumped-up charges, condemned to death and executed. His body, together with those of ten men condemned at the same trial, was incinerated and the ashes scattered on an icy road. The trial was a parody of justice; the execution a judicial assassination.

We do not intend to investigate whether or not Slansky's activities were in line with the politics of the Czechoslovak Communist Party as one understood it in 1952, or even as it is at the present time, but must point out that at his trial the prosecuting counsel strongly emphasised the fact that Slansky and most of the other accused were of 'Jewish origin'. It seems therefore, both fitting and just to place Rudolf Slansky, holder of the Czechoslovak Order of the Revolt, first class, among the members of the Jewish Resistance.

Another figure who stands out among the Partisans who fought in Slovakia is young Edith Katz. She was arrested in 1941, at the age of twenty-one, for 'anti-national activities'. Early in 1944 she was transferred to Novaky because of a heart condition, it being no doubt considered that a camp life was better for her health than prison regime. At all events, she took the opportunity to escape and join the Communist Partisans.

After the uprising she led a detachment of the Slovak Partisan brigade, *Jan Zizka*, and also took part in the combats in the Trencin region, but she was forced to beat a retreat to Jastrabie Banovce. It was here Edith Katz fell, on 26 September 1944 dying a hero's death: she remained behind her machine-gun, covering the retreat of her companions, until she was captured and shot.

Like a great many Communist Jews of all nationalities, Edith Katz had been a member of the Zionist youth movement *Hachomer Hatzair*. She belonged to a family of extremely devoted and devout Jews. Her uncle was, and still is Chief Rabbi in Bratislava.

Other Jewish combatants, such as Emil Fürst (Knieza), commander of a reconnaissance platoon, belonged to the *Stalin* Partisan brigade of the 9th battalion, with which we are already familiar. Fürst distinguished himself by capturing a German captain.

Eugen Neumann-Novak commanded the *Stalin* Partisan detachment. He, too, had fought in Spain, and the French MOI resistance group headed by Arthur London had helped him to get back to Slovakia in 1941.

Fürst-Knieza and Neumann-Novak survived, but Karol Adler, chief of the *Petöfi* Partisan detachment was captured by the enemy and publicly hanged in the village square of Dobcina on 20 December 1944.

How many Jews took part in the Slovak national uprising? A Jewish investigator from Bratislava, Ladislav Lipscher, estimated as many as 1,566, of which 169 were women: by no means a negligible figure when compared to the total of around 20,000 Jews living in Slovakia at that date.

The reflux of the uprising began about the middle of September 1944. The Soviet Army had conquered Eastern Galicia, but was halted at the Dukla Pass while attempting to cross the Carpathians. At the same time the rebels were cut off behind the German front and reinforcements of men and materials parachuted by the Soviet command were insufficient to permit a real battle.

Among the men parachuted in was the Russo-Jewish officer Leonide Bernstein, who took command of a Partisan detachment; but there was not a great deal he could do.

The German counter-attack was launched by the *Waffen SS*. Berger failed to quell the uprising and was replaced by SS general Hoffle who seized the rebel capital of Banska Bystrica and forced the Partisans to withdraw to the mountains.

Two Jews from Slovakia, Haviva Raik and Shloma Ben Yaakov, had reached the city just ahead of the Germans. They were among the thirty-five Palestinian paratroopers dropped on occupied Europe. They tried to round up their former comrades of *Hachomer Hatzair*, and other non-organised Jews. The Haviva Raik mission, like the Anglo-American one, where several dozen English and American military men were parachuted into Slovakia, ended tragically. The bodies of Haviva Raik and Shloma Ben Yaakov were discovered after the war in a communual grave in Kremenica. Those English and Americans who were not killed there and then finished up in Mauthausen and Buchenwald.

The failure of the rebellion meant death to most of the Jews remaining in Slovakia. Following his instructions, Hoffle dispatched to Auschwitz all those he had not shot on the spot.

The Weissmandel-Fleischmann group was also deported to Auschwitz, apart from a few members who had gone into hiding. Rabbi Weissmandel, despite his advanced age, jumped out of the deportation train. Gizi Fleischmann was shot the moment she arrived at the extermination camp, at the personal request of Eichmann's deputy, Gunther.

When Czechoslovakia was eventually liberated there was only a handful of Jews left in the country, among them several young men in military uniform who had joined the Czechoslovak Army on their liberation from Auschwitz. Several thousand Jews from all over the world had had the same idea. A Czechoslovak unit that had fought in France in 1939—1940 reconstituted itself in Great Britain and, strengthened with reinforcements, took part in the Normandy landing, and in the battle of Falaise and the siege of Dunkirk. The Jewish contingent in these units accounted for an average of 25 per cent of the total, varying according to the period, while there was an even higher proportion of Jewish volunteers in the Czechoslovak armed forces levied in Palestine. These units participated in the Eritrea campaign of 1940—1941, and in the defence of Tobruk.

In the USSR a Czechoslovak army corps, under the command of the future President of the Socialist Republic of Czechoslovakia, General Ludvik Svoboda, was set up in 1942. The nucleus of this corps was the remains of the Czech armed group that had been set up in Polish territory in September 1939. After several battles with the Germans, this group — composed mainly of Jews — had reached what was then the eastern part of Poland, where it was captured by the Red Army. Other Czech Jews who had sought refuge in Soviet territory at different periods were reunited in the Czechoslovak corps that was eventually set up there. This corps fought in Sokolov (1943), in Bielaïa Tzerkov (1944) and in the Dukla Pass. After the war, General Svoboda gave high praise to the Jewish combatants who fought under him.

NOTES

1. Records of Jewish suffering in Warsaw and Theresienstadt have been carefully preserved. The latter consist of works of art which the life of the ghetto inspired, such as the famous children's drawings — children who, with rare exceptions, died in the Auschwitz gas chambers. Drawings of men like Bedrych Frita are less well known. The Gestapo arrested him one day and imprisoned him in the little fortress, where he eventually died. His companions walled up his work so that it could be recovered after the liberation.

2. See p. 288.

CHAPTER 35

THE JEWISH PARTISANS IN THE BALKANS

THE war extended to the Balkans on 28 October 1940, when the Italian Army crossed from Albania into Greece: Albania had been occupied by the Italians since she succumbed to their lightning raid on Good Friday 1939.

Mussolini, piqued at having so far had to play the unenviable supporting role in the Axis, embittered at having been thwarted in June 1940 by the French Alpine army and defeated in the Mediterranean — though the Libyan defeats were still to come — decided to try his hand at *blitzkrieg*, and without even taking the trouble to seek a valid pretext and, worse still, without informing the *Führer* of his intentions, marched into Greece.

Previous Italian military efforts had not inspired Hitler with confidence; moreover, unknown to Mussolini, he was just then preparing his attack on the USSR, and complications in the Balkans could lead to the Allies landing in Greece, which was the last thing he wanted. However, he had no desire to confide his plans to the *Duce*, knowing that, if he did, Great Britain would be informed within the hour.

Hitler's misgivings were soon justified: the Italian armies were defeated in Epirus and forced to abandon Greek territory and even part of Albania. By the end of 1940 Hitler was obliged to come to the aid of his unfortunate Italian ally. The *Wehrmacht* had entered Romania in September 1940, under cover of 'military training formations', and moved on to Bulgaria in February 1941, after having forced her to join the tripartite pact. It was now preparing to invade Greece. The code name of the operation was *Marita*. But first of all the rear non-operational zone had to be protected by forcing Yugoslavia to join the pact as well.

Yugoslavia yielded, but the Yugoslav people did not. A group of senior officers overthrew both the government and the regency, seizing power in the name of the young king, Peter II, who was declared of age. The head of the *putsch*, General Douchan Simovitch, became Prime Minister.

Simovitch did not denounce the pact — there was hardly time: Hitler struck on 6 April 1941. After three days of battle, Yugoslavia lost half its territory. The whole of Croatia seceded. The Italians captured Ljubljana and advanced into Dalmatia. The German army forced the Greek frontier fortifications and seized Salonica. Within thirteen days the organised resistance of the Yugoslavian army was no more. On May 1 the Germans entered Athens, and a few weeks later launched a large-scale airbone operation on Crete and seized the island.

Greece was divided into two zones of occupation: the Italians occupied the centre and the south, Athens included; the Germans occupied the north. Yugoslavia was simply cut to pieces. The Italians annexed Slovenia and most of Dalmatia; the Germans took possession of a little territory along the Austrian frontier, and the towns of Maribor and Bled. Hungary received the Bacska and Baranya zones. Croatia was turned into an independent state under the thumb of Ante Pavelitch and his Ustasas, divided into two zones of influence — more like zones of occupation — one German and the other Italian. Montenegro was handed over to Italy, who hastened to make it an independent state (that never saw the light of day); and the territories inhabited by Albanian minorities were allotted to Albania, that is to say, again to Italy. A few days later, Bulgaria was recompensed with the Yugoslav town of Pirot, the whole of Yugoslav Macedonia, Greek Macedonia and Thrace. In this region the Germans retained only the town of Salonica, a strip of territory along the Turkish frontier, and two Aegean islands: Thasos and Samothrace.

So Yugoslavia was parcelled out, or rather cut to shreds, although Serbia which was under military occupation, did retain a semblance of autonomy. A collaborator was installed at the head of it: a general whom someone had succeeded in fishing out of the wreck of the Yugoslav army. The lot of the 70,000 Jews living in the country[1] was not a happy one, although those living in Italian-occupied territories were much better off than the rest.

The Germans did not call upon General Neditch when they began moving the Serbian Jews to concentration camps in and around Belgrade, which had been occupied on 24 April 1941. On 16 April the first anti-Jewish decree was published, bringing with it the obligation to register. The various subsequent measures: forced labour, yellow armbands, curfew, blocking of fortunes, administration of sequestered property, etc., followed each other in rapid succession as they did everywhere else.

The execution of the prisoners in the Belgrade internment camps began in July (Jajinca, Sajmiste), first on the pretext of reprisals for earlier Partisan actions, then without any explanation whatsoever. As these camps were thus relieved of their Jewish prisoners, others swiftly took their place.

In Vojvodina, the occupying Hungarian authorities massacred Serbs and Jews, particularly in Novi Sad and Subotica. An early Communist Resistance organisation was broken up and several of its members: Adolf Singer, Lily Bem, and Otto Blam, to mention only the Jewish members of the network, were hanged in the public square.

Things were much the same in Croatia, although there, to begin with, at least, the Ustasas of Pavelitch did not massacre the Jews but were content simply to rob them and throw them into prison. They only began executing them later, in the camps, and from 1943 onwards they were handed over to the Germans and deported to Auschwitz.

The reason why the Croatian Jews were not massacred in 1941 was simple: the Ustasas were far too busy exterminating the Serbian population of the country — and the Bosnia Moslems as well whenever they could get their hands on them. These massacres assumed a religious character, unusual in the twentieth century. The Ustasas were profoundly Catholic, and theirs was a particularly violent form of Catholicism. When they entered a Serbian village — that is to say, one of Orthodox religious convictions — they massacred the villagers in the name of Christ, only leaving alive those who had the happy inspiration to recognise *in extremis* the intrinsic superiority of the Ustasa type of Roman Catholicism. There were quite enough priests and monks among the Ustasas to baptise the forced converts, when the moment came.

It is hardly surprising that when Josip Broz — known then under the name of Tito — gave the signal for a national insurrection, he found willing supporters, eager to fight for their patriotic and political convictions, perhaps because they knew they had nothing to lose. On 7 July 1941 the Yugoslav Communists decided to revolt, and five days later a nationwide appeal was launched, with the help of a Jewish engineer, Josip Engel, who built the first radio transmitter and broadcast the call to arms.

Many former combatants of the International Brigade in Spain are listed as leading the Yugoslav national uprising, headed, of course, by Tito himself; and a number of Jews such as Robert Domani, Nissim Albahari, Pavle Goranin and Iljia Andzic (Engel) figure among the 'national heroes' of Dalmatia, Bosnia and Serbia. All these received this military distinction posthumously, for they were swiftly captured and executed.

The great Barouh family, three brothers and three sisters, were all Communists and intellectuals. When the Germans entered Belgrade Isodore, the eldest of the family, was imprisoned, but managed to escape. He and his brother Joseph joined one of the very first Partisan groups in the region of Uzice and took part in the opening combats. Isodore was killed and Joseph was seriously wounded and lost a hand. The Croatian Ustasas captured the hospital in which he was recovering and dispatched him by means of an injection.

Rachel, the eldest of the sisters, was arrested together with her husband when there was an explosion in the laboratory where they were employed. Both were shot in the Sajmiste camp near Belgrade. The last of the brothers, Boria, who had been one of the leading members of a Partisan brigade, was captured by General Mihailov's *chetniks* and handed over to the Germans. He, too, was shot in Sajmiste, in July 1942. Boria Barouh was a talented painter who had made a name for himself in France before he was expelled in 1939 for his Communist activities.

The youngest of the sisters, seventeen-year-old Batia fought with the Belgrade Resistance. She was arrested and shot in Sajmiste on 13 March 1943.

When the Partisans learned the fate of the rest of the family, they took Sonja, the only remaining member, under their wing and provided her with particularly foolproof identity papers and a very safe job. She managed to survive.

A street named after the Barouhs, in the former Jewish quarter of Belgrade, commemorates the fighting spirit and sacrifice of this particularly stricken family.

Two Jewish youth organisations, the Belgrade group of *Hachomer Hatzair* and the mainly Communist *Matatja* association of Sarajevo, took to the underground *en bloc* and fought so desperately and under such dangerous conditions that it is surprising any of them survived at all.

Another all-Jewish formation that distinguished itself in the struggles to liberate the country only came into being in the autumn of 1943 on the Dalmatian island of Rab, previously occupied by the Italians.

In Croatia, as in France, the Italians refused to hand over the Jews either to the Germans or to their henchmen, who put on the pressure both locally and at government level, but in vain. Matters were slightly different in Rome, where Ribbentrop himself intervened and complained to Mussolini that the Italian generals in Croatia refused to deliver up 'their' Jews to the Germans, and that they were supported in their refusal by senior officials in the Italian Ministry of Foreign Affairs as well as by leading members of the military administration. Mussolini did not let the Germans down: he issued directives, but, knowing perfectly well that these directives were ignored, took no steps to enforce their application. He did nothing whatsoever in November 1942, when General Pieche cabled him that the Croatian Jews deported by the Germans, from their own zone of occupation had been gassed, nor did he show any reaction when he received an appeal from General Mario Roatta, former chief of military intelligence, who was not squeamish himself about spilling blood when the occasion arose. He had been responsible for the massacre of the brothers Rosseli in Bagnoles de l'Orne in 1937, among others, and had certainly not spared the executions during the Italian occupation of Yugoslavia. Roatta protested that since the Jews trusted the Italian soldiers, it was against the traditions, and would harm the image of the Italian army if it should have to hand them over to their executioners.

In the end, the Italians set up a number of what were more internment and reception camps than concentration camps in their own zone of occupation, and the Jews of the region were accommodated in these. Jews from all over the country came to seek refuge there when they heard the good news.

Some of these camps were established on the islands, on Rab, in particular. Later, an enormous number of Yugoslav Jews managed to infiltrate into Italy.

When the Italian army surrendered on 8 September 1943, several thousand Italian soldiers united with Tito's Partisans. Others — much more numerous —

allowed themselves to be disarmed by the Partisans. The Jewish internees liberated from their camp on the island of Rab set up a very large Partisan detachment and hastened to take part in the Banja combats in Bosnia where most of them were lost.

Apart from these Jewish combatants, who joined the Resistance movement in more or less organised groups, others played an important part at the head of it. Mocha Pijade, at that time 'number 2' of the Yugoslav Communist movement, was put in charge of political activities by Tito, and it was not the least of Pijade's merits that he managed to make the great mass of the country's patriots see the nationalist character of Tito's movement. The 'anti-Fascist Council of National Liberation of the Yugoslav Peoples' owes much to Mocha Pijade.

After the war, Pijade became one of the most distinguished theoreticians of what was at one stage called Titoism. Although he had never been an Orthodox Jew Pijade vaunted his Jewishness and never ceased to do so up to his disappearance in 1957.

The number of the 70,000 or so Yugoslav Jews who took part in the Partisan war is estimated at around 2,000; but in addition there were young men like the 17-year-old Haim Almozlino who went around the towns setting fire to German military vehicles. Esther (Estreja) Ovadija, a young militant Communist Jewess from Macedonia, was killed by the Bulgarian secret police. We stress the fact that Esther Ovadija was Jewish, for at present she is claimed by both Yugoslav and Bulgarian Resistance pantheons.

The Jews of both Yugoslav and Greek Macedonia played a prominent part in the Resistance movements of the region. The Bulgarian army occupied the entire country and had no compunction in delivering up the local Jews to the Germans. Some twenty thousand Jews from Macedonia and Bulgarian-occupied Greek Thrace were deported in the spring of 1943, most of them straight to Treblinka. Trains transported them directly to the camp, or unloaded them at the Danubian ports, Vidin and Lom-Palanka, where they were taken by boat to Vienna, and on by rail from there.

Hundreds, if not thousands, of Macedonian Jews took to the Resistance with the help of the Communists, who were particularly well represented in the region, and who issued proclamations and appeals to the population, condemning the persecution of the Jews and urging them to go to their aid. The people responded.

Some hundreds of Jews sought refuge further to the west in the Yugoslav territories populated by Albanians, which Italy had incorporated into Albania, as well as in Albania itself; and those who were physically capable later integrated themselves into the Albanian Partisan movement. Many Jewish women and children were given shelter by the Albanian people.[2]

The Jews as such were unable to play any particular role in the Partisan movements of these regions if only because of their very limited numbers. There was, however, one Jewish general — Zechariah Lehrer, known under the *nom de guerre* of Vojo Todorovic — and a largely Jewish medical service, the Jewish doctors and nurses playing *mutatis mutandis* the same role as their Jewish colleagues in the Soviet Partisan ranks.

The Greek Jews — almost all 'Spanish' Jews — were completely out of touch with other Jewish centres, but during the early years of Nazism they did all they could for the Central European Jews when they were striving to seek refuge elsewhere, but preferably in Palestine.

Greece, maritime country *par excellence*, became the centre of transit for some ten thousand Jews, and when Italy attacked her, the Greek Jews took up arms with the rest of the population. While their activities at that period could hardly be described as Resistance, they certainly became so after April—May 1941, that is to say from the beginning of the total occupation of the country.

Incidentally, the first Jews to stand up to the enemy in Greece were not the Greek but the Palestinian Jews. In fact the British Expeditionary Force that was obliged to abandon Greece without having done anything worthwhile to defend it, included several thousand Jews from what was still Palestine. These were not primarily combatants, much as they longed to be, but the main body of the engineering and transport divisions. Most of them were able to re-embark, others were taken prisoners, but quite a few sought refuge with Greek peasants on the mainland and on the islands, especially Crete. There was a serious language problem; for although the Jews had the reputation of knowing several languages, few knew modern Greek; but this obstacle was eventually overcome and a great many soldiers from the land of Palestine fought alongside the Greek Partisans against the common enemy. Later, those who were living in Crete managed to establish radio contact with the British Command in the Middle East and used Cretan Partisan leaders for some operations required by the British.

More than two-thirds of the 75,000 or so Greek Jews were concentrated in Salonica, while there were several thousand in Athens and a few in the provincial towns. As Athens was in the Italian zone, the Jews enjoyed a respite until September 1943; those in the north, especially in Salonica, were most bitterly persecuted after the occupation of the country.

We are only too familiar with the tedious cycle of registration, distinctive signs, on persons and on shops, exclusion from public functions, spoliations of all types — the whole accompanied by individual maltreatment and atrocities and ending in deportation. The vast majority of the Jews in Salonica took the road to Auschwitz. They went to their doom even more ignorant of what awaited them than their fellow Jews in other European countries, the Germans having pushed callousness to the extent of selling Salonica-Auschwitz railway tickets, and handing over letters of credit in exchange for Greek drachmas. They even went so far as to sell the Jews plots of land in Auschwitz.

In Salonica, as in a great many other Jewish communities in occupied Europe, the self-appointed leaders, or those imposed by the Germans, played an unsavoury role, to say the least. That said, they are now as dead as the other Jews.

There was quite a large number of Resistance fighters among the Jews of Salonica, the first five Greeks shot as hostages and Resistance fighters belonging to this community, and later, Jews were to be found in all the various Greek Resistance groups; but in 1944, soon after the liberation of Greece, a particularly merciless civil war broke out, in the course of which the principal anti-Nazi Resistance Movement ELAS found itself on the losing side. Most of the Jewish combatants who had belonged to the ELAS network accused, often unjustly, of Communism, preferred, when the war was over, not to let it be known that they had fought in the Resistance, and the part the Jews played in the principal Resistance groups remains a mystery. We know, however, that some of them helped to plan the most famous operation in the history of the Greek Resistance: the destruction of the Gorgos-Potamos viaduct.

At that period Rommel's *Afrika-Korps* were using the Greek ports as supply bases, for the Germans thought that the Royal Air Force would delay a little longer before attacking Greek and Italian ports. Jacques Costis, an Athenian Jew, who had created an important maritime sabotage force, was ordered to blow up the German ships both in the port of Piraeus and at sea. He carried out these orders with remarkable success, contributing greatly to Rommel's defeat.

The large number of the Jewish medical personnel paid their blood tribute like their colleagues in Yugoslavia, for the Germans made no differentiation between Partisan doctors and Partisan fighters.

The Greek Jews cherish the memory of Robert Mitrani, a medical student who was known under the apt *nom de guerre* of Hippocrates.

The Germans may have prevented Robert Mitrani from completing his studies, but they could not prevent 'Hippocrates' from doing his duty — even though he hadn't taken the oath. He was captured while tending the wounded and shot in Salonica on 5 January 1944.

On the same day, two Jewish combatants, 'the two Davids' (David Cohen and David Rousso), both nineteen years old, perished in the skirmish of Agia Triada.

Further up the scale, Mimi Cabelis from Trikkala in Thessaly, mobilised a large proportion of the Jews in his town, organising sabotage operations on a provincial scale. In Verroia, in Macedonia, many Jews joined the Resistance, and, an agricultural expert called Eliezer Azaria (*nom de guerre*, Tripotamite), was responsible for the logistics of a large number of Partisan detachments in the north and south of the country, from Rumelia and Thessaly to the Peloponnese. Wherever they went the Jews tried to establish contact with the Resistance where they were usually welcomed with open arms.

'I could do with a great many men like you,' said one Partisan leader to five Jews who had managed to track him down: 'Why are there not fifty of you?'

While the Jews who managed to stay in Greece and unite with the Partisans were playing their part in the Resistance, those Greek Jews who had been deported had not abandoned the struggle. There was a high proportion of Greek Jews in the *Sonderkommando* that rose up in Auschwitz in October 1944, among them Henri Nehama Cappon, former leader of the Jewish Scouts in Salonica.

The situation of the Bulgarian Jews was altogether different from that of their fellows in the neighbouring countries, there being only 50,000 Jews in Bulgaria with nothing to distinguish them from the rest of the population, so that it was a case of basic assimilation. Apart from a sizeable intellectual stratum, the Bulgarian Jews were simple working people who had never even heard of anti-Semitism until the Nazis entered their country.

Historically speaking, certain affinities existed between Bulgaria, or at least its leaders, and Germany. During the First World War the King of Bulgaria, the German Tsar Ferdinand, had dragged his country into war alongside the Central Powers, Bulgaria hoping to recapture territories that Serbia, Greece and Romania had seized from her. In the event she lost more than she gained, including access to the Aegean Sea, and when Bulgaria signed the tripartite pact in 1941, she hoped to make good part of her losses; German influence having already enabled her to recover territory from Romania in August 1940.

When we say 'Bulgaria' we mean the leaders of the country, for the Bulgarian masses sided with Russia, rather than Germany. This predilection was based on the affinity of the two languages and perhaps even more on the fact that the Russian conquest of Turkey in 1877—1878 had enabled Bulgaria to recover her national independence.

Besides being sentimentally attached to Russia, a great many Bulgarians were more directly linked to the Soviet Union through the Communist Party. Although illegal, the latter had a stronghold in the country. It was a powerful, well-structured organisation with a long-standing Bolshevist tradition,[3] and despite setbacks and tough repressive measures, the Bulgarian Communist Party remained a politically important factor.

Heading it was Georges Dimitrov who had become quite widely known after the 1933 Reichstag trial at which he not only stood up to Hermann Goering but went to the extent of ridiculing him. Georges Dimitrov had become secretary-general of the Communist International (*Komintern*) and this heightened the prestige of the party in the country.

Dimitrov had great personal sympathy and understanding for the persecuted

Jews, and was one of the rare Communist leaders of the time who also understood their national aspirations. While communist parties sprang to the defence of the hunted Jews everywhere in occupied Europe, they were more vigilant in Bulgaria than elsewhere.

The country had a constitutional monarchy and its government was answerable to parliament. The first anti-Semite measures were introduced there in 1941 and were debated at great length being adopted only after particularly tumultuous parliamentary scenes. Similar measures had already been adopted in other countries but in Bulgaria they produced strong public reaction which the Communist Party supported. The Bulgarian parliament was assailed with petitions, addresses, motions of all descriptions and from every sort of social background. The one thing they had in common was strong Communist influence. Thus the Writers' Union protested energetically; a great many workers in factories throughout the country voiced their indignation; the legal and medical associations also protested; even the Orthodox Church manifested its displeasure.

The general situation of the country changed after the German attack on the USSR. Bulgaria alone among Hitler's allies and puppet states did not break off diplomatic relations with Moscow, and there continued to be a Soviet embassy in Sofia. Not, one suspects, that it was particularly active.

The Communist Party did not consider itself at all bound by the attitude of neutrality adopted by the Bulgarian government in the Germano-Soviet war; on the contrary, it sprang into action against the Germans stationed in the country and also, naturally, against the Bulgarian government allied to Nazi Germany, for the Germano-Bulgarian alliance had led to the Bulgarian military occupation of Greek and Yugoslav territories.[4]

Among the numerous Jewish members of the Bulgarian Communist Party, one of the first to distinguish himself was Leon Tadger ben David, who in the autumn of 1941 succeeded in setting fire to the German fuel depots in Ruse on the Danube, and other enemy installations. Captured and tried, Tadger declared to the tribunal that he considered himself much more a Bulgarian patriot and a Communist than a Jew. He was sentenced to death, and executed on 14 December 1941.

This point of view of Leon Tadger was certainly not shared by Zionist youth movements in Plovdiv which were not even remotely connected with Communism, though they still played a prominent part in Partisan activities.

Partisan action began to expand from 1943 onwards. On the orders of the National Front, a Communist-directed organisation, hardly a week passed without some notable German collaborator being shot. The former Minister of Home Affairs, General Loukov, led the way, followed by the director-general of the police, an individual called Pantev. Belev himself, that all-powerful commissary of Jewish affairs, narrowly escaped being killed.

It was a young girl, Violetta Yacova, and her comrade Miko Leon Papo, both Jewish, who were responsible for executing all these prominent people. Both were eventually killed in their turn by the Bulgarian political police.

But the decisive action in the rescue of the Bulgarian Jews took place on 24 May 1943 in the third district of Sofia. It was a Communist project and a large number of Communist Jews participated.[5]

Nearly 20,000 Jews in Bulgarian-occupied territories had been deported in the spring of 1943, under the Danneker-Belev agreements. Now these agreements had been left open, so that the Bulgarian Jews were still under threat. In fact, the Jews of Sofia already knew that they were going to be deported and the Orthodox Metropolitan of the capital had invited the Chief Rabbi to take refuge in his palace.

So it was that on 24 May 1943, in the middle of the war, the citizens in their tens of thousands — and Sofia had at the time 300,000 inhabitants — demonstrated in the streets against the threatened deportations of the Jews.

The demonstration had its effect: the Jews of Sofia were forced to leave the city, though they were allowed to remain in Bulgaria[6] and were simply asked to choose residences outside the capital; so that Bulgarian Jewry suffered no particular hardship during the war.

There were still a large number of Jewish Partisans taking part in the combats, the best known among those who perished being Emile Chekerdjiski.

Bulgarian governments fell in quick succession as the Red Army drew nearer and nearer and a German defeat became more and more probable. When the Red Army entered Bucharest on 30 August, after the capitulation of neighbouring Romania, the Bulgarian government abolished all anti-Jewish measures in a desperate, and fruitless, attempt to clear its name. As the Red Army reached the Bulgarian frontier, the USSR declared war on Bulgaria; its army entered the country without a shot being fired and was given a triumphant welcome. Georges Dimitrov, just back from Moscow, resumed his leadership of the Bulgarian government.

Thus the Bulgarian Jews were spared the fate of their brothers in other European countries. But the story does not end there.

Prior to 1939 the Bulgarian Jews had felt themselves as Bulgarian as the other inhabitants and were accepted as such. But by 1945 the situation had changed. The Bulgarian Jews had survived; but in their own eyes, and in the eyes of their fellow citizens they were no longer Bulgarians like the rest.

When the State of Israel was created in May 1948, about 90 per cent of Bulgarian Jewry moved to Israel. Although nothing in official Communist policy had ever advocated this type of emigration the Bulgarian Jews received the personal encouragement of Dimitrov. The brother of Emile Chekerdjiski, a prominent militant Communist like himself, promptly decided that he, too, would move to Israel, and has been there militating in the ranks of the Israeli Communist Party ever since.

1. The Jews of Yugoslavia were classified as Spanish Jews because they were the descendants of the Jews driven from Spain in the fifteenth century. The others, the German Jews, were originally from Central Europe.
2. Macedonia may be a country of racial and national hatreds but anti-Semitism is practically unknown there. As for Albania, it was not aware of the Jews as such, still less of any problem regarding them.
3. In 1941, the Bulgarian Socialist Party (the future Communist Party) was one of the few European Socialist parties to approve Lenin's attitude to World War I. Its adherence to Leninist policy continued after 1917.
4. This occupation satisfied the irredentist claims of Bulgaria and at the same time saved the German army the trouble of taking possession of hostile territories.
5. Todor Jivkov, future head of the Bulgarian Communist Party, was at that time secretary of the Communist Party branch in the third district of the Bulgarian capital, where the Jewish quarter of Iuchbounar was situated.
6. Stalingrad had been completely retaken by the Red Army on 2 February 1943, and Tunisia completely liberated about a fortnight before that, which seems to explain, partly at least, why the Bulgarian government gave in to the people. The part the king played in all this has long been open to discussion. Some say it was his influence that prevented the Jews from being deported, adding that the death of the king, which took place a few weeks later on his return from paying a visit to Hitler, could have been provoked by the Germans. They had played up his 'treachery'. Others, basing their opinions on Bulgarian documents that we have not been able to consult, declare that Boris III disliked the Jews intensely and would have been only too pleased to hand them over to the Germans. Others, again, remark upon pressures brought to bear by parliamentary circles and other groups allied to the government. Others think that certain financial outlays approved by the representatives of Palestinian Jewry stationed in Constantinople had something to do with the decision. One cannot help recalling the Chinese maxim: 'Victory has a hundred fathers; defeat is an orphan ...'

CHAPTER 36

ROMANIA: SUCCESS (MORE OR LESS) WITH TRADITIONAL METHODS

B ETWEEN the two wars, it was the Romanian Jews, 800,000 of them, who constituted the biggest Jewish concentration in Europe after Poland, with the exception, naturally, of the USSR. They were frequently victims of persecution, more often by one or other of the extremist groups, than by the State. These groups had been influenced at an early stage by Nazi theories and usually worked hand in glove with the local authorities. When the Ministers were alerted, they either made light of the matter or promised to take action but, needless to say, at local police section or rural police force level these promises were rarely kept.

Romania was an extremely rich country and the middle-class Jews, at least, made a very comfortable living. As in the rest of Eastern Europe most of them held well-established positions in both business and industry, which all things considered, few people grudged them, and while the anti-Semite press violently attacked Jewish businessmen, there were very few Gentiles keen to replace them. The wealthiest Gentiles were generally the big land-owners and, anti-Semites or not, at least got on with 'their' Jews; as did non-Jewish industrialists and financiers.

There was much more bitter competition in the professional classes where the Jews had to face open hostility from their colleagues; this often took the form of physical violence. The same sort of thing cropped up in the universities and even in secondary schools where the Jew was a dangerous rival who had to be shoved out of the way by fair means or foul. Whereas in most European countries the students were, and are, generally more to the left of public opinion, in Romania most were to the extreme right.

In order to cope with this state of affairs Romanian Jewry had gradually worked out a number of defence mechanisms. Its leaders were past masters in the art of drawing up memoranda, reports, protests etc. To lend weight to those documents, all they had to do was to pull a few strings —inside as well as outside the country — and when necessary, to oil the machine by means of financial sops, the sum being proportional to the importance of the demand and of the person solicited.

The situation of the Romanian Jews deteriorated towards the end of 1937 when King Carol II invited Octavian Goga to take over the premiership. Goga may have been a talented poet but he was also an anti-Semite and moreover was subsidised by Berlin. His government imposed a series of anti-Jewish measures which the Jewish people opposed with passive, but even so quite effective, resistance. While international Jewish organisations launched appeal after appeal to the SDN, the Jews of Romania waged a sort of economic strike action. Whether they did so in answer to instructions, or simply because they feared what the future would bring, the tradespeople stopped buying; the importers left their goods in the bonded warehouses; and individual Jews withdrew their money from the banks and sold their shares, bringing about a fall in the stock exchange. The restaurants, theatres, and cinemas saw their turnover rapidly decline. Then taxes stopped coming in.

A few months later, in February 1938, King Carol II yielded to Anglo-French pressure, parted company with Goga and took over the reins of government himself. Most of the anti-Jewish measures ceased to be applied, whether or not they were officially abolished.

It was only a respite. On 27 June 1940, after the military defeat of France, traditional protector of Romania, the USSR demanded the restitution of Bessarabia. This was by way of being an ultimatum; and she wanted northern Bukovina as well. Carol II, abruptly deprived of the support of London and Paris, turned to Berlin, where he was advised to exercise restraint and was given to understand that Germany would not come to his aid. Carol gave in.

With Bessarabia and part of Bukovina gone, Romania fell within the Reich's sphere of influence. Anti-Jewish hostility now took the form of a series of laws and administrative measures. At the same time there was a renewal of anti-Communist repression.

Late in the summer of 1940 Romania suffered further hardships. Under pressure from Germany and Italy she was obliged to cede to Hungary that part of Transylvania she had annexed in 1918. The general effect of these territorial losses resulted in the Jewish population of Romania being reduced by half.

A few days later, on 6 September 1940, Carol was forced to abdicate. A rather curious twosome took over from him: part of it was a single individual, General Ion Antonesco, former Romanian military attaché in London and Paris, an extremely ambitious person and something of a paranoid. His sparse red hair encouraged his enemies — and he had a great many — to dub him the Red Dog. He nursed a personal grievance against Carol II who, instead of delegating him the power which Antonesco regarded as his right, had had him shut up in a monastery. In view of this, the general became reconciled to Hitlerian Germany.[1]

The other half of the twosome was the political movement of the Iron Guards, a Nazi-inspired movement with a strong admixture of Christian-Orthodox mysticism which had been deprived of its leadership two years earlier when its captain, Corneliu Codreanu, and some of his adjutants were done away with by Romanian security forces. Officially they had attempted to escape; in fact, they had simply been strangled.

A year later, in September 1939, it was the turn of the members of this organisation to dispose of Carol II's prime minister. Carol reacted by taking rather unusual reprisal measures, even for Romania: he had the culprits shot without trial on the same spot as the assassination had been committed — and left them there in full public view for a whole day. At the same time he had the most notorious members of the Iron Guard movement in all the chief provincial towns shot and their bodies exhibited on the public square. So that the militants of the Iron Guard associated with General Antonesco in September 1940 were left with individuals of minor importance.

The Iron Guards practised Nazi-style anti-Semitism but served it in a Romanian sauce. In other words, it could be toned down, depending upon the individual, by timely voluntary contributions. Although Antonesco had been on good terms with Codreanu, his was an old Romanian-style anti-Semitism. He detested the Jews, yet when he had a villa built he had recourse to a Jewish architect, and he was still on friendly terms with W. Filderman, principal leader of the Jewish communities in Romania. Filderman was certainly a 'dirty Jew', but the two men had been schoolfriends.

The only real strength of the Iron Guards was the support they received from the SS, but the SS refused to intervene when relations between Antonesco and the movement became strained four months later.

Hitler had received a visit from the general a few days previously and was very impressed by him. He was already preparing his attack on the USSR and he preferred to have a general in power in Romania rather than a movement of dubious character, for Hitler distrusted foreigners who claimed to be Nazis.

The whole of the last part of 1940 was punctuated by acts of brutality perpetrated by the Iron Guard, and by memoranda and visits from Filderman to Antonesco. As time passed the visits became less frequent but the memoranda continued to arrive regularly.

On 21 January 1941, the Iron Guards made a vain attempt to overthrow Antonesco. They had more success with the Jews, whom they arrested in large numbers, slaughtering 120. The Romanian variant of the pogrom, says Hannah Arendt, was to hang the victims' bodies on meat hooks.

The Jews enjoyed a slight breathing space after the failure of the *putsch*, whose leaders fled to Germany; and for several months there was no more violence, though economic measures followed each other in swift succession. When war against the USSR broke out on 22 June 1941, decrees had already been promulgated 'nationalising', among other things, all real estate owned by the Jews in town and country.

The months that followed this short respite were the bloodiest of all for Romanian Jewry. On 29 June 1941, the male Jews in Jassy, the second largest town in the country, situated immediately behind the eastern front, were summoned to the local prefecture. A few judiciously positioned machine-gun nests made short work of several thousand of them. The survivors were packed into goods wagons and their train meandered across Romania in obedience to the contradictory orders that kept reaching it. From time to time the doors were opened and the corpses removed. Occasionally, the prisoners were given something to drink and even food, and a fortnight later, the train drew to a halt in Calarasi station, just over 300 miles from Jassy. Surprisingly, there were a few survivors and these were even allowed to return to their home towns. Ten thousand of the Jews from Jassy, men aged from sixteen to sixty-five, were no more.

As the Germans and Romanians gradually advanced eastwards, first Bukovina then Bessarabia were recaptured from the USSR. *Einsatzgruppe D*, operating behind the southern front, vied with the Romanian forces in a sort of competition to see who could kill the largest number of the Jews resident in the provinces. In the Germans' opinion the Romanians were too preoccupied with money: whenever they saw an opportunity for pillaging they forgot all about shooting the Jews; nevertheless tens of thousands of Jews living beyond the River Prouth fell victims to the Romanians and a comparable number to *Einsatzgruppe D*. Later, in October 1941, when the Romanian army conquered Odessa, a further 80,000 Jews were slaughtered by Romanian units.

The Jewish leaders of Bucharest were thunderstruck. Had the memoranda lost their effect? They began sending them again. Occasionally they served some purpose.

At the end of 1941, some 120,000 Jews of the eastern and western territories of Romania were deported beyond the Dniester river to Transnistria, the annexed Soviet territory between it and the southern reaches of the Bug. The region was under Romanian military rule. There were no gas chambers certainly — but neither was there proper living accommodation, food, hospitals, nor even the prospect of employment, yet more than half the deportees survived, thanks to Romanian Jewry, its leaders and — especially after 1942 — the International Red Cross. Tens of thousands of Jews managed to set up virtual self-government in a number of Transnistrian ghettos, creating workshops of all kinds, working the land and enabling the Young Zionists to complete their agricultural and ideological training for life in Israel, which had been their one and only aim for years. Whatever they lacked, the deportees struggled to obtain from the Romanians. After a few months the Romanian State Police no longer ventured into ghettos such as Shargorod, for example, whose *de facto* autonomy was recognised. The leader of this ghetto, Meyer Teich, even managed to get in touch with the Soviet Partisans in the region, hid some of them in the ghetto and supplied others with food. The Soviet authorities undoubtedly recognised these services, and though when the

Red Army recaptured Shargorod in the spring of 1944 and Teich was arrested, he was very swiftly released and complimented on his good services.

In Romania proper, the period of pogroms and massacres had practically drawn to a close by the end of 1941, but the fact was not known until the Liberation so that right to the end the Jews did not for an instant stop fearing the worst. There was nothing to indicate that they would be spared, considering the tradition of anti-Semitism in Romania and the massacres just described, not to mention those perpetrated by the *Einsatzgruppen* in the USSR and by the SS in the death camps of Poland. The Jewish population in the country was very well informed of these matters.

While the Zionist youth organisations[2] continued as before, adapting their activities to the circumstances, but without compromising the first objective: to preserve their collective life, the structures of Judaism were badly shaken. The counsellor for Jewish affairs in the German Embassy, and Eichmann's personal delegate, was *SS-Hauptsturmführer* Gustav Richter. This individual, who had the rank of police attaché, prided himself upon being something of a journalist. He had managed to get his hands on the *Bukarester Tageblatt*, the daily paper of the embassy, and used it to make regular attacks on the Romanian Jews.

Richter decided to introduce into Romania a Jewish organisation, modelled on the German one, which all the Jews in the country would be forced to join, and this organisation, the Jewish Central Office, was effectively established, while all other Jewish organisations were abruptly dissolved and their assets transferred to the Central Office.

The Germans placed a certain Dr. N. Gingold at the head of the organisation. Originally from Transylvania, but educated in Germany, Dr. Gingold had always kept well away from Judaism, and had even been received into the Catholic Church about a year after the anti-Jewish racial law came into force in Romania which took away all 'material advantages' from such a late baptism.

Gingold was known to the Germans both in his capacity as embassy doctor and as doctor to von Rintgen, Richter's predecessor in Bucharest.

Gingold, who asked for nothing better than to help the Jews, with whom he was quite unfamiliar, turned to the traditional counsellors of the Jewish way of life, who did not refuse him their co-operation, so that the Bucharest Central Office did not become a *Judenrat* of the sort found in Poland, Hungary and elsewhere. The Zionist organisation, although officially banned, did not disperse, but simply removed its president, the lawyer M. Benveniste, and replaced him by a man of quite a different calibre, A. L. Zissu, a well-known thinker, writer and poet, as well as head of the sugar combine. His wide interests enabled him to discuss matters on an equal footing with almost everyone of note in Romanian political circles. Gingold could not hold a candle to him: he did not even try and

Richter was granted authority to appoint Radu Lecca, former director-general of the ministry to a position above Gingold. Lecca thus became representative for Jewish affairs, though he was not in the same category as Zissu either.

The Romanian authorities did not share the German conception of the role of the *Judenrat*. When they created their organisations the Germans preferred to have dealings with one structure only, and preferably with only one person within it, while the Romanian authorities could not see why they should have to deal only with the representatives of the Jewish Central Office, or why it was necessary for them to negotiate through Lecca's office of Jewish affairs all the time.

Jewish youth organisations took more direct action. The young Communists who co-operated with the Zionist movement *Hachomer Hatzair*, began by distributing leaflets. Someone had the bright idea of printing anti-war slogans on banknotes. There were about fifteen arrests. The shortest sentence was the one passed on a twelve-year-old girl: ten years' hard labour. Three of the accused, the oldest eighteen years old, were sentenced to death and shot. May the author be permitted to give the names of his childhood companions: Elias, Zalman, Moscovici. They perished in the spring of 1942.

A few weeks earlier a military tribunal had tried a group of young Communists who had been distributing propaganda material among the peasants. These young people finished up in a forced-labour camp in Fierbinti, east of Bucharest. Two of them, Meirovici and Mihalovici were condemned to death and shot. The others were thrown into prison and remained there until the Liberation.

The last serious alert received by the Romanian Jews was in the summer of 1942, when they learned that the Jews of Romanian Transylvania were to be deported to Poland. The matter was, of course, a secret, but the Jewish organisations got wind of it and a campaign of visits and wide-ranging appeals were launched. The Chief Rabbi Alexander Safran succeeded in gaining the co-operation of the Metropolitans and the Orthodox and Catholic bishops. Even the Nuncio rallied to his call. All of them spoke to Antonesco. Other Jewish leaders forced the hand of the leaders of the principal opposition parties, the liberals and the peasants. They, too, made representations to Antonesco. Others again turned to the Court; some even made direct representations to Antonesco.

It was the month of August 1942. The battle of Stalingrad had not long begun. Germano-Romanian relations had improved a little. Antonesco gave in.

The year 1943 began with the Stalingrad débâcle and saw a rapid deterioration in Germano-Romanian relations. Stalingrad was an even worse disaster for Romania than it was for Germany, for Romania had lost two entire armies in the battle, and Antonesco went personally to Hitler's headquarters to request him to make peace, for in his eyes all hope of victory had gone.

Hitler would not commit himself.

At that point, Marshal Antonesco — he had promoted himself after the capture of Odessa — sent his Foreign Minister, Mihail Antonesco (the two men were not related) on a tour of Europe. The emissary tried to influence the Italians, urging the *Duce* to withdraw from the war. He even made some vain move in the direction of Vichy. The war went on.

Then Zissu had a flash of inspiration. As acting president of the Zionist organisation, he took over the position of representative of the Jewish Agency for Palestine. This agency, through the intervention of its delegation in Istanbul, gave him its official sanction and he set about negotiating directly with Mihail Antonesco to obtain permission for the evacuation of as many Jews as possible to Palestine.

He managed to collect funds — from Geneva and Constantinople — then boats, then the green light from the Romanian government, and from the spring of 1944 boats filled to overflowing left the Romanian port of Constanta for Istanbul. Several thousand Jews were saved in this way.

The Jewish Agency now had Palestinian parachutists dropped in pairs on Romania, who were to establish contact with the Zionist youth movements and organise armed resistance in case the enemy might decide at the last moment to get rid of the Jews.

The operation was not a great success. The first parachutists were captured, some being interned in a prisoner-of-war camp inhabited mainly by RAF crews, and managed to continue their activities inside. A few escaped capture and were able to collaborate with the youth movements.

The operation failed for lack of resources. The organiser, Eliahou Golomb, then commander-in-chief of the *Haganah*, had planned to drop the whole of *Palmach*, that is the whole of the *Haganah* mobile force of about 2,000 men, on occupied Europe, heading the operation himself. These 2,000 combatants were to have made their way into the ghettos and other Jewish agglomerations, organise military groups and lead them into battle. They would thus have mobilised tens and hundreds of thousands of Jews and to have put the non-operational German zone — and the Balkans and Poland in particular — to fire and sword.

To send 2,000 men behind enemy lines required both equipment and strategy and *Haganah* did not even have the essential aeroplanes and radio transmitters. The Royal Air Force could have supplied these and other necessary equipment but, for political rather than military reasons, Great Britain had no desire to get involved in the Jewish struggle to this extent: or this is the argument officially put forward in Israel today.[3]

In the end, therefore, no more than 35 parachutists took part in the operation, and these had to be divided between six countries. They were able to play a limited part in Italy, Czechoslovakia and Hungary; those who were sent to Bulgaria reached their destination only after the Red Army had entered the country, while those who landed in Yugoslavia had only to arrive there to attain their objective. But Romania was the prime target of the Palestinian parachutists, more than a third of them being dropped in her territory.

Those who stayed free managed to give basic training to a number of the younger Jews.

Zissu, who at this period had his finger in several pies, tried to get some of these parachutists out of their difficulties.

He spoke to the Jewish Agency for Palestine and luckily, the Antonesco pair had formed a very high opinion of the power of 'international Jewry'. It was clear to them that the war was lost and that there was a good chance of the Red Army invading Romania. They knew that the Jewish Agency was an Anglo-American affair — if more British than American — and so when a respected gentleman came to speak to them in the name of such an organisation, at what was for them a very critical moment, they were all ears. In the circumstances the Antonesco pair put Germany and its orders firmly to one side. The Jewish Central Office was simply ignored and the Office of Jewish matters received strict injunctions to place itself virtually at the disposal of Zissu. As for SS-*Hauptsturmführer* Richter, he was, so to speak, out of circulation. He tried hard, by invoking his diplomatic functions, to impose the views of the Grand Mufti of Jerusalem on the Romanian Government, which had taken refuge in Berlin and sent regular notes to Ribbentrop reporting the departures of the various batches of European Jews to Palestine and asking him to intervene. The Great Mufti added this suggestion: since the Jews had to leave in any case, why not send them to Poland? Germany had demonstrated that it had found a practical solution to the problem there.

Mihail Antonesco, informed of the Mufti's notes in 1944, was inclined to disregard them, and stated that the great ally, Germany, seemed most concerned with the interests of the 'noble Arabian nation', while ignoring the interests of the Romanians. As Antonesco's first responsibility lay in defending the interests of the latter; there was no question of his refusing the aid offered by the Jewish Agency.

The Red Army had recaptured the Crimea and destroyed the German 7th army, largely composed of Romanian divisions. On 20 April 1944, the Russians took over part of Romania on recapturing Bukovina and half of Bessarabia. Odessa was no longer Romanian, nor was Transnistria.

Meanwhile, the Romanian Communist Party became more and more active. It had succeeded in emerging from its political ghetto and had set up a national democratic bloc with the Social Democrats, which even included the traditional parties. The former would have preferred to be liberated by the Allies but could not afford to ignore the proximity of the Red Army. Not only that, it had even managed to secure the co-operation of several generals and superior officers, some of whom, like General Damaceanu, commander of the capital, held leading strategic positions.

Zissu thought it good policy to keep up relations with the Communists, and in addition offered official financial contributions to the Red Cross.

On a different level, the Communist Party set up an armed combat network in Bucharest: *Patriotic Defence*. This group, led by the Communists, had to take military action against both the loyalist troops of Antonesco and the Germans in the event of a German or pro-German *putsch*. The example of the German Occupation of Hungary on 19 March 1944 was in everybody's minds.

Patriotic Defence and its leader Emil Bodnares naturally counted upon the co-operation of the young Jews of the capital who were already regrouped in the structure of the former forced labour detachments, and since the Anglo-American bombardments at the beginning of spring 1944, had been engaged in passive resistance and rescue operations.

The Red Army, which had halted its advance in April 1944, went into action again on 20 August, and the German armies were crushed, while the Romanians allowed the Russians to continue their advance.

The German defeat soon looked as though it would end in disaster, which the events of 23 August 1944 promised to hasten.

On that day Marshal Antonesco was invited by King Michael to the royal palace, an armed detachment supplied by Emil Bodnares guaranteeing the personal safety of the Marshal and his Minister for Foreign Affairs; and a coalition government was set up which proclaimed the end of the state of war with the Allies, both Western and Soviet.

When the remainder of the German allies thus found themselves in a trap, their troops stationed near Bucharest tried to seize the capital.

They were too late. The Romanian army was far superior in strength. Moreover the detachments of *Patriotic Defence* and the Jewish detachments had swiftly armed themselves. The German offensive was crushed.

The Zionist youth movements had also managed to arm themselves and elected to station themselves in the Jewish quarters, ready to confront any possible pogrom. There was no pogrom.

On 31 August 1944, the Red Army entered Bucharest. There was no resistance, since the Romanians had disarmed the last of the German troops, and Romania carried on the war at the side of the Red Army, backed by forces far superior to those France had at her disposal in 1944—1945.

As for the Jews, once the Germans had gone they knew they had escaped the threat of massacre that had been haunting their leaders. By playing on the antagonism Romania nursed for her powerful German ally, the Jewish leaders had succeeded in turning the circumstances to their own account. Romania was the only country in the German sphere of influence where old-fashioned Jewish political methods, personal intervention, solicitation of third parties, baksheesh, etc. had had results.[4] It cannot fairly be claimed that the end justified the means.

Suffice it to recall the comment attributed to Marshal Joffre referring to the battle of the Marne: 'I do not know who won it, but I know who would have lost it if it had been lost.'

The attitude of the Jewish Councils in Poland and elsewhere has often been severely criticised, but it is impossible to place Judaeo-Romanian organisations, the Central Office, the illegal Zionist organisation, the associated illegal committees, on the same level as the Jewish Councils of other countries.

The Romanian attitude was different because it was not the Germans who applied the anti-Jewish policy, but the Romanians. The Jewish leaders in Romania had to face up to Romanians who practised classic anti-Semitism and successfully opposed them by traditional methods.

The same traditional methods were applied in Hungary, Romania's nearest neighbour. These seem to have ended in utter failure because the Hungarian Jews were not up against anti-Semites of a traditional brand, but Nazi Germans, the Gestapo and its service IVB, in particular.

NOTES

1. A political *rapprochement* maybe, but certainly not an intellectual or moral one. When Antonesco went to see Hitler (as he did several times during the war), the general expressed himself in French. He was one of the very few foreign politicians that made an impression on Hitler, and even more rare, one whose advice Hitler sought. He did not follow it, of course, but that is beside the point.

2. The Zionist movement, and indeed the whole of the Zionist organisation (which included adults as well as youth movements) was looked upon quite favourably by the Romanian authorities, for they tended in the long run to diminish the numbers in the Jewish community. The youth movements, however, were more suspect than the rest, for some of them were situated very much to the left — even to the extreme left. Although the Zionist movement, especially in Romania, was theoretically incompatible with Communism, Romanian Security (*Siguranta Generale*) was on its guard. It thought that 'real' Communists could easily infiltrate into these movements which were already, in their opinion, rather too 'red' for comfort.

3. There is no doubt that the sending of 2,000 agents behind German lines at that period was no little matter. The British did not send that number of agents into France in the whole four years of the country's occupation.

4. Ion Antonesco thought nothing of taking the credit for saving the Romanian Jews. At the time of his trial (he was sentenced to death and shot) he said to the prosecutor, 'The fact that the Jews are alive today is all due to Marshal Antonesco!' The prosecutor, Stoican, simply replied: 'But how many are still alive? How many?' (Hearing of 6 May 1946.) In fact, there were more than 100,000 Jewish victims. And we are only referring to those that died in the Romanian and Soviet territories ruled by Antonesco.

CHAPTER 37

HUNGARY: IS IT POSSIBLE TO BARGAIN WITH THE SS?

I N 1938 there were about 440,000 Jews resident in Hungary. This figure doubled following the annexations that it succeeded in carrying out with the aid of Germany: southern Slovakia and sub-Carpathanian Russia, former Czechoslovak territories, in 1938 and 1939; northern Transylvania; and, following the defeat of the Yugoslav army in May 1941, the Yugoslav territories of Bacska and Baranya.

The hazards of war had it that these conquests, effected by one of Hitler's allies with his blessing, gave all these Jews a respite: at least until 19 March 1944, when the German army actually occupied Hungary and installed a puppet government there[1].

The more or less peaceful existence of the Hungarian Jews came to an abrupt end, and from this date onwards nearly 450,000 of them were exterminated.

Various Jewish measures had already been taken by the Magyar government, the most devastating of which had been the mobilisation of a large part of the men (some thirty categories) for compulsory paramilitary service. This consisted of statutory labour behind the Hungarian and German front lines in the USSR. Slave labour would be a better description. Between the end of 1941 and 19 March 1944, 42,000 Jewish conscripts had perished.

A few conscripts were able to get in touch with the Soviet Partisans and even managed to join them. Relations were facilitated because of the number of Jews in the Partisan ranks. Hundreds of Hungarian Jews succeeded in slipping over to the Soviet side. Others caught in the act were hanged, often in front of their assembled comrades.

Richard Holzer — whom we know from the Herbert Baum affair — was more fortunate. After his escape from Germany and his arrival in Budapest, he was called up from compulsory service. He was probably quite relieved, for this put him even further out of the reach of the Gestapo. In the spring of 1944 he spent several months in Volhynia in western Ukraine, where he managed to make friends with Ukrainian and Polish sympathisers who put him in touch with a number of Jews whom they had hidden here and there in the vicinity. The detachments of Hungarian Jews drew upon their own scant rations to help their fellow Jews in hiding.

Later Holzer suffered the same fate as many other members of these paramilitary services: he and his fellow Jews were captured in a Soviet sortie. For Holzer, a German Communist, there was no problem; it was just what he wanted: he managed to have his true position recognised by the Soviet officers, who used his services in psychological warfare against Germany.

The Judaeo-Hungarian soldiers were not so lucky, the Soviet military authorities refusing to consider them as victims of racism: they were prisoners of war like the others. Not a single Jewish institution in Hungary or in any Western democratic country, least of all the anti-Fascist Jewish Committee of Moscow, bothered about the fate of these men in the course of the war. They were lucky to be alive. It was more than other Hungarian Jews were.

At this time a rescue network for the Jewish refugees of occupied territories was set up in Budapest and several thousand Jews from Poland, Slovakia, the protectorate of Bohemia-Moravia, even from Germany and Austria, managed to find refuge in Hungary. Financial backing, coming not so much from Hungarian Jewry as from foreign Jewish organisations — bought them legal status and shielded them from German persecution. At the head of this rescue committee, known under the Hebrew name of *Vaadah le'ezra ve-lehatzala* (rescue and life-saving committee) was the junior lawyer Reszo Kasztner, also known under the names of Rudolf and Israël.

This group was in close contact with the Workers' Group of Bratislava which it supplied with funds and from which it received refugees. A network of escape agents had been set up including frontier guards who had been bribed to ensure the safe passage of the refugees.

When it came to obtaining funds from abroad, *Vaadah* had no choice: it had to use the couriers of German *Abwehr* headed by Admiral Canaris. The Budapest branch of this German intelligence agency, led by Dr. Schmidt, delivered letters to Constantinople and collected them from there. The couriers had to be generously recompensed even though they had undertaken these operations with the tacit authorisation of the Admiral himself.

The principal spokesmen of *Vaadah* were men like Captain Winninger; the Viennese dentist, Sedlaeck, and a few others, including a rather suspicious individual called Gyorgy Grosz, nicknamed Bandi. *Vaadah* had also established contact with the Hungarian colleagues of *Abwehr*, with the help of financial inducements, but these contacts became uncertain, when Canaris was dismissed and the men of *Abwehr* were integrated into the SD under Schellenberg who was directly responsible to Heinrich Himmler.

The members of *Vaadah* were not what one would call representative of Hungarian Judaism, whose leaders were very conservative[2] and motivated by a very special form of Grand Hungarian patriotism.

As early as the nineteenth century, the Hungarian Jews had played an active part in the Hungarian *renaissance* and resolutely opposed the whole of the central Viennese government. Later, under the double monarchy, they considered themselves first and foremost Hungarians; so that when the Transylvanian, Croatian, Slovak and Ruthenian territories were annexed in 1918 by Romania, Yugoslavia and Czechoslovakia respectively, the Jews who inhabited these territories were — at least in the beginning — caught off their balance. The result was that when Hungary recovered a large part of this territory in 1938—1941, the Jews had not the feeling of being annexed at all, but rather of returning to the Motherland[3].

This perhaps explains why even in 1944 the Hungarian Jews, and also their leaders, were not really aware of the dangers that lay ahead. Even when the young men were sent as conscripts to the Eastern front; even when, in 1941, around 20,000 Jews, mostly from sub-Carpathian Russia, were sent to the Kemenets-Podoskiy region of the Ukraine and killed off by the *Einsatzgruppen*, the Hungarian Jews continued to lead a normal life.

The *Vaadah* group must have known what a menace Germany was to Hungarian Judaism: it was in contact with the neighbouring countries, it took in refugees, sent couriers, received messages — such as the report of the two Auschwitz escapees — and transmitted them. That the *Vaadah* group knew perfectly well what was happening in the Grand Reich is proved by Dr. Kasztner's report published after the war[4].

Kasztner, a militant Zionist of the majority party *Poalei Sion* acted as vice-president of *Vaadah*, the president being Otto Komoly, a moderate Zionist. Soon after the group was founded in January 1943, Joel Barand, a young man whose name was to become very well known, was given the task of organising the life-saving network, which, beginning with Poland, was to rescue around 7,000 people.

On 14 March 1944 Dr. Kasztner was faced with a supremely difficult situation. Winninger, captain of *Abwehr*, informed *Vaadah* that German military occupation of Hungary was imminent. The group held a meeting and, according to Kasztner, took three decisions: to tell the Palestinian delegation in Istanbul what was about to happen; to send Winninger and Schmidt as emissaries from *Abwehr* to Bratislava to contact Wisliceny, Eichmann's man who had 'agreed' in 1942, to suspend deportations from Slovakia, and discuss with him whether it was possible to avoid the inevitable in Hungary; finally, to take defence measures.

These measures were not in fact taken. Kasztner reels off a number of reasons that prevented the formation of a Resistance organisation. The most plausible seems to have been the immediate arrest of Moshe Schweiger, whom the Palestinian *Haganah* had ordered to direct Zionist Resistance. Kasztner also accuses the Hungarian Jews of having wasted time in sterile conflicts, of having exhausted themselves in partisan and personal feuds etc. He also asserts that the Zionist movement was divided, and complains finally that Istanbul had promised to send him a secret military mission in February 1944, which was to have organised the Resistance, and that this mission had not arrived.

In our opinion, the main difficulty was an entirely different one: Kasztner himself. A man who first tries to reach an understanding with the enemy and to bargain with him on a financial basis, considering resistance only as an after-thought, could never lead a Resistance movement, let alone give it the necessary impetus.

On March 1944, an *SS-Sondereinsatzkommando*, led by Eichmann himself, turned up in Budapest. Apart from Eichmann it comprised almost all the German delegates who had been responsible for organising deportations in Europe: Wisliceny (Slovakia and Salonica), Dannecker (France, Bulgaria and Italy), Burger (Theresienstadt), Krumey (Lodz), Hunsche, legal expert of the Eichmann service in Berlin, and several other leading lights of lesser brilliance.

Kasztner tells us in his report not what was done to meet this threat, but what was not done. He describes as follows the action of what he considers the most combative element: the young Zionists:

> The Zionist nucleus, the youth movement, was the only organisa-
> tion even in Jewish circles, to make preparations for resistance. It
> could not act on its own initiative: that would have been too fool-
> hardy. Nor could it accept responsibility for creating a situation that
> would encourage the Germans to present anti-Jewish measures in the
> form of reprisals for 'irresponsible Jewish activities'.

Kasztner and the *Vaadah* members themselves decided to see Wisliceny in Budapest and come to a financial agreement with him.

The *Sondereinsatzkommando* for its part was delighted with this approach. Eichmann had received express orders from Himmler to avoid a repetition of the Warsaw ghetto uprising, in view of the fact that the Red Army had already reached the Carpathians, the frontiers of Hungary. Eichmann, therefore, set up a *Judenrat* in Budapest. At that point what should he see but the leaders of what the SS them-selves considered their mortal enemies, the only ones capable of organising a 'second Warsaw ghetto', coming towards him bound and gagged; a sight to gladden his heart.

The events that followed were so complex that it is difficult to unravel them.

Though Himmler had not given up the idea of annihilating the Jews it had begun to dawn on him that the war was lost, or at least that there was no hope of Germany defeating the Anglo-American forces and the Soviets at the same time; and the idea that through the Hungarian Jews in Hungary he could enter into contact with the Allies, and even separate the West from the East, began to appeal to him.

Eichmann, for his part, was not so far-sighted. He had been ordered to annihilate the Hungarian Jews, but also to allow certain contacts. He fulfilled the first part of his mission, if not exactly with enthusiasm, at least in a competent manner. During the second part of his mission he acted basically in the same way. If Kasztner and his colleagues got the impression that Eichmann had let his hand be forced by Himmler, it could be nothing but a tactical ruse on the part of the SS: Eichmann had to be made the incarnation of 'evil' while other SS had to represent the 'good'. The 'good SS', according to Kasztner and his kinsman, and assistant in the *Vaadah*, André Biss[5], were the *SS-Standartenführer* Kurt Becher, his assistants and collaborators, and in a lesser measure Wisliceny who played the part of the corruptible SS while Eichmann appeared as the incorruptible SS. Wisliceny had persuaded the Jews of Bratislava that it was he, and he alone, who had halted the deportations from Slovakia in 1942, and this because he had been paid a substantial sum of money. In actual fact, he had not kept the money for himself at all and the halting of the deportations was due to the reticence of the Slovak authorities who were strongly influenced by the Vatican. The Jews of Bratislava did not know this, but only that they had paid up and that the deportations had ceased: *post hoc ergo propter hoc.*

The Germans, with the co-operation of the Hungarian police, now set about establishing ghettos in all the provincial towns, beginning with the regions nearest the frontier: first sub-Carpathian Russia and Upper Hungary, then Hungarian Transylvania and the eastern regions, then the south and the west of the country. Last of all the capital.

During this period, the usual anti-Jewish measures were adopted by the Hungarian authorities. The Jewish Council did the only possible thing, bombarding the German and Hungarian authorities with memoranda, calling upon their sense of humanity. The results were what one would expect.

Kasztner and Brand had better results: Eichmann presented them with the famous barter plan of a million Jews against 10,000 lorries to be used in the East.

Brand was sent to Istanbul to submit this plan to the local Zionist authorities, and through them to the Allies. He believed in his mission, as did his colleagues in Budapest.

In Transylvania, tens of thousands of Jews found themselves in the ghettos of Cluj, Oradea Mare, Tirgul Mures (in Hungarian, Koloszvar, Nagyvarad, Marosvasarhely). Now these ghettos and several others were within nine miles of the Romanian frontier. The *Vaadah* group took care not to advise those inhabitants with whom it was in contact to flee to Romania. Some of them did so on their own initiative and were saved, for Romania took them in without protest. Two years before things would have been different, but in 1944 it received the refugees.

Kasztner himself paid more than one visit to his home town of Koloszvar to plead with the Jews there to use caution and patience. The great rescue scheme must not be wrecked by attempts to escape.

The Kasztner plan had never been taken seriously by Eichmann. When Brand set off on his mission to Istanbul in a German plane and under cover of a German passport the deportations had already begun and were not to stop for a single instant. Brand was transported from Istanbul, where he had entered into contact with the Palestinian delegates, to Aleppo in Syria, at that time British-occupied territory. There he had to get in touch with Moshe Shertok (Sharett) who was head of the political department of the Jewish Agency for Palestine. Brand would have preferred to meet him in Istanbul so that he might go straight on to Budapest, but Shertok did not receive the necessary authorisations for entering Turkey, and Brand felt it was up to him to go to Syria. There he was interned by the British authorities and as far as we are concerned left the scene.

Kasztner, having had no part in the appointment of Brand, of which he did not approve, continued his negotiations with the SS.

The Germans began the deportations to Auschwitz in mid-May 1944, speeding them up by establishing ghettos in brickyards linked to the stations and railways where ovens were available. Others higher up the hierarchical scale were also making provision for these deportations.

Albert Speer, Minister of Munitions to the Reich, had ordered Marshall Milch to make preparations for the mass production of fighter-bombers, and for this project he needed 100,000 workers. Thoughts, naturally enough, turned to the Jews. But where could one find 100,000 Jews in 1944? Himmler had the answer: he had 500,000 Hungarian Jews deported to Auschwitz. Out of these 500,000 there would be a good 100,000 who could be handed over to Speer. As for the others, the Auschwitz installations were there to be used, weren't they? Thus several birds could be killed with one stone: the Hungarian Jews would be done away with, the Reich would have its workers, and Speer would be under an obligation to Himmler.

Jeno Levai, historian of the catastrophe of Hungarian Judaism, speaks of 618,000 deportees and 121,000 repatriates up to 31 December 1945, which puts the number of victims at over 450,000.

The influx of Jews from Hungary was such that the crematoria could not meet the demand and the gas chambers were not able to cope with the surplus.

The former commandant of the camp, Rudolf Höss, who had been promoted, was sent back to Auschwitz to deal with the situation. He ordered out the firing squads. The gas chambers had been invented to spare the nerves of the execution officials, and here they were, back where they started.

What was the *Vaadah* group doing when the deportations were at their height?

M

It had ordered its president Komoly, hero of the First World War, to negotiate with the Hungarian authorities in Budapest; as for Kasztner he continued his discussions with Eichmann and later with the 'good SS' Kurt Becher.

The best part of the outcome of all these discussions was that 1,648 Jews were taken from the various ghettos and sent to Bergen-Belsen where they were treated as priviliged prisoners, while a few hundred others were withdrawn from Cluj and sent to Budapest.

From this point onwards, the thought uppermost in the minds of the ghetto inhabitants was not Resistance, nor even individual attempts to escape, but the hope of figuring on the 'miraculous' list. It is not difficult to imagine the sort of disputes that followed, and, when Eichmann offered, at a price, to send fifteen to eighteen thousand Jews to Austria, where they would be liable to forced labour but kept, according to Eichmann in cold storage (*auf Eisgelegt*) awaiting the delivery of the promised lorries, there was fierce competition for these places though the results were not always what Kasztner had anticipated.

The problem took on a new slant with the appearance on the Budapest scene of Kurt Becher, SS cavalry colonel, who was familiar with Hungary where most of his regiment's horses had been purchased. Soon after the occupation of the country, Himmler made him responsible for an important SS financial transaction: the purchase of the Manfred-Weiss metallurgical and iron and steel combine.

The Manfred-Weiss family had been converted to Catholicism in the course of the generations, but there were still a few Jews left among them. The most striking aspect of the affair was that although, in accordance with racial laws, the property belonged to the Hungarian State, Becher succeeded in persuading the family to sell their assets to the SS. The other side of the transaction was simple: a token financial compensation, of course, but also permits to enable the whole family to enter Portugal. The deal was concluded on these terms.

Himmler, like his *Führer*, liked to make two or more people responsible for one and the same affair, believing that this encouraged everybody to give of his best; he therefore ordered Becher to negotiate with Kasztner.

While Kasztner imagined that he was saving the remnants of Judaism, all Himmler really wanted was to establish some sort of liaison with the Americans, and the name of *Joint* runs through the whole affair like a red thread. It is very evident that Himmler overestimated this organisation, attributing to it a power it had never possessed, espccially in 1944.

Kasztner's account of events and the reports of his apologists brand Saly Mayer, *Joint*'s delegate in Switzerland, as a villain. This Swiss businessman was also a philanthropist. When, at Kasztner's request, he journeyed to the Austrian frontier he was greeted by Kasztner and Becher with demands for enormous sums of money. He reacted as any normal Swiss businessman would, protesting vehemently against the marketing of human flesh and saying that he would have no hand in it. What he omitted to say, but what seems clear to us, is that he did not know where to find five million dollars, and anyway he did not believe a word the Nazis said.

That the Nazis did not really want the money is proved by the fact that when they did get their hands on a certain amount, they gave it all back. Their principal aim was to negotiate with the Americans, and Becher attained this end on 5 November 1944 when the American representative, Roswell McClelland, agreed to see him. McClelland was President Roosevelt's personal delegate, and Swiss representative of the War Refuge Board, an organisation created by Roosevelt to aid hunted Jews[6].

Little did Becher and Himmler care what happened to a few Jews; or to some thousand Jews; still less to the Jews *en masse*. All they were interested in was to save what could be saved. By November 1944 the Western Allies had almost liberated France and Belgium; they occupied the south of The Netherlands and had penetrated the Siegfried Line. Aix-la-Chapelle had fallen. In Eastern Prussia, the Red Army had reached the frontiers of the Reich, occupied half of Poland, and laid siege to Budapest.

We know that Himmler had failed in his plans to divide the Allies and ensure a position for himself at the top, ousting Adolf Hitler if need be. The same thing cannot be said of Kurt Becher, who quietly had himself de-Nazified after the war, with Kasztner testifying for him. André Biss, a relative of Becher, and his ex-adjutant, heaps tributes on him in a book published in France and Germany. Fortune has smiled on the old cavalryman in other ways too: today he is one of the most prosperous coffee merchants in the Bremen market.

At this stage Himmler decided to suspend the execution of the Jews, hoping that it was not too late to forge an alibi for himself while Eichmann, for his part, did not, or would not, understand this sudden change of tactics on the part of Himmler, knowing that he himself was beyond help[7]. Kasztner and Biss had no compunction in taking credit for the whole affair.

Kasztner already flattered himself that he had 'saved' the Jews he had sent to Austria, and whom Eichmann had said he would put in cold storage. In fact these Jews were to have dug trenches along the stretch of the Austro-Hungarian frontier that the Red Army was expected to attack. A private letter from Ernst Kaltenbrunner, Heydrich's successor at the head of the Security Police and of the SD, to his personal friend the *SS-Brigadeführer* Blaschke, Mayor of Vienna, dated 30 June 1944, makes it clear that these Jews were sent to Vienna, or rather to the concentration camp of Vienna-Strasshof, on Blaschke's express request. According to Kaltenbrunner, experience had shown that only 30 per cent of the Jewish convoys contained able-bodied Jews (3,600 out of a total of 12,000) and that consequently:

> *Since the women and children of these convoys are incapable
> of working, they will be retained for a special operation. Prepara-
> tions must therefore be made for their impending departure.*

The military collapse of the Reich had a lot to do with the eventual cancellation
of this 'special operation', the nature of which is not difficult to guess. And perhaps
the chief of Gestapo in Vienna also had a hand in events. From the time he took
up his duties in 1943 the few Jews who had not been deported from the city found
their living conditions a little more tolerable.

To return to the three Palestinian Jewish officers whose absence Kasztner
regretted in February 1944: there was one very young woman, Hanna Szenes, who
was also a distinguished poet, and two men, Fritz (Peretz) Goldstein and Joel
Nussbecher (Palgi). They were parachuted into a part of Yugoslavia that was held
by the Partisans and had orders to proceed to Budapest. Hanna Szenes was
detailed to leave first, followed by the two men, or rather youths; all three were
to get in touch with a certain Hungarian official who was to help them on their way.

Hanna Szenes had a radio transmitter with her and managed to contact the
escape agent, who lost no time in warning the Hungarian counter-espionage agency.
The mere fact that she had a radio transmitter in her possession was proof enough
of her guilt and she was tried, sentenced to death, and executed.

When her companions, unaware of what had happened, arrived in their turn, the
escape agent passed on the news but the Hungarian special services preferred to let
the young men alone. Hanna Szenes had revealed nothing about the mission, although the Gestapo had not hesitated to employ its usual interrogation technique.

The young men entered Budapest, oblivious of the fact that they were being
closely followed, and tried to get in touch with — of all people — Kasztner. It was
the natural thing to do since he was, after all, a militant Zionist leader of *Vaadah*.
They did succeed, but the Hungarian police finally arrested Nussbecher, and Goldstein went into hiding. Kasztner states in his report that he was questioned by the
Hungarian police, who were determined to find the missing man and threatened
to have Nussbecher shot if Goldstein was not handed over to them. According to
Kasztner, when he told Goldstein about the Hungarian threats he gave himself up.

The outcome was that Goldstein was dead, while Nussbecher escaped and was
able to take part in various minor Resistance actions during the last period of the
German occupation.

Another type of Resistance group, concentrated mainly in Budapest, was much
more down-to-earth than Kasztner's and perhaps for this reason superior. Instead
of negotiating with the Nazis, these young Zionists took all action possible within
their limited means, and in the end were able to account for several thousand Jews
saved — and really saved. Leading them were Hungarian and Slovak refugee

members of *Hachomer Hatzair*, while the principal leader of both the young
Zionists and *Hachomer Hatzair* was Rafi[8].

Rafi Friedl had come to Budapest from Czechoslovakia at the beginning of
1944. He looked like a pure-blooded Aryan — tall, blond and blue-eyed. He still
looks like this, in fact, even though he has changed his name to Raphael Ben
Shalom. He was Israeli Ambassador in Mali, Cambodia, and Romania.

Rafi and his fellow refugees were astounded at the 'normal' life led by the
Budapest Jews and even more so at their absolute lack of concern, and unshaken
confidence that what had happened to the Jews in Austria, Czechoslovakia, Yugoslavia and Romania could not possibly happen in Hungary. Such feelings were
prevalent not only among the 'bourgeois' but among the Communists as well.

Rafi and his comrades did not share this feeling. As refugees living outside the
law they were obliged to procure false papers for themselves. By the time the
Germans occupied the country they had at their disposal not only a considerable
stock of false papers, but better still the necessary equipment to produce them *en
masse*.

Unlike their elders, the young Zionists pushed their distrust of the Nazis to the
extent of repudiating all possibility of reaching an 'understanding' with them.
They gave the signal for artificially induced panic, organised chaos, and systematic
disobedience. It goes without saying that none of the members of these movements
wore the yellow star imposed by the Germans the moment they entered the city.
They next proceeded with 'Aryanisation' of all the members of the movement, the
'native' members, that is, for, of course, the refugees themselves had been 'Aryan-
ised' from the start.

The second stage was the setting up of escape channels to Romania in particular — and back again to Slovakia. In fact, for several months the situation of the
Jews in Slovakia had shown a steady improvement. The passage of several hundred
militants to Romania was organised by Moshe Pil (Moshe the elephant).

Imre Hertz (Mimisch), a brilliant forger saw to the liberation of some of his
comrades as well. With the help of some Serb friends — and large cash payments —
he helped quite a number of them to escape from the German Bacstopolya
camp.

Rafi himself made a very useful contact in Budapest in the person of Fritz.
Eighteen-year-old Fritz was a native of Cologne and a harmonica enthusiast. He
was also an SS officer, but according to Rafi, his harmonica was more important
to him than Hitler's war and the SS put together. One day one of his new Jewish
friends persuaded him to drive out to Kistarcse camp and asked him to rescue his
fiancée who was interned there. Fritz was happy to oblige and an hour later the
couple were reunited. The good offices of Fritz were called upon quite often after
that until eventually several dozen prisoners were liberated.

This information comes from Rafi's report. He did not know then and cannot say even now what led Fritz to act in this way; nor does he even know his surname.

Escape channels to Romania were closed on 23 August 1944 when the country changed sides, but a new situation had developed in Budapest itself when another name, Miklos Krausz, came to the fore.

Krausz was at the head of the Palestine Office of Budapest, the representative body in Hungary of the Jewish Agency for Palestine: officially recognised by the British government as the legal representative of the Palestinian Jewish community. Anglo-Hungarian diplomatic relations having long since been broken off, British interests in Hungary were safeguarded by Switzerland, the protector power.

Like Zissu, his opposite number in Bucharest, Krausz had a flash of inspiration: he had a collective passport made up for several thousand 'candidates for emigration to Palestine' and this with the authority of Switzerland. Furthermore he leased a building and affixed a plate to it inscribed in Hungarian, French and German: *Swiss Legation — Representation of Foreign Interests — Emigration Service.*

Of course this 'annex' of the Swiss Legation could not have come into being without their authority and especially not without the consent of the Swiss Consul, Charles Lutz.

The 'glass house' — so named because it belonged to the glass magnate Arthur Weiss — situated at 29 Vadasz-Utca, rapidly became a veritable hive of activity. The fact that it enjoyed extra-territorial status encouraged employees of the Palestinian Office, their families, their friends and their friends' families, then all the leading militant Zionists and their families, to settle there permanently. Very soon, nearly 2,000 persons were in residence, walking all over each other, queueing up for the lavatories, etc., living in literally suffocating conditions.

A very young militant Zionist, Erszi (Elisabeth) Eppler, saved the situation. She discovered that a party-wall divided the glass house from the headquarters of the Hungarian Football Federation. The siege of Budapest meant that very little activity was going on there, and Erszi simply had a gap made in the wall.

The same young woman had shown her mettle earlier in the Occupation at the time the *Judenrat* was set up, when she managed to get herself employed there in a very junior capacity and kept a close watch on the proceedings. When the *Judenrat* summoned certain categories of Jews, the intellectuals for example, with the intention of handing them over to the Germans, Erszi saw to it that the persons concerned were warned. In so doing the young librarian was simply carrying out the instructions of the young Zionists: never obey German orders; counter them if possible.

The 'glass house' rapidly became the centre of activities for all the Jewish organisations in Budapest. The success of this sanctuary led to the setting up of others, and soon, under cover of Switzerland, and later of the International Red Cross, and of a series of other consulates (Spain, Portugal, El Salvador, and Sweden) 'protected houses' began to spring up all over the city. The Holy See itself offered its protection to the Jews of Budapest.

But the practical work, the manufacture of safe-conducts and permits devolved upon the young Zionists; and if a particular consulate ordered five hundred safe-conducts, the young Zionists had at least three times as many made. The number of recipients of these miraculous papers is reckoned to have been around 90,000, but the fact that it was impossible to distinguish between bearers of genuine papers and the others makes an exact assessment impossible.

Everything went more or less smoothly so long as the situation in Budapest remained as it were normal, but at the beginning of December 1944 it began to deteriorate. The capital was suddenly besieged on all sides by the Red Army while at the same time Fascist elements in the city grasped the opportunity to take the law into their own hands. Ferenc Szalasi, chief of the *Nyillas* (Slashed Cross), was at the head of the government, but his men were completely out of his control. One day a group of *Nyillas* attacked the 'glass house' and set about turning the inhabitants out onto the street in the bitter cold. Rafi was immediately alerted and hastened to inform the Hungarian civil and military authorities of this flagrant violation of international law — and the miracle happened: the Hungarian military police and a detachment of the army went to the spot and drove off the *Nyillas*, who had their revenge by arresting and killing a large number of Jews in the street. Arthur Weiss, Otto Komoly and the Zionist leader Simcha Hohnwald were among them.

Fascist violence was rapidly succeeded by equally flagrant Jewish retaliation, especially among the younger members. Deciding to sell their lives dearly they set about procuring arms and rigging themselves out in the most extraordinary variety of Fascist uniforms. Rafi points out in his report that there were several hundred young Jews involved, but that for want of organization they were unable to take any concerted action. Worse still, the Hungarian police eventually arrested a large number of the most belligerent, seizing three of their bunkers in the process.

It fell to Rafi to come to their aid, and he succeeded in saving over a hundred young Jews, as well as some dozens of Jewish and non-Jewish militant Communists. A boy of twenty or so, he had already learnt the judicious use of boldness, *sang-froid*, and hard cash.

Relations between the young Zionists and the militant Communists could not have been better. The Hungarian Communists were weak and divided at that period and in their relations with the Zionists they were the hangers-on. Hampered as the young Zionists were, they were the stronger of the two parties. They were able to help the Communists by supplying them with the false papers of Rafi and

Co. and by the time the siege was nearing its close Rafi's workshops were turning out documents for every nationality: Hungarian, German, Slovak, Bulgarian, Turkish, Spanish, South American, even North American[9].

While Kasztner was still deeply involved in his highly political negotiations, the fate of the Jews of Budapest was becoming more and more precarious.

However, there had been no more deportations since July, international intervention on an unprecedented scale having weighted the balance in favour of the Jews. The Vatican had made its voice heard in no uncertain manner, as had the Swedish King Gustaf V. The Western press like the neutral press had broken its self-imposed silence on the fate of the Jews and news of Auschwitz was splashed over all the newspapers. In the face of such opposition, the Hungarian chief of state Admiral Horthy took it upon himself to put an end to the deportations. The Hungarian military police stopped co-operating with the Germans and the two Hungarian officials charged with helping Eichmann in his enterprise, Endre and Baky, were prevented from doing so. Eichmann himself was obliged to leave Hungary.

As the front drew nearer and nearer Budapest, more and more prominent people, organisations, foreign and international authorities, hastened to the aid of the Jews. The consulates of Sweden, Switzerland, Portugal and El Salvador — even the consulate of Spain — delivered certificates of protection to them. The Papal Nuncio did likewise and so did the International Red Cross. The Hungarian authorities finished by creating a ghetto in Budapest, attached to which were a number of 'protected houses' where holders of certificates might live.

The regent, Horthy, seeing that the game was up, tried to negotiate a separate peace. Following the example of his Italian colleague Badoglio, he proclaimed the surrender of the Hungarian army. But like Badoglio, he had not foreseen the German reaction, which was particularly violent. Otto Skorzeny was sent specially to Budapest to seize the person of Horthy, which he did without firing a shot. A Nazi-Hungarian government headed by Ferenc Szalasi, chief of the pro-Nazi organisation *Nyillas*, was set up in his place. The Hungarian army such as it was continued the fight on the side of the Germans.

Just before the Soviet circle closed around Budapest, Eichmann succeeded in dispatching several thousand Jews on foot to Austria. Even Rudolf Höss, chief of the Auschwitz camp, and the SS general Juttner, head of the mobilisation of the *Waffen-SS* were moved to voice their disapproval.

During the last phases of the siege of Budapest, the *Nyillas* shot a number of Hungarians guilty of harbouring Jews, while the Germans shot several of their own soldiers, guilty of the same crime.

The epilogue of the Kasztner affair was acted out in 1957. Reszo Kasztner, now known as Israel Kastner, had emigrated to Israel and become a top-ranking official there. When one of the survivors of Hungarian Judaism wrote a pamphlet in which he denounced the role that Kasztner had played in Budapest, declaring that his attitude had contributed to the extermination of the Hungarian Jews, an action for libel was brought against the pamphleteer, not by Kasztner, but by the Public Prosecutor of Israel.

The action of the State of Israel against Malkiel Grunwald caught the public imagination. The participants and witnesses of the drama, and there were a great number of them, took their stand one after another in the witness-box during the months that followed. Soon the Grunwald trial turned into the Kasztner trial, for Grunwald was acquitted on several of the charges while it was assessed that Kasztner 'sold his soul to Satan'.

The State appealed against the verdict, and Grunwald was finally found guilty on all counts, which was equivalent to exonerating Kasztner; but to all intents and purposes Kasztner was a finished man, and shortly afterwards a handful of 'terrorists' shot him down in the street. His murderers, who were not Hungarians, alleged that the trial had convinced them that Kasztner was a traitor. They were given very heavy sentences, but were reprieved after a short time.

NOTES

1. A similar paradox had it that the Jews of the anti-German countries (that is to say of Greece and Yugoslavia) suffered heavy losses while the Jews of pro-German countries such as Bulgaria, Romania (and even if one wishes, Albania) were generally able to survive. The reason for this was that the local Fascist regimes, the Italian one, for example, were much less efficient than the German National Socialist machine.

2. Some Jews militated in the (illegal) Communist Party and in the clandestine (if not illegal) Social Democratic Party; but neither category was very large.

The Zionist movement, on the other hand, had never been very powerful in Hungary although it had been reinforced to a certain extent by the annexation of Northern Transylvania.

3. This was particularly true of the upper classes. The Jews of Ruthenian territory (sub-Carpathian Russia) and of the extreme north of Transylvania (Maramourech in Romanian; Marmaros in Hungarian) lived in Jewish villages, or constituted very closely knit and extremely devout groups in the towns. These bore a strong resemblance to Judaeo-Polish communities. The brothers Jérôme and Jean Tharaud described them in far from flattering terms between the two wars, and perhaps there is some truth in what they say. Certainly they lived entirely outside the twentieth century.

4. Eichmann trial exhibit T/1113. See also *Der Kastner-Bericht uber Eichmanns Menschenhandel in Ungarn*, (Munich, Kindler Verlag, 1961).

5. See André Biss's *Echec à la solution finale. Un Million de Juifs à sauver* (Paris, Grasset, 1967). Biss shares the illusions of Kasztner.

6. This organisation only came into being as late as 1944 but was extremely efficient right from the start. Its delegates were authorised to employ any techniques and methods they wished. McClelland, for example, could meet enemy agents; whereas Allied organisations, public or private, were strictly forbidden to do so.

7. Himmler could very well have followed the same line of reasoning, but at times he betrayed a totally lacking sense of reality: he could go as far as believing in his own propaganda, an eccentricity one would certainly not have encountered in Eichmann.

8. Rafi Ben Shalom's report was published anonymously and undated in Budapest in 1945. Its author was in hospital at the time. The original is in the Moreshet archives, Tel Aviv (ref. D 2-88), and we have a copy. It is a simple typed report corrected by hand.

9. Strictly speaking there was no Jewish armed resistance in Hungarian territory, but a number of Jews did try to join the Partisans. There were hardly any in Hungarian territory proper; so the Hungarian Jews escaped to Tito's Partisans, or north to the Ukrainian Partisans of sub-Carpathian Russia. The latter was formed in the spring of 1944 around a number of parachuted Soviet agents.

CONCLUSION

WHEN I undertook to write this book, I intended to show the reader not what the Jews had suffered at the hands of the Germans, but how they had stood up to them and fought them; but as I have advanced in my task I have realised that the accounts of the persecution of the Jews, the massacres of the Jews, and of Jewish suffering in general, have taken up more and more space.

Nothing was further from my mind than arousing the compassion of the reader. Compassion, pity, commiseration are often tinged with contempt — and the Jewish people have suffered rather too much of this in the last two centuries.

There is therefore an apparent contradiction. Resistance was never an end in itself. Various peoples have offered resistance both *for* something and *against* something, having had positive as well as negative reasons for doing so. On the whole, the peoples of occupied countries resisted the occupying enemy forces in order to gain or regain national independence and liberty, or liberties. In the allied countries of the Third Reich, the Resistance forces aimed at overthrowing the Fascist regimes in order to regain their liberty, or liberties. This, too, was the aim of members of the German Resistance movement, although their conception of liberty, or liberties, often seems curious to me. And wherever the Communists took part in the Resistance, and they took part almost everywhere, they injected it with fresh energy. They were also fighting to gain acceptance for their own views, even when they thought that the society for which they were fighting would only come into being much later on. For them the matter in hand was to overcome 'German Fascism'.

The Jews' position was entirely different. Perhaps one can begin to understand it by citing the proud motto of Colonel Fabien: 'Conquer and live'. As far as the Jews were concerned, if they wished to live, they had to conquer.

A great Jewish poet echoed Fabien's words on the other side of Europe. On 24 August 1941, David Bergelson, one of the protagonists of the Judaeo-Soviet anti-Fascist Committee, speaking on Moscow radio, declared proudly:

> *Today the vandals are destroying everything, they are determined to annihilate every living soul, beginning with the Jews, but we — the people of Maimonides, Spinoza, Heine, Mendelssohn — we shall not die. The people who for thousands of years have replied to its oppressors: 'I will not die, I will live', give the same response today:*
> *I WILL NOT DIE, I WILL LIVE!*

They ask us to commit suicide, to take the quickest way out. Bar-
barians make no distinction between believers and atheists, they wish
to exterminate them all. But we, the Jewish people, are a stubborn
race. We choose the roughest road, the road of life.

The European Jews who took part in the Resistance, whether in the ranks of
more or less autonomous Jewish structures or in national Resistance movements,
did so for varying motives, with varying plans in mind. But wherever they fought,
the main reason for doing so was in order that the Jews might survive. Even the
most French of the French Israelites, those who indignantly rejected the notion of
'Jewish people', refusing to admit to any motive other than their fidelity to France,
desired that the liberation of the country be accompanied by the rescission of anti-
Jewish measures.

The Western European Jews — whatever form their Resistance took — can give
a more successful account of themselves: a very large proportion of Western European Jewry managed to outlive Hitler, and this thanks to the Resistance of the
Jews. Of course, without the assistance of the non-Jewish Resistance it would have
been impossible.

The Eastern European Jews, as a whole, could not have been saved by the
Jewish Resistance because the non-Jewish Resistance was inadequate to say the
least.

Generally speaking, the Jews of the ghettos only fought to prevent themselves
from being led to their death 'like lambs to the slaughter' (the expression much
used by the ghetto fighters does not come from anti-Semites, nor from somewhat
masochistic Jews. We owe it to the prophet Jeremiah.) Are these Jews then the
conquered ones? I do not think so.

The combatants of Warsaw, Vilna, Bialystok and of other ghettos, big and small,
the members of the Jewish Resistance in Sachsenhausen, Treblinka, Sobibor and
Auschwitz, the Eastern European Partisan Jews, won another type of victory: like
their Jewish brothers in Western, Southern, Central and Northern Europe they
succeeded in preserving the collective existence of the Jewish people. History gives
us many examples of peoples who completely disappeared after some terrible
blood-letting simply because they had lost the will to live. By fighting for their
honour, the Eastern European Jews kept the will to survive alive in the Jewish
people.

It is also true that, even though the Jews played a large part in the Resistance
in other European countries, it is the Warsaw ghetto uprising that is most remembered by them all — more than any local episodes in which the Jews distinguished
themselves. To the Parisian Jews, Mordekhai Anielewicz is much more the symbol
of Jewish Resistance than any of the Jews in the French Resistance movement.

The same goes for the Italian Jews. Mordekhai Anielewicz symbolises the Jewish Resistance fighter much more than Emanuele Artom and Eugenio Curiel, for example. All Jews are deeply cognisant of the fact that the sacrifice of the Warsaw ghetto combatants has allowed them to live and to live like Jews — *whatever interpretation they give to the notion of Jew*.

From the Jewish point of view, two basic facts emerge, the well-being of individuals — only partially successful — and the affirmation of collective existence, which did not reach its height until after the Liberation.

Can one go any further? Can one draw any further lessons from this terrible equation: on the one hand six million dead; on the other hand some tens of thousands of Resistance fighters?

In our opinion one cannot and one must not. Tens of thousands of Jews proved by their revolt something of universal value and significance: *resistance alone can save*.

About four centuries ago the Prince of Orange declared: 'It is not necessary to hope in order to undertake; nor to succeed in order to persevere.'

The Jewish Resistance fighters have given a new sense to this noble thought: those who undertake the most desperate actions and persevere with them in spite of the absence — apparent or real — of success, end by carrying them off.

By revolting against the Hitler regime which intended to exterminate the entire Jewish population, the Jews were not engaging in an act of heroism, they simply wished to preserve the material and moral substance of their people. Their success won them immortality.

SOURCES

A. ARCHIVES

Listed below are the principal archives consulted.

Naturally the author assumes full responsibility for the use he has made of the documents and for his interpretation of them.

German Democratic Republic.
Institut Für Marxismus-Leninismus Beim ZK Der SED, Berlin.
Sachsenhausen Museum.

German Federal Republic
Ministry of Foreign Affairs archives, Bonn.
Bundesarchiv, Koblenz. (We are particularly grateful to the *Oberarchivrat* Dr. Heinz Boberach for his particulary helpful and profitable suggestions.)
Friedrich-Ebert-Stiftung, Bad Godesberg.
Institut Für Zeitgeschichte, Munich.
West Berlin Senate.

Austria
Dokumentationsarchiv Der Osterreichischen Widerstandsbewegung, Vienna.
International Resistance Federation, Vienna.

Belgium
Archives of the Jewish Defence Committee, Brussels.
M. José Gotovitch, Brussels.
Ministry of Public Health, Brussels.

France
Centre De Documentation Juive Contemporaine, Paris.

Great Britain
Weiner Library, London.

Israel
Lochamey Haghettaot Kibbutz ('The ghetto combatants').
Moreshet Mordekhai Anielewicz Memorial building, Tel Aviv.
Yad Vashem, Jerusalem and Tel Aviv.

Italy
Centro Di Documentazione Ebraica Contemporanea, Milan. (I am particularly grateful to the secretary of the Centre, Doctor Eloisa Ravenna, not only for allowing me free access to the archives but for kindly reading the chapter devoted to Italy and giving me the benefit of her most valuable suggestions and criticisms.)
Istituto Nazionale Per la Storia Del Movimento Di Liberazione In Italia, Milan and Turin.

Switzerland
Juna, Basle.

Czechoslovakia
Jewish State Museum, Prague.

B. INTERVIEWS

I interviewed a great many people (witnesses and participants) who were on one side or the other of the barricades in the last war. Their accounts varied greatly and some were more valuable than others, but I am most grateful to everybody for their co-operation.

C. PUBLISHED MATERIAL

I. General

I know of no book that gives an overall picture of the part the Jews played in the Resistance. However, there is an anthology by Yuri Suhl, *They fought back* (327 pp. New York, Crown Publishers, 1967) containing 33 accounts and surveys of the various aspects and episodes of the Resistance.

If one searches carefully through the immense bibliography devoted to the catastrophe of the European Jews, a few passages, even entire chapters can be found describing the part the Jews played in the Resistance. Almost without exception, they refer to the Warsaw ghetto uprising.

Still, there are a few books that give a general picture of the persecution of the Jews under Hitler and develop the theme of the Jews in the Resistance. Most of these contain substantial bibliographies:

HILBERG, Raul. *The Destruction of the European Jews*, 788 pp. Chicago, Quadrangle Books, 1961. (A monumental work, but unfortunately the author is so overcome by the scale of the disaster that he is almost indifferent to the part the Jews played in the Resistance.)

POLIAKOV, Léon. *Bréviaire de la Haine*, 385 pp. Paris, Calmann-Lévy, 1951. (The Third Reich and the Jews.)

Procès des Grands Criminels de Guerre, 42 volumes. Nuremberg, International Military Tribunal, 1949.

REITLINGER, Gerald. *The Final Solution: the Attempt to Exterminate the Jews of Europe*, 1939—1945. New York, Beechurst Press, 1953; and London, Vallentine Mitchell, 1953. (Reitlinger has the same failing as Hilberg and his book contains a large number of inaccuracies.)

ROBINSON, Jacob. *And the Crooked Shall Be Made Straight: a New Look at the Eichmann Trial*, 406 pp. New York and London, Macmillan, 1965. (This book contains an exhaustive list of the catalogues of books devoted to the various aspects of the Jewish catastrophe in Europe during the Second World War.)

BERNARD, Henri. *Histoire de la Résistance Européene: la 'quatrième Force' de la Guerre 1939—1945*, 283 pp. Verviers, Marabout-Université, 1968.

European Resistance Movements. Paris-London, Pergamon Press, 1960.

KUEHNRICH, Heinz. *Der Partisanenkrieg In Europa 1939—1945*, 768 pp. East Berlin, Dietz Verlag, 1968.

MICHEL, Henri. *Les Mouvements Clandestins en Europe 1938—1945*, 127 pp. Que sais-je? Paris, PUF, 1965.

ZENTNER, Kurt. *Illustrierte Geschichte Des Widerstands In Europa 1933—1945*, 608 pp. Munich, Südwest Verlag, 1966.

Here are two more catalogues of books (most of them French) which deal with the Jewish problem as a whole and the Jewish (and general) situation in Europe after 1933. (One even commences with the Dreyfus affair.)

La France de l'Affaire Dreyfus à Nos Jours, catalogue (no. 1), 266 pp. CDJC Library, Paris, 1964.

La France — Le Troisième Reich — Israël, catalogue (no. 2), 254 pp. CDJC Library, Paris, 1968.

The following are the most important books of the vast collection dealing with the repression:

Anatomie Des SS-Staates, 2 vols. Munich, DTV, 1967. (The articles of Hans Buchheim, Martin Broszat, Hans Adolf Jacobsen and Helmut Krausnick cover a wide variety of aspects of the repression.)

BILLIG, Joseph. *L'Hitlérisme et le Système Concentrationnaire*, 331 pp. Paris, PUF, 1967.

DELARUE, Jacques. *Histoire de la Gestapo*, 473 pp. Grandes Etudes contemporaines. Paris, Fayard, 1962.

HOHNE, Heinz. *Der Orden Unter Dem Totenkopf: die Geschichte Der SS*, 600 pp. Gütersloh, Sighert Mohn, 1967.

REITLINGER, Gerald. *The SS — Alibi of a Nation*, London, 1956.

WORMSER-MIGOT, Olga. *Le Système Concentrationnaire Nazi (1933–1945)*, 600 + VII pp. Paris, PUF, 1968.

WORMSER-MIGOT, Olga. *Essai sur les Sources de l'Histoire Concentrationnaire Nazi (1933–1945)*, 363 pp. roneoed. Complementary thesis, no address and undated, Paris, 1968.

2. Sources in individual countries*

Germany

Damals In Sachsenhausen, 172 pp. East Berlin, Kongress-Verlag, 1961.

Erkämpft Das Menschenrecht, 694 pp. East Berlin, Dietz, 1958.

GRUNDIG, Gustav. *Zwischen Karneval Und Aschermittwoch*, 429 pp. East Berlin, Dietz, 1959.

LEBER, Annedore; BRANDT, Willy; BRACHER, Karl Dietrich. *Das Gewissen Entscheidet*, 303 pp. Berlin-Frankfort, Mosaik-Verlag, 1957.

MAAS, Hermann and RADBRUCH, Gustav. *Den Unvergessenen, Opfer Des Wahns 1933 bis 1945.* pp. 11–18, Heidelberg, Lambert Scheider-Verlag, 1952.

MARK, Bernard. 'The Herbert Baum group. A Jewish Resistance group', in *Bleter Far Geszychte* (Yiddish), vol. XIV. pp. 27–65, Warsaw, 1961.

PIKARSKI, Margot. *Die Rolle Der Parteiorganisation Der KPD In Der Herbert Baum-Gruppe, Berlin 1939–1942.* Thesis, 73 p. text, 43 p. notes, 43 p. documents and photos. Franz Mehring Institute of the Karl Marx University, 1964.

RIESENBURGER, Martin. *Das Licht Verlöscht Nicht*, 87 pp. East Berlin, Union-Verlag, 1960.

SACHSENHAUSEN, *Erlauterungen zur Nationalen Mahn-und Gedenkstatte*, Potsdam, 1962.

Spiegelbild einer Verschwörung. Die Kaltenbrunner-Berichte an Bormann und Hitler uber das Attentat vom 20. Juli 1944, VII-587 pp. Stuttgart-Degerloch, Seewald Verlag, 1961.

STEINBERG, Lucien. 'Der Anteil der Juden am Widerstand in Deutschland', in *Studien und Berichte aus dem Forschungsinstitut der Friedrich-Ebert-Stiftung-Stand und Problematik des Widerstandes gegen den Nationalsozialismus.* pp. 113–143, Bad Godesberg, 1965.

WEISENBORN, Günther. *Der Lautlose Aufstand*, 2nd edition, 347 pp. Hamburg, Rowohlt, 1954.

Italy

ALLASON, Barbara. *Memorie di una Antifascista*, 339 pp. Milan, Avanti, 1961.

*Only the principal titles are mentioned in the Hebrew and Yiddish books. For further details see Robinson, op. cit.

ARTOM, Emanuele. *Diari, Gennaio 1940—Febbraio 1944*; edited by Paola de Benedetti and Eloisa Ravenna, 182 pp. Milan, CDEC, 1966.

BATTAGLIA, Roberto. *Storia della Resistenza Italiana*, 621 pp. Turin, Einaudi, 1953.

CONSOLO, Edi. *La Glass e Cross attraverso le Alpi*, 307 pp. Turin, Teca, 1965.

DEAKIN, F. W. *The Brutal Friendship: Mussolini, Hitler and the Fall of Fascism*, 896 pp. London, Wiedenfeld & Nicholson, 1962.

Ebrei in Italia durante il Fascismo (gli). 3 vol. to date: vol. 1, 123 pp. Turin, FGEI, 1961: vol. 2, 177 pp. Milan, CDEC, 1962; vol. 3, 230 pp. Milan, CDEC, 1963.

Fascismo e Antifascismo: *Lezioni e Testimonianze*, 2 vols., 346 and 356 pp. Milan, Feltrinelli, 1962–1963.

FELICE, Renzo de. *Storia degli Ebrei Italiani sotto il Fascismo*, 697 pp. Turin, Einaudi, 1962.

KESSELRING, Albert. *Memorie di Guerra*, 366 pp. Milan, Garzanti, 1954.

LATIS, Giorgio. *Un Popolo alla Macchia*, 503 pp. Verona, Mondadori, 1947.

MILAN, M. and VIGHI, F. *La Resistenza al Fascismo*, 246 pp. [abridged]. Milan, Feltrinelli, 1955.

MONTAGNANA, Mario. *Ricordi di un Operaio Torinese*, 437 pp. Rome, Rinascita, 1952.

SECCHIA, Pietro. *I communisti e l'Insurrezione (1943–1945)*, 513 pp. Rome, Edizioni di Cultura Sociale, 1954.

SERENI, Emilio. *CLN*, 265 pp. Milan, Percas, 1945.

SERENI, Marina. *I Giorni della Nostra Vita*, 125 pp. Rome, Editori Riuniti, 1956.

SIMONI, Leonardo (pseud. of Magistrati). *Berlin, Ambassade d'Italie*, 492 pp. Paris, Robert Laffont, 1947.

SPERCO, Willy. *L'Ecroulement d'une Dictature: choses Vues en Italie durant la Guerre 1940–1945*, 292 pp. Paris, Hachette, 1946.

TREVES, Benvenuta. *Artom—Tre Vite dall'Ultimo '800 alla Meta del '900*, 254 pp. [abridged]. Rome, Edizioni Israel, 1954.

VALIANI, Leo. *Dall'Antifascismo alla Resistenza*, 269 pp. Milan, Feltrinelli, 1959.

WOLFF, Karl. 'Ecco la Verità', *Tempo*, nos. 5–11, 40 pp. Milan, 1951.

ZANGRANDI, Ruggero, *1943–25 Luglio–8 Settembre*, 1129 pp. Milan, Feltrinelli, 1964.

France

Only the books most frequently used are mentioned.

ABOULKER, Marcel. *Alger et ses Complots*, 277 pp. Paris, Jour et Nuit, 1945.

ANSKI, Michel. *Les Juifs d'Algérie du Décret Crémieux à la Libération*, 374 pp. Paris, Editions du Centre, 1940.

Au Service de la France, 156 pp. Paris, UEVACJ, n. d.

COOKBRIDGE, E. H. *Inside SOE*, 640 pp. London, Arthur Barker, 1966.

COOKBRIDGE, E. H. *Missions Spéciales*, 240 pp. Paris, Fayard, 1966.

DIAMANT, David. *Héros Juifs de la Résistance Française*, 245 pp. Paris, Renouveau, 1962.

DREYFUS-SCHMIDT, Pierre. *Captivités et Evasions*, 183 pp. Belfort, 1955.

KNOUT, David. *Contribution à l'Histoire de la Résistance Française*, 245 pp. Paris, Renouveau, 1962.

LAZARUS, Jacques, (Captain Jacquel). *Juifs au Combat*, 153 pp. Paris, CDJC, 1947.

LISSNER, Abraham. *Un Franc-Tireur Juif Raconte*, 93 pp. Paris, (in the author's possession) 1969.

LONDON, Arthur. *L'Aveu. Dans l'Engrenage du Procès de Prague*, 455 pp. Paris, Gallimard, 1968.

MAYER, Daniel. *Les Socialistes dans la Résistance*, 248 pp. Paris, PUF, 1968.

MICHEL, Henri. *Bibliographie Critique de la Résistance*, 223 pp. Paris, IPN, 1964.

NOGUERES, Henri; DEGLIAME, Marcel; VIGIER, J. P. *Histoire de la Résistance en France*. Paris, Laffont. n. d.

OUZOULIAS, Albert. *Les Bataillons de la Jeunesse*, 489 pp. Paris, Editions Sociales, 1967.

Parti Communiste Français dans la Résistance (Le), 354 pp. Paris, Editions Sociales, 1967.

PIERRE-BLOCH, Jean. *Le Vent Souffle sur l'Histoire*, 332 pp. Paris, SIPEP, 1956.

POLIAKOV, Leon. *L'Hostellerie des Musiciens*. Unpublished manuscript written in 1945.

Presse Antiraciste sous l'Occupation Hitlérienne (La), Preface by A. Rayski 329 pp. Paris, UJRE, 1950.

STEINBERG, Lucien. *Les Autorités Allemandes en France Occupée*, 352 pp. Paris, CDJC, 1966.

———— 'The French Jews in the Anti-Hitlerite War' (in Hebrew). In *Moreshet*, no. IX. pp. 78–105. Tel Aviv, October 1968.

———— 'The Jews in the French Resistance Movement' (in Hebrew). In *Le Soldat Juif dans les Armées du Monde*. pp. 42–55 Tel Aviv, Editions de l'Armée d'Israël, Maarachot, 1967.

TILLON, Charles. *Les FTP*, 646 pp. Paris, Juillard, 1962.

VALLAT, Xavier. *Le Nez de Cléopâtre*, 308 pp. Paris, Quatre Freres Aymon, 1957.

WIGHTON, Charles. *Le Saboteur*, 298 pp. Paris, Fayard, 1967.

Belgium

BERNARD, Henri. *La Résistance 1940–1945* (the Belgian Resistance, that is), 141 pp. Brussels, La Renaissance du Livre, 1968.

GERMAIN, E. [Ernest Mandel], *La Conception Matérialiste de la Question Juive*, preface by Abraham Léon. Paris, EDI, 1969.

GRYNBERG-NINIO, Gisele. *Déportation et Résistance Nationale — Persécution et Résistance Juive*, 55 pp. Brussels, 1969.

OFIPRESSE. Brussels, 1945–1946. (press bulletins.)

STEINBERG, Lucien. 'L'Attaque du XXe Convoi.', *Regards*, Brussels, Sept.–Oct. 1968.

————— *Les Autorités Allemandes . . .* op. cit., pp. 317–323.

————— 'Le Sauvetage à Main Armée.' In *Le Monde Juif*, Paris, Oct.–Dec. 1968.

Netherlands

PRESSER, Jacques. *Ondergang*, 2 vols. La Hague, 1965. Translated into English under the title *Ashes in the Wind*, London, 1968.

SABILLE, Jacques. *Lueurs dans la Tourmente*, 165 pp. Paris, ed. du Centre, 1956.

SIJES, B. A. *The February Strike, 25–26 February* (in Dutch, with a resumé in English). La Hague, Rijksinstituut voor Oorlogsdocumentatie, 1954.

THE ZONE OF THE GHETTOS AND
THE EXTERMINATION CAMPS

DVORJETSKI, Dr Marc. *La Victoire du Ghetto* (translated by Arnold Mandel), 319 pp. Paris, France-Empire, 1962.

GARFUNKEL, L. *The Destruction of Kovno Judaism* (in Hebrew), 330 pp. Jerusalem, Yad Vashem, 1959.

KAHANOVICH, Moshe. *The War of the Jewish Partisans in Eastern Europe* (in Hebrew), 435 pp. Tel Aviv, Ayanot, 1954.

Lachwa, The First Revolt, (in Hebrew) Collective work. Tel Aviv, 1957.

ZUCKERMAN, Itzhak and BASOK, Moshe. *The Book of the Ghetto Combats* (in Hebrew), 812 pp. Tel Aviv, Kibbutz Hameoukhad, 1956.

Unpublished sources include:

DVORJETSKI, Dr Marc. *History of the Nazi Camps in Estonia (1941–1944).* (thesis). Tel Aviv, Paris, n. d. [1967].

Eichmann Trial — Verbatim Report of the Proceedings (in French, English, Hebrew, German).

Eichmann Trial — Exhibits (in their original language, most often German, Hebrew, or Yiddish).

The Ghetto of Warsaw

The main printed source to date is the report of General Stroop, published in the original in volume XXVI of *Procès des Grands Criminels de Guerre devant le Tribunal Militaire International.*

B. Mark (who died in 1966) remains the most important ghetto historian. His basic work, *The Warsaw Ghetto Uprising*, was published in Warsaw in 1953 (translation and French adaptation by Jean Noaro, Paris, 1955, Editions Sociales). This first edition, which goes back to the so-called Stalinist era exaggerates the importance of the part played by the Jewish and non-Jewish Communists. A German edition (the third) of the same work ensures that non-Communists, Jewish and non-Jewish, also receive due credit.

In 1966, Michel Borwicz, himself a former officer of the AK, published a book bearing the same title in Paris (Julliard).

We also suggest to interested readers Joseph WULF's book: *Das Dritte Reich und seine Vollstrecker — Die Liquidation von 500,000 Juden im Ghetto Warschau.* Berlin-Grünewald, Arani Verlag, 1961.

All these works contain generous notes and bibliographies as well as other sources of reference.

I interviewed General Erich von dem Bach-Zelewski on 2 May 1961 in Nuremberg prison where he was (and still is) for activities which, I may say, have nothing to do with what he did between 1939 and 1945.

The Memoirs of Emmanuel Ringelblum were first introduced to the Western world in the form of a novel by John Hersey, *The Wall*, New York, 1950. Recently a German edition of the Memoirs was published entitled *Ghetto Warschau — Tagebücher aus dem Chaos*, Seewald Verlag (Stuttgart, 1967). This edition, prepared by Professor A. Tartakower and the Yad Vashem Institute in Jerusalem, is based on the original work and is far superior to the two preceding ones.

The two principal publications in Hebrew (with English summaries) are as follows:

BLUMENTAL, Nachman and KERMISH, Joseph. *Resistance and Revolt in the Warsaw Ghetto, A Documentary History*, 481 pp. in Hebrew + XLVIII pp. English summary. Jerusalem, Yad Vashem, 1965.

CZERNIAKOW, Adam. *Warsaw Ghetto Diary*, edited by Nachman, Blumental, Nathan Eck, Joseph Kermish, Aryeh Tartakower. Jerusalem, Yad Vashem 1968. (This book is made up of three distinct parts: an introduction in English and in Hebrew by Joseph Kermish; the fascimile of Czerniakow's diary, 264 pp. in Polish; his translation into Hebrew, 329 pp., together with a bibliography and five different indexes.)

CENTRAL EUROPE AND THE BALKANS

Czechoslovakia

LOBL, Eugen. *Proces à Prague*, preface by André Fontaine, trans. by Amber Bousouglou, 223 pp. Paris, Stock, 1969.

ROTHKIRCHEN, Livia. *The Destruction of the Jews of Slovakia* (in Hebrew), English summary. Jerusalem, Yad Vashem, 1964.

SLANSKA, Josefa. *Rapport sur Mon Mari*, 222 pp. Paris, Mercure de France, 1968.

Romania

CARP, Matatias. *Cartea Neagra* ('The Black Book'), 3 vols., in Romanian. Bucharest, 1945–1947.

LAVI, Theodore. *Roumanian Jewry in World War II. Fight for Survival*, 191 pp. in Hebrew and 9 pp. English summary. Jerusalem, Yad Vashem and the Association of Romanian Immigrants, 1965.

Procesul Marii Tradari Nationale ('The Antonesco Trial'), (in Romanian.) Bucharest, 1946.

România în Rasboiul Antihitlerist ('Romania in the Anti-Hitlerite War, 23 August 1944–9 May 1945'), 815 pp. Bucharest, Military Editions, 1966.

Hungary

BISS, André. *Echec à la 'Solution Finale' — Un Million de Juifs à Sauver*, translated from German by François Carrare, 395 pp. Paris, Grasset, 1967.

BRAHAM, Randolf L. *The Destruction of Hungarian Jewry, a Documentary Account*, 971 pp. New York, World Federation of Hungarian Jews, 1963.

Der Kastner-Bericht über Eichmanns Menschenhandel in Ungarn. Munich, Kindler, 1961.

KASZTNER, Dr. R. *Der Bericht des Judischen Rettungskomitees aus Budapest, 1942–1945*. Roneoed, of no address and n. d.

LEVAI, Jenö. *Eichmann in Hungary*, 324 pp. Budapest, Pannonia, 1961.

Some of the unpublished sources are:

EPPLER, Erszebet [Dr Elisabeth], statements made in 1946 and 1947 (in Hungarian).

FRIEDL-BEN SHALOM, Raphael. . . . *weil Wir Leben Wollten: Errinerung an 10 Monate Schonungslosen Kampfes*, 152 pp. Budapest, n. d. [1945]. Photocopy of a typed text, corrected by hand.

Procès Eichmann, transcript of proceedings.

Finally, the author would like to express his profound gratitude to Constantin Melnik, for his unfailing encouragement and valuable advice while the book was in preparation.

Without his help and encouragement it would never have seen the light of day.

INDEX

356

Partisans' War in the East   258—67
Patriotic defence (Bucharest)   319
Pechorski, Alexander   271—8
Perelman, Chaim   137, 139, 144, 148, 150, 153
Perelman, Fela   137, 144
Pétain, Marshal, Henri Philippe   88, 125—6
Petrol bombs   140
Pijade, Mocha   304
Pikarski, Margot   27
Pilafoot, Capt.   123, 125
Pincherle, Bruno   62—3
Pius XII, Pope   66—8
Poalei Sion (Socialist Party)   112, 145, 195, 209, 244, 324
Pohl, SS General   208—9
Pol, Monsieur, *see* Polonski, Abraham
Poland   179, 189; *see also* Warsaw ghetto
Poliakov, Léon   108
Polonski, Abraham   111—17
Poner camp   229, 237
Pourim, feast of   266
Presse nouvelle (French Communist newspaper)   93
Purwin, Adolf   22

Rabinovitch, Jacques   110
Rachet, Lucien, *see* Rachline, Lazare
Rachline, Lazare   85
Rafi, *see* Shalom, Raphael Ben
Raik, Haviva   298
Railways, sabotage of   92—3
Rappaport, David   107
Rath, Ernest von   27
Ratner, Simon   243
Rauter, Hans Albin   156—7, 160
Rayman, Marcel   102—3
Rayski, A.   101—3, 108
Registration cards, burning of Jewish (1942)   140

Registration of Jews: France (1940)   86; Holland (1940)   157; Serbia (1941)   301
Reich Central Security Office, *see* RSHA
Reichsvereinigung   11—13
Resnik, Ber   188
Ribbentrop, Joachim von   141, 303
Richter, Gustav   315—18
Riga   32, 262
Ritter, Julius   103
Robota, Rosa   286
Rochczyn, Icchak   183—4
Romania   300, 311—20
Romanovitch   154
Rosani, Rita   72
Rosenberg report   287—8, 296
Rosenthal, Jean   84
Roselli, Carlo and Nello (brothers)   59—60
Rotam-Rathauser, Simha   215—18
Rotholz, Heinz   35—6
Rotholz, Lotte   35—9
RSHA (Abb. for Reich Central Security Office)   10, 45, 86
Rubel, Lucien   117
Rufeisen, Oswald Samuel   187—90

Sachsenhausen (1942)   27, 47, 48—53
Safran, Chief Rabbi Alexander   316
Saliège, Archbishop   104
Sammern-Frankenegg, Ferdinand von   204—5, 210, 212
Saragat, Giuseppe   66
Sarajevo   303
Scharff, Gertrude   46—7
Scharff, Werner   44—7
Scheinbaum, Jechiel   233
Schlossberg, Pnina and Haim   187
Schmidt, Corporal Anton   232
Schulstrasse Jewish prison   46
Schulze-Boysen, Harro   29, 34